Practical Java Programming with ChatGPT

Develop, Prototype and Validate Java Applications by integrating OpenAI API and leveraging Generative AI and LLMs

Alan S. Bluck

Orangeava.com

First published: November 2023

Published by: Orange Education Pvt Ltd, AVA™

Address: 9, Daryaganj, Delhi, 110002

ISBN: 978-81-19416-79-0

www.orangeava.com

Dedicated to

My Beloved Wife, **Jenny**

My Children, **Julie** *and* **Rosalie**
and their families

About the Author

Alan S. Bluck is the Director of ASB Software Development Limited and also, provides consultancy as a systems architect, providing a broad range of services, from high-level technical design, through mentoring for code development and installation and configuration of FileNet's core products.

Nominated as an IBM Champion in 2022 and re-elected in 2023, the Author has already published 5 technical books and over 30 ResearchGate papers which are available for free download.

He is responsible for high-level analysis and configuration of existing and new FileNet systems. He is also responsible for mentoring and troubleshooting high-level systems and issues.

He has over 45 years of Software Development experience in both business and scientific systems; 5 years of experience as a Project Manager / Analyst Developer, 11 years as a Software Development Manager for a team of 12 Software Engineers, 11 years as a Technical Consultant and 20 years as a Solutions Architect.

About the Reviewer

Gil Metcalf has had a long and varied career, initially qualifying as an industrial microbiologist working for an oil company on projects relating to microbial mining of heavy metals as well as enhanced oil recovery from spent wells. Following this he worked for many years for a large pharmaceutical company where he fulfilled several roles, including project manager, development team leader and network administrator. During this time he developed software for clinical trials management, as well as critical tools used in hospitals for the management of cancer patients. During his many years working in the software industry as a solutions architect, he has gained a wealth of experience in many fields and sectors, particularly financial technologies, but also including manufacturing, logistics, and energy markets. He has an in-depth knowledge of many software fields, including those that relate to modern business practices. These include documents and content management, case management, business process management and process automation, document lifecycle management, identity management and online banking technologies. He is widely regarded as an expert within the industry. Working with many well-known banks and institutions, he brings a wide knowledge and keen eye for detail to bear, whilst at the same time being able to see and understand the wider picture. This enables him to successfully tackle problems that large financial organizations have struggled with. His perceptive and innovative approach has been applied in many cases and applications to deliver success across the industry.

He is now a software architect with over 25 years of experience in the software industry. He has been instrumental in designing and implementing solutions for many blue-chip enterprises, and has spent the last ten years working mainly with fintech solutions. He has many qualifications in the document capture, document management, business automation and identity management fields. He has recently been working on profile management and passwordless authentication methods for mobile banking applications. Gil believes that the key to successful software architecture rests on a number of primary skills; an understanding of the software being just one of those. Also important are softer abilities such as being able to explain complex software concepts to less technicallyminded audiences (such as users and executives!), being able to see a broad picture of the solution (along with the risks and pitfalls), and being able to tease out requirements from what is often a vague wish list. He says that preparing for solution design is often "an exercise in extrapolation and interpolation at the same time!". He is a member of several professional associations, including the Chartered Institute for IT, the Identity Management Institute, and the International Association for Software Architects.

Acknowledgement

There are a few people whom I want to thank for the continued and ongoing support that they gave me while I wrote this book. First and foremost, I would like to thank my wife, Jenny, for continuously encouraging me to write the book–I could never have completed this book without her support.

I am grateful for the support of the ResearchGate website, which has held over 30 of my free publications since 2019, most of which I have referenced in this book

I also extend my gratitude to the team at AVA Orange for their support and dedication allowing me to publish this book in such a short time and update the material during the production process as AI Software is such a rapidly expanding area covering a broad range of applications.

I would also like to thank Giles Metcalf, the Technical Reviewer of this book, for his diligence and helpful suggestions.

Preface

The questions in this book, relating to Java program software development, were posed to the ChatGPT android phone app.The questions were based on previous developments (many algorithms originally took days to write). The responses were astonishing and appeared in seconds!In this book,we take the example Java code supplied by ChatGPT and implement it using the latest available Eclipse IDE. We have also established that all the base code generated by ChatGPT is free to use!

ChatGPT provides a fantastic opportunity for Java programmers to turbocharge their code writing. Software developers, programmers and software engineers can spend days writing code for applications. In this book we describe, using examples, the prompts which can be used for ChatGPT to automate the process of ChatGPT Java code generation.

This book contains questions relating to software development, which I posed (in bold) to the ChatGPT Android phone app. We then describe the detailed steps to implement the working Java code and validate the results.

This book is divided into **13 chapters**, designed to provide examples for use by Java Programmers, IT consultants, Systems and Solution Architects, with basic general IT knowledge, The book provides working templates for the development of Java programming solutions with examples using the OpenAI ChatGPT server system and the front end AI systems to support the development of programs for use by Developers for Data processing, Mathematical Analysis and Document Management, for implementation for Manufacturing Industries, Banks and Insurance Companies.

Chapter 1: covers questions relating to software development, which were posed (in bold) to the ChatGPT 3.5 AskAI 'phone app. We also cover the installation of ChatGPT as a web application and the Android mobile 'phone application install. The issue of copyright of the responses and the basic use of ChatGPTis described.

Chapter 2: covers the ChatGPT prompt used to test its knowledge of good programming practice. We asked it to define what it knew about the "SOLID" principles, which it did almost instantaneously.The following output was just the introduction:

"SOLID is a set of five principles for object-oriented programming that were introduced by Robert C. Martin (also known as Uncle Bob). These principles aim to make software designs more robust, flexible, and maintainable. Here's a brief overview of the SOLID principles and how they apply to Java:"

Chapter 3: covers the Java Code required to use the OpenAI Java API to interface with the ChatGPT AI system. ChatGPT provided an example of how to make a request to the API using the OkHttp library. In order to use the API,we describe the method required to obtain the OpenAI API key.

Chapter 4: covers the questions posed to provide a code for a Java program for using Binary Search. The Binary Search method takes a sorted array of integers and a target integer to search for. It returns the index of the target integer in the array if it is found, or -1 if it is not found.

Chapter 5: We cover the download and installation of the latest Open-Source Eclipse Java IDE (Eclipse IDE 2023-06 R – Eclipse IDE for Java Developers) and the step-by-step installation on MS Windows 10 and RedHat Enterprise Linux, RHEL 8.x. We then describe the detailed implementation and validation of the Binary Search program by creating the Java BinarySearch project and examining the Java Program output.

Chapter 6: covers the Fourier analysis of an MP4 music file to separate instruments and vocals.This is a complex task, involving multiple steps like decoding the MP4 file, performing signal processing, and applying source separation techniques. ChatGPT provided an outline guide for the steps required and suggested some libraries for each step.A simpler task, which ChatGPT did provide the full working code for, was for the Fourier analysis of a sine wave using Java code.

Chapter 7: describes theChatGPT-generated Java code for the Fast Fourier Transform. ChatGPT was asked to provide example Java code to demonstrate the Fast Fourier transform. An example Java code was displayed that demonstrated the Fast Fourier Transform (FFT) using the Apache Commons Math library.

Chapter 8: covers an example Java code generated by ChatGPT,for indexing a document with an output of a list of keywords with the associated document page numbers. The code provided by ChatGPT created an index of documents and their associated keywords using the Lucene library. It also allowed searching for documents based on keywords and returned the document path.

Chapter 9: describes how ChatGPT was prompted to provide a Java code for the Saltikov determination of the size distribution of particles in an opaque material from a measurement of the size distribution of their sections. This code generated by ChatGPT prompted the user to input the number of sections measured, the size of each section, and the area under the curve. It then calculated the particle size distribution using the Saltikov determination and printed the results.

Chapter 10: explains how ChatGPT generated Java code to invert a triangular matrix to obtain the coefficients of a polynomial.ChatGPT was prompted for an example Java program with code to invert a triangular matrix to obtain the coefficients of a polynomial as the result of a set of polynomial equations. The Java code created prompted the user to input the degree of the polynomial and the coefficients of a set of polynomial equations. It then used Gaussian elimination to invert the resulting matrix and obtain the coefficients of the polynomial. Finally, it printed the coefficients of the polynomial.

Chapter 11: covers the use of ChatGPT to generate an example Java code to store a document in the latest IBM FileNet Document Management system, using the FileNet Java API. The code, generated by ChatGPT, after some additional download libraries, established a connection to the FileNet server, created a new document, set the document properties, added content to it, saved the document, and then filed it in the specified Object Store folder.

Chapter 12: covers the conclusions and the future of ChatGPT for program development.We describe the ChatGPT 3.5 knowledge cutoff in September 2021, and the subsequent ongoing developments by the OpenAI Foundation to enhance this knowledge base and therapid development of the beta ChatGPT 4.0 currently released.We also give some indications for the road map of future versions of ChatGPT 5.0.

Chapter 13: provides Appendices with references and additional ChatGPT questions including information on other IBM systems supporting AI development, including the impact of Quantum Computing developments on AI processing.

Downloading the code bundles and colored images

Please follow the link to download the
Code Bundles of the book:

https://github.com/OrangeAVA/Practical-Java-Programming-with-ChatGPT

The code bundles and images of the book are also hosted on
https://rebrand.ly/6821ed

In case there's an update to the code, it will be updated on the existing GitHub repository.

Errata

We take immense pride in our work at **Orange Education Pvt Ltd,** and follow best practices to ensure the accuracy of our content to provide an indulging reading experience to our subscribers. Our readers are our mirrors, and we use their inputs to reflect and improve upon human errors, if any, that may have occurred during the publishing processes involved. To let us maintain the quality and help us reach out to any readers who might be having difficulties due to any unforeseen errors, please write to us at :

errata@orangeava.com

Your support, suggestions, and feedback are highly appreciated.

DID YOU KNOW

Did you know that Orange Education Pvt Ltd offers eBook versions of every book published, with PDF and ePub files available? You can upgrade to the eBook version at **www.orangeava.com** and as a print book customer, you are entitled to a discount on the eBook copy. Get in touch with us at: **info@orangeava.com** for more details.

At **www.orangeava.com**, you can also read a collection of free technical articles, sign up for a range of free newsletters, and receive exclusive discounts and offers on AVA™ Books and eBooks.

PIRACY

If you come across any illegal copies of our works in any form on the internet, we would be grateful if you would provide us with the location address or website name. Please contact us at **info@orangeava.com** with a link to the material.

ARE YOU INTERESTED IN AUTHORING WITH US?

If there is a topic that you have expertise in, and you are interested in either writing or contributing to a book, please write to us at **business@orangeava.com**. We are on a journey to help developers and tech professionals to gain insights on the present technological advancements and innovations happening across the globe and build a community that believes Knowledge is best acquired by sharing and learning with others. Please reach out to us to learn what our audience demands and how you can be part of this educational reform. We also welcome ideas from tech experts and help them build learning and development content for their domains.

REVIEWS

Please leave a review. Once you have read and used this book, why not leave a review on the site that you purchased it from? Potential readers can then see and use your unbiased opinion to make purchase decisions. We at Orange Education would love to know what you think about our products, and our authors can learn from your feedback. Thank you!

For more information about Orange Education, please visit **www.orangeava.com**.

Table of Contents

CHAPTER 1
Getting Started with ChatGPT

Introduction

This book features questions relating to Java software development which were posed (in bold) to the **OpenAI** organization, **AI** software, **ChatGPT 3.5**, using the Android phone app, **Ask AI**.

The questions were based on my previous developments (many algorithms originally taking days to write, and most were written in the **Fortran IV** language).

The responses were astonishing and appeared in seconds!

In this chapter, we cover the installation of **ChatGPT** as a web application and also use the **Ask AI ChatGPT** front-end interface application, installed on an Android mobile 'phone.

We also cover the current legal copyright ownership of the responses and the basic use of **ChatGPT**.

Structure

In this chapter, we will discuss the following topics:

- AI Suggested book titles

- Current copyright laws for AI-Generated Java code
- Create an account for the Free ChatGPT 3.5 version
- Create an account for the Subscribed ChatGPT-4 Version

AI Suggested book titles

To illustrate the prompts and responses of the mobile phone Application, **Ask AI**, which uses **ChatGPT 3.5** (which has an internet knowledgebase cut-off of September 2021), the following question was asked. (All questions are in bold and the **ChatGPT AI** responses are in italics)

I want to write a book about using ChatGPT to assist Java programmers. Can you suggest a book title which would be of interest to them?

Certainly! Here are a few book title suggestions for a book about using ChatGPT to assist Java programmers:

1. *"Java Mastery with ChatGPT: Unleashing AI to Enhance Your Programming Skills"*
2. *"ChatGPT for Java Programmers: Revolutionizing Your Coding Experience"*
3. *"The AI-Driven Java Developer: Unleashing the Power of ChatGPT"*
4. *"Java Programming Made Smarter: Harnessing ChatGPT for Efficiency and Productivity"*
5. *"ChatGPT Companion: Empowering Java Programmers with AI-Powered Assistance"*
6. *"Conversational Coding: Mastering Java with ChatGPT's Intelligent Guidance"*
7. **"Enhancing Java Development with ChatGPT: Your AI-Powered Programming Assistant"**
8. *"The Intelligent Java Developer: Leveraging ChatGPT for Enhanced Efficiency"*
9. *"AI-Assisted Java Programming: Unlocking New Frontiers with ChatGPT"*
10. *"Java Programming in the Age of AI: Harnessing ChatGPT for Success"*

Feel free to customize these suggestions or let me know if you need more options!

The title in bold was selected (the seventh title suggested by the **Ask AI** app). This title was selected because it emphasizes the role of the human programmer. Care should be taken to validate the code produced by the AI software. (It has been known to produce results with mistakes!)

Copyright laws for AI-Generated Java code

There is some controversy in the media over the legal status of the responses provided by **ChatGPT**. There are a number of specific areas where the legality of the **AI** responses is currently being challenged, for example, authors who think their copyright may have been broken from the reproduction of response data obtained during the web "scraping" which was used to train **ChatGPT** in 2021.

This position is complicated by the current legal status of **AI** software output in **UK** copyright law:

"UK *law would currently prohibit an* AI *from owning copyright (or even recognising that an* AI *created it), as it is not a human and therefore cannot be treated as an author or owner under the* Copyright, Designs *and* Patents Act. *It is also unlikely that this position is going to change anytime soon, given the* UK *government's response to the* AI *consultation*"

See: https://www.port.ac.uk/news-events-and-blogs/blogs/security-and-risk/chatgpt-what-the-law-says-about-who-owns-the-copyright-of-ai-generated-content

---

Note

A *number of other websites were found which discussed the legal requirements with reference to copyright, as follows:*

WIPO, the World Intellectual Property Organisation, currently states (amongst many other statements and even more relevant questions!) that:

"AI *applications are increasingly capable of generating literary and artistic works. This capacity raises major policy questions for the copyright system, which has always been intimately associated with the* ***human creative spirit*** *and with respect and reward for, and the encouragement of, the expression of* ***human creativity***. *The policy positions adopted in relation to the attribution of copyright to* AI-*generated works will go to the heart of the social purpose for which the copyright system exists.* ***If AI-generated works were excluded from eligibility for copyright protection, the copyright system would be seen as an instrument for encouraging and favoring the dignity of human creativity over machine creativity***. *If copyright protection were accorded to* AI-*generated works, the copyright system would tend to be seen as an instrument favoring the availability for the consumer of the largest number of creative works and of placing an equal value on human and machine creativity.*"

The full paper is freely available for download from **WIPO** covering many aspects of the **AI** intellectual property rights, and asking many more additional, and very interesting questions. This can be downloaded as a pdf file (**wipo_ip_ai_2_ge_20_1_rev.pdf**) from:

https://www.wipo.int/edocs/mdocs/mdocs/en/wipo_ip_ai_2_ge_20/wipo_ip_ai_2_ge_20_1_rev.pdf

The following reference **https://sprintlaw.com.au/articles/chatgpt-copyright-issues/** has the following statement concerning the law on Copyright in **Australia** as far as **AI**-generated content is concerned:

"*Australian case law has ruled that an AI system cannot own intellectual property (IP) as it is not a natural person. This was discussed extensively in the case of Thaler v Commissioner Of Patents [2021] – we've written more about the case here.*

So, when it comes to copyright, the general rule is that AI-generated content is not protected by copyright laws."

The Journal of Intellectual Property Law Practice has an article at the following link:

See: (**Volume 17, Issue 3, March 2022, Pages 321–326, https://doi.org/10.1093/jiplp/jpac013**)

Also, at **https://academic.oup.com/jiplp/article/17/3/321/6550465**

Has the following paragraph:

"The European Patent Office (EPO), for example, has recently confirmed on appeal the rejection of the DABUS applications EP 18 275 163 and EP 18 275 174. While the decision has yet to be made publicly available, **the EPO made it clear that 'only a human inventor could be an inventor' and 'a machine could not transfer any rights to the applicant.'**[23]Unless harmonization is sought–and hopefully achieved–via international law, interventions at the national level will only risk inconsistency. Rather, the current UK position, following the Court of Appeal's judgement in *Thaler v Comptroller General of Patents*,[24]is one of relative legal certainty–**we do know that AI *cannot* be named as inventor and, empirically, nothing suggests there is a pressing need for this to be changed**."

To get the **AI** view on the copyright issue, the following question of content ownership was asked to **Ask AI**, which uses **ChatGPT 3.5**, for its opinion on the use of **AI**-generated content for commercial purposes.

Can I use output from ChatGPT for commercial uses?

The **Ask AI** mobile 'phone app, using **ChatGPT 3.5,** gave the following response to this question:

"The use of output from OpenAI's GPT models, such as ChatGPT, for commercial purposes may be subject to certain restrictions and require appropriate licensing or permission from OpenAI.

OpenAI's GPT models are covered by several licenses, including the Creative Commons Attribution-NonCommercial-ShareAlike 4.0 International (CC BY-NC-SA 4.0) license.

This license allows for non-commercial use and distribution of the output generated by the models, as long as appropriate attribution is given and the resulting work is distributed under the same or a similar license.

If you intend to use the output from ChatGPT for commercial purposes, you should consult with OpenAI or a legal professional to ensure that you have the appropriate licenses and permissions to do so. Additionally, you should be aware of any potential ethical or legal concerns surrounding the use of AI-generated content in commercial applications."

The **CC BY-NC-SA 4.0 *Creative Commons*, Attribution-ShareAlike 4.0** license lets others modify and build upon the licensed material, even for commercial purposes, as long as the author is credited and the material is published under identical terms. This license is effectively "copyright" free and an open-source software license.

Creating an account for the Free ChatGPT V. 3.5

Having established that the Java code output from **ChatGPT** is free to use, as far as **UK** law and the **OpenAI** organization is concerned, we need to sign up for the free account access to **ChatGPT V3.5**, so the following steps were used:

1. Use a web browser to go to the **ChatGPT** website at **https://chat.openai.com/auth/login** to give the Welcome Login prompt as shown in *Figure 1.1*:

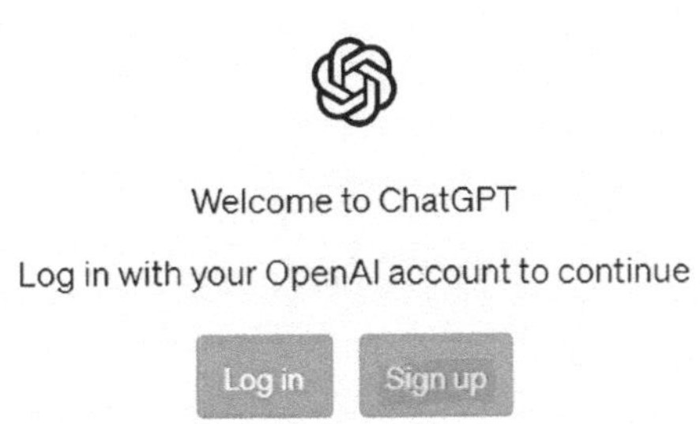

Figure 1.1: *The* ***ChatGPT*** *Login web page*

2. First, we need to select the **Sign up** button highlighted above, in *Figure* 1.1.
3. Next, we have to provide an email address, choose a strong password, and accept the terms of service, as shown in *Figures* 1.2 and 1.3 following:

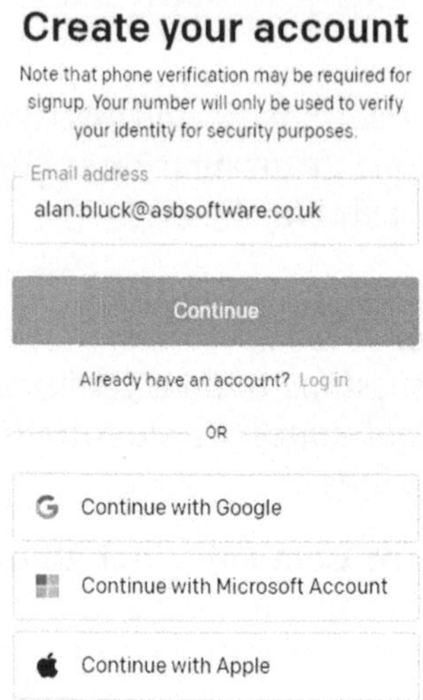

Figure 1.2: *The* **ChatGPT** *account creation web page*

A valid email address, that you have access to, is required because OpenAI uses a two-factor authentication mechanism, which requires you to click on a verification link in the email that is sent to you. A strong password must be entered, as requested in *Figure* 1.3.

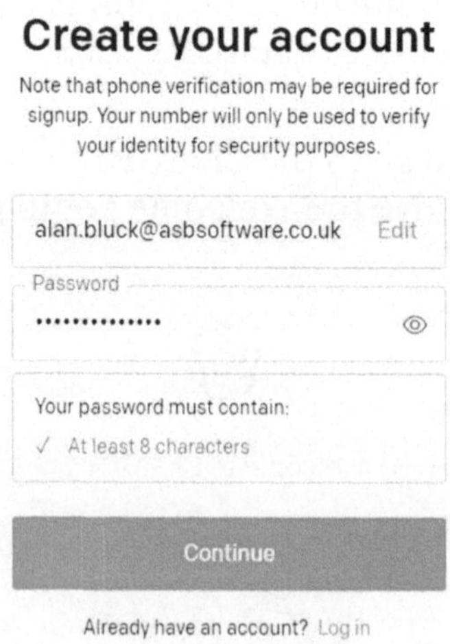

Figure 1.3: *The ChatGPT account password is entered*

As explained earlier, you are then prompted to verify the email you have been sent to complete the account creation, as shown in *Figure 1.4*:

Figure 1.4: *The ChatGPT account must be verified*

4. Next, you need to check your email inbox for a verification message and click the link to verify your email address, as shown in *Figure 1.5*.

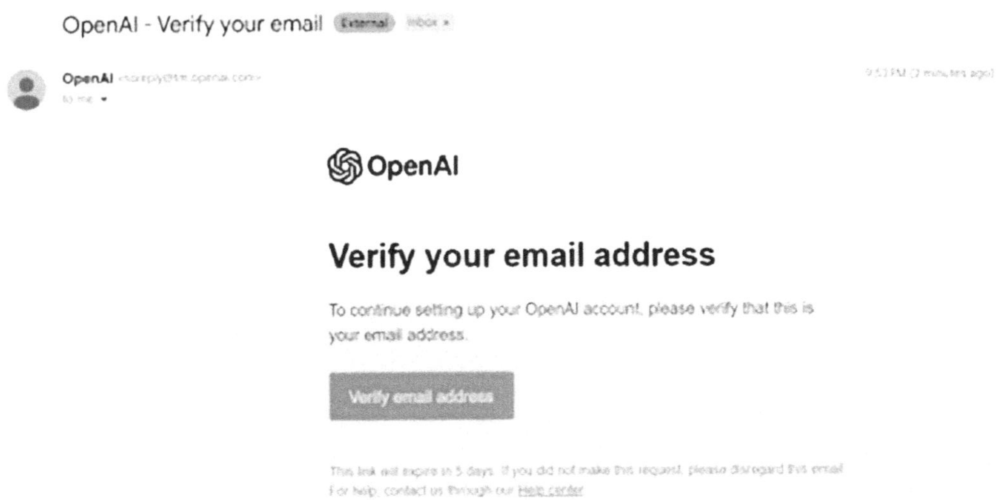

Figure 1.5: *The ChatGPT account is verified using the Verify email address button*

After the **Verify email address** button is clicked you will get a message as shown in *Figure* 1.6, as follows:

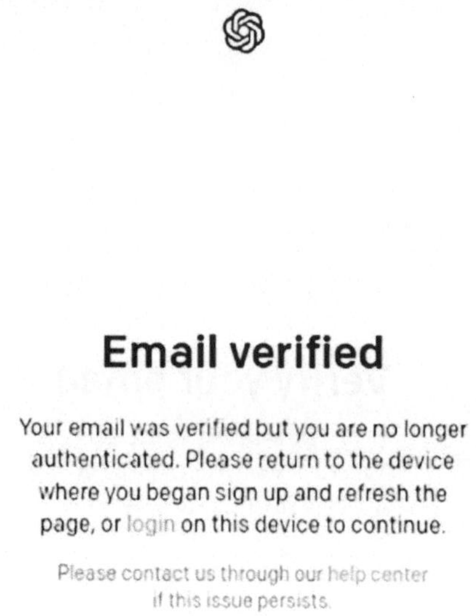

***Figure* 1.6**: *The* **ChatGPT** *account verification is confirmed*

The following web page is shown as displayed in *Figure* 1.7:

***Figure* 1.7**: *The verified page is now displayed*

5. Fill in your first and last names on the sign-up page, then click the **Continue** button, as shown in *Figure 1.8*.

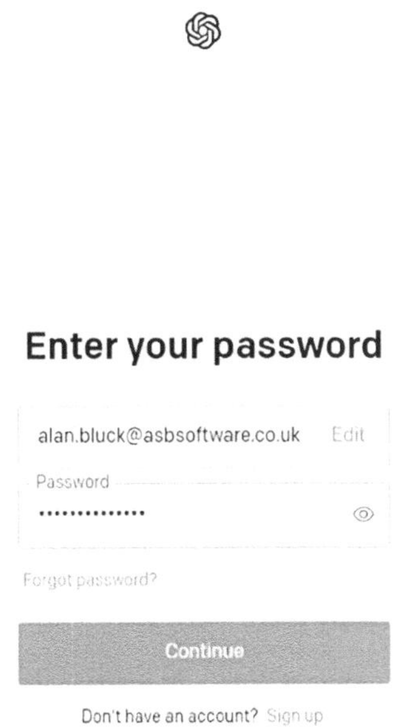

Figure 1.8: *The Login page is now shown for logging into the new account*

The new account requires additional **GDPR** protected (General Data Protection Regulations) biographical information as shown in *Figure* 1.9.

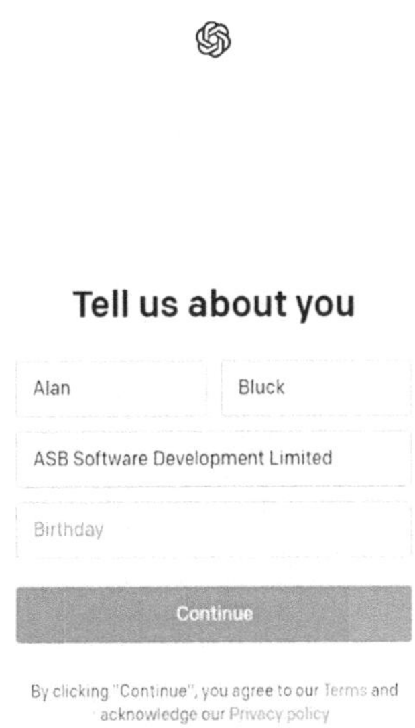

Figure 1.9: *The ChatGPT account prompts for further specific information*

6. To verify your phone number, you have to enter a 6-digit OTP (One-Time Password) code that will be sent to your phone.

   Developing Java Code for Utilizing the ChatGPT API

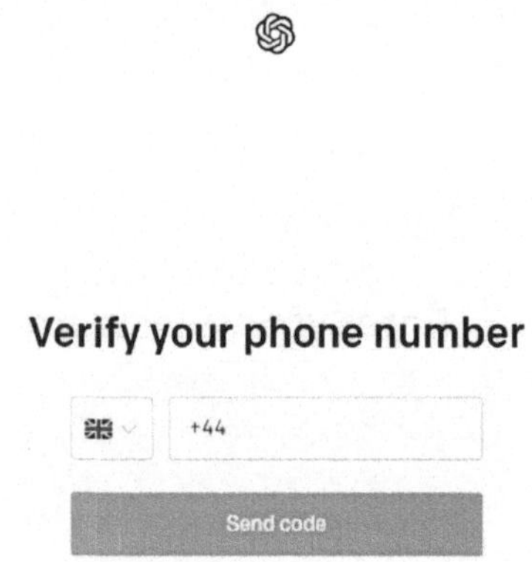

***Figure 1.10**: The ChatGPT account prompts for the user's mobile phone number*

You mobile 'phone should be switched on and connected to your service provider, since an **SMS** text message is sent to the 'phone number you enter. Remember to select your country of residence from the drop-down list. The text message you receive will contain the code you are prompted to enter, as shown in *Figure* 1.11.

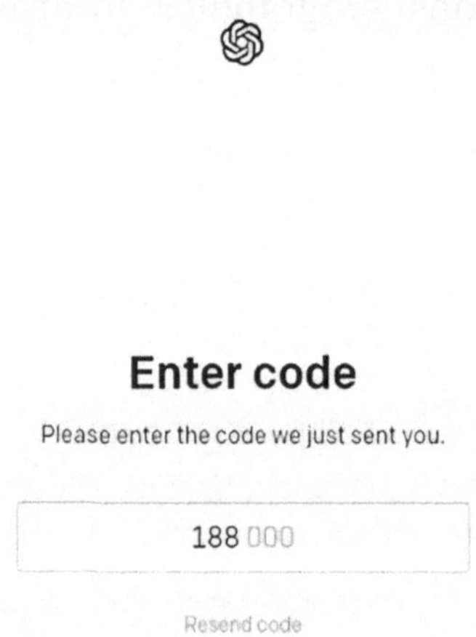

***Figure 1.11**: The **ChatGPT** account, two-factor code, is entered from the **SMS** text*

1. After completing these steps, you will have successfully signed up for **ChatGPT** and can begin using it with the dashboard, as shown in *Figure* 1.12.

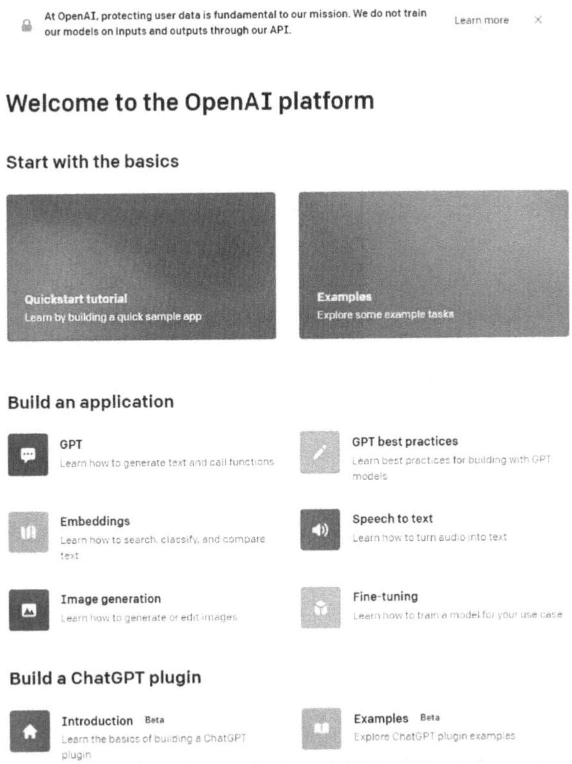

Figure 1.12: *The* **ChatGPT** *Dashboard is displayed on successfully logging in*

It is recommended to start by running the **Quickstart** tutorial:

https://platform.openai.com/docs/quickstart

By following the instructions, you will be able to create an account and start using **ChatGPT** successfully.

Using the playground:

https://platform.openai.com/playground/p/default-qa?model=gpt-3.5-turbo-0301

Note

I found that over time the model (currently chosen as **gpt-3.5-turbo-0301***) which can be used will change, so you may have to select another from the available dropdown list.*

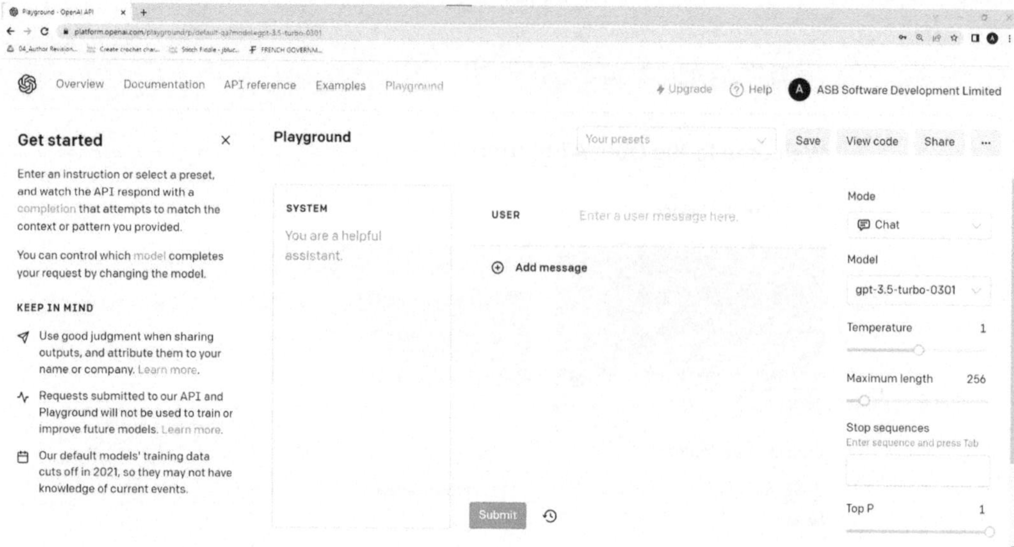

***Figure 1.13**: The ChatGPT OpenAI playground for questions.*

So, the following question was asked, using the text:

"Have you got a java code method for a binary search program"

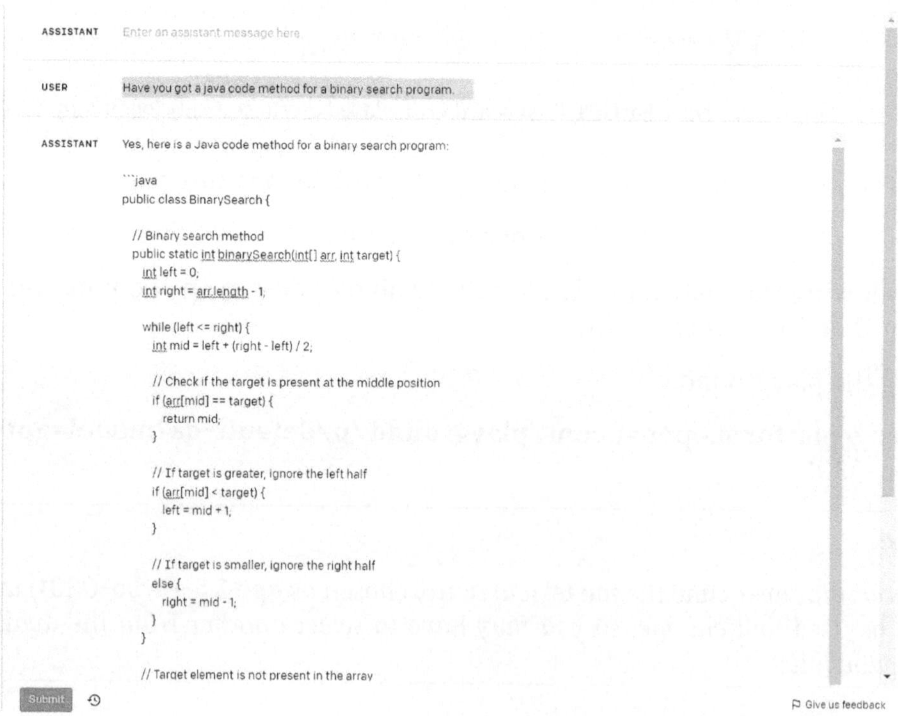

***Figure 1.14**: The ChatGPT response example for Binary Search java code*

Or, select the following link which takes you to **ChatGPT**:

https://chat.openai.com/

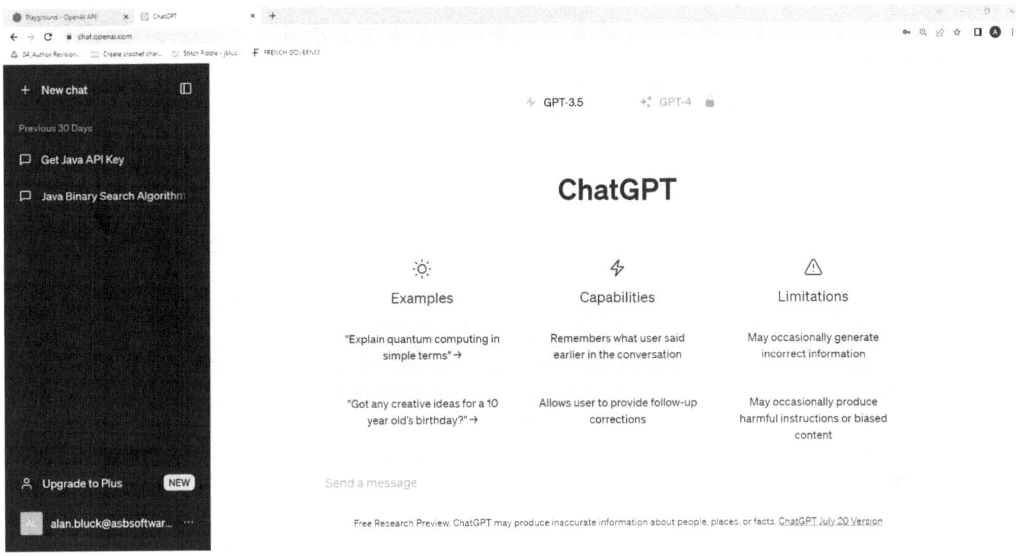

Figure 1.15: *The message window is displayed for entry (contains* **Send a message**, *by default)*

The **`Send a message`** grey font text, indicates where you need to type your question, as shown in *Figure 1.16*:

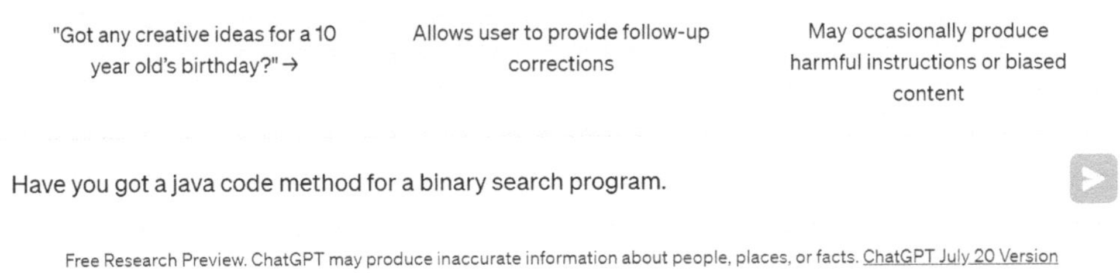

Figure 1.16: *The message window can be used, as shown above, click the white arrow icon*

Clicking the white arrow (on a green background as shown in *Figure 1.16*), gives the display as shown in *Figure 1.17*:

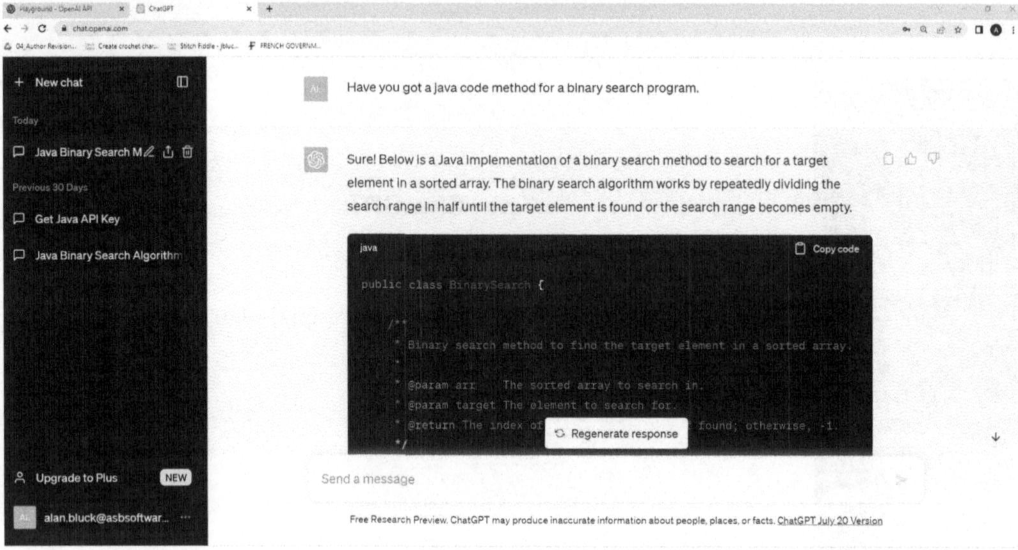

***Figure 1.17**: The **ChatGPT** code generated is copied using the **Copy code** button*

This gives the output code and text description (for the code, click on **Copy code** top right in the inset window, shown in *Figure 1.17*.) The code generated is as follows:

> **Note**
>
> The actual code generated may very well change over time. As an example, we have emboldened some of the additions made from an earlier response given.

```
public class BinarySearch {

    /**
     * Binary search method to find the target element in a sorted array.
     *
     * @param arr    The sorted array to search in.
     * @param target The element to search for.
     * @return The index of the target element if found; otherwise, -1.
     */
    public static int binarySearch(int[] arr, int target) {
        int left = 0;
        int right = arr.length - 1;
```

```
        while (left <= right) {
            // If the middle element is the target, return its index
            if (arr[mid] == target) {
                return mid;
            }
            // If the target is in the left half, discard the right half
            if (arr[mid] > target) {
                right = mid - 1;
            } else { // If the target is in the right half, discard the
left half
                left = mid + 1;
            }
        }

        // If the target is not found, return -1
        return -1;
    }

    public static void main(String[] args) {
        int[] arr = {2, 5, 8, 12, 16, 23, 38, 45, 56, 72, 91};
        int target = 23;

        int index = binarySearch(arr, target);

        if (index != -1) {
            System.out.println("Element found at index: " + index);
        } else {
            System.out.println("Element not found in the array.");
        }
    }
}
```

We can scroll down past the code window to show the **ChatGPT AI** description, as follows:

*In this example, we have a sorted array **arr**, and we're searching for the target element using the **binarySearch** method. If the target element is found, the method* *will return its index; otherwise, it will return -1 to indicate that the element is not present in the array. The provided main method demonstrates how to use the* ***binarySearch*** *method with a sample array.*

Installing and using the Android phone App, Ask AI

This other option, which gives similar responses, is to use the Android phone app, **Ask AI**, created by **Codeway Dijital**.

(This can be used for up to three questions per day for free)

It costs £4.89/week or £39.99 for Lifetime unlimited access.

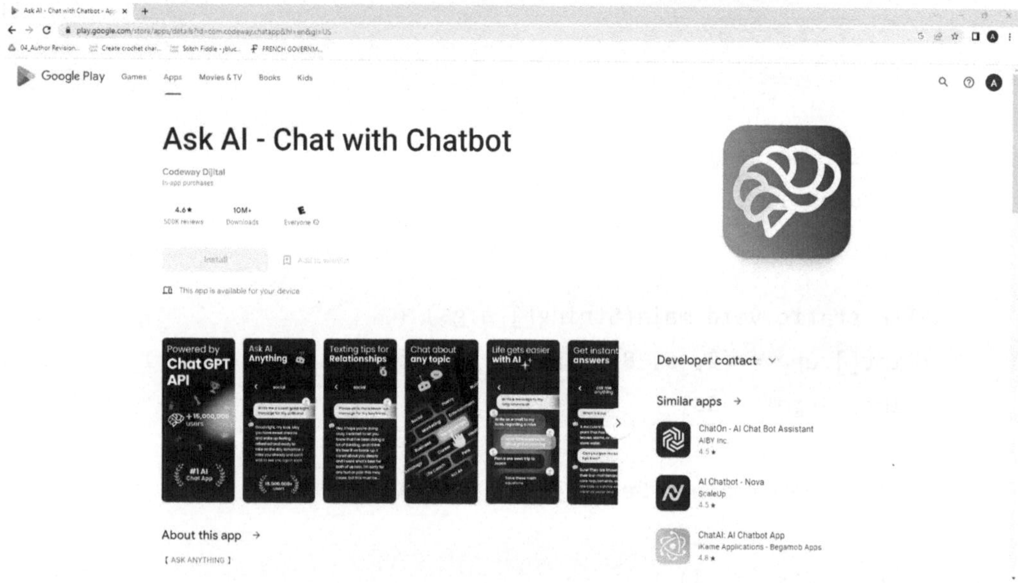

Figure 1.18*: The ChatGPT Android app on Google Play*

The **Install now** option is clicked as shown in *Figure 1.19 (a)* and opened as shown in *Figure 1.19 (b)*.

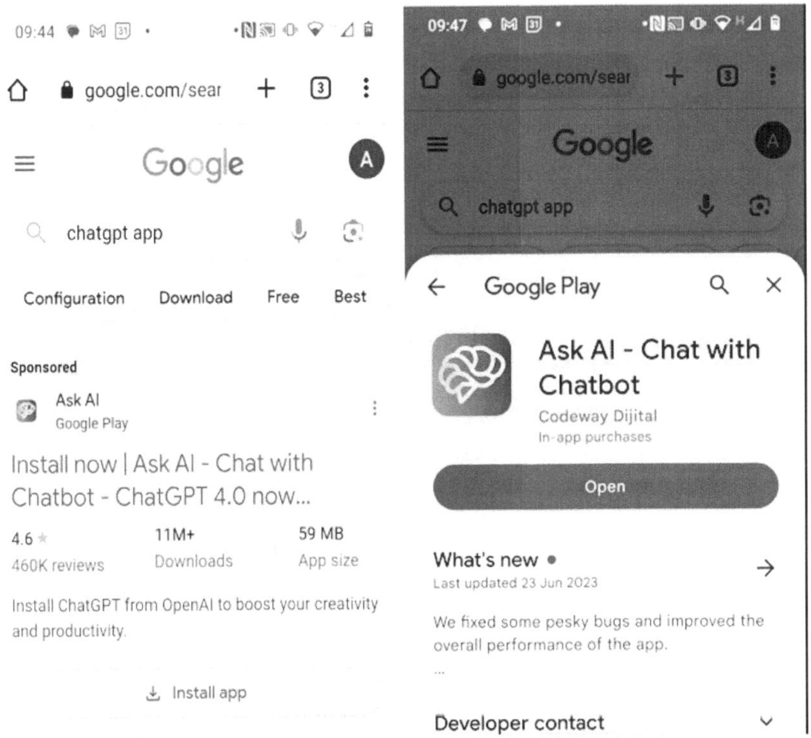

(a) (b)

Figure 1.19: *(a) The* **Ask AI ChatGPT** *app is installed from the Google Play web site. (b) The installed* **Ask AI ChatGPT** *app is started with the* **Open** *button*

On the Android mobile phone we can now tap on the newly installed **Ask AI** icon as shown in *Figure 1.20*.

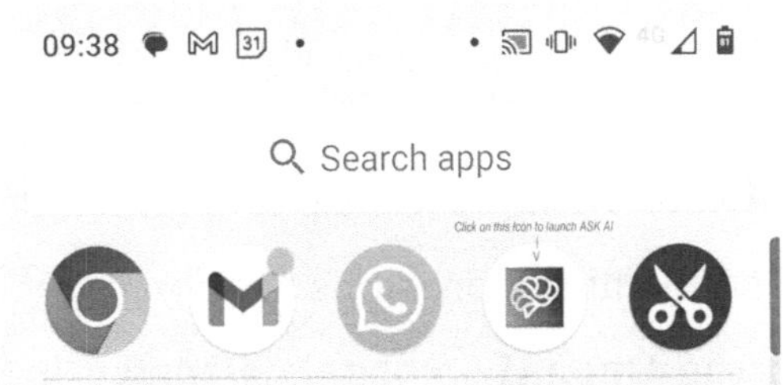

Figure 1.20: *The* **Ask AI ChatGPT** *app icon is shown in the Android 'phone screen*

The icon highlighted in *Figure* 1.20 is tapped to display the window shown in *Figure* 1.21:

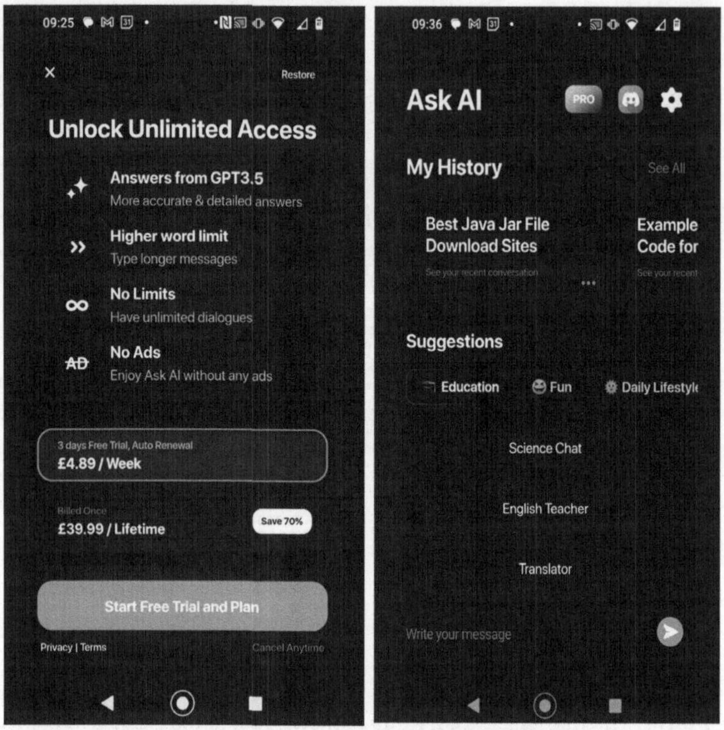

Figure 1.21: *(a) The X close on the top left, gives the "free" default screen (b) Three free questions are allowed*

Creating an account for the Subscribed ChatGPT-4

To log in to GPT-4, the following steps are recommended:

1. Sign up for **OpenAI** in the previous section.

   After loading the **OpenAI** website, as shown in **Figure 1.15**, mouse-over on the "**GPT-4**" button located in the upper-center of the screen, as shown in **Figure 1.22**.and then select the **Upgrade to ChatGPT Plus** button. Follow the prompts to create your **OpenAI** account.

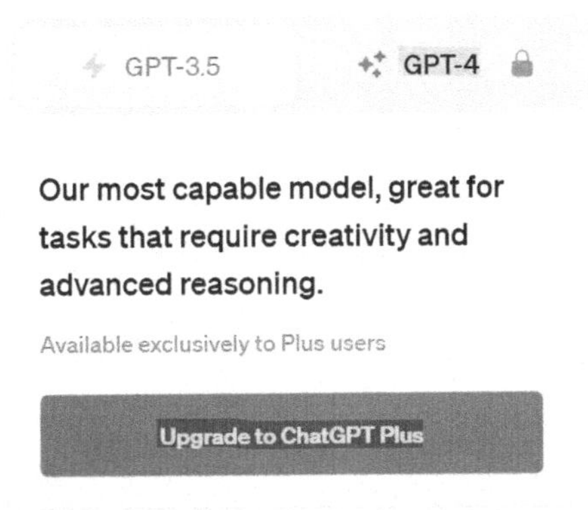

Figure 1.22: *The option to upgrade to ChatGPT Plus*

2. You can now Subscribe to **Chat GPT Plus**: You will be prompted to subscribe to the **Chat GPT Plus** plan, which costs $20 per month. Follow the instructions to complete the subscription process. By subscribing to **Chat GPT Plus**, you will gain access to the **GPT-4** version.

   But, why pay for this when you can get the power of **ChatGPT Plus** from the **Microsoft Windows Bing** search engine?

   You will notice that the latest **MS Windows 10** version (kindly updated for free by Microsoft) has a new search box:

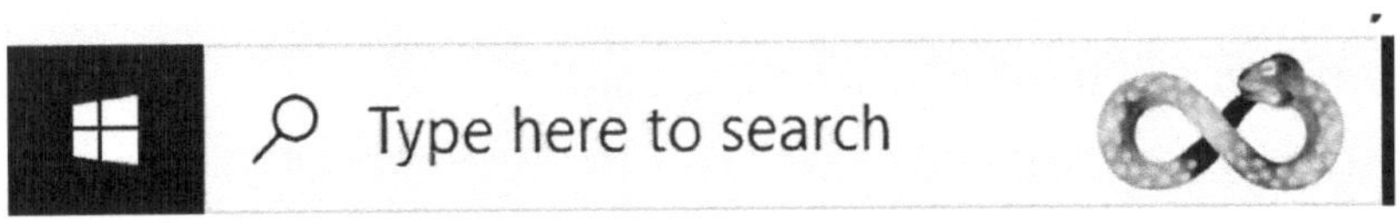

Figure 1.23: *The latest Windows Search box with its Ouroboros snake logo*

So, just knowing Microsoft's search engine is called **Bing**, we entered the following text into the Box in *Figure* 1.24

"**What does Bing use for its AI**"

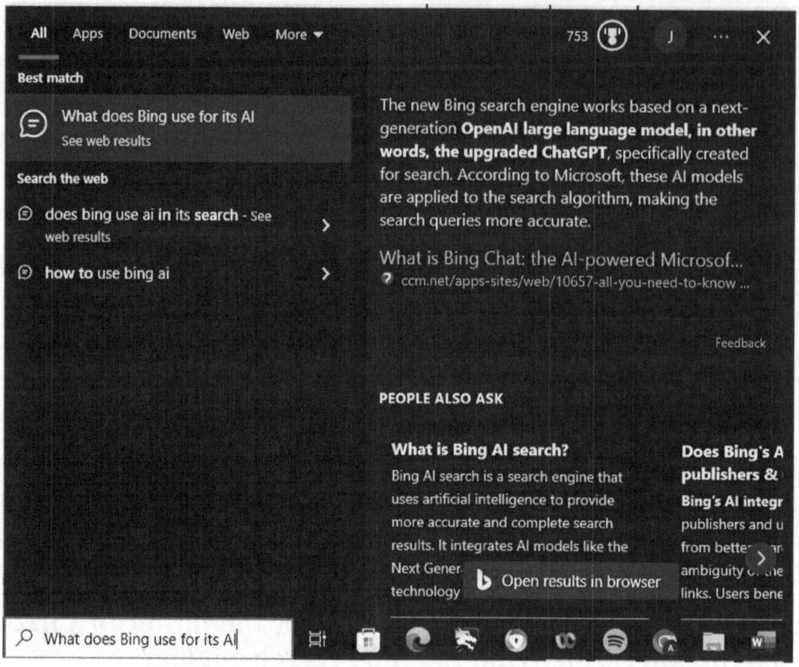

***Figure 1.24**: The Bing search engine reply to "What does Bing use for its AI"*

Then we asked:

"Which version of ChatGPT does Bing use?"

Which gave the response:

"ChatGPT 3.5, *which is what powers the chatbot that's gained notoriety since launching last November, relied on information from 2021 and before. The new OpenAI large language model that powers Bing has been optimized for search. It's built on learning from ChatGPT and GPT-3.5."*

Disappointing, but just as the snake is shown eating its tail, if you paste this response as a search, back into the text box, you get

"There has been speculation that Bing Chat uses GPT-4, and Microsoft confirmed that's the case after OpenAI announced the launch of ChatGPT-4."

Just to confirm this amazing response, we feed this reply text back again into the search box too, with the response from the Bing search engine, as shown in *Figure 1.25*:

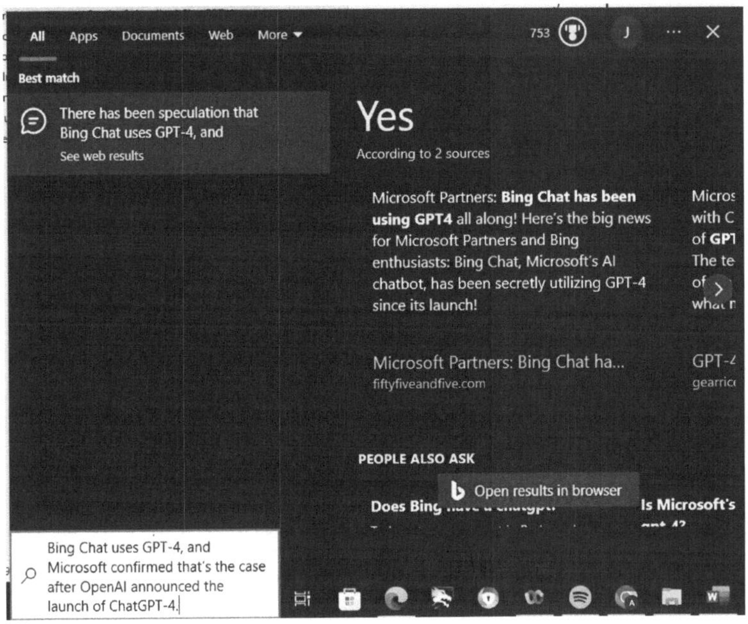

Figure 1.25: *The confirmation that we are using* **ChatGPT Version 4** *through* **MS Bing** *search*

Out of curiosity, we repeated the question asked earlier in **ChaptGPT 3.5**:

Have you got a java code method for a binary search program?

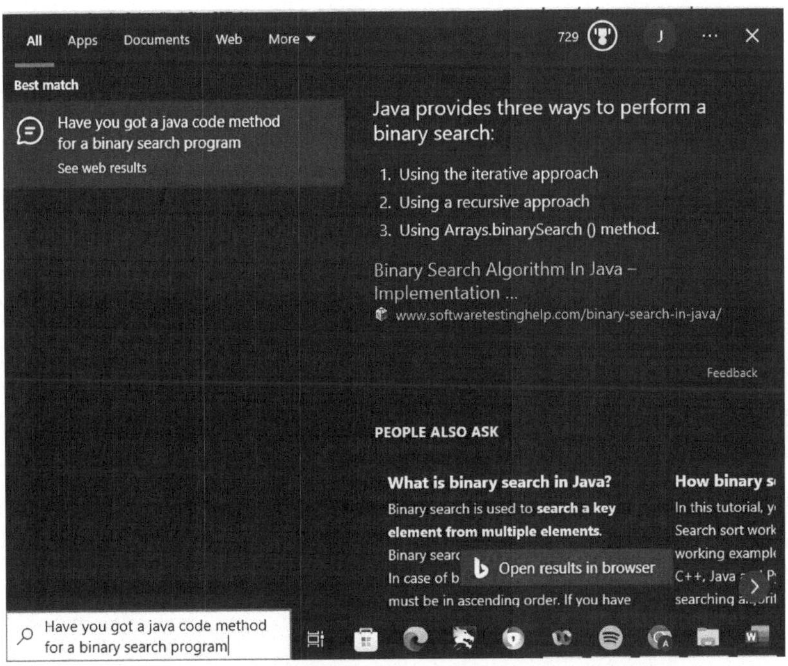

Figure 1.26: *We ask Bing the question we asked previously for a Binary search code method*

This gives the link:

https://www.softwaretestinghelp.com/binary-search-in-java/

(Updated on June 25, 2023)

This link has a full tutorial, so provides a very good introduction for a student Java programmer. It also uses a smarter version of the Binary Search code, using the standard Java **Arrays.binarySearch** method.

Note

You may have noticed in the code example given, that the Array position of the number 50 is the fifth number in the list, so you might think the program has given the wrong answer for the index of 4.

Here you have to remember that Java array elements are numbered with the first element indexed from zero.

Be sure to check the use of any of the code given in this link as the material is copyright protected!

We found the following on their website (**https://www.softwaretestinghelp.com/copyright-policy/**):

"Fair use allowed:

If you want to refer to any article from this website you can post article excerpts or summaries **generally not more than one paragraph** and a link back to Softwaretestinghelp.com original article."

Conclusion

There are a number of options available to use **OpenAI**'s **ChatGPT AI** application as a free tool for assisting a Java software developer as described, step-by-step in this first chapter.

The Java code for the Binary Search example we used was requested in the Free Bing search engine as shown in **Figure 1.26,** the link provided gives a full description of the algorithm and examples of the Java code we require.

In the next chapter, we will look at Java programming best practices as stated by **ChatGPT**.

Points to remember

- For copyright, it is important to use due diligence and research yourself to confirm the code you wish to use is really in the public domain.
- The web pages supplied by **ChatGPT** are regularly updated by **OpenAI**. This **AI** system is always evolving, so be aware that the examples supplied in this book may change over time. The book attempts to focus on making the best use of **AI** systems, to suit the expertise of the Java programmer, so we have covered access to bare code and the use of the **Bing** search engine for in-depth assistance.
- The actual code generated may very well change over time. As an example, we have emboldened some of the additions made from an earlier response given in the code listed for the Binary Search code shown in this Chapter.

Multiple choice questions

1. **Which version of ChatGPT is charged at $20 per month?**
    a. **ChatGPT** model **GPT-4**
    b. **ChatGPT** model **GPT-3-5**
    c. **gpt-3.5-turbo-0301**
    d. Microsoft **Bing**
2. **GDPR is the pneumonic for?**
    a. **General Digital Processing Regulations**
    b. **General Digital Protection Requirements**
    c. **General Data Protection Regulations**
    d. **General Data Processing Regulations**
3. **Which of the following is the name for the Android mobile 'phone app?**
    a. ChatGPT
    b. Ask AI
    c. Bing
    d. OpenAI

Answers

1. **a**
2. **c**
3. **b**

Questions

1. Which is the most expensive option for using the ChatGPT AI, also describe the limitations of each of the 'free' versions.
2. What are the main reasons that Copyright is not assignable to the content produced by an AI program?
3. Why should you still be careful to validate the responses created by **ChatGPT**?
4. Why is it important to provide a valid email address when applying for an OpenAI account?

Key terms

- **AI**: Artificial Intelligence Software that mimics the responses you might expect to questions supplied by a human operator.
- **OpenAI**: is the American artificial intelligence research laboratory that developed **ChatGPT** comprising the non-profit **OpenAI** organization and its for-profit subsidiary corporation **OpenAI Limited**.
- **API**: Application Programmer's Interface - a set of callable methods to allow a server system to be accessed for functionality using code used for a client-based program.
- **Ask AI**: The Android mobile phone app is available for access to **ChatGPT** 3.5.
- **CC BY-NC-SA**: Creative Commons, by NonCommercial-ShareAlike Attribution, effectively a copyright-free software license providing the content is correctly attributed with a reference link to the original software source.
- **ChatGPT**: **ChatGPT** is a language model developed by **OpenAI**. It is based on the **GPT** (Generative Pre-trained Transformer) architecture, specifically **GPT-3.5** for the free use option. The model is designed to generate human-like text responses to user inputs, making it capable

of engaging in interactive and natural-sounding conversations. **ChatGPT** has been trained on a massive amount of diverse textual data from the internet, allowing it to acquire a broad understanding of language and context. It uses deep learning techniques, particularly **transformers**, which enable it to process and generate text effectively. This language model has a wide range of applications, including answering questions, providing explanations, giving recommendations, offering creative writing assistance, language translation, and code generation. It can be integrated into various software operating systems and hardware platforms and can be used to create software applications to offer interactive and conversational experiences for users using the **ChatGPT API** interface.

- **EPO**: The European Patent Office.
- **EU**: The European Union
- **Fortran**: Early scientific computer language, derived from **For**mula **Tran**slation.
- **GDPR:** General Data Protection Regulations,
- **SMS:** Short Message Service, used to send the text through to a cell mobile phone, from another cell 'phone, or a computer server.
- **WIPO**: The World Intellectual Property Organisation.

CHAPTER 2
Java Programming – Best Practices as Stated by ChatGPT

Introduction

In this chapter, we prompt ChatGPT to test its knowledge of good programming practice. We asked it to define what it knew about the "SOLID" principles which it did almost instantaneously, the following output was just the introduction:

"*SOLID is a set of five principles for object-oriented programming that were introduced by Robert C. Martin (also known as Uncle Bob). These principles aim to make software designs more robust, flexible, and maintainable. Here's a brief overview of the SOLID principles and how they apply to Java:*"

Structure

In this chapter, we will discuss the following topics:

- The principles of SOLID
- Best Practice for Java code indentation
- SOLID Code Examples
    - o Single Responsibility Principle (SRP)
    - o Open/Closed Principle (OCP)

- o Liskov Substitution Principle (LSP)
- o Interface Segregation Principle (ISP)
- o Dependency Inversion Principle (DIP)

The principles of SOLID

The response from ChatGPT on the five principles for using Object-Oriented Programming were numbered as follows, when we asked the question

"What are the principles of SOLID for Java program development?"

1. **Single Responsibility Principle (SRP):** A class should have only one reason to change. This means that a class should have only one responsibility or job to do. If a class has multiple responsibilities, it becomes difficult to change, test, and maintain. In Java, you can apply SRP by creating smaller, more focused classes that do one thing well.

2. **Open/Closed Principle (OCP):** Software entities (classes, modules, functions) should be open for extension but closed for modification. This means that you should be able to add new functionality to a program without modifying existing code. In Java, you can apply OCP by using interfaces and abstract classes to provide a stable interface for clients while allowing implementation details to vary.

3. **Liskov Substitution Principle (LSP):** Subtypes should be substitutable for their base types. This means that any subclass should be able to be used in place of its parent class without causing problems. In Java, you can apply LSP by following the "is-a" relationship between classes and ensuring that subclass methods do not violate the contracts of their parent class.

4. **Interface Segregation Principle (ISP):** Clients should not be forced to depend on interfaces they do not use. This means that you should design interfaces that are specific to the needs of their clients. In Java, you can apply ISP by creating smaller interfaces that have a clear purpose and only contain the methods that are relevant to their clients.

5. **Dependency Inversion Principle (DIP):** High-level modules should not depend on low-level modules. Both should depend on abstractions. Abstractions should not depend on details. Details should depend on abstractions. This means that you should design your code so that high-level modules are decoupled from low-level modules, and both depend on abstractions. In Java, you can apply DIP by using dependency injection to provide objects with their dependencies, and by programming to interfaces rather than concrete classes.

Best Practice for Java code indentation

In the following question, we used the **ChatGPT 3.5** available using the web-based link:

https://chat.openai.com/ :

Can you describe the best practice for Java code indentation?

Proper code indentation is essential for writing clean, readable, and maintainable Java code. Consistent and well-formatted code improves collaboration among developers and reduces the chances of introducing errors. Here are some best practices for Java code indentation:

- **Use Consistent Indentation Style:** Choose a specific indentation style (e.g., 2 spaces, 4 spaces, or tabs) and stick to it throughout your codebase. Consistency is key to readability.
- **Indentation for Blocks:** Indent each block of code (such as classes, methods, loops, and conditionals) to visually indicate their hierarchy. The contents of the block should be indented one level further.

```java
public class Example {
    public void doSomething() {
        if (condition) {
            for (int i = 0; i < 10; i++) {
                // Indent further for inner blocks
            }
        }
    }
}
```

***Figure 2.1**: The ChatGPT Java code indentation example*

- **Vertical Alignment:** Align similar elements vertically to improve readability. This is particularly useful for assignments, method calls, or multiple variable declarations.

```java
int x                    = 5;
int veryLongVariableName = 10;
```

***Figure 2.2**: The ChatGPT Java code vertical alignment example*

- **Chaining and Method Calls:** When chaining method calls, align the dots for better clarity. You can also align parameters if they don't fit comfortably on a single line.

```java
StringBuilder builder = new StringBuilder()
        .append("Hello")
        .append(" ")
        .append("World");
```

***Figure 2.3**: The ChatGPT Java code vertical alignment example*

- **Indentation for Wrapped Lines:** When a line is too long and wrapped onto multiple lines, the subsequent lines should be indented to indicate their continuation.

```java
String longText =
        "This is a long text that cannot fit on a single line, " +
        "so we wrap it to improve readability.";
```

***Figure 2.4**: The ChatGPT Java code Indentation for Wrapped Lines example*

- **Indentation for Nested Constructs:** When dealing with nested constructs, increase the indentation level accordingly to show their nesting level.

```java
for (int i = 0; i < 5; i++) {
    if (condition) {
        // Nested code block
    }
}
```

***Figure 2.5**: The ChatGPT Java code Indentation for Nested Constructs example*

- **Comments and Annotations:** Comments and annotations should typically share the same indentation level as the code they're associated with.

```java
public class MyClass {

    @Override
    public void doSomething() {
        // Comment aligned with the code
    }
}
```

Figure 2.6: *The ChatGPT Java code Indentation for Comments and Annotations example*

- **Aligning Parameters:** For method calls with multiple parameters, consider aligning the parameters for improved readability.

```java
someMethod(firstParameter,
           secondParameter,
           thirdParameter);
```

Figure 2.7: *The ChatGPT Java code Indentation for Aligning Parameters example*

- **Indentation in Switch Statements:** Indent the case labels within a switch statement, and indent the code inside each case block.

```java
switch (value) {
    case 1:
        // Code for case 1
        break;
    case 2:
        // Code for case 2
        break;
    default:
        // Code for other cases
}
```

Figure 2.8: *The ChatGPT Java code Indentation for Switch Statements example*

- **Use an IDE's Formatting Tools:** Most modern Integrated Development Environments (IDEs) provide automatic code formatting tools. Configure your IDE's settings to follow your preferred indentation style, and use the auto-formatting feature regularly.
- By following these best practices, you can create Java code that is easy to read, understand, and maintain, leading to a more efficient and collaborative development process.

SOLID Code Examples

The five "**SOLID**", best practice Java Coding for Object-Oriented programming principles, were examined in detail, by asking the **ChatGPT Ask AI** mobile 'phone app the following questions for each of the principles it listed as shown in the following sections:

Single Responsibility Principle (SRP)

Do you have a Java Code example that illustrates the SOLID Single Responsibility Principle?

Certainly! The Single Responsibility Principle (SRP) states that a class should have only one reason to change, meaning it should have a single responsibility. Here's a Java code example that demonstrates the SRP:

```
```java
// UserService class responsible for user-related operations
public class UserService {
   public void registerUser(String username, String password) {
      // logic for registering a user
      }
      public void authenticateUser(String username, String password) {
      // Logic for authenticating a user
     }

     public void resetPassword(String username) {
     // Logic for resetting a user's password
     }

     // other user-related methods...
}
```
```

```
// EmailService class responsible for sending emails
public class EmailService {
      public void sendEmail(String recipient, String message) {
     // logic for sending an email
     }

     // other email-related methods...
}
```

In the above example, we have two classes: **UserService** and **EmailService**. The **UserService** class is responsible for user-related operations such as user registration, authentication, and password reset. It follows the SRP because it has a single responsibility of managing user-related operations.

On the other hand, the **EmailService** class is responsible for sending emails. It follows the SRP because it has a single responsibility of managing email-related operations.

By separating the concerns into two separate classes, we adhere to the SRP and achieve better maintainability and flexibility in our code. If there are changes required in user-related operations, we only need to modify the **UserService** class without affecting the **EmailService** class, and vice versa.

Open/Closed Principle (OCP)

Do you have a Java Code example that illustrates the SOLID Open/Closed Principle?

Certainly! The Open/Closed Principle (OCP) states that classes should be open for extension but closed for modification. In other words, you should be able to add new functionality to a class without modifying its existing code. Here's a Java code example that demonstrates the OCP:

```java
// Shape interface representing a geometric shape
     public interface Shape {
        double calculateArea();
     }

// Rectangle class implementing the Shape interface
   public class Rectangle implements Shape {
```

```
        private double width;
        private double height;

    public Rectangle(double width, double height) {
        this.width = width;
        this.height = height;
    }

    public double getWidth() {
        return width;
    }

    public double getHeight() {
       not
       return height;
    }

    public double calculateArea() {
       return width * height;
    }
}

// Circle class implementing the Shape interface
      public class Circle implements Shape {
        private double radius;

        public Circle(double radius) {
            this.radius = radius;
       }

        public double getRadius() {
            return radius;
       }

       public double calculateArea() {
           return Math.PI * radius * radius;
       }
}
```

```
// AreaCalculator class responsible for calculating the total area of shapes
public class AreaCalculator {
    public double calculateTotalArea(Shape[] shapes) {
        double totalArea = 0;
        for (Shape shape : shapes) {
            totalArea += shape.calculateArea();
        }
    return totalArea;
    }
}
```

In the above example, we have an **AreaCalculator** class that is responsible for calculating the total area of shapes. It follows the OCP because it is open for extension. If we want to add a new shape, such as a **Triangle**, we can create a new class that implements the `Shape` interface without modifying the existing code.

The **Rectangle** and **Circle** classes are examples of shapes that implement the **Shape** interface. They are closed for modification because their code does not need to be changed when adding a new shape.

By adhering to the OCP, we can easily introduce new shapes by creating new classes that implement the **Shape** interface, without modifying the **AreaCalculator** class or existing shape classes. This promotes code reusability and maintainability.

Liskov Substitution Principle (LSP)

The response to this question by **ChatGPT Ask AI,** uses the same example Java code, as a base that was used in the previous section, entitled **Open/Closed Principle (OCP)** so, we have highlighted the additional Java code that was added in the response below, in **bold italic**.

Do you have a Java Code example that illustrates the SOLID Liskov Substitution Principle?

Certainly! The Liskov Substitution Principle (LSP) states that objects of a superclass should be replaceable with objects of its subclasses without affecting the correctness of the program. Here's a Java code example that illustrates the LSP:

````
```java
// Shape interface representing a geometric shape
public interface Shape {
      double calculateArea();
}

// Rectangle class implementing the Shape interface
      public class Rectangle implements Shape {
      private double width;
      private double height;

      public Rectangle(double width, double height) {
         this.width = width;
         this.height = height;
      }

      public double getWidth() {
        return width;
      }

      public void setWidth(double width) {
        this.width = width;
      }

      public double getHeight() {
        return height;
     }

     public void setHeight(double height) {
       this.height = height;
     }

     public double calculateArea() {
       return width * height;
     }
}

// Square class extending the Rectangle class
````
````

```
public class Square extends Rectangle {
   public Square(double sideLength) {
      super(sideLength, sideLength);
   }

@Override
   public void setWidth(double width) {
      super.setWidth(width);
          super.setHeight(width);
   }

@Override
   public void setHeight(double height) {
       super.setWidth(height);
       super.setHeight(height);
   }
}

// AreaCalculator class responsible for calculating the total area of
shapes
public class AreaCalculator {
    public double calculateTotalArea(Shape[] shapes) {
        double totalArea = 0;
        for (Shape shape : shapes) {
        totalArea += shape.calculateArea();
    }
return totalArea;
   }
}
```

In the above example, we have an **AreaCalculator** class that calculates the total area of shapes. The **Shape** interface represents a geometric shape and includes a **calculateArea()** method.

The **Rectangle** class implements the **Shape** interface and represents a rectangle with a width and height. The **Square** class extends the **Rectangle** class and represents a square with equal side lengths.

The **Square** class overrides the **setWidth()** and **setHeight()** methods from the **Rectangle** class to ensure that the width and height are always the same for a square. While this contradicts the usual behavior of a rectangle, it adheres to the LSP because objects of the `Square` class can be substituted for objects of the `Rectangle` class without affecting the correctness of the program.

By following the LSP, we can safely substitute objects of a superclass (**Rectangle**) with objects of its subclasses (**Square**) without introducing unexpected behavior or breaking the functionality of the program.

Interface Segregation Principle (ISP)

In the following question, we used the ChatGPT 3.5 available using the web-based link:

https://chat.openai.com/ :

You will notice that, in this example, ChatGPT illustrates code that violates the principle as a way of describing the basis of the concept.

Do you have a Java Code example that illustrates the SOLID Interface Segregation Principle?

Certainly! The Interface Segregation Principle (ISP) is one of the SOLID principles that states that a class should not be forced to implement interfaces it doesn't use. Instead of having a large, monolithic interface, you should create smaller, more specific interfaces that cater to the needs of individual classes. This promotes better separation of concerns and avoids unnecessary dependencies.

Here's a Java code example that illustrates the Interface Segregation Principle

```
// Interface Segregation Principle Violation


// Suppose we have a monolithic interface that contains multiple
methods.
interface Worker {
    void work();
    void eat();
    void sleep();
}


class Employee implements Worker {
    @Override
    public void work() {
```

```
        System.out.println("Employee is working.");
    }

    @Override
    public void eat() {
        System.out.println("Employee is eating.");
    }

    @Override
    public void sleep() {
        System.out.println("Employee is sleeping.");
    }
}

class Robot implements Worker {
    @Override
    public void work() {
        System.out.println("Robot is working.");
    }

    @Override
    public void eat() {
        // Robots don't eat, so this method is irrelevant and violates
ISP.
        throw new UnsupportedOperationException("Robots don't eat.");
    }

    @Override
    public void sleep() {
        // Robots don't sleep, so this method is irrelevant and violates
ISP.
        throw new UnsupportedOperationException("Robots don't sleep.");
    }
}
```

```
public class Main {
    public static void main(String[] args) {
        Worker employee = new Employee();
        employee.work();
        employee.eat();
        employee.sleep();

        Worker robot = new Robot();
        robot.work();
        robot.eat();  // This call doesn't make sense for a Robot and
may cause errors.
        robot.sleep(); // This call doesn't make sense for a Robot and
may cause errors.
    }
}
```

In this example, the Worker interface violates the Interface Segregation Principle because it forces all implementing classes to provide implementations for methods like eat() and sleep(), even though those methods are not relevant for all types of workers (such as robots).

To adhere to the Interface Segregation Principle, you would need to break down the monolithic Worker interface into smaller, more focused interfaces based on the specific responsibilities of each type of worker, such as Workable, Eatable, and Sleepable. This way, each class would only need to implement the interfaces that are relevant to its behavior.

Dependency Inversion Principle (DIP)

In the following question, we also used the **ChatGPT 3.5** available using the web-based link:

https://chat.openai.com/ :

Do you have a Java Code example that illustrates the SOLID Dependency Inversion Principle?

Certainly! The Dependency Inversion Principle (DIP) is one of the SOLID principles that states that high-level modules should not depend on low-level modules. Both should depend on abstractions. Additionally, abstractions should not depend on details; details should depend on abstractions. In simpler terms, this principle encourages the use of interfaces or abstract classes to define high-level structures and relationships between components, promoting loose coupling and flexibility.

Here's a Java code example that illustrates the Dependency Inversion Principle:

In this example, the Dependency Inversion Principle is demonstrated by introducing the Switchable interface. Both the LightBulb and Fan classes implement the Switchable interface. The Switch class depends on the Switchable abstraction rather than concrete implementations. This allows you to easily switch between different types of devices (light bulbs, fans, and more) without modifying the Switch class.

```
// Dependency Inversion Principle Example


// High-level module that depends on an abstraction.
class LightBulb {
    void turnOn() {
        System.out.println("LightBulb: Bulb turned on.");
    }

    void turnOff() {
        System.out.println("LightBulb: Bulb turned off.");
    }
}

// Another high-level module that also depends on the same abstraction.
class Switch {
    private final Switchable device;

    Switch(Switchable device) {
        this.device = device;
    }

    void turnOn() {
        System.out.println("Switch: Turning on...");
        device.turnOn();
    }
```

```
    void turnOff() {
        System.out.println("Switch: Turning off...");
        device.turnOff();
    }
}

// Abstraction (interface) that both high-level modules depend on.
interface Switchable {
    void turnOn();
    void turnOff();
}

// Low-level module that implements the abstraction.
class Fan implements Switchable {
    @Override
    public void turnOn() {
        System.out.println("Fan: Fan turned on.");
    }

    @Override
    public void turnOff() {
        System.out.println("Fan: Fan turned off.");
    }
}

public class Main {
    public static void main(String[] args) {
        Switchable fan = new Fan();

        Switch fanSwitch = new Switch(fan);
        fanSwitch.turnOn();
        fanSwitch.turnOff();

        LightBulb bulb = new LightBulb();
```

```
        Switch bulbSwitch = new Switch(bulb);
        bulbSwitch.turnOn();
        bulbSwitch.turnOff();
    }
}
```

By adhering to the Dependency Inversion Principle, the code becomes more flexible, maintainable, and easier to extend. High-level modules are not tightly coupled to low-level modules, and changes in low-level modules do not affect the high-level modules.

Conclusion

In this chapter, we prompted **ChatGPT** to test its knowledge of good programming practice. We asked it to define what it knew about the "SOLID" principles which it did almost instantaneously. The AI program also provided code examples to illustrate the best practice for Java code indentation. (The following link covers the reasons why the **ChatGPT AI** can be very slow: **https://ecoagi.ai/topics/ChatGPT/why-is-chatgpt-slow**)

In the next chapter, we try using the OpenAI Java API to interface with the **ChatGPT AI** system. **ChatGPT** provided an example of how to make a request to the **API** using the **OkHttp** library.

We also try the **REST API** service provided for **ChatGPT** and the new **Whisper** speech to text feature.

Points to remember

- SOLID is a set of five principles for object-oriented programming, aim to make software designs more robust, flexible, and maintainable.
- Proper code indentation is essential for writing clean, readable, and maintainable Java code
- Take advantage of your Java Integrated Development Environments (IDE) auto-formatting feature to provide automatic code formatting, configured to follow your organizations indentation style.
- A Java class should have one single responsibility.
- You should be able to add new functionality to a Java class without modifying its existing code.

- Objects of a Java superclass should be replaceable with Objects of its subclasses without affecting the correctness of the program.
- Create smaller, more specific interfaces that cater to the needs of individual classes to promote better separation of concerns and avoid unnecessary dependencies.
- High-level Java modules should not depend on low-level modules. Both should depend on abstractions.

Multiple choice questions

1. **Which of the following is the best description of the Liskov Substitution Principle (LSP)?**
   a. A Java class should have one single responsibility.
   b. You should be able to add new functionality to a Java class without modifying its existing code.
   c. Objects of a Java superclass should be replaceable with Objects of its subclasses without affecting the correctness of the program.
   d. Create smaller, more specific interfaces that cater to the needs of individual classes to promote better separation of concerns and avoid unnecessary dependencies.
   e. High-level Java modules should not depend on low-level modules. Both should depend on abstractions.

2. **Which of the following is the best description of the Interface Segregation Principle (ISP)?**
   a. A Java class should have one single responsibility.
   b. You should be able to add new functionality to a Java class without modifying its existing code.
   c. Objects of a Java superclass should be replaceable with Objects of its subclasses without affecting the correctness of the program.
   d. Create smaller, more specific interfaces that cater to the needs of individual classes to promote better separation of concerns and avoid unnecessary dependencies.
   e. High-level Java modules should not depend on low-level modules. Both should depend on abstractions.

3. **Which recommendation best describes the indentation for Chaining and Method Calls?**
    a. Indent the case labels.
    b. Subsequent lines should be indented to indicate their continuation.
    c. Align the parameters for improved readability.
    d. Align the dots for better clarity.

Answers

1. **c**
2. **d**
3. **d**

Questions

1. Describe three different examples of Java code which displays the use of the SOLID principles.?
2. Can you think of one advantage of using the **ChatGPT 3.5** AI available using the web-based **OpenAI** link, **https://chat.openai.com/** compared with the **ChatGPT 3.5** AI available through the Ask AI Mobile 'phone App??
3. There are a couple of methods missing from the Java code example which illustrates the **SOLID Open/Closed Principle** compared with the code given for the **SOLID Liskov Substitution Principle**. Can you describe the purpose of these two methods?

Key terms

- **AI**: Artificial Intelligence Software that mimics the responses you might expect to questions supplied by a human operator.
- **OpenAI**: is the American artificial intelligence research laboratory that developed **ChatGPT** comprising the non-profit **OpenAI** organization and its for-profit subsidiary corporation **OpenAI Limited**.
- **Ask AI**: The Android mobile phone app is available for access to **ChatGPT** 3.5.
- **SOLID**: A set of five principles for object-oriented programming that were introduced by Robert C. Martin (also known as Uncle Bob).
- **SRP:** Single Responsibility Principle – the first listed principle.
- **OCP:** Open/Closed Principle– the second listed principle

- **LSP**: Liskov Substitution Principle– the third listed principle
- **ISP**: Interface Segregation Principle– the fourth listed principle
- **DIP**: Dependency Inversion Principle – the fifth listed principle
- **ChatGPT**: **ChatGPT** is a language model developed by **OpenAI**. It is based on the **GPT** (Generative Pre-trained Transformer) architecture, specifically **GPT-3.5** for the free use option. The model is designed to generate human-like text responses to user inputs, making it capable of engaging in interactive and natural-sounding conversations. **ChatGPT** has been trained on a massive amount of diverse textual data from the internet, allowing it to acquire a broad understanding of language and context. It uses deep learning techniques, particularly **transformers**, which enable it to process and generate text effectively. This language model has a wide range of applications, including answering questions, providing explanations, giving recommendations, offering creative writing assistance, language translation, and code generation. It can be integrated into various software operating systems and hardware platforms and can be used to create software applications to offer interactive and conversational experiences for users using the **ChatGPT API** interface.

CHAPTER 3
Developing Java Code for Utilizing the ChatGPT API

Introduction

This chapter describes the use of the **OpenAI** Java **API** to interface with the **ChatGPT AI** system. **ChatGPT** provided an example of how to make a request to the **API** using the **OkHttp** library.

Structure

In this chapter, we will discuss the following topics:

- The **ChatGPT API** overview
- **ChatGPT's AI**-Generated Java code **API** examples
- Validation of the suggested **API** Code
    - Accessing the **ChatGPT**-referenced **OkHttp** Java Library Jar files
    - Accessing the **ChatGPT** Secret **API** Key
    - Using **ChatGPT** Model Ids

The ChatGPT API overview

An overview of the **ChatGPT** and **OpenAI** organization systems available can be found, after obtaining an **OpenAI** account, using the link:

https://platform.openai.com/overview

There is a "quick start" link for developers, accessible from this web page:

https://platform.openai.com/docs/quickstart/build-your-application

Originally, most GPT models processed unstructured text, presented to the model as a sequence of "tokens". ChatGPT models operate differently, using a sequence of messages together with metadata. Although the input is rendered to the model as a sequence of "tokens" for the model to process, the raw format used is in a format, which **OpenAI** refers to as Chat Markup Language ("**ChatML**").

OpenAI uses a pay-as-you-go system per 1,000 tokens. For the initial three months of use, they provide **$5** in free credit to developers. They use the **text-davinci-003** model in their javascript code example, but they suggest that the new **gpt-3.5-turbo** model may be best for initial testing. Later, you can progress to check other models to compare the efficiency of the responses, as different models might perform better depending on the required functionality.

The total number of tokens processed in a single request (both prompt and completion) can't exceed the model's maximum context length. For most models, this is 4,096 tokens or about 3,000 words (1 token is approximately 4 characters or 0.75 words for English text).

OpenAI has recently announced that **ChatGPT** can now be integrated with its **Whisper** models, through the **ChatGPT API**.

The **Whisper** models give access to language and speech-to-text functionality. **OpenAI** has provided programmers with complete access to their open-source **Whisper large-v2** model in the **API**, giving much faster (and more efficient processor) results.

OpenAI has developed a **REST API** endpoint to interact with their **ChatGPT** models.

The example code pattern they provide for this interaction is as follows:

```
curl https://api.openai.com/v1/chat/completions \
 -H "Authorization: Bearer $OPENAI_API_KEY" \
 -H "Content-Type: application/json" \
 -d '{
 "model": "gpt-3.5-turbo",
```

```
 "messages": [{"role": "user", "content": "What is the OpenAI
mission?"}]
 }'
```

Note: There is a free-to-download publication from ResearchGate (copyright **ASB Software Development Limited**), which you can use to install a free RedHat RHEL 8.x Linux operating system, including the supporting **VMware** virtual server running on an MS Windows operating system: **https://doi.org/10.13140/RG.2.2.14590.95049**

This REST URL gives the following result, after posting, when we use our **OpenAI** key in a Linux command window:

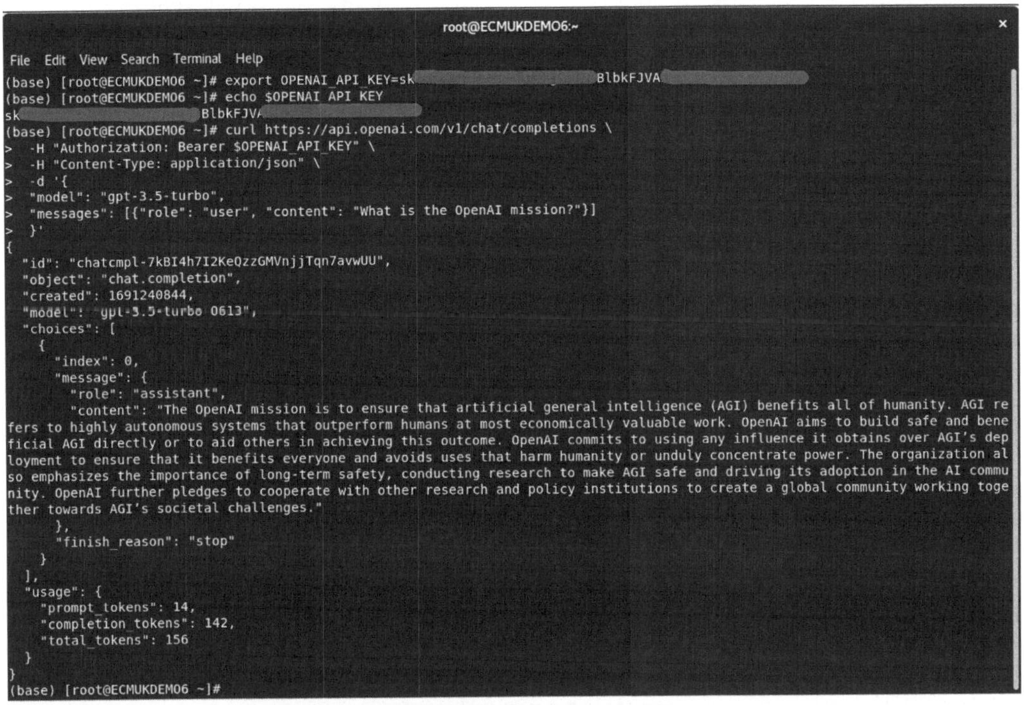

Figure 3.1: *The OpenAI REST API endpoint example*

The **$OPENAI_API_KEY** environment variable just needs to be set with a unique key, as shown in the redacted example. This involves using the **OpenAI** key, which we will show how to download from your **OpenAI** account later in this chapter, in the section **Accessing the ChatGPT Secret API Key**.

I have highlighted in **bold** the JSON formatted response returned by the **ChatGPT AI.**

```
(base) [root@ECMUKDEMO6 ~]# export OPENAI_API_
```

```
KEY=skxxxxxxxxxxxxxxxxxxxxxxxBlbkFJVAxxxxxxxxxxxxxxxxxxx
(base) [root@ECMUKDEMO6 ~]# echo $OPENAI_API_KEY
skxxxxxxxxxxxxxxxxxxxxxxxBlbkFJVAxxxxxxxxxxxxxxxxxxx
(base) [root@ECMUKDEMO6 ~]# curl https://api.openai.com/v1/chat/
completions \
>  -H "Authorization: Bearer $OPENAI_API_KEY" \
>  -H "Content-Type: application/json" \
>  -d '{
>  "model": "gpt-3.5-turbo",
>  "messages": [{"role": "user", "content": "What is the OpenAI
mission?"}]
>  }'
```


```
{
  "id": "chatcmpl-7kBI4h7I2KeQzzGMVnjjTqn7avwUU",
  "object": "chat.completion",
  "created": 1691240844,
  "model": "gpt-3.5-turbo-0613",
  "choices": [
    {
      "index": 0,
      "message": {
        "role": "assistant",
        "content": "The OpenAI mission is to ensure that artificial
general intelligence (AGI) benefits all of humanity. AGI refers to
highly autonomous systems that outperform humans at most economically
valuable work. OpenAI aims to build safe and beneficial AGI directly or
to aid others in achieving this outcome. OpenAI commits to using any
influence it obtains over AGI's deployment to ensure that it benefits
everyone and avoids uses that harm humanity or unduly concentrate power.
The organization also emphasizes the importance of long-term safety,
conducting research to make AGI safe and driving its adoption in the
AI community. OpenAI further pledges to cooperate with other research
and policy institutions to create a global community working together
towards AGI's societal challenges."
      },
      "finish_reason": "stop"
    }
  ],
```

```
  "usage": {
    "prompt_tokens": 14,
    "completion_tokens": 142,
    "total_tokens": 156
  }
}
(base) [root@ECMUKDEMO6 ~]#
```

Whisper, the speech-to-text model, was released in September 2022 by **OpenAI** and was recently updated to the **large-v2** model available through the **Whisper API** (this is charged as $0.006/minute).

Whisper API currently accepts the following sound file formats:

m4a, mp3, mp4, mpeg, mpga, wav, webm

OpenAI has also supplied an example code pattern for **Whisper AI**:

```
curl https://api.openai.com/v1/audio/transcriptions \
  -H "Authorization: Bearer $OPENAI_API_KEY" \
  -H "Content-Type: multipart/form-data" \
  -F model="whisper-1" \
  -F file="@/path/to/file/openai.mp3"
```

We used a mobile phone to record a **.wav** file and copied it to use on the Linux system.

(This sound file, **`Recording9.wav`**, was converted to text (highlighted in **bold**) with 100% accuracy!)

First, we copied the original emailed file (**`Recording 9.wav`**) to the Linux VMWare server **`/root`** directory and removed the space from the file name using the **`mv`** command to rename it:

```
(base) [root@ECMUKDEMO6 ~]# cp /mnt/hgfs/Installs/Recording\ 9.wav .
(base) [root@ECMUKDEMO6 ~]# mv Recording\ 9.wav Recording9.wav
(base) [root@ECMUKDEMO6 ~]# pwd
/root
```

The command was then run (with the key already set in the **`OPEN_API_KEY`** environment variable) using the following:

```
(base) [root@ECMUKDEMO6 ~]# curl https://api.openai.com/v1/audio/
transcriptions \
>   -H "Authorization: Bearer $OPENAI_API_KEY" \
```

```
>    -H "Content-Type: multipart/form-data" \
>    -F model="whisper-1" \
>    -F file="@/root/Recording9.wav"
{"text":"This is a very short example file to show the availability of ChatGPT to translate a voice file into a text stream."(((((base) [root@ECMUKDEMO6 ~]#
```

***Figure 3.2**: The **OpenAI** REST **API** endpoint example using the **whisper-1** model*

For additional links, please visit **https://openai.com/blog/introducing-chatgpt-and-whisper-apis**.

In this link, **OpenAI** restates for developers that they are:

"Simplifying our Terms of Service and Usage Policies, including terms around data ownership: **users own the input and output of the models.**"

ChatGPT's AI-Generated Java code API examples

Using **Ask AI** on the mobile phone, we asked **ChatGPT** for a Java program example for using the **API** interfacing to the server-based **AI**.

Is there an example of a Java program code to interface with the ChatGPT AI system?

*Yes, you can use the **OpenAI API** to interface with the **ChatGPT AI** system in Java. Here is an example of how to make a request to the **API** using the **OkHttp** library:*

```
```java
import okhttp3.*;


public class ChatGPTApi {
    private static final String API_KEY = "YOUR_API_KEY";
    private static final String MODEL_ID = "YOUR_MODEL_ID";
    private static final String API_URL = "https://api.openai.com/v1/
engines/" + MODEL_ID + "/completions";


    public static String getResponseFromGPT(String prompt) throws
Exception {
```
```

```
        OkHttpClient client = new OkHttpClient().newBuilder()
                .build();
        MediaType mediaType = MediaType.parse("application/json");
        RequestBody body = RequestBody.create(mediaType, "{\"prompt\":
\"" + prompt + "\",\"temperature\":0.7,\"max_tokens\":60}");
        Request request = new Request.Builder()
                .url(API_URL)
                .method("POST", body)
                .addHeader("Content-Type", "application/json")
                .addHeader("Authorization", "Bearer " + API_KEY)
                .build();
        Response response = client.newCall(request).execute();
        String responseJson = response.body().string();
        response.close();
        return responseJson;
    }

    public static void main(String[] args) throws Exception {
        String responseJson = getResponseFromGPT("Hello, how are you?");
        System.out.println(responseJson);
    }
}
```

In this example, you need to replace `YOUR_API_KEY` with your actual OpenAI API key and `YOUR_MODEL_ID` with the ID of the ChatGPT model you want to use. You can find the model ID in your OpenAI dashboard.

The `getResponseFromGPT` method takes a prompt string as an argument and returns a JSON string containing the response from the ChatGPT model. The `main` method, in this example, demonstrates how to use the `getResponseFromGPT` method to get a response from the ChatGPT model.

Note that using the OpenAI API requires that you have an OpenAI API key, which you can obtain by signing up for an OpenAI account and creating an API key.

Validation of the suggested API Code

We must now test the Java code created by **ChatGPT** to validate that we have working code. So, we need to load this code into a suitable Java program development **IDE**. For this book, we used the latest available **Eclipse IDE**. The download and installation of **Eclipse IDE 2023-06** is covered step-by-step in **Chapter 5, Installation of the latest Open-Source Eclipse Java IDE**.

ChatGPT, like many other **LLM**-based **AI** systems, can give incorrect results (There can also be issues with the generation of **AI Hallucinations**). See the free pdf file article available at: **https://assets.cureus.com/uploads/editorial/pdf/138667/20230219-28928-6kcyip.pdf**

In this article on medical diagnosis, from a **ChatGPT** response, they quoted:

ChatGPT defines artificial hallucination in the following section. "Artificial hallucination refers to the phenomenon of a machine, such as a chatbot, generating seemingly realistic sensory experiences that do not correspond to any real-world input. This can include visual, auditory, or other types of hallucinations. .... there have been instances where advanced AI systems, such as generative models, have been found to produce hallucinations, particularly when trained on large amounts of unsupervised data."

Accessing the ChatGPT-referenced OkHttp Java Library Jar files

This raises the question about how to access the Java Library jar files, such as **OkHttp**, which are referenced in the **ChatGPT** responses. So, I asked **ChatGPT**:

What are the best Java Jar file Download Sites?

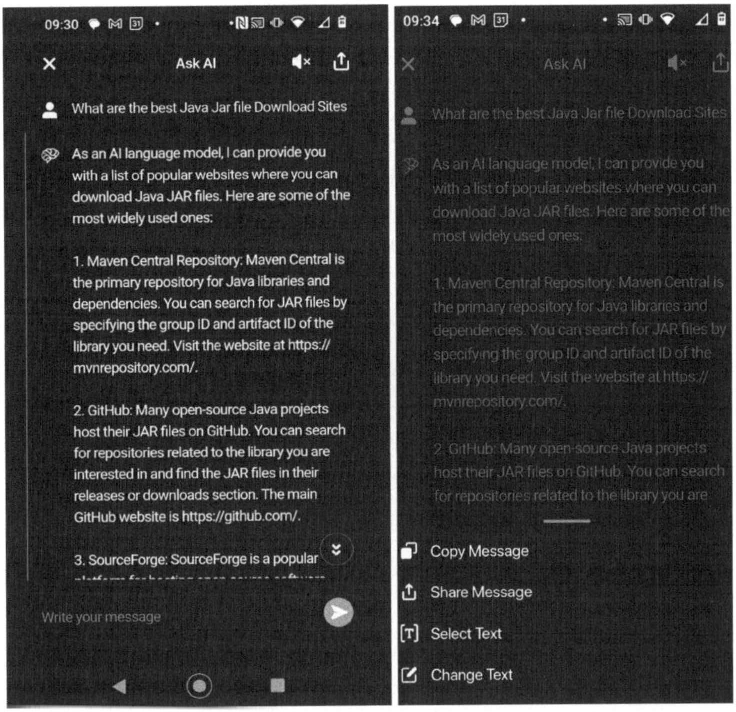

Figure 3.3: *(a) ASK AI Phone App question 2 (b) Press down on the window areas to copy*

The Android phone **Ask AI** mobile phone application responses (and questions) can be copied, as shown in *Figure 3.3 (b)*, by pressing a finger on the question or response window area and then selecting **Copy Message** to obtain the following response:

"As an AI language model, I can provide you with a list of popular websites where you can download Java JAR files. Here are some of the most widely used ones:

1. ***Maven Central Repository:*** *Maven Central is the primary repository for Java libraries and dependencies. You can search for JAR files by specifying the group ID and artifact ID of the library you need. Visit the website at* ***https://mvnrepository.com/****.*
2. ***GitHub:*** *Many open-source Java projects host their JAR files on GitHub. You can search for repositories related to the library you are interested in and find the JAR files in their releases or downloads section. The main GitHub website is* ***https://github.com/****.*
3. ***SourceForge:*** *SourceForge is a popular platform for hosting open-source software, including Java projects. You can search for Java libraries and download JAR files from the project's files section. Visit SourceForge at* ***https://sourceforge.net/****.*

4. JCenter: JCenter was a popular repository for Java libraries, but it has been sunsetted and is no longer recommended for new projects. However, existing projects may still have JAR files available on JCenter. Visit the website at **https://bintray.com/bintray/jcenter**.
5. Apache Maven Repository: Apache Maven also hosts a repository for Java libraries and dependencies. You can search for JAR files using the Maven coordinates of the library you want. The website for Apache Maven Repository is **https://repository.apache.org/**.

Please note that when downloading JAR files from external websites, it's important to verify the integrity and authenticity of the files to ensure they are from trusted sources. Additionally, consider using a build automation tool like Maven or Gradle, which can manage dependencies and automatically download JAR files from reputable sources."

We used the first option, using the following link:

https://mvnrepository.com/

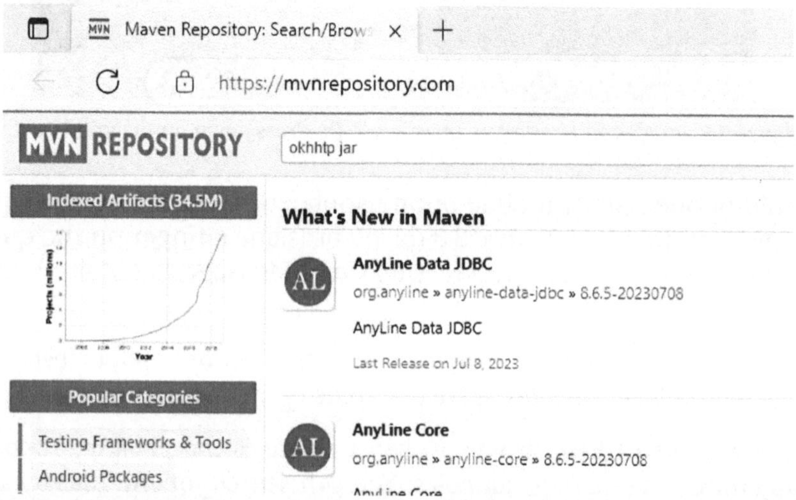

***Figure 3.4**: The Maven repository search field is used to search for the **okhttp.jar** file*

Searching for the **okhttp3 jar** gives:

https://mvnrepository.com/artifact/com.squareup.okhttp3/okhttp

Note

We had to use **Version 3.2** eventually, as some features we needed were removed in the later versions of the **okhttp.jar** file.

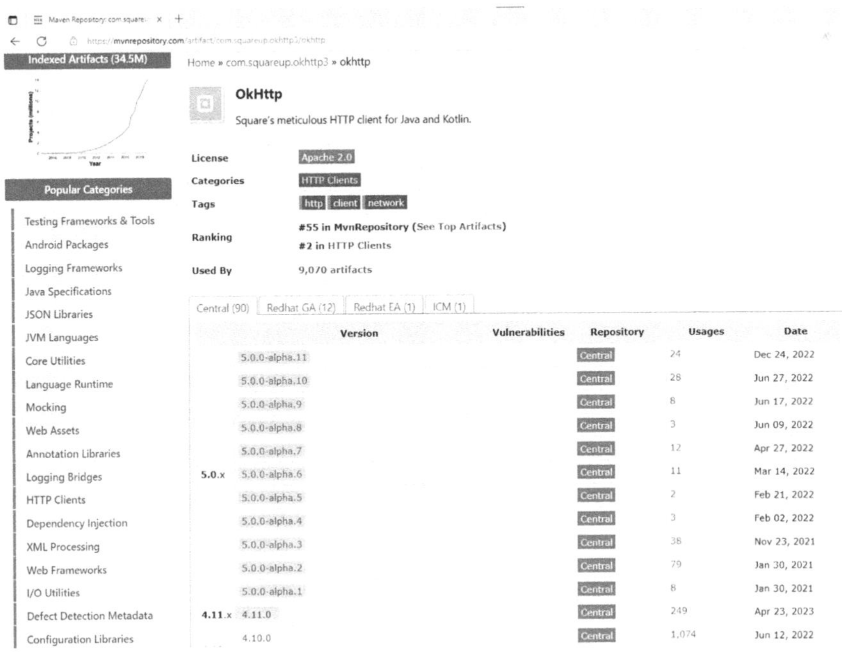

Figure 3.5: *The maven repository web page showing the* **OkHttp3 jar** *download page*

This gave the highlighted link, as shown in *Figure* 3.5. Clicking on this link gives the Jar, which is selected using the highlighted link in *Figure* 3.6.

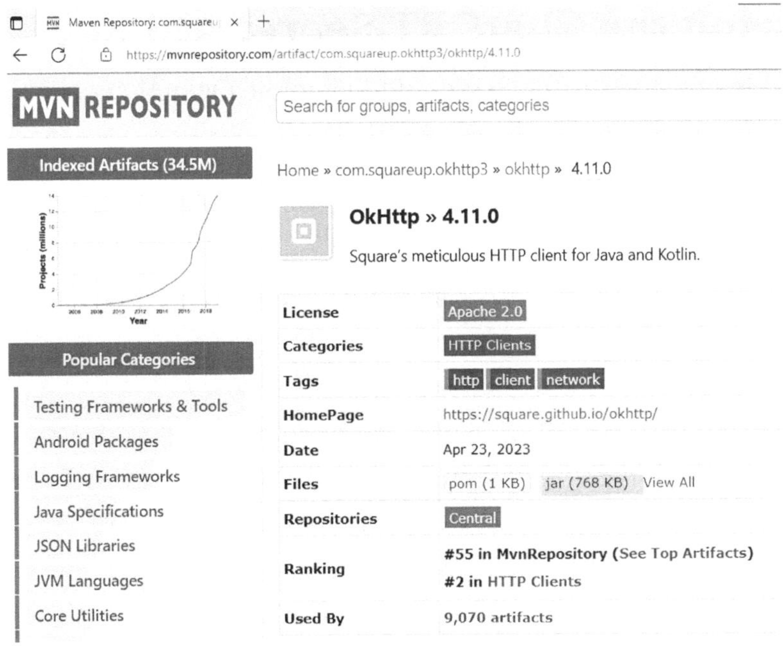

Figure 3.6: *The highlighted link is clicked to download the* **ChatGPT-***referenced* **OkHttp3** *jar*

When this version failed, we used the earlier version 3.2, available at the following links:

https://mvnrepository.com/artifact/com.squareup.okhttp3/okhttp/3.2.0

and

https://repo1.maven.org/maven2/com/squareup/okhttp3/okhttp/3.2.0/okhttp-3.2.0.jar

Note

We also found we had to change the Eclipse project **JVM** from Java 17 to Java 11

The Chrome browser prompted us to ensure that we were happy to download a .jar file (which could contain malware). We selected the **Keep** option, as shown in *Figure 3.7*.

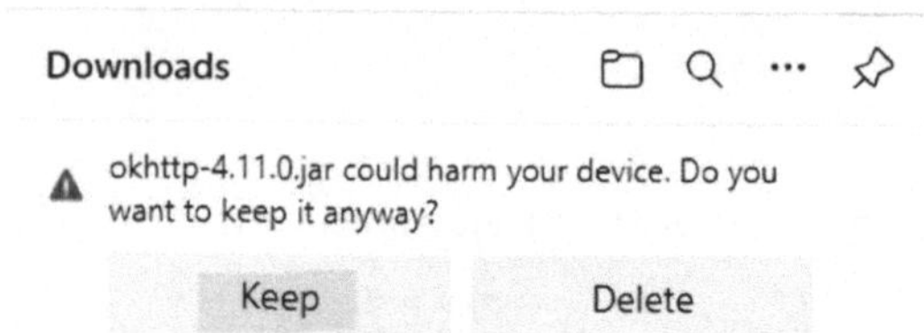

Figure 3.7*: The Chrome browser warns about the download of jar files, we selected* **Keep**

Accessing the ChatGPT Secret API Key

The next thing we need is the Secret API Key in the OpenAI Account. The steps are as follows:

Log in using **https://platform.openai.com/**

1. Once logged in, click on your profile name or Icon to open the menu.

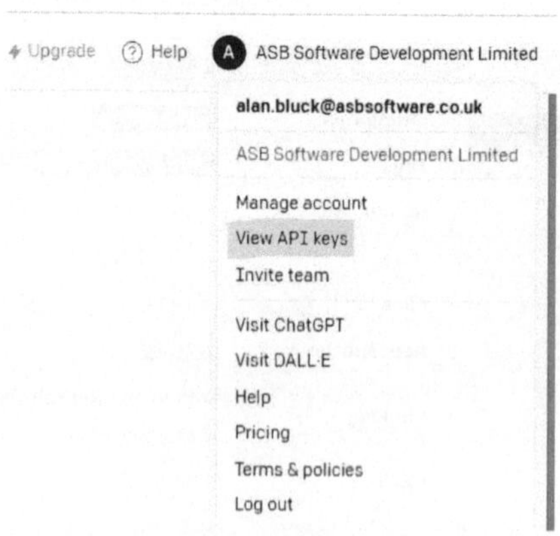

Figure 3.8*: The* ***View API keys*** *dropdown menu item is selected*

2. On the **API** Keys page, you will see a list of existing Secret Keys.

   The first time into the profile, you need to select the **Create new secret key**, as highlighted in *Figure* 3.9.

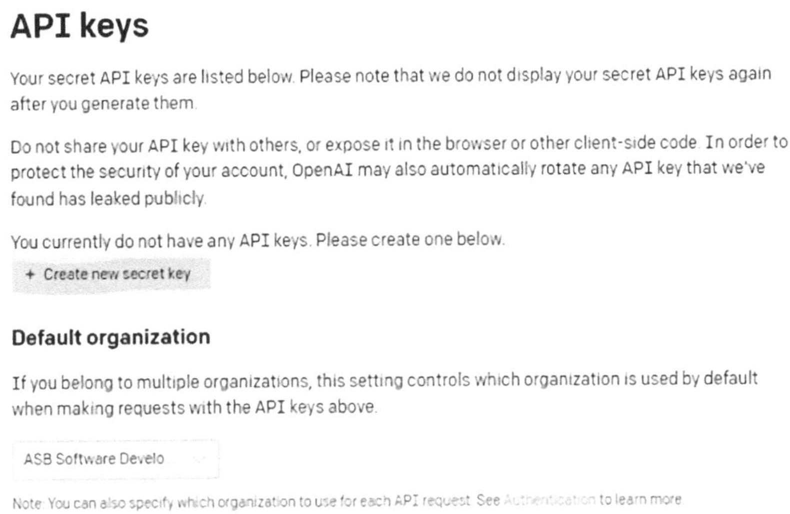

***Figure* 3.9**: *The Create new secret key link is clicked as highlighted*

3. Then, click the green icon on the popup page to copy your **OpenAI** secret key to a safe place, as shown in *Figure* 3.10.

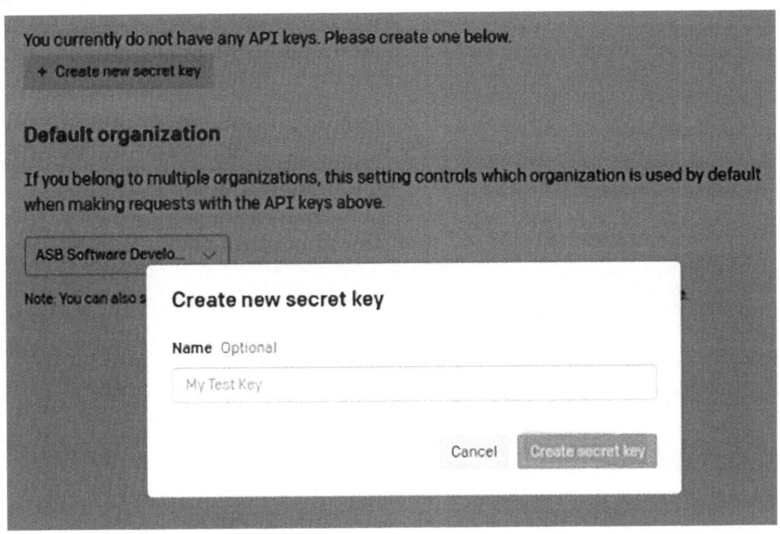

Figure* 3.10**: *The* ***Create secret key *button is clicked*

First, select the  icon to copy the generated key, as shown in *Figure 3.11*.

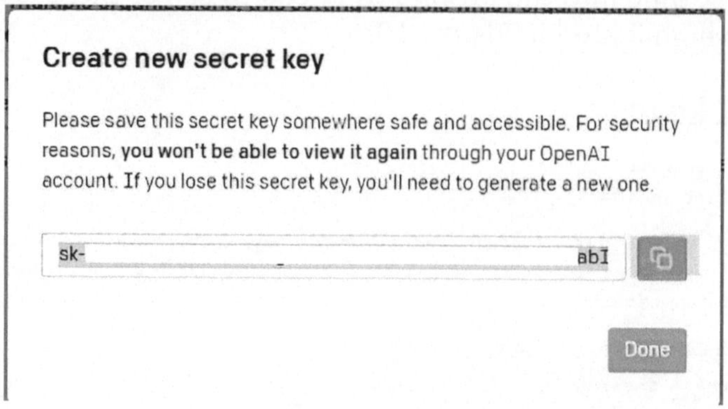

Figure 3.11: *The new key can now be copied using the highlighted icon*

Next, we need to paste the copied key to a suitable safe text file and save it for use in the Java code.

After you have a secure copy of the key, you can click **Done.**

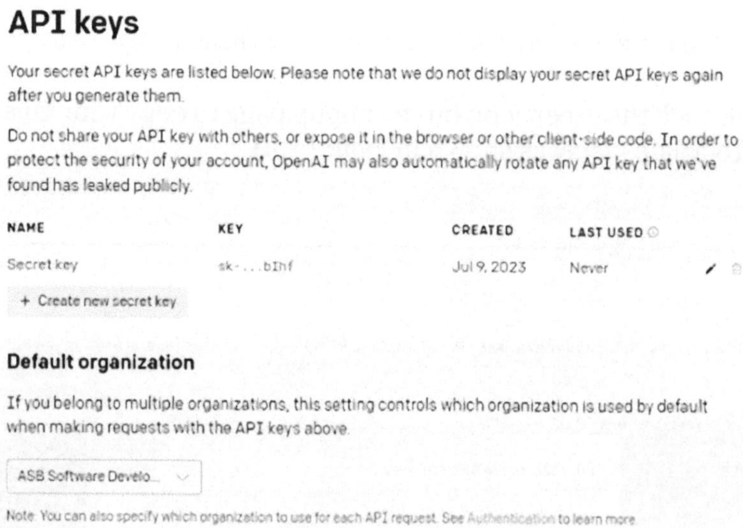

Figure 3.12: *The generated key is now listed*

A link to the API introduction tutorial can be accessed by clicking on the green "Authentication" link, as shown in *Figure* 3.12.

(This links to **https://platform.openai.com/docs/api-reference/introduction**)

There is a link on the OpenAI website as follows:

https://openai.com/blog/gpt-4-api-general-availability

This shows the status of the ChatGPT version available for access.

Using ChatGPT Model Ids

ChatGPT models are described in detail in the link **https://platform.openai.com/docs/models/overview**

The model used for our example queries was **gpt-3.5-turbo**. The installation of the **Eclipse IDE** is shown step-by-step in *Chapter* 5, *Installation of the latest Open-Source Eclipse Java IDE.*

Running the **ChatGPT API** code example, we create a project in the **Eclipse IDE** by following these steps and clicking on the Create a Java project link, as shown in *Figure* 3.13.

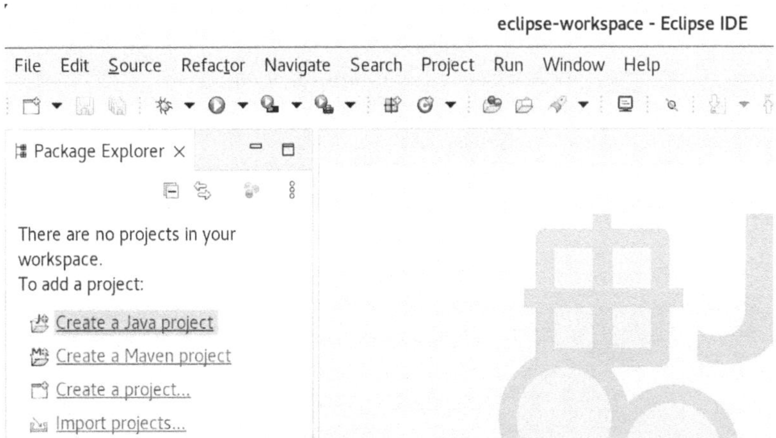

***Figure* 3.13**: *The Create a Java project was selected in the new Eclipse installation*

We enter the **Eclipse IDE** Project name as **ChatGPTAPI_ExampleChapter3**, highlighted in *Figure* 3.14.

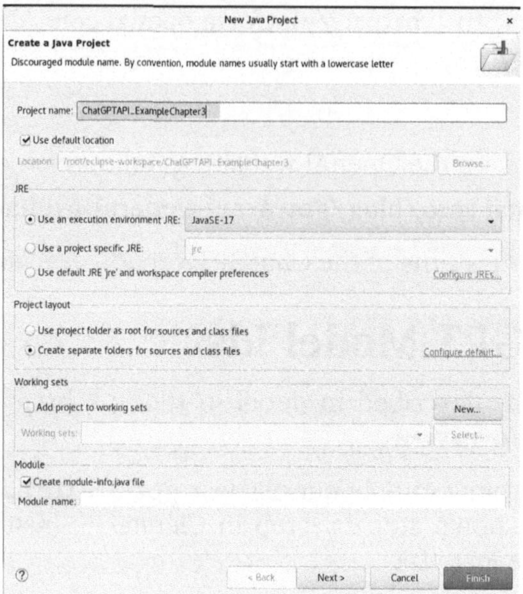

Figure 3.14: *The Project name is entered as* **ChatGPTAPI_ExampleChapter3**

The new project is created once we click the Finish button, as shown in *Figure* 3.15.

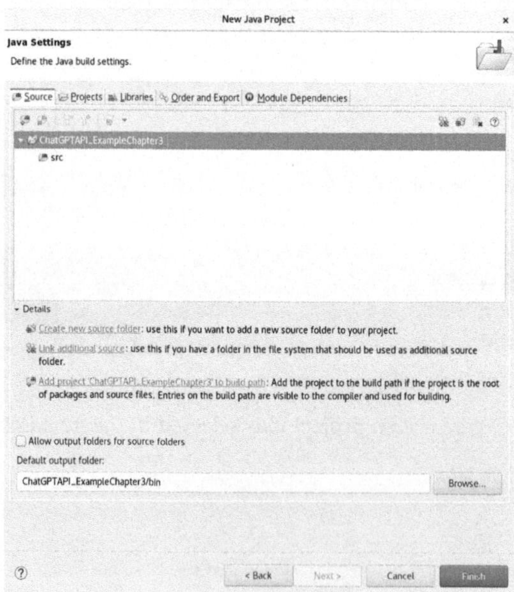

Figure 3.15: *The Finish button is clicked to create the Eclipse project in the IDE*

We now create a new class called **ChatGPTApi**, with a package name of **com.asb**, as highlighted in *Figure 3.16*.

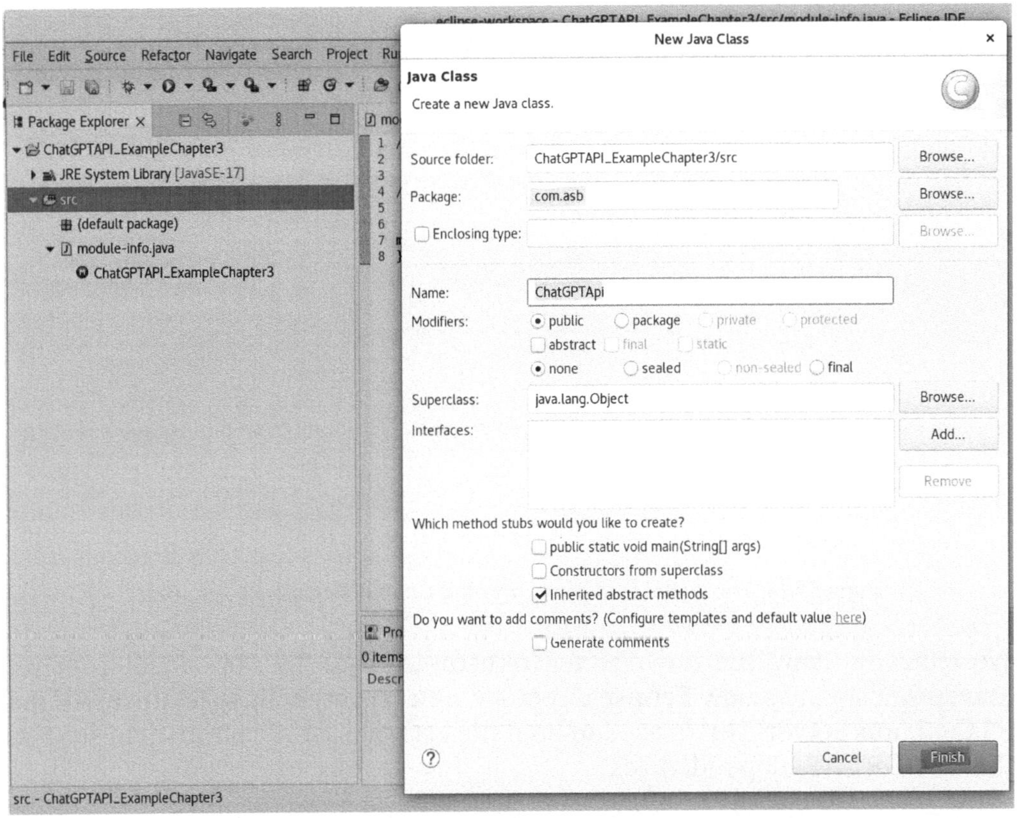

Figure 3.16*: A new Java class called* ***ChatGPTApi*** *is created*

After the **Finish** button is clicked, the new **ChatGPTApi** Java class is given an empty "skeleton" structure, ready for pasting code into, as shown in *Figure 3.17*.

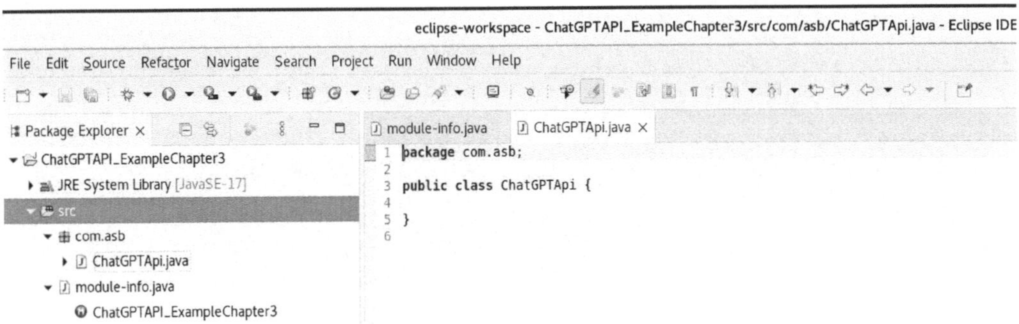

Figure 3.17*: The empty code structure is displayed*

As shown in *Figure* 3.18, the loaded code has a number of issues. First, we need to provide a valid version of the **okhttp3.jar** file, as this is missing from the **Class Path** of the project.

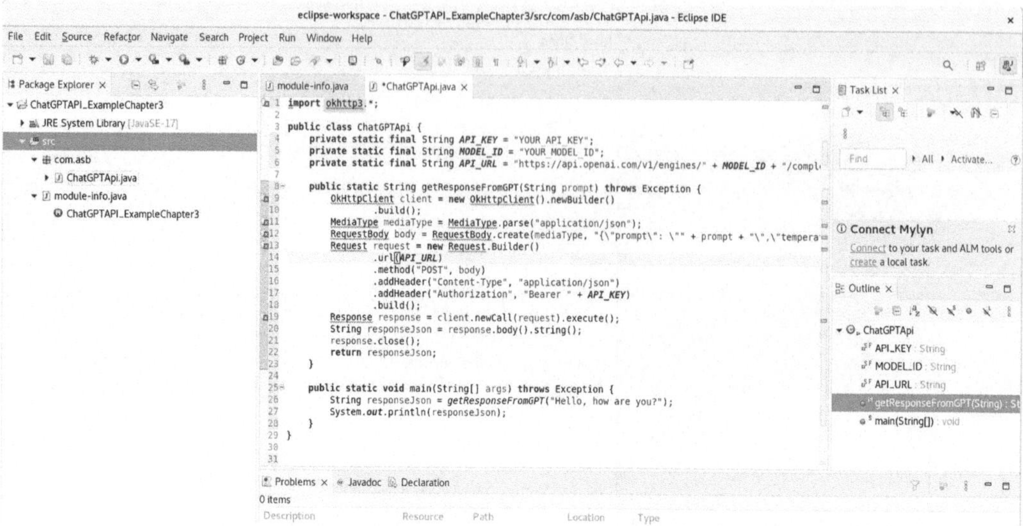

Figure 3.18: *The initial load of the original* **ChatGPT** *response Java code*

We can now copy the downloaded **okhttp-4.11.0.jar** file, obtained from the **Maven** website, to a new **Eclipse** directory area, **/root/eclipse/eclipse/AILibs,** on the **Linux** server. This is used to hold the external .jar file libraries to support the **ChatGPT API** dependencies.

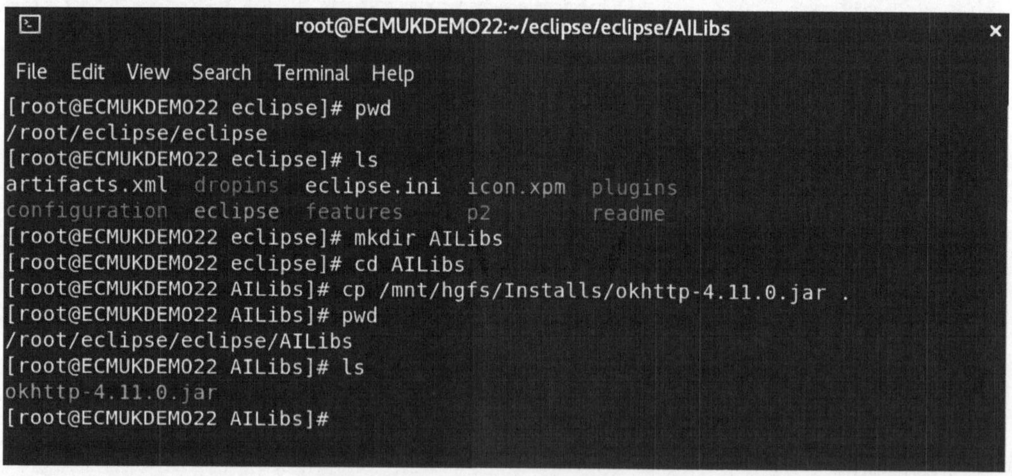

Figure 3.19: *The recommended* **ChatGPT** *jar file,* **okhttp-4.11.0.jar,** *is copied to an* **Eclipse** *area*

The Project properties are selected to update the project Class path, as shown in *Figure* 3.20.

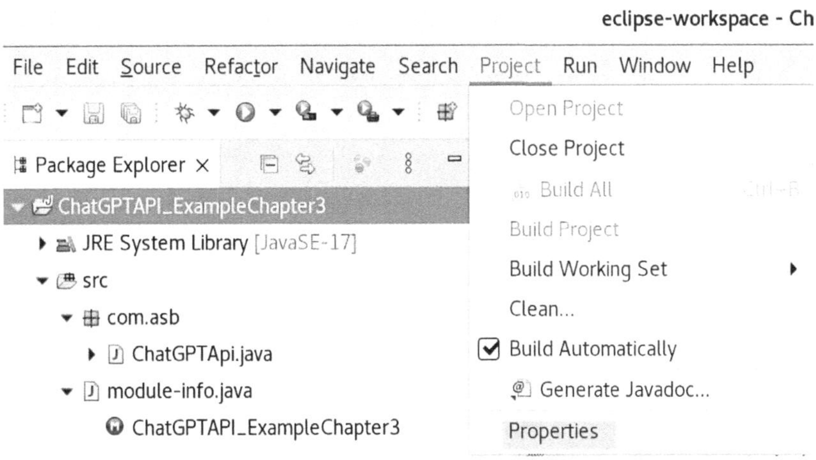

Figure 3.20: *The Project properties are selected to update the project Class path*

The Add External jars option is used to update the Class path, as shown in *Figure* 3.21.

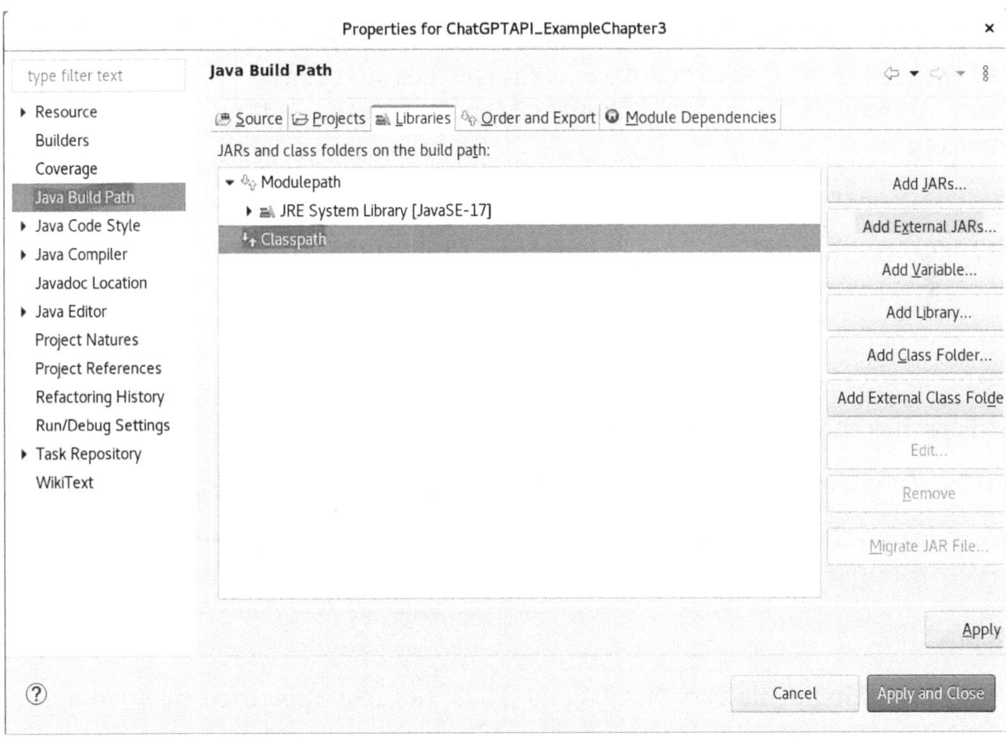

Figure 3.21: *The* **Add External JARs** *button is clicked*

We can now add the jar file we downloaded and copied by browsing the Eclipse jar area we created, as shown in *Figure* 3.22.

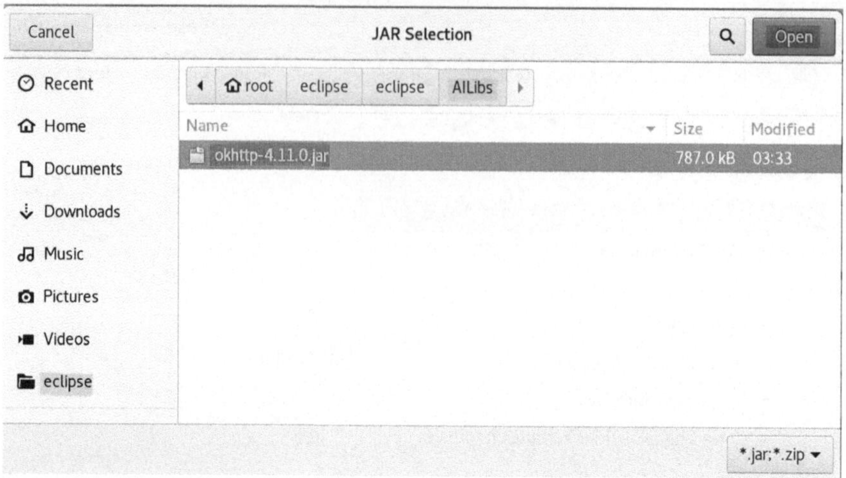

Figure* 3.22**: *The* **okhttp-4.11.0.jar** *file is selected from the directory* ***/root/eclipse/eclipse/AILibs

We discovered the need for another supporting Java library. While running the program, an error occurred:

"`The type` **`okio.ByteString`** `cannot be resolved. It is indirectly referenced from required type okhttp3.RequestBody ChatGPTApi.java /ChatGPTAPI_ExampleChapter3/src/com/asb line 1J a v a Problem`"

which we searched finding the link:

https://stackoverflow.com/questions/35329028/okhttp-error-cannot-access-bytestring

So, we needed to download the **okio jar** file. We used the link: https://mvnrepository.com/artifact/com.squareup.okio/okio

This jar has the highlighted link:

https://mvnrepository.com/artifact/com.squareup.okio/okio/2.8.0

We selected the latest working stable version, which is 2.8 (as shown in the blog error response).

> **Note**
>
> *The later* **okio** *jar file versions 3.4 and 3.5 do not work (we tried them) and also are much smaller.*

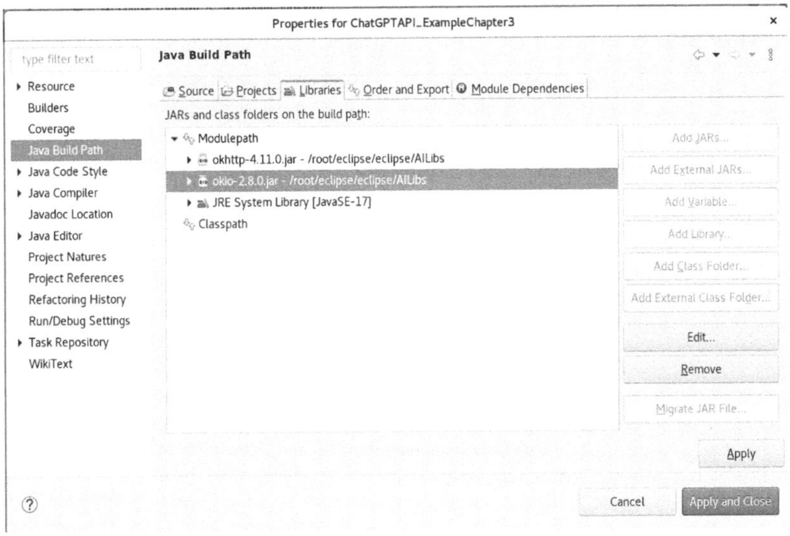

Figure 3.23**: The **okio-2.8.0.jar** file was added from **/root/eclipse/eclipse/AILibs

On the first run, we get:

```
Exception in thread "main" java.lang.NoClassDefFoundError: kotlin/
jvm/internal/markers/KMappedMarker
```

Internet searches suggested that we needed **kotlin-stdlib-1.3.41.jar.** (This can be found on the page: **https://mvnrepository.com/artifact/org.jetbrains.kotlin/kotlin-stdlib-jdk7/1.3.41**)

Then, we also added **kotlin-runtime-1.2.71.jar** using the following URL links:

https://mvnrepository.com/artifact/org.jetbrains.kotlin/kotlin-runtime

https://repo1.maven.org/maven2/org/jetbrains/kotlin/kotlin-runtime/1.2.71/kotlin-runtime-1.2.71.jar

Now, we get the error message:

```
Error caused by: java.lang.ClassNotFoundException: kotlin.collections.
AbstractList
```

We selected the following link for some ideas on how to fix this:

https://beginnersbook.com/2017/12/kotlin-in-eclipse-ide/

So, we realized that we need to install the **Kotlin** plugin framework for Eclipse to satisfy the project dependencies. We selected the **Help** drop-down menu, **Eclipse Marketplace...** menu option, as shown in *Figure* 3.24.

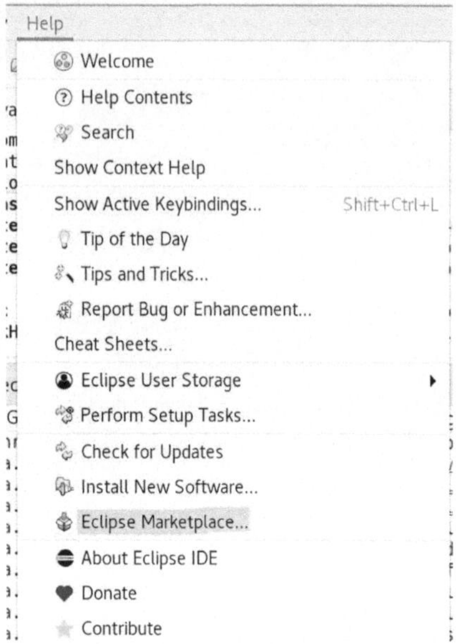

***Figure 3.24**: The **Help** drop-down menu, **Eclipse Marketplace...** menu option is clicked*

We select the **Enhanced Kotlin for Eclipse** in the search results, as shown in *Figure* 3.25, and select all the boxes.

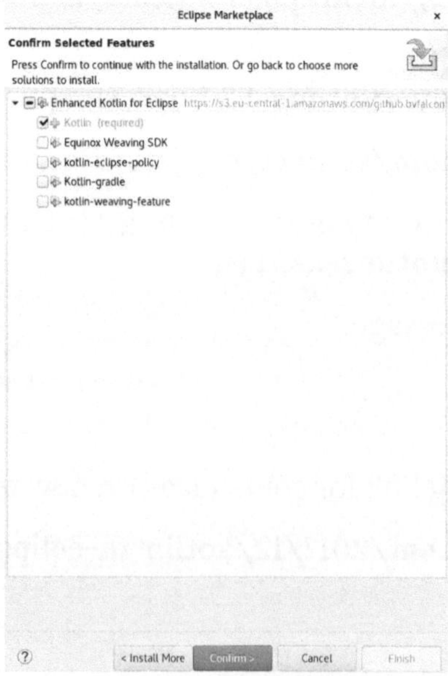

***Figure 3.25**: The Kotlin install options are displayed*

All the supporting packages for Kotlin are selected, as shown in *Figure 3.26*.

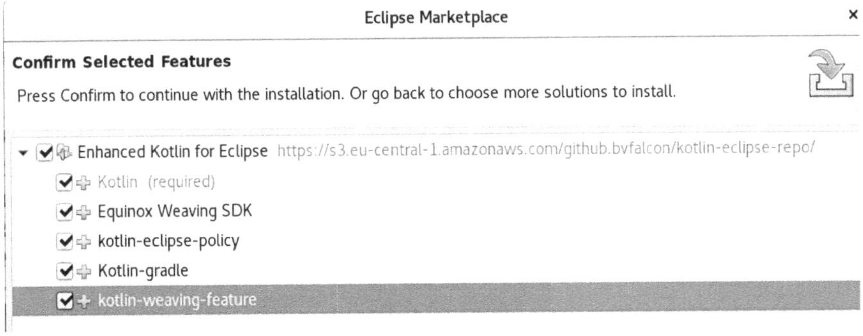

Figure 3.26: *The full set of Kotlin installation option tick boxes are selected*

The License text is displayed, and we click the highlighted **I accept** radio button option, as shown in *Figure 3.27*.

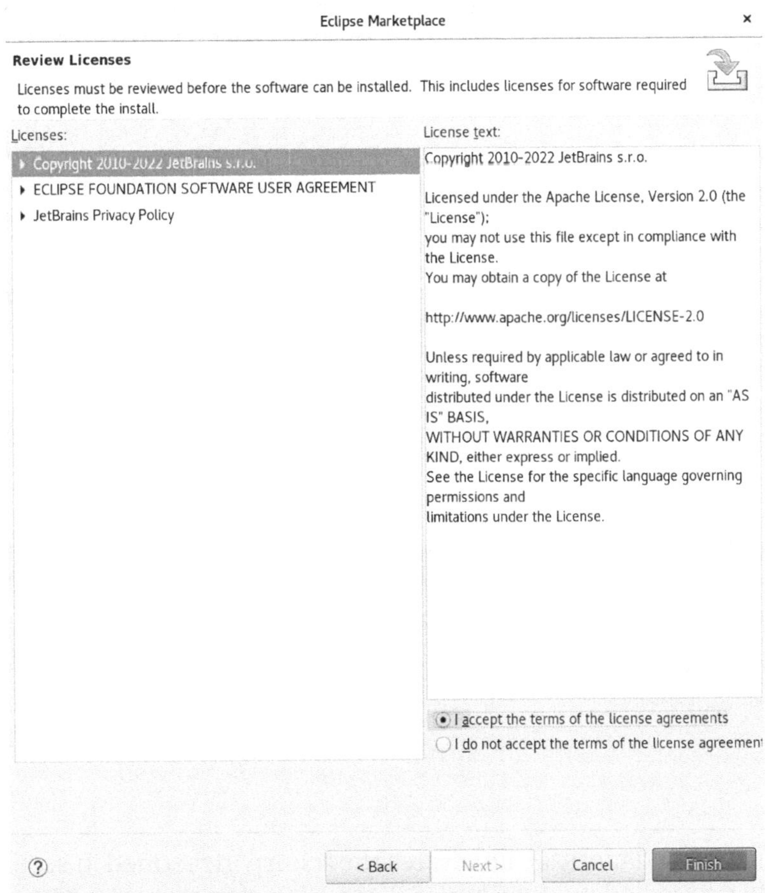

Figure 3.27: *The* ***I accept*** *option is selected and the* ***Finish*** *button is clicked*

The next screen displays the Trust authorities, which we can select to allow updates, as shown in *Figure* 3.28.

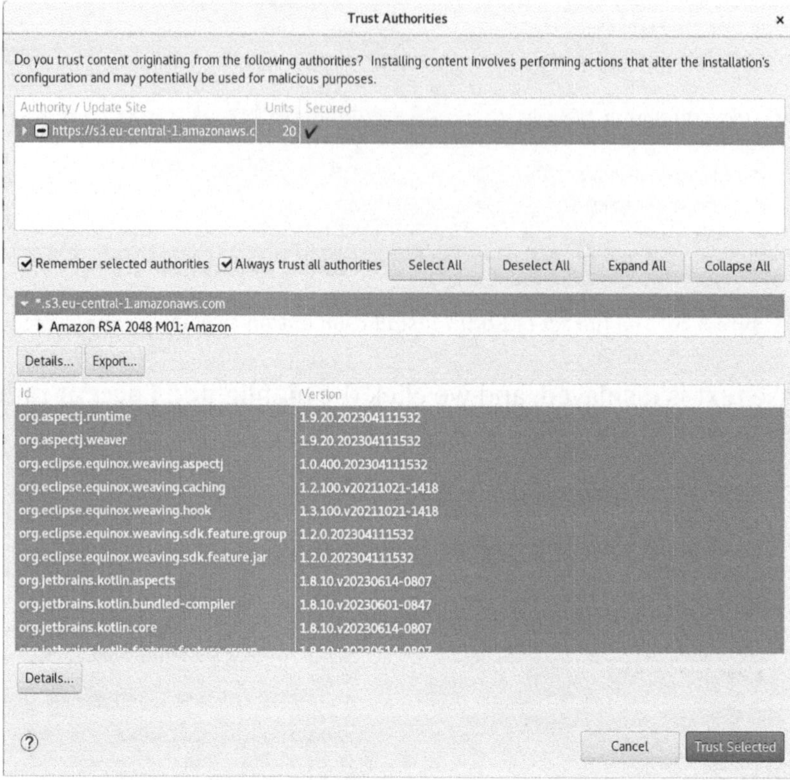

Figure 3.28: *The Trust Authorities are required to be selected to allow updates as required*

On the first (partly successful) run of the code suggested by **ChatGPT**, we got:

```
{
  "error": {
    "message": "This is a chat model and not supported in the v1/
completions endpoint. Did you mean to use v1/chat/completions?",
    "type": "invalid_request_error",
    "param": "model",
    "code": null
  }
}
```

The aforementioned message illustrates the "churn" described in several articles on the code supported by the **ChatGPT API**. Unfortunately, the **API** parameters are not at all stable. The model reference names and web links are regularly changed by **OpenAI,** causing the **ChatGPT** responses for example **API** code given in responses to quickly become outdated.

However, even given this limitation, there are very useful **ChatGPT** responses to more stable requirements such as the algorithms for Java code we are using as examples in the rest of this book.

The preceding issues were still present, even after updating several imports for libraries, as shown in *Figure* 3.29, and using the **Kotlin** plugin for **Eclipse**.

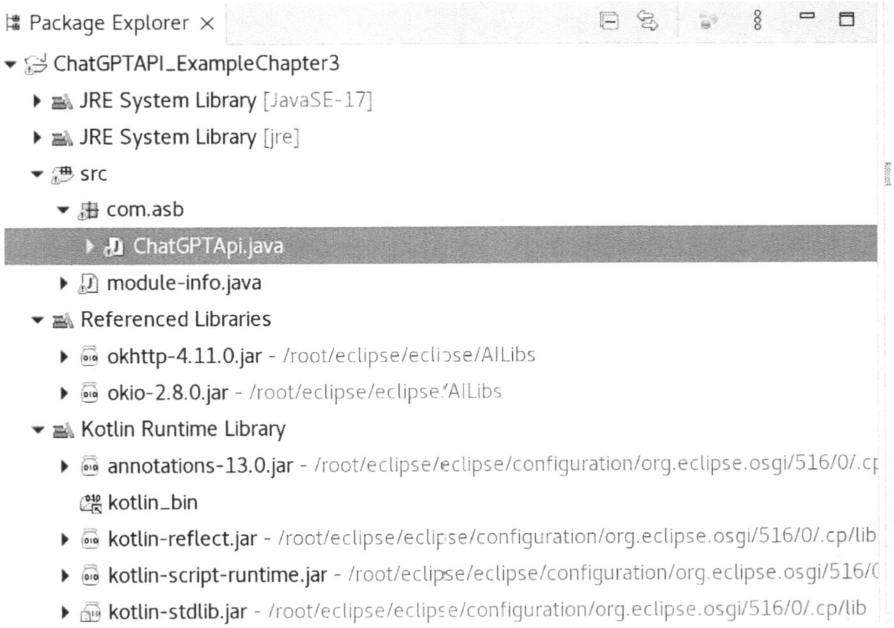

***Figure 3.29**: The final Project jar file list allowing the code to be run*

To even get this far, we had to follow these steps:

1. Add the following imports:

```
package com.asb;
import okhttp3.MediaType;
import okhttp3.OkHttpClient;
import okhttp3.Request;
import okhttp3.RequestBody;
import okhttp3.Response;
```

2. Then run the Enhanced Kotlin plugin installation for Eclipse using the Eclipse Market Place.

3. Finally, we have the libraries required to run the program code, without error, but still not with a valid JSON structure,

   We finally get:

```
Request=Request{method=POST, url=https://api.openai.com/v1/chat/
completions, headers=[Authorization:Bearer sk-xxxxxxxxxxxxxxxxxx
xxxxxxxxxBlbkFJVAxxxxxxxxxxxxxxxxxxxx, Content-Type:application/
json, messages:[{"role": "user", "content": "What is the OpenAI
mission?" }]}{
    "error": {
        "message": "We could not parse the JSON body of your
request. (HINT: This likely means you aren't using your HTTP
library correctly. The OpenAI API expects a JSON payload, but
what was sent was not valid JSON. If you have trouble figuring
out how to fix this, please contact us through our help center at
help.openai.com.)",
        "type": "invalid_request_error",
        "param": null,
        "code": null
    }
}
```

   The final version of the code we had, using the preceding libraries, was as follows:

```
package com.asb;
import okhttp3.MediaType;
import okhttp3.OkHttpClient;
import okhttp3.Request;
import okhttp3.RequestBody;
import okhttp3.Response;
public class ChatGPTApi {
    private static final String API_KEY = "sk-xxxxxxxxxxxxxxxxxxxx
xxBlbkFJVAxxxxxxxxxxxxxxxxxxx";
    private static final String MODEL_ID = "\"gpt-3.5-turbo\"";
/*
 * ASB Software Development Addition and URL change we know the
following URL works:
 *
 * https://api.openai.com/v1/chat/completions -H "Authorization:
```

```
Bearer sk-xxxxxxxxxxxxxxxxxxxxxxBlbkFJVAxxxxxxxxxxxxxxxxxx" -H
"Content-Type: application/json" -d '{"model": "gpt-3.5-turbo",
"messages": [{"role": "user", "content": "What is the OpenAI
mission?"}] }'
 *
 */
// Original    private static final String API_URL = "https://api.
openai.com/v1/engines/" + MODEL_ID + "/completions";
// NEW    private static final String API_URL =
 "https://api.openai.com/v1/chat/completions/";
    private static final String API_URL = "https://api.openai.com/
v1/chat/completions";
    public static String getResponseFromGPT(String prompt) throws
Exception {
        OkHttpClient client = new OkHttpClient().newBuilder()
                .build();
        MediaType mediaType = MediaType.parse("application/
json");
        // ASB Original line gave the error "message": "you must
provide a model parameter",
        //RequestBody body = RequestBody.create(mediaType,
"{  \"prompt\": \"" + prompt + "\",\"temperature\":0.7,\"max_
tokens\":60}");
        RequestBody body = RequestBody.create(mediaType, "{
\"\"model\"\":  \"" + MODEL_ID + "\",\"messages\": [{\"role\":
\"user\", \"content\":" + prompt + "\",\"temperature\":0.7,\"max_
tokens\":60}");
        Request request = new Request.Builder()
                .url(API_URL)
                .method("POST", body)
                .addHeader("Authorization", " Bearer " + API_KEY)
                .addHeader("Content-Type", "application/json")
                .addHeader("messages", " [{\"role\": \"user\",
\"content\": \"What is the OpenAI mission?\" }") //}]
                .build();
        System.out.print("Request=" + request.toString());
        Response response = client.newCall(request).execute();
        String responseJson = response.body().string();
```

```
            response.close();
            return responseJson;
        }

        public static void main(String[] args) throws Exception {
            String responseJson = getResponseFromGPT("Hello, how are 
    you?");
            System.out.println(responseJson); // ASB for debug output
        }
    }
```

Note

The following link gives a more useful example:

https://www.infoworld.com/article/3697151/build-a-java-application-to-talk-to-chatgpt.html

Conclusion

The example Java code we received from **ChatGPT** in this Chapter illustrates the "churn" described in several articles on the code supported by the **ChatGPT API**.

We need to be aware that the model reference names are regularly changed by **OpenAI** and so the **ChatGPT** responses for the example **API** code given in responses are outdated very quickly.

However, even given this limitation, there are very useful responses to more stable requirements, such as the algorithms for Java code that we are using as examples in the rest of this book.

The aforementioned issues were still present, even after updating several imports for libraries. In the next chapter, we will look at the response obtained for our question on a Binary Search algorithm. We will see that the response from ChatGPT for this is much more useful.

Points to Remember

- To use the OpenAI API, you need an OpenAI API key, which can be obtained by signing up for an OpenAI account. This allows the creation of an API key to use the ChatGPT API.

- There is a free-to-download publication from ResearchGate (copyright ASB Software Development Limited), which can be used to install a free RedHat RHEL 8.x Linux operating system, including the supporting VMware virtual server running on an MS Windows operating system: **https://doi.org/10.13140/RG.2.2.14590.95049**
- We had to use Version 3.2 of the okhttp.jar file eventually, as some features we needed were removed in the later versions.
- In Eclipse, we also found that we had to change the Eclipse project JVM from Java 17 to Java 11 to get the OkHttp system to run.
- The later okio jar file versions 3.4 and 3.5 do not work (we tried them) and also are much smaller than the 2.8 version. The kotlin-stdlib-1.3.41.jar is also required. (This can be found on the page: **https://mvnrepository.com/artifact/org.jetbrains.kotlin/kotlin-stdlib-jdk7/1.3.41**).

Multiple Choice Questions

1. **Which ChatGPT model can be used for sound file to text translation?**
    a. text-davinci-003
    b. gpt-3.5-turbo
    c. whisper-1
    d. ChatML3
2. **Which supporting Java library is required for the I/O used by OkHttp?**
    a. annotations-13.jar
    b. kotlin-reflect.jar
    c. okio-2.8.0.jar
    d. kotlin-stdlib.jar
3. **Which of the following are the current list of file extensions of sound files supported by Whisper?**
    a. m4a, mp3, mp4, mpeg, mpga, wav, webm
    b. mtm, ec3, sf2, midi, mpga, wav, webm
    c. m4a, mp3, mp4, mpeg, mtm, ec3, sf2
    d. vpw, sds, dct, vag, mp4, mpeg, mtm

4. **What Linux command can be used to remove the space from a file name by renaming it?**
   a. pwd
   b. cp
   c. ls
   d. mv
5. **Which of the following Java download sites did we use for the download of the ChatGPT java library files used in this Chapter?**
   a. GitHub
   b. Maven Central Repository
   c. SourceForge
   d. JCenter

Answers

1. **c**
2. **c**
3. **a**
4. **d**
5. **b**

Questions

1. What are the main drawbacks to the use of ChatGPT to develop Java code for its own API interface?
2. Why is it important to validate the responses from ChatGPT? What does the term **Hallucination** mean?
3. Describe the steps you would use to validate the **Java** code generated from a **ChatGPT** response.
4. What is the **Kotlin** plugin framework for Eclipse used for? What advantages are there in using this language in a Java project?

Key Terms

- **HTTP:** Hypertext Transfer Protocol (HTTP) is an internet communications protocol for use between a web browser or client program and a server to post and get data in standard formats (XML, HTML, and JSON), which can be interpreted by any system.
- **Eclipse IDE: Eclipse** is an integrated development environment (**IDE**) used in computer programming, which has been demonstrated for use with **Java** and **Kotlin** languages in this chapter. It contains a base workspace and an extensible plug-in system, which provides the **Kotlin** plugin, which we also showed how to install.
- **HTML:** Hypertext Markup Language.
- **JSON:** JavaScript Object Notation (JSON) is a standard nested text-based format, with tags similar to XML, but with curly bracket delimiters, rather than the angle brackets used for XML; both standards are used for representing structured data.
- **JVM:** Java Virtual Machine runs Java class files, which are then compiled into machine-specific Java **JVM** binary code, called bytecode, which the machine interprets, but can also be compiled for faster execution.
- **Kotlin:** Kotlin is a language, very similar to Java, which can be run with Java code, as it uses the same jar file structure. It is a high-level programming language, designed to interoperate fully with Java, and the JVM version of Kotlin's standard library depends on the Java Class Library. It is said to be around 40% more condensed in coding lines than Java and so more efficient.
- **LLM:** This stands for Large Language Model (LLM) used by **ChatGPT** and other **AI** systems to train their knowledge databases. They are nearly always huge data sets, often measured in petabytes used to generate and predict new content.
- **REST API:** A **REST API**, which is sometimes called a "**RESTful**" **API**, is a type of **API** (Application Programmers Interface) that posts commands from a program or web browser to an **HTTP**-based target web server, which is designed to process the data and return a result. **REST** stands for **Representational State Transfer**. The sent and returned data is usually structured into an **XML** or **JSON** message. We have covered the use of this, in the examples in this Chapter, for the **ChatGPT AI API** interface, which is **REST** based.

- **URL:** Uniform Resource Locator identifies a specific web server and usually a web page or a downloadable file or document and links to content online, which can be accessed from a browser or client program.
- **XML:** Extensible Markup Extensible (**XML**) is a markup language, with a very similar use as **JSON**, which is used for holding structured data. The angle brackets used for XML allow the structured data to be easily parsed to enable the extraction of subsets for further processing. **XML** is used for some older **REST API** services, but **JSON** is the most frequently used.

CHAPTER 4

Java Program for Using Binary Search

Introduction

In this chapter, we prompt **ChatGPT** for a Java program for using Binary Search. The Binary Search method takes a sorted array of integers and a target integer to search for. It returns the index of the target integer in the array if it is found, or -1 if it is not found. The method starts by initializing two variables, `left` and `right`, which represent the left and right boundaries of the search space. Initially, the search space is the entire array. The method then enters a loop that continues as long as the search space has not been exhausted.

Structure

In this chapter, we will discuss the following topics:

- AI prompt and response
- Java code validation using Eclipse Java code

AI prompt and response

We first asked the **Ask AI** mobile 'phone App, the following question and received the response (which is based on **ChatGPT 3.5**) as follows:

1. **Have you got a java code method for a program to use a binary search?**

   "Sure! Here's an example Java code method for a binary search:"

```java
public static int binarySearch(int[] array, int target) {
    int left = 0;
    int right = array.length - 1;
    while (left <= right) {
        int mid = left + (right - left) / 2;
        if (array[mid] == target) {
            return mid;
        } else if (array[mid] < target) {
            left = mid + 1;
        } else {
            right = mid - 1;
        }
    }
    return -1;
}
```

"This method takes in an array of integers and a target integer to search for. It returns the index of the target integer in the array if it is found, or -1 if it is not found.

By

The method starts by initializing two variables, `left` and `right`, which represent the left and right boundaries of the search space. Initially, the search space is the entire array.

The method then enters a loop that continues as long as the search space has not been exhausted (i.e., `left <= right`). Inside the loop, it calculates the midpoint of the current search space using the formula `mid = left + (right - left) / 2`. It then compares the value at the midpoint of the array to the target value.

If the value at the midpoint is equal to the target, the method returns the index of the midpoint. If the value at the midpoint is less than the target, the method updates `left` to be `mid + 1`, effectively narrowing the search space to the right half of the current search space. If the value at the midpoint is greater than the target, the method updates `right` to be `mid - 1`, effectively narrowing the search space to the left half of the current search space.

If the method completes its loop without finding the target value, it returns -1 to indicate that the target value was not found in the array."

In the preceding example, **ChatGPT 3.5**, accessed through the **Ask AI** mobile 'phone app, did not supply a **main** Java program method for testing the algorithm. When we asked the same question for the **ChatGPT** web application (**https://chat.openai.com/**)we got the following code, which did include a main method, but the description was very much less detailed.

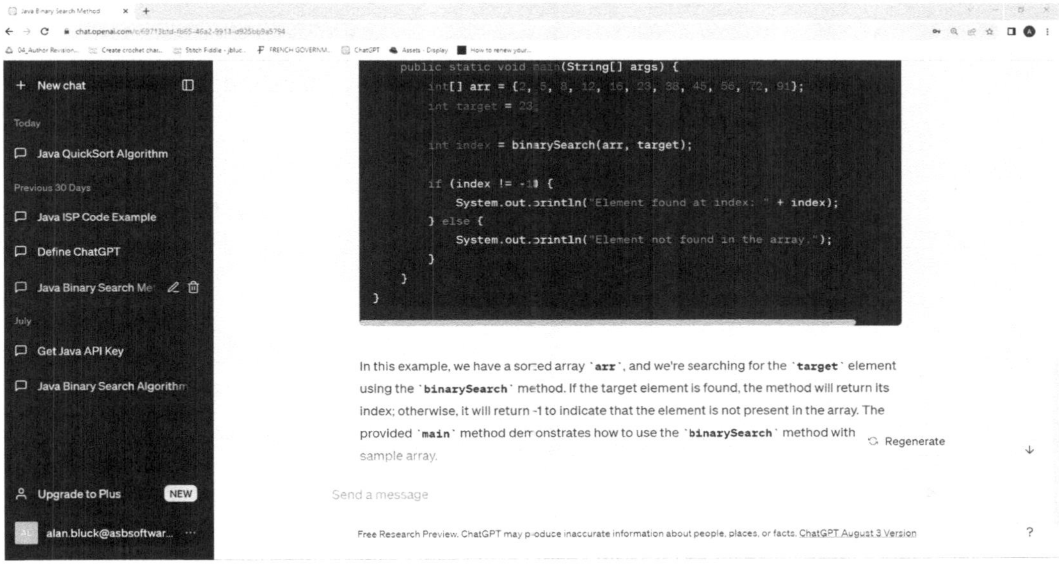

Figure 4.1: *The Main java code is supplied here but with a shorter description*

Note

The actual code generated may very well change over time. As an example, I have emboldened some of the additions made from an earlier response given.

```
public class BinarySearch {

    /**
     * Binary search method to find the target element in a sorted array.
     *
     * @param arr    The sorted array to search in.
     * @param target The element to search for.
     * @return The index of the target element if found; otherwise, -1.
     */
```

```
    public static int binarySearch(int[] arr, int target) {
        int left = 0;
        int right = arr.length - 1;
        while (left <= right) {
            // If the middle element is the target, return its index
            if (arr[mid] == target) {
                return mid;
            }
            // If the target is in the left half, discard the right half
            if (arr[mid] > target) {
                right = mid - 1;
            } else { // If the target is in the right half, discard the
left half
                left = mid + 1;
            }
        }

        // If the target is not found, return -1
        return -1;
    }

    public static void main(String[] args) {
        int[] arr = {2, 5, 8, 12, 16, 23, 38, 45, 56, 72, 91};
        int target = 23;

        int index = binarySearch(arr, target);

        if (index != -1) {
            System.out.println("Element found at index: " + index);
        } else {
            System.out.println("Element not found in the array.");
        }
    }
}
```

We can scroll down past the code window to show the **ChatGPT AI** description, as follows:

In this example, we have a sorted array ***arr****, and we're searching for the target element using the* ***binarySearch*** *method. If the target element is found, the method will return its index; otherwise, it will return -1 to indicate that the element is not present in the array. The provided main method demonstrates how to use the* ***binarySearch*** *method with a sample array.*

Java code validation using Eclipse Java code

One requirement that we need to supply in order to fully validate the algorithm for the Binary Search, is a sorted array. So, we posed the question for the **ChatGPT** web application (**https://chat.openai.com**). This question and the response are as follows:

Do you have an example of an efficient sort algorithm using a Java program to sort an array of integer values into ascending numeric order?

We get the response as follows:

"Certainly! One efficient sorting algorithm is the QuickSort algorithm. It's a divide-and-conquer algorithm that works by selecting a 'pivot' element and partitioning the array into two sub-arrays, one containing elements less than the pivot and the other containing elements greater than the pivot. The sub-arrays are then recursively sorted.

Here's a Java program that implements the QuickSort algorithm to sort an array of integer values into ascending numeric order:

```
public class QuickSort {
    public static void main(String[] args) {
        int[] arr = { 9, 7, 5, 11, 12, 2, 14, 3, 10, 6 };

        System.out.println("Original array:");
        printArray(arr);

        quickSort(arr, 0, arr.length - 1);

        System.out.println("Sorted array:");
        printArray(arr);
```

```
}

public static void quickSort(int[] arr, int low, int high) {
    if (low < high) {
        int pi = partition(arr, low, high);

        quickSort(arr, low, pi - 1);
        quickSort(arr, pi + 1, high);
    }
}

public static int partition(int[] arr, int low, int high) {
    int pivot = arr[high];
    int i = (low - 1);
    for (int j = low; j < high; j++) {
        if (arr[j] < pivot) {
            i++;
            int temp = arr[i];
            arr[i] = arr[j];
            arr[j] = temp;
        }
    }
    int temp = arr[i + 1];quickSort

    arr[i + 1] = arr[high];
    arr[high] = temp;

    return i + 1;
}

public static void printArray(int[] arr) {
    for (int num : arr) {
        System.out.print(num + " ");
    }
```

```
        System.out.println();
    }
}
```
"

In this program, the quickSort method is the main driver for the QuickSort algorithm, and the partition method is responsible for rearranging the elements around the pivot. The printArray method is just for displaying the array before and after sorting.

Remember, while **QuickSort** *is efficient on average, its performance can degrade in the worst-case scenario. Other sorting algorithms like* **MergeSort** *or* **TimSort** *might be better suited for scenarios where worst-case performance is a concern."*

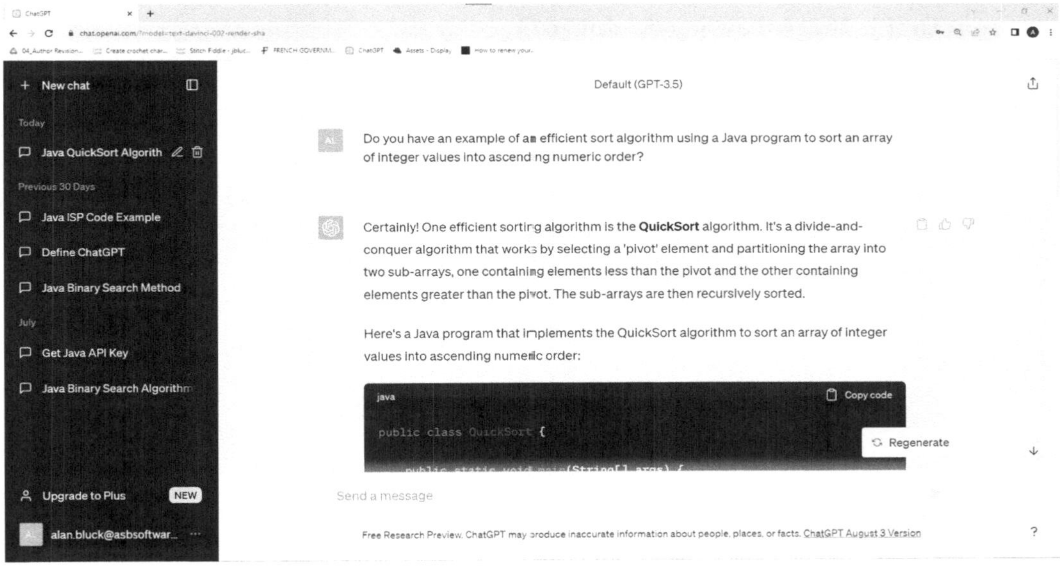

Figure 4.2*: The ChatGPT response to our sort algorithm question*

If we want to get the most efficient sort, we need to be able to check the other sort algorithms referenced by **ChatGPT** and also ask it for additional code to provide timings.

So, we asked the questions as follows:quickSort

Do you have an example of the MergeSort algorithm using a Java program to sort an array of integer values into ascending numeric order including code to measure the performance of the sort?

Certainly! Here's an example of the MergeSort algorithm implemented in Java, along with code to measure the performance of the sort using the **System.**

***currentTimeMillis()** method. MergeSort is a divide-and-conquer sorting algorithm that divides the unsorted list into smaller sublists until each sublist contains a single element. It then repeatedly merges these sublists to produce a sorted output.*

```
import java.util.Arrays;

public class MergeSortExample {

    public static void merge(int[] arr, int left, int mid, int right) {
        int n1 = mid - left + 1;
        int n2 = right - mid;

        int[] leftArray = new int[n1];
        int[] rightArray = new int[n2];

        System.arraycopy(arr, left, leftArray, 0, n1);
        System.arraycopy(arr, mid + 1, rightArray, 0, n2);

        int i = 0, j = 0, k = left;

        while (i < n1 && j < n2) {
            if (leftArray[i] <= rightArray[j]) {
                arr[k++] = leftArray[i++];
            } else {
                arr[k++] = rightArray[j++];
            }
        }

        while (i < n1) {
            arr[k++] = leftArray[i++];
        }

        while (j < n2) {
            arr[k++] = rightArray[j++];
        }
    }
```

```
    public static void mergeSort(int[] arr, int left, int right) {
        if (left < right) {
            int mid = left + (right - left) / 2;

            mergeSort(arr, left, mid);
            mergeSort(arr, mid + 1, right);

            merge(arr, left, mid, right);
        }
    }

    public static void main(String[] args) {
        int[] arr = {12, 11, 13, 5, 6, 7};

        System.out.println("Original array: " + Arrays.toString(arr));

        long startTime = System.currentTimeMillis();
        mergeSort(arr, 0, arr.length - 1);
        long endTime = System.currentTimeMillis();

        System.out.println("Sorted array: " + Arrays.toString(arr));
        System.out.println("Time taken: " + (endTime - startTime) + "
milliseconds");
    }
}
```

In this example, the merge method merges two sorted subarrays, and the mergeSort method divides the array into smaller parts recursively. The main method demonstrates how to use these methods to sort an array of integers and measure the time taken for the sorting process. Keep in mind that for more precise performance measurement, you might consider using System.nanoTime() instead of System.currentTimeMillis().

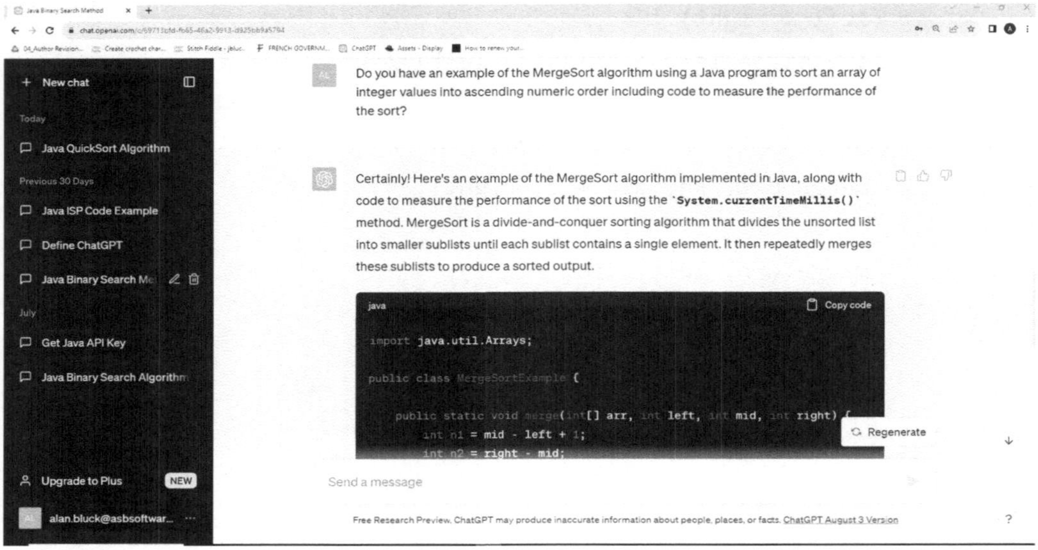

***Figure 4.3**: The ChatGPT response to the MergeSort question*

We also posed a similar question for the **TimSort** algorithm, referenced in the first **ChatGPT** response:

Do you have an example of the TimSort algorithm using a Java program to sort an array of integer values into ascending numeric order including code to measure the performance of the sort?

Certainly! TimSort is a hybrid sorting algorithm derived from merge sort and insertion sort. It has been Python's standard sorting algorithm since version 2.3 and is also used in Java's Arrays.sort() and Collections.sort() methods. Here's an example of using TimSort to sort an array of integer values in Java, including code to measure the performance of the sort:

```
import java.util.Arrays;


public class TimSortExample {


    public static void main(String[] args) {
        int[] arr = {12, 11, 13, 5, 6, 7};


        System.out.println("Original array: " + Arrays.toString(arr));
```

```
        long startTime = System.currentTimeMillis();
        Arrays.sort(arr);
        long endTime = System.currentTimeMillis();

        System.out.println("Sorted array: " + Arrays.toString(arr));
        System.out.println("Time taken: " + (endTime - startTime) + "
milliseconds");
    }
}
```

In this example, the Arrays.sort() method is used to perform the TimSort algorithm on the input array. The main method demonstrates how to use this method to sort an array of integers and measure the time taken for the sorting process. Keep in mind that for more precise performance measurement, you might consider using System.nanoTime() instead of System.currentTimeMillis().

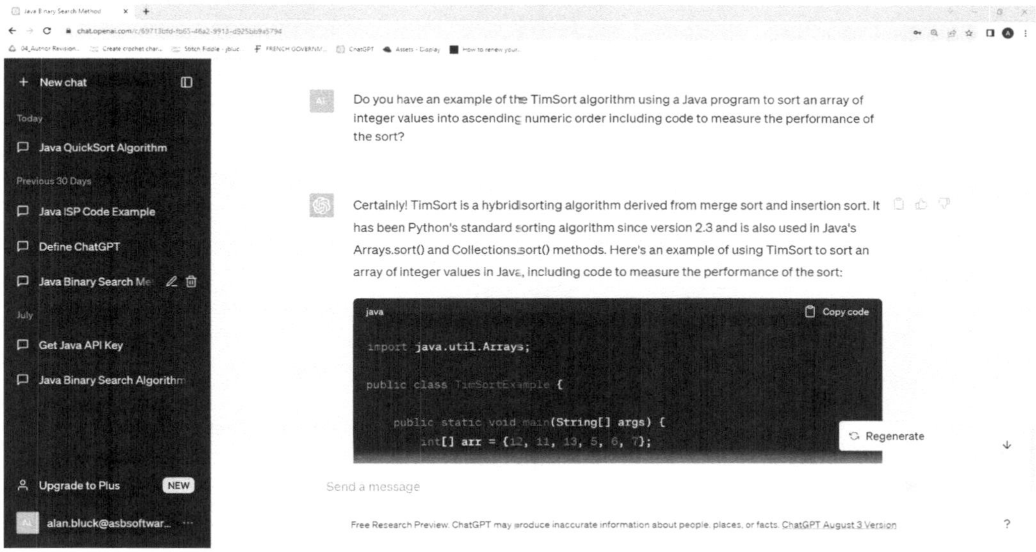

***Figure 4.4**: The ChatGPT response to the TimSort question*

You will notice that the last Java code array sorting example we obtained from **ChatGPT** was much more concise and also made use of the industry standard built-in method for sorting an array in Java.

This illustrates the importance of following up with further questions and also, that the **ChatGPT AI** does not necessarily give the best response first!

Now we can test each of the sort algorithms supplied by ChatGPT and validate the code supplied to sort the array we will use, using the **Eclipse IDE** (the installation for this is covered in the next chapter, **Installation of the latest Open-Source Eclipse Java IDE**).

So, first, we will test the first program given by **ChatGPT**, **QuickSort,** by creating a new Java project in the **Eclipse IDE, QuickSortValidation_Chapter4** as illustrated in *Figure* 4.5:

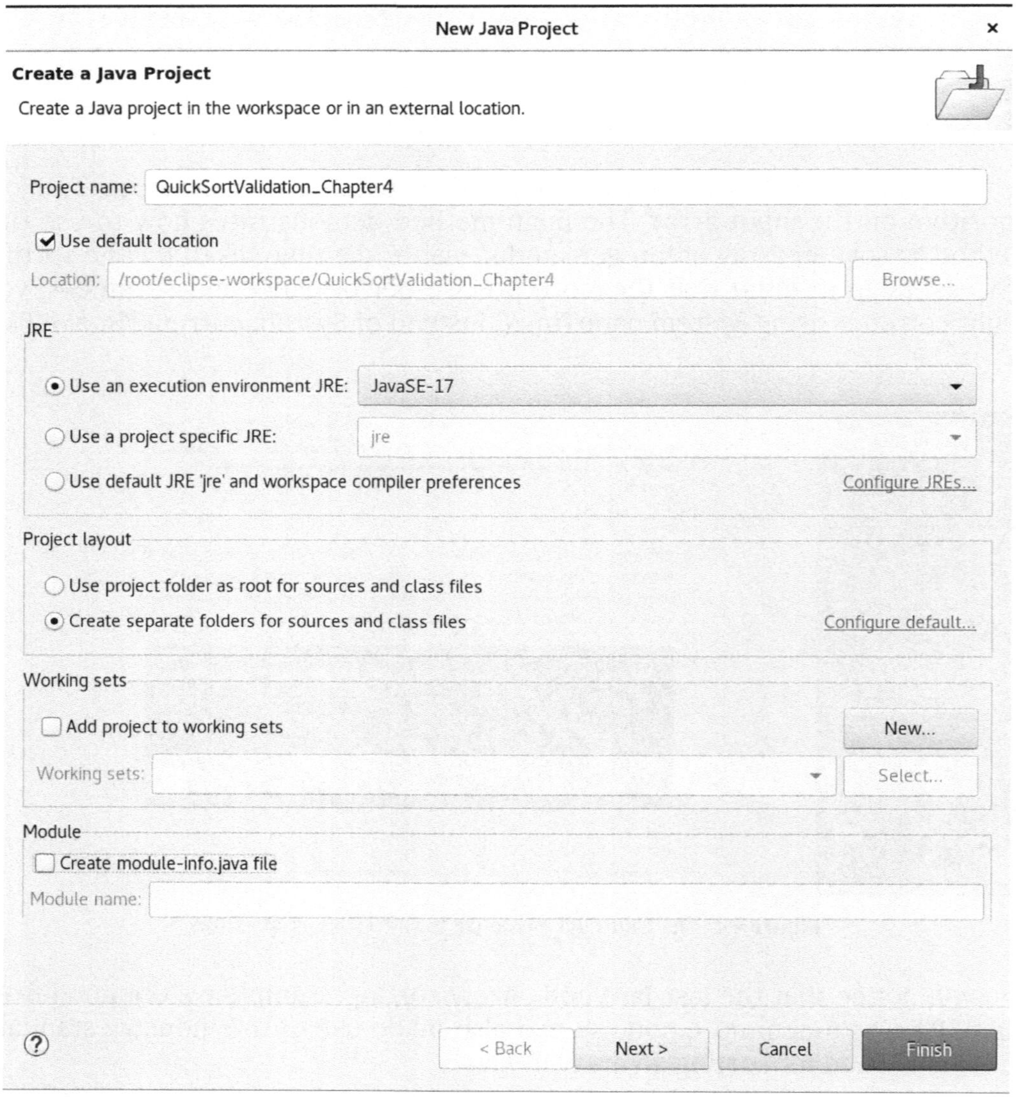

Figure 4.5**: The **ChatGPT QuickSortValidation_Chapter4** project is created in the **Eclipse IDE

Clicking on the **Next>** button shows the basic src folder structure as shown in *Figure* 4.6:

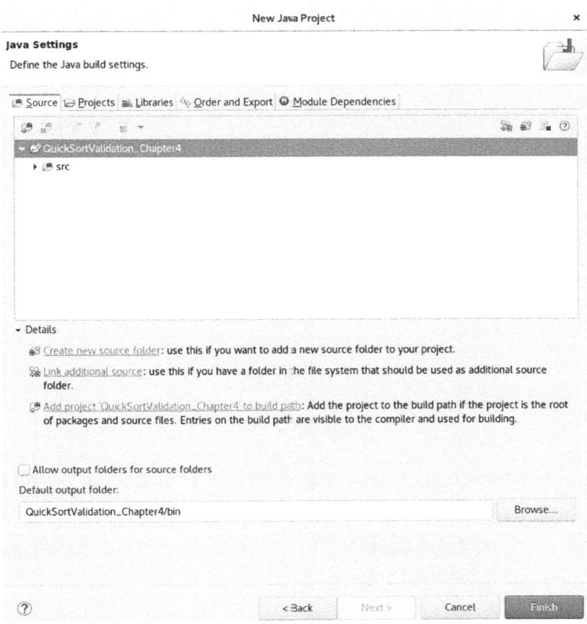

***Figure 4.6**: The ChatGPT **QuickSortValidation_Chapter4** project folder structure is shown*

On Clicking the **Finish** button in *Figure 4.6*, we can add a Java Class of **QuickSort**, with a package name of **com.asb**, as shown in *Figure 4.7*:

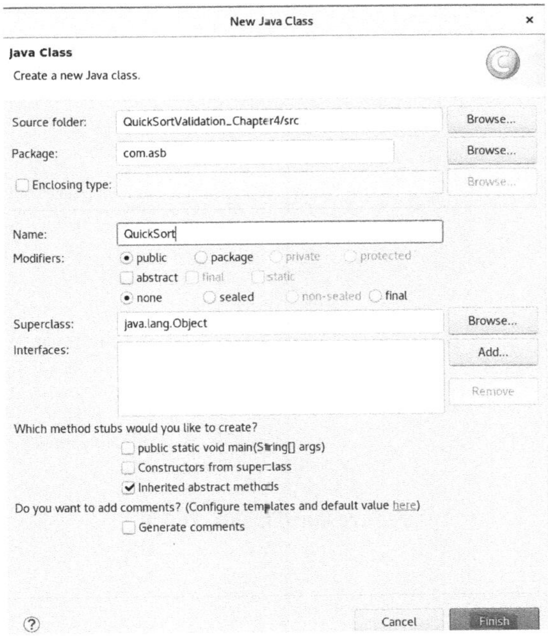

***Figure 4.7**: The **ChatGPT QuickSort** class is added under our **com.asb** package*

On Clicking the **Finish** button in *Figure* 4.7, we get the "skeleton" java shown in *Figure* 4.8, which we can update by pasting in the **QuickSort** code given by **ChatGPT:**

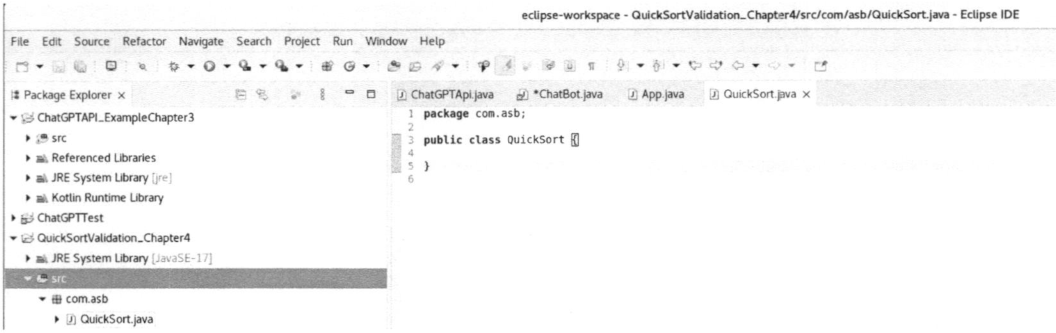

***Figure 4.8**: The **QuickSort** skeleton code, created by the **IDE**, before pasting the **ChatGPT** code*

The **QuickSort** code from **ChatGPT** is pasted into the **Eclipse IDE** as shown in *Figure* 4.9:

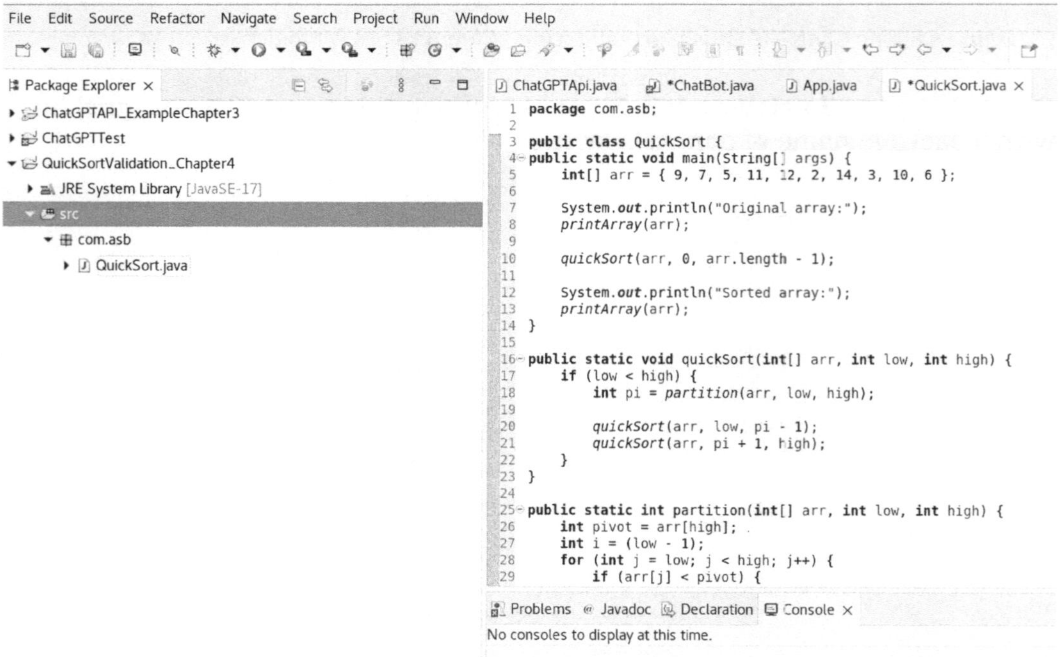

***Figure 4.9**: The ChatGPT*

The **QuickSort** Java code pasted into the class as shown in *Figure* 4.9 can be seen to compile with no syntax errors and is run as a Java application as shown in *Figure* 4.10:

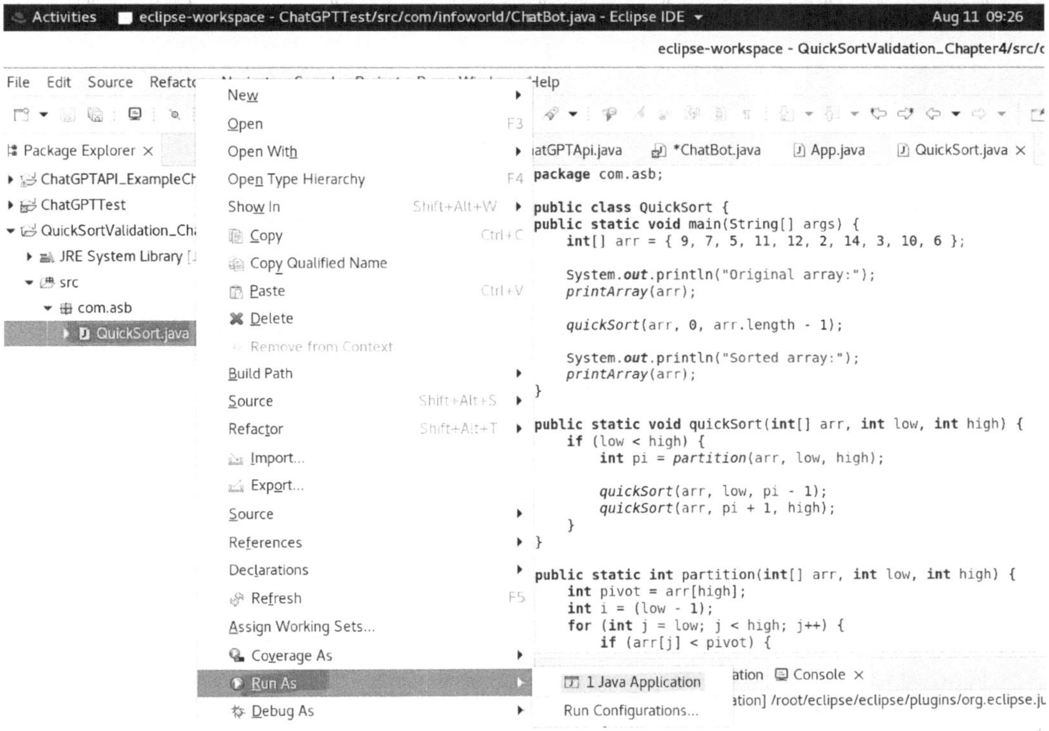

Figure 4.10: *The ChatGPT* **QuickSort** *example Java code is run in the* **Eclipse IDE**

The code in *Figure* 4.10 runs successfully, giving the output in *Figure* 4.11:

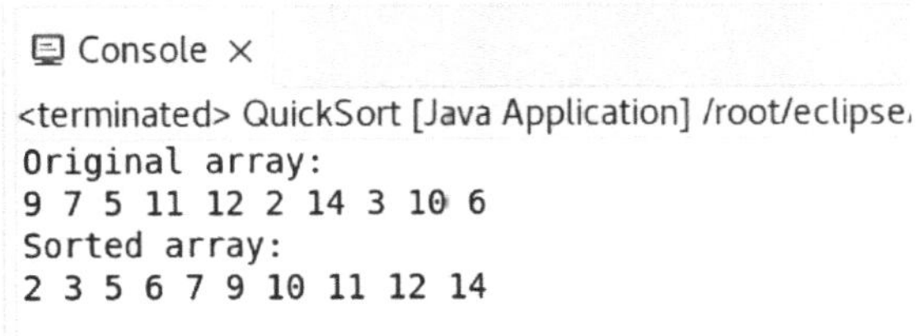

Figure 4.11: *The ChatGPT* **QuickSort** *run output, showing the sorted array of integers*

We can now repeat the above procedure from the creation of the **QuickSort** Class in *Figure* 4.7, for the **MergeSort** and **TimSort** classes.

We made just one small change to the code just to alter the class name from **MergeSortExample** to **MergeSort** as highlighted in *Figure* 4.12:

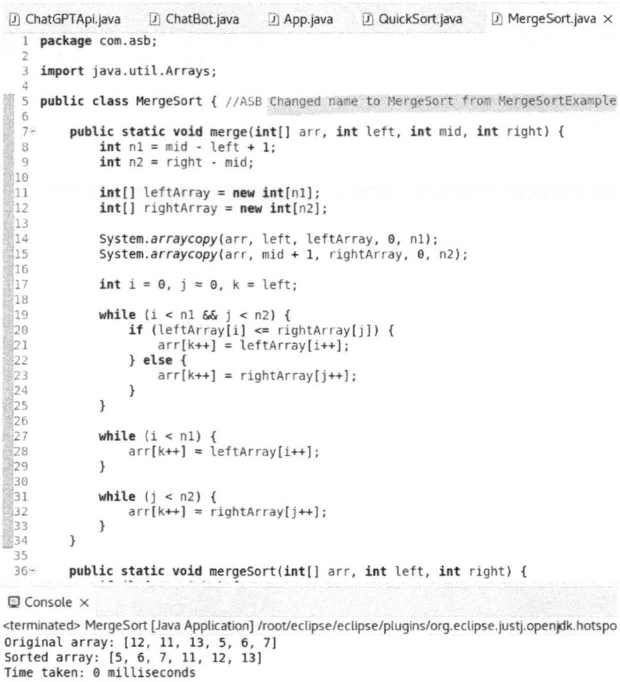

***Figure 4.12**: The ChatGPT **MergeSort** run output, showing the sorted array of integers*

We also made a similar small change to the code just to alter the class name from **TimSortExample** to **TimSort** as shown in the highlighted run of the code in *Figure* 4.13:

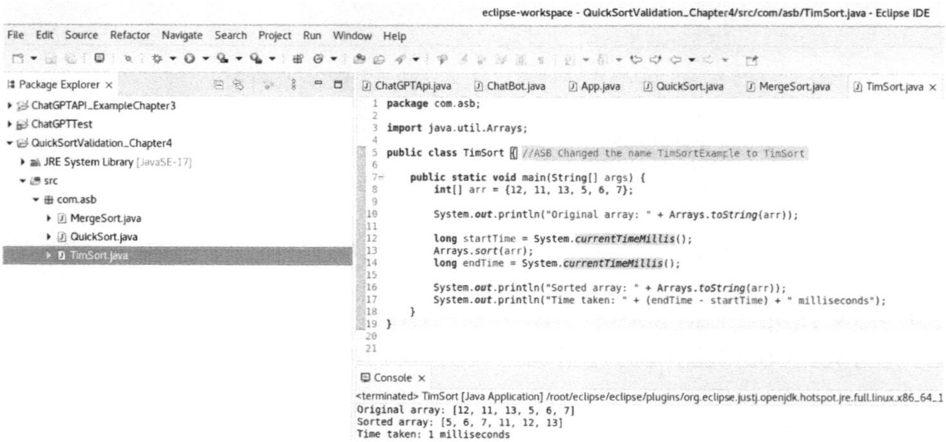

***Figure 4.13**: The ChatGPT **TimSort** run output, showing the sorted array of integers*

Just one more test was made to use the ChatGPT suggested change for the timings to *System.nanoTime()*

This gave the following result, as shown in *Figure 4.14*:

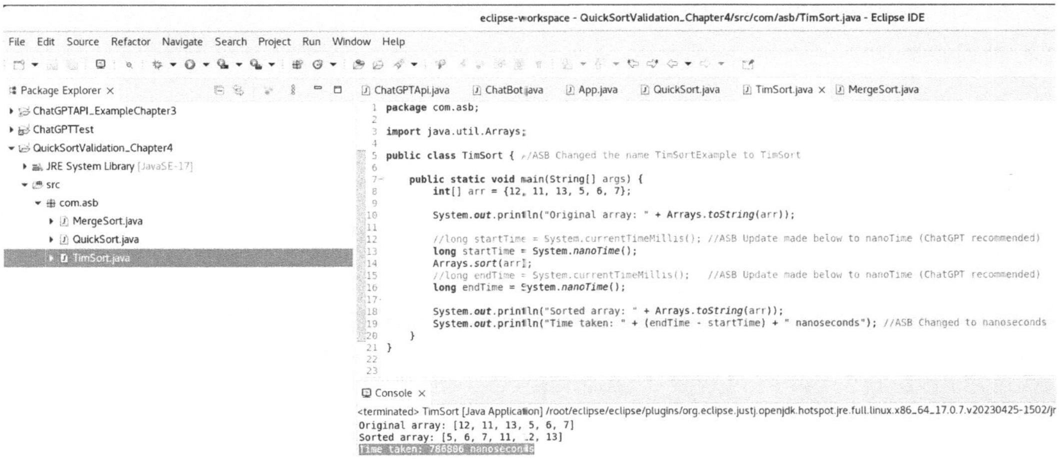

Figure 4.14: *The results when the code was updated to use* **System.nanoTime();**

This change to using **System.nanoTime();** was repeated for the other two sort algorithms:

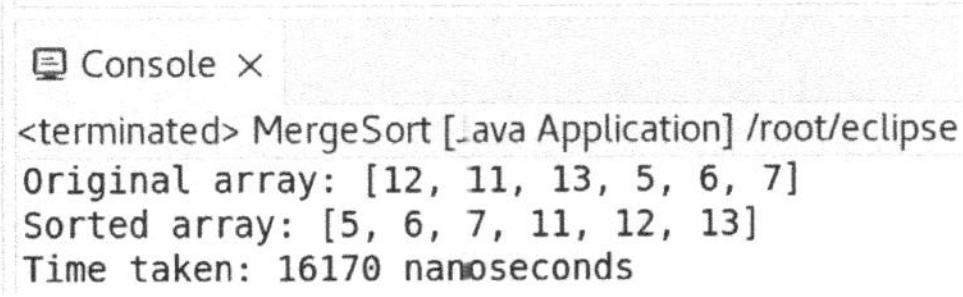

Figure 4.15: *The results of the timing for the MergeSort is now in nanoseconds*

So, the MergeSort on a short 6-element array is around 50 times faster than the TimSort.

> **There is one other small change that we made since the reported time differences should be named as nanoseconds. Also, it is worth repeating the runs several times to get an average. We also need to test with much larger arrays to compare the impact of larger data arrays on the timings.**

For the QuickSort, we added the code for timing and got the output as follows:

```
Original array:
9 7 5 11 12 2 14 3 10 6
Sorted array:
2 3 5 6 7 9 10 11 12 14
Time taken: 1829824 nanoseconds
```

So, the MergeSort is over 100 times faster than the QuickSort.

But you may notice that there are 10 elements in the QuickSort test data, so we changed this to match the other two code examples, we got.

```
Original array:
12 11 13 5 6 7
Sorted array:
5 6 7 11 12 13
Time taken: 1739028 nanoseconds
```

So, it is faster but still over 100 times slower than the MergeSort.

So, on the tests we tried, the fastest algorithm is the **MergeSort**, it is also the longest algorithm at 60 lines, next fastest is the **TimSort**, although around 50 times slower than the **MergeSort**, it is the shortest in code length at 21 lines of code. The originally suggested **QuickSort** code is the slowest and uses around 50 lines of code.

Conclusion

In this chapter, we have covered the algorithm created by **ChatGPT** for the Binary Search java method. We compared the different codes created by the web-based **ChatGPT** with the **Ask AI** version. We asked additional questions for sorting an array as the input for the Binary Search algorithm and discovered that the first response from **ChatGPT** isn't always the best response.

In *Chapter 5, Installation of the latest Open-Source Eclipse Java IDE*, we introduce the latest available version of the **Eclipse Java IDE** (**Eclipse IDE 2023-06 R - Eclipse IDE** for Java Developers), which is downloaded and we describe the step-by-step installation on MS **Windows 10** and **RedHat** Enterprise Linux, **RHEL 8.x**.

Points to remember

- The actual code generated by **ChatGPT** may very well change over time.
- It is important to follow up with further questions since **ChatGPT AI** does not necessarily give the best response first!
- It is recommended to test each of the algorithms supplied by **ChatGPT** and validate the code supplied and its efficiency.

Multiple choice questions

1. **Which sort algorithm takes the fewest lines of code?**
    a. QuickSort
    b. MergeSort
    c. TimSort
    d. partition
2. **Which sort algorithm is the most efficient?**
    a. QuickSort
    b. MergeSort
    c. TimSort
    d. partition
3. **In the example QuickSort program given by ChatGPT which method is responsible for rearranging the elements around the pivot?**
    a. The quickSort method
    b. The partition method
    c. The printArray method
    d. The main method

Answers

1. **c**
2. **b**
3. **b**

Questions

1. Which algorithm would you use to presort an integer array for the Binary Search program we are testing?
2. How would you validate that the algorithm you have chosen is the best one to use?
3. What question would you ask ChatGPT to establish that you were using the fastest sort algorithm? (You could try this and see what response you get from the AI).

Key terms

- **AI**: Artificial Intelligence Software that mimics the responses you might expect to questions supplied by a human operator.
- **OpenAI**: is the American artificial intelligence research laboratory that developed **ChatGPT** comprising the non-profit **OpenAI** organization and its for-profit subsidiary corporation **OpenAI Limited**.
- **Ask AI**: The Android mobile phone app is available for access to **ChatGPT 3.5**.
- **ChatGPT**: **ChatGPT** is a language model developed by **OpenAI**. It is based on the **GPT** (Generative Pre-trained Transformer) architecture, specifically **GPT-3.5** for the free use option. The model is designed to generate human-like text responses to user inputs, making it capable of engaging in interactive and natural-sounding conversations.

CHAPTER 5

Installation of the Latest Open-source Eclipse Java IDE

Introduction

In this chapter, we introduce the latest available version of the **Eclipse Java IDE** (**Eclipse IDE 2023-06 R** - **Eclipse IDE** for Java Developers), which is then downloaded. We subsequently describe the step-by-step installation process on **MS Windows 10** and RedHat Enterprise Linux (**RHEL 8.x**).

Structure

In this chapter, we will discuss the following topics:

- Downloading the Eclipse Java IDE
- Eclipse IDE validation of the Binary Search code
    - Perplexity
- Creating the Java BinarySearch project
- Running the Eclipse Java program
- Binary Search validation Java Program output

Downloading the Eclipse Java IDE

The latest available version of the Eclipse Java IDE was downloaded (at the time of writing in June 2023) from the Eclipse organization webpage as follows:

https://www.eclipse.org/downloads/

Click on the **Download x86_64** button on the home webpage, as shown in *Figure* 5.1, to open the webpage link for the **eclipse-inst-jre-win64.exe** Windows installation program, as shown in *Figure* 5.2.

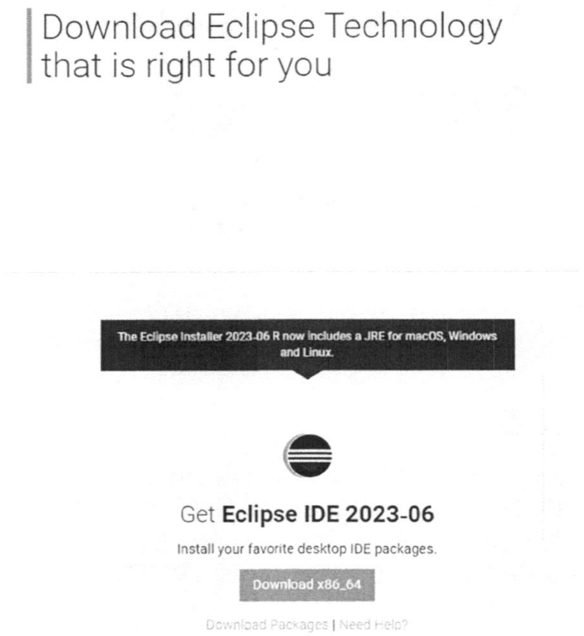

***Figure 5.1**: The **Download x86_64** button on the home page is selected*

As shown in **Figure 5.2**, the **eclipse-inst-jre-win64.exe** Windows installation program is now available by clicking the **Download** button. The mirror site is randomly selected, for example, **Germany – dogado GmbH** based on our location in the European zone. However, if needed, you can choose another server by clicking the **Select Another Mirror** link and selecting from the list as follows:

Europe

Germany: dogado GmbH

Czech Republic: UPC Ceska republika, a.s.

Russian Federation: Tomsk State Pedagogical University

Germany: University of Applied Sciences Esslingen
Sweden: Academic Computer Club, Umea University
France: CNRS IBCP
Germany: University of Erlangen-Nuremberg
Germany: RWTH Aachen University
Italy: Consortium GARR
Netherlands: SNT, University of Twente
Turkey: Linux Kullanicilari Dernegi

North America

Canada: Rafal Rzeczkowski
United States: Jevin Canders
United States: Clarkson University Open Source Institute
Canada: University of Waterloo Computer Science Club
United States: University of Maryland
United States: XMission Internet
United States: OSU Open Source Lab

Asia

Republic of Korea: Kakao Corp.
China: Dalian Neusoft University of Information (大连东软信息学院)
Cyprus: University of Cyprus, Library
Japan: Japan Advanced Institute of Science and Technology
Japan: Yamagata University
Japan: Yamagata University
China: eScience Center, Nanjing University

Australia/Oceania

Australia: Australian Academic Research Network

South America

Brazil: C3SL - Federal University of Parana

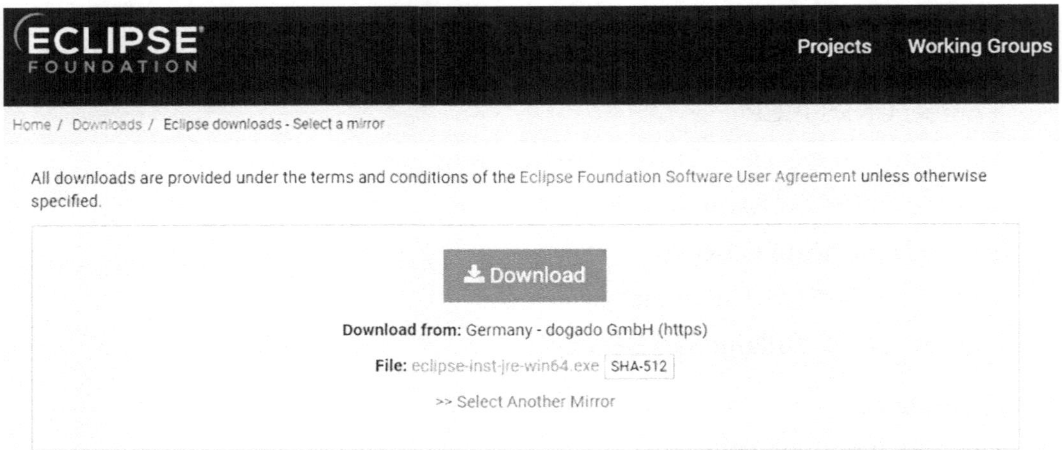

Figure 5.2: *Click the Download button to get an* **eclipse-inst-jre-win64.exe** *Windows version*

The progress of the 123 Mbyte download can be viewed in the browser's status bar window, as shown in *Figure* 5.3.

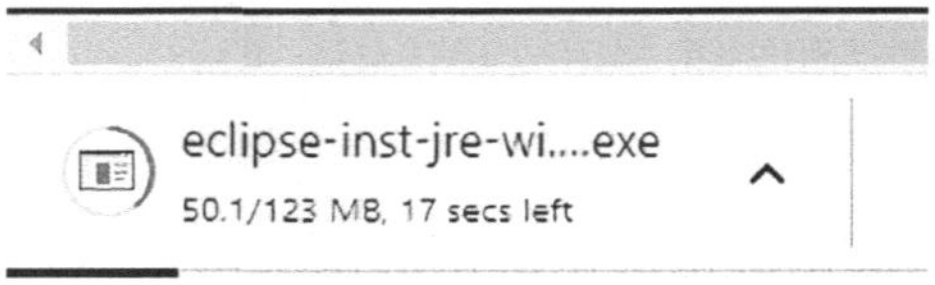

Figure 5.3: *The progress of the 123 Mbyte download can be viewed*

For Linux installs, we can use the following link as a starting point:

https://www.eclipse.org/downloads/packages/

This displays the following webpage, as illustrated in *Figure* 5.4.

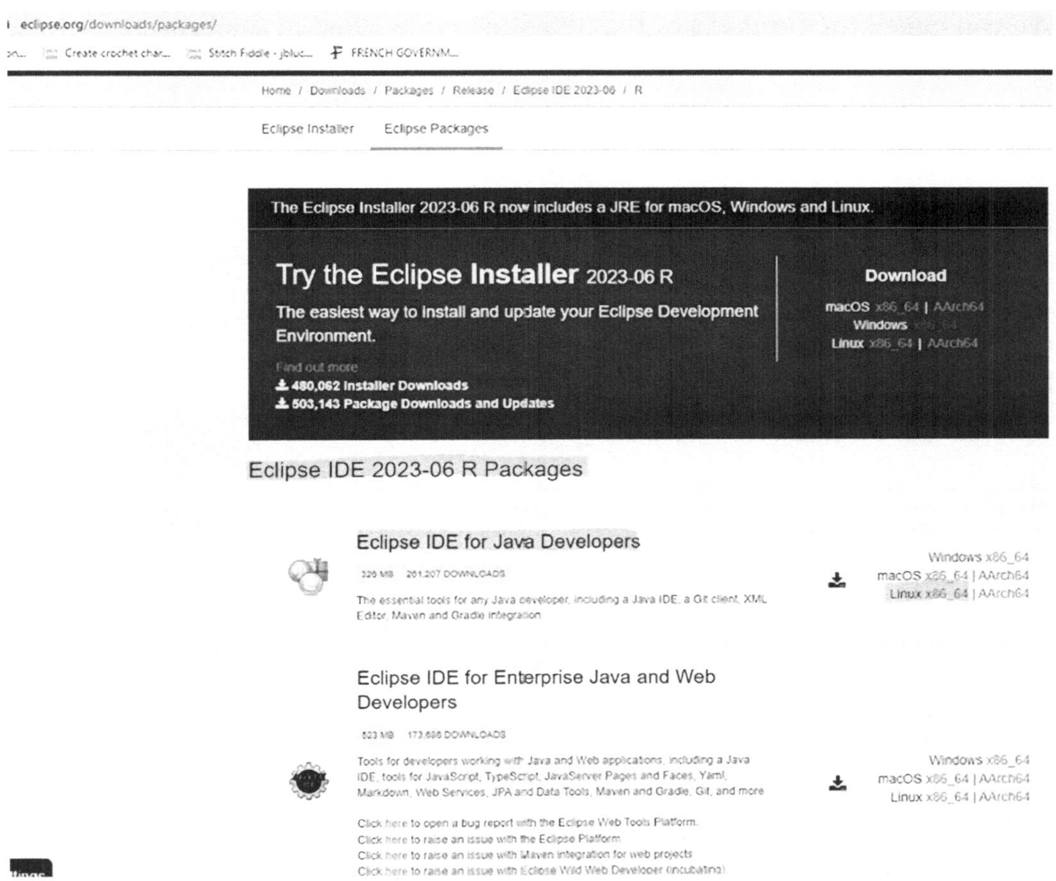

Figure 5.4: *The highlighted* **Linux x86_64** *is selected to download for our* **RHEL 8.x** *server*

The Linux tar and gzipped Eclipse file, **eclipse-java-2023-06-R-linux-gtk-x86_64.tar.gz** file, is obtained by clicking on the highlighted **Download** button, as shown in *Figure* 5.5.

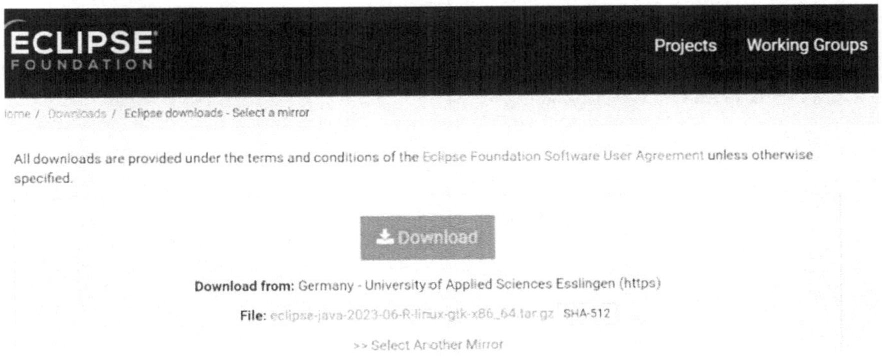

Figure 5.5: *The Linux file,* **eclipse-java-2023-06-R-linux-gtk-x86_64.tar.gz**, *is downloaded*

We can check the progress of the 326 Mbyte download in the browser's status window, as shown in **Figure 5.6**.

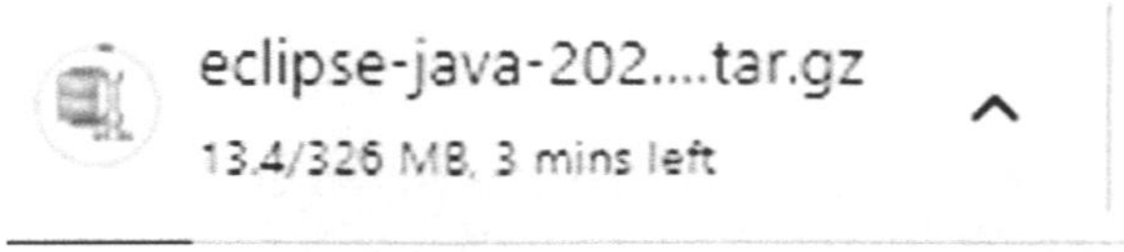

Figure 5.6: *The progress of the 326 Mbyte download can be viewed*

The downloaded **eclipse-java-2023-06-R-linux-gtk-x86_64.tar.gz** file is copied from the mapped Windows **Installs** directory area to our VMware RedHat Linux RHEL 8 server and then unpacked, as shown in *Figure* 5.7.

Figure 5.7: *The downloaded* ***eclipse-java-2023-06-R-linux-gtk-x86_64.tar.gz*** *file is extracted*

We have created an **eclipse** directory under the **/root** folder of the root users and then copied and unpacked the **Eclipse IDE** program using the following commands:

```
mkdir eclipse

cp /mnt/hgfs/Installs/eclipse-java-2023-06-R-linux-gtk-x86_64.tar.gz .

tar -zxvf eclipse-java-2023-06-R-linux-gtk-x86_64.tar.gz
```

The eclipse program can now be launched from the unpacked **/root/eclipse/eclipse** folder by using the command **./eclipse**, as shown in *Figure* 5.8.

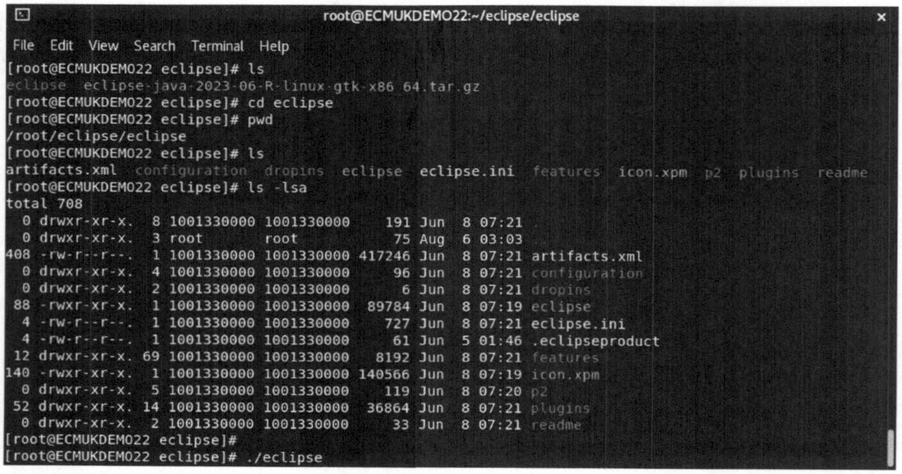

Figure 5.8: *The eclipse program is launched from* ***/root/eclipse/eclipse*** *using* ***./eclipse***

The splash screen of the **Eclipse** program is displayed on the launch of the program, showing the version and the load progress status bar, as shown in *Figure 5.9*.

Figure 5.9*: The Eclipse 2023-06 version splash screen*

The **Launch** button is clicked (we use the default **Eclipse** workspace directory area), as shown in *Figure 5.10*.

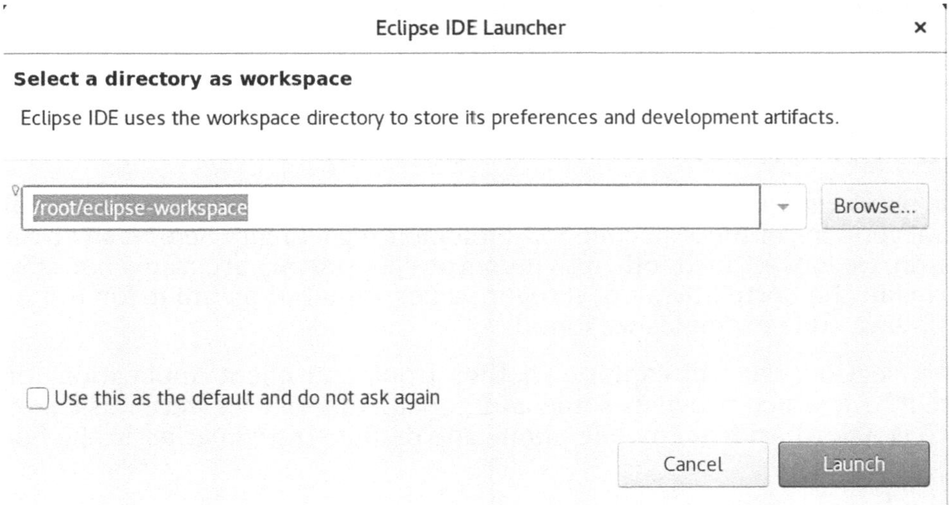

Figure 5.10*: The* **Eclipse** *program* **Launch** *button is clicked (using the default workspace area)*

Finally, the Welcome page is displayed for the launched **Eclipse IDE** program, as illustrated in *Figure* 5.11.

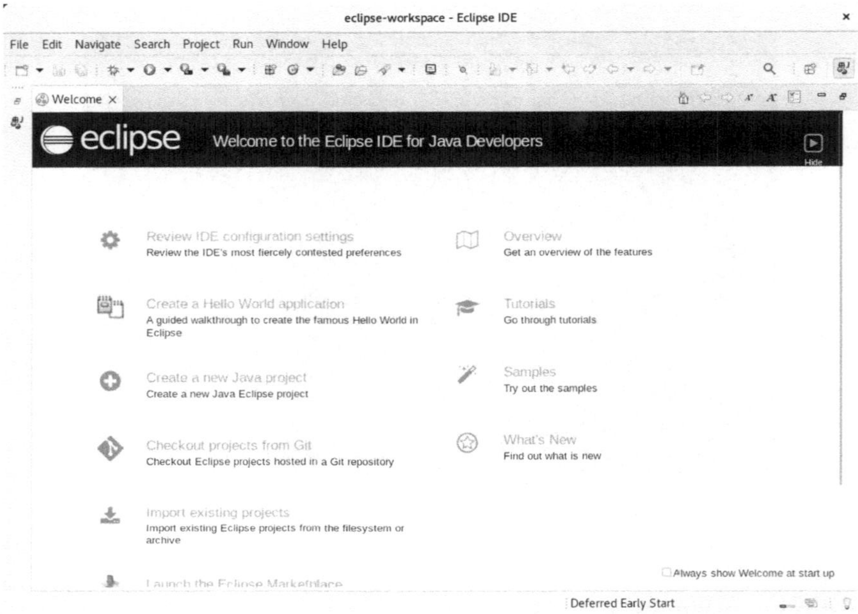

***Figure 5.11**: The Welcome page is displayed for the launched Eclipse IDE program*

Eclipse IDE validation of the Binary Search code

In the previous Chapter 4, Java Program for using Binary Search, we were shown several versions of the Java code for implementing a Binary Search algorithm. In addition, we looked, in-depth, into numerous supporting program code snippets to provide the sorted array of integer values required as input for the Binary Search Java code examples we found.

In this section, we will explore another front-end client application for the **ChatGPT AI**, which provides some additional features that were missing in the previous **Ask AI Android** mobile phone app demonstrated earlier in the book.

Perplexity

There is another mobile phone app available for free to use in its default mode, which has even more useful features than the **Ask AI** we have been using.

There is a comparison site that lists several **AI** application options, as follows:

https://sourceforge.net/software/product/Perplexity-AI/alternatives

Although this link is informative, its comparison tables, as shown in *Figure* 5.12, were out of date for **Perplexity**, as it has no tick box for an **Android** mobile phone app or **Apple iPad** support (which, as of 12th August 2023, we will demonstrate is fully supported).

There was a review of **Perplexity** on 31st March 2023 at the following link, entitled

"*How to use Perplexity, the only iPhone ChatGPT app that matters (bgr.com)*":

https://bgr.com/entertainment/how-to-use-perplexity-the-only-iphone-chatgpt-app-that-matters/

However, things have obviously changed since the March release of **Perplexity**. The article states:

"*The best part of Perplexity AI is that, unlike the ChatGPT clients for iPhone or the ChatGPT web experience, you don't need to set up an account. Perplexity AI will work as soon as you load it in a browser or install the iPhone app.* ***But Perplexity will not offer other ChatGPT features. It won't write code or essays for you.***"

The first statement is true: the **Perplexity** App from the Apple store is free and doesn't require an **Open AI** account. The last point in the statement is demonstrably not true, at least when using the current release of **Perplexity**, as we will show in this section of the chapter.

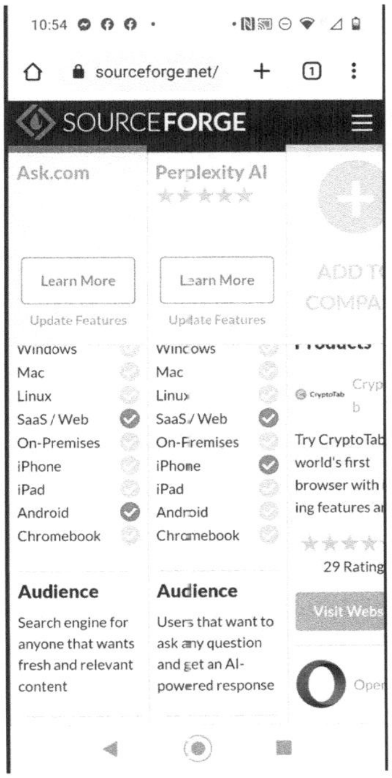

Figure 5.12: *The SourceForge website (12/08/2023) comparison table for* **Perplexity**

Perplexity AI was established in August 2022 by a group of **AI** software engineers: Denis Yarats, Aravind Srinivas, Johnny Ho, and Andy Konwinski.

The **Perplexity** app now runs on **iPhone, Android,** and **iPad** and has a search interface powered by **OpenAI's GPT 3.5** and **Microsoft Bing**, which answers user questions (and currently uses **GPT 4**).

Perplexity is very fast and has very useful features, which are not currently available from the **Ask AI** App. It displays the internet search sources for all of its responses. In addition, it has a **Copilot** mode option, which provides additional clarification and summarizes search results.

Another really useful feature is that each resource is flagged as a subscript number in the descriptive text that is displayed under the code that is produced.

The **iPad** version of **Perplexity** can be installed by searching in the **Apple** store to show the following screen, as illustrated in *Figure* 5.13.

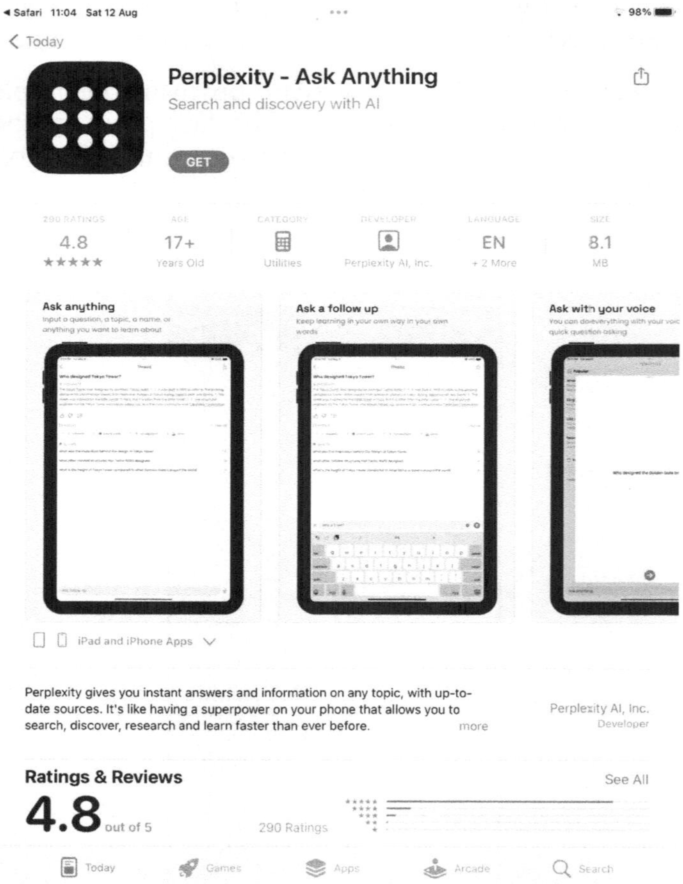

Figure 5.13**: The **Perplexity App** for download in the **Apple** store for the **iPad

Upon selecting the **Get** button on the **iPad**, as shown in *Figure* 5.13, we get the pop-up window, as shown in *Figure* 5.14.

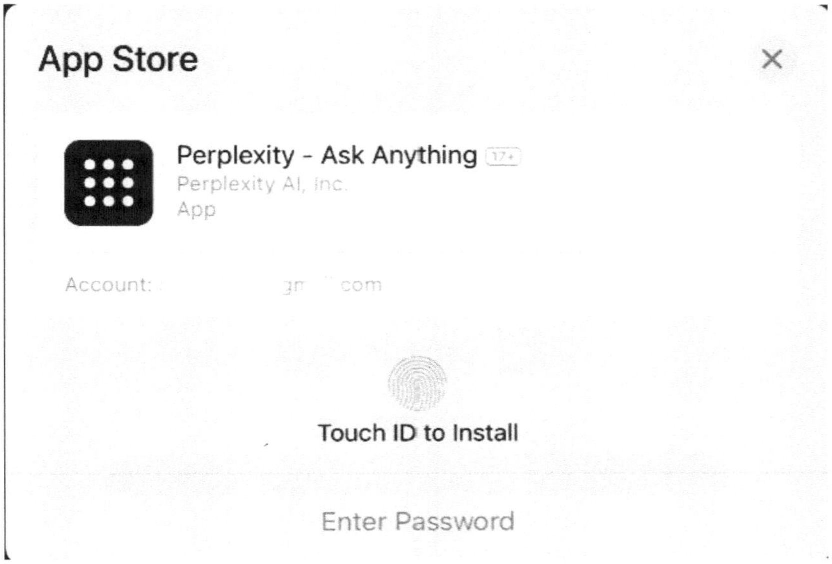

***Figure 5.14**: The **Touch ID** or a password for the **Apple** store can be entered with the keyboard*

The sign-in is prompted for the **Apple ID** email password to allow the **Perplexity App** to be installed, as shown in *Figure* 5.15.

***Figure 5.15**: The sign-in is prompted for the **Apple ID** email password*

We then proceed to download **Perplexity** and receive a prompt to launch the **App**, with a choice of authentication mechanisms, through a **Google** account, an existing **Apple** account, or another email address, as illustrated by *Figure* 5.16.

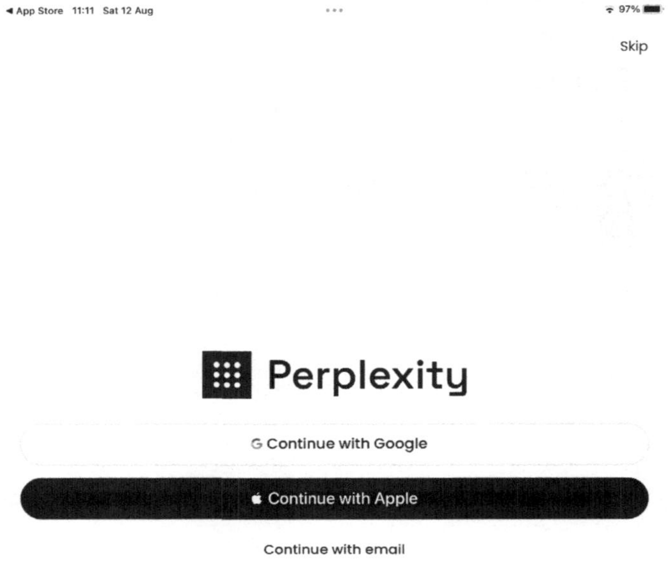

***Figure* 5.16**: *The* **Continue with email** *option is selected*

The email address (redacted) is entered, as shown in *Figure* 5.17.

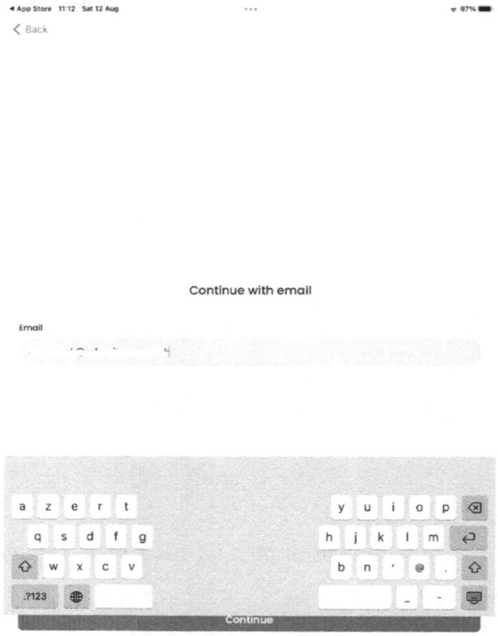

***Figure* 5.17**: *The email address is entered to launch the* **Perplexity AI App** *prompt screen*

We entered the question, which was originally posed to **Ask AI** and also to the **Open AI ChatGPT** web application, on the newly installed **Perplexity App** on the **iPad**, as shown in *Figure* 5.18.

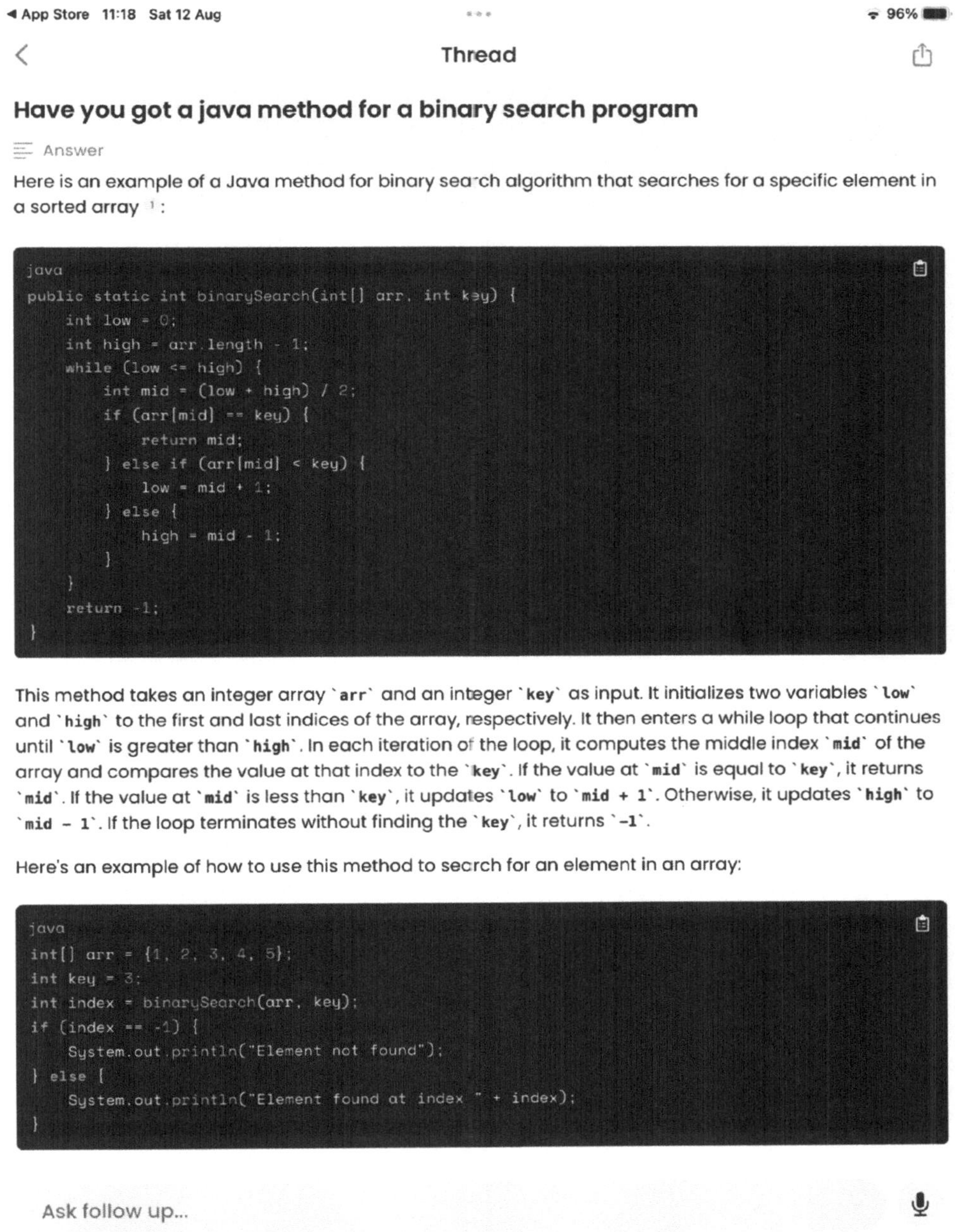

Figure 5.18: *The question, on the example for a* **Binary Search**, *posed to the* **Perplexity App** *on the* **iPad**

The **Perplexity AI App** provides not only the standard features of the **OpenAI ChatGPT** in its response page but also provides, as is illustrated in *Figure* 5.19, the list of further resource links available

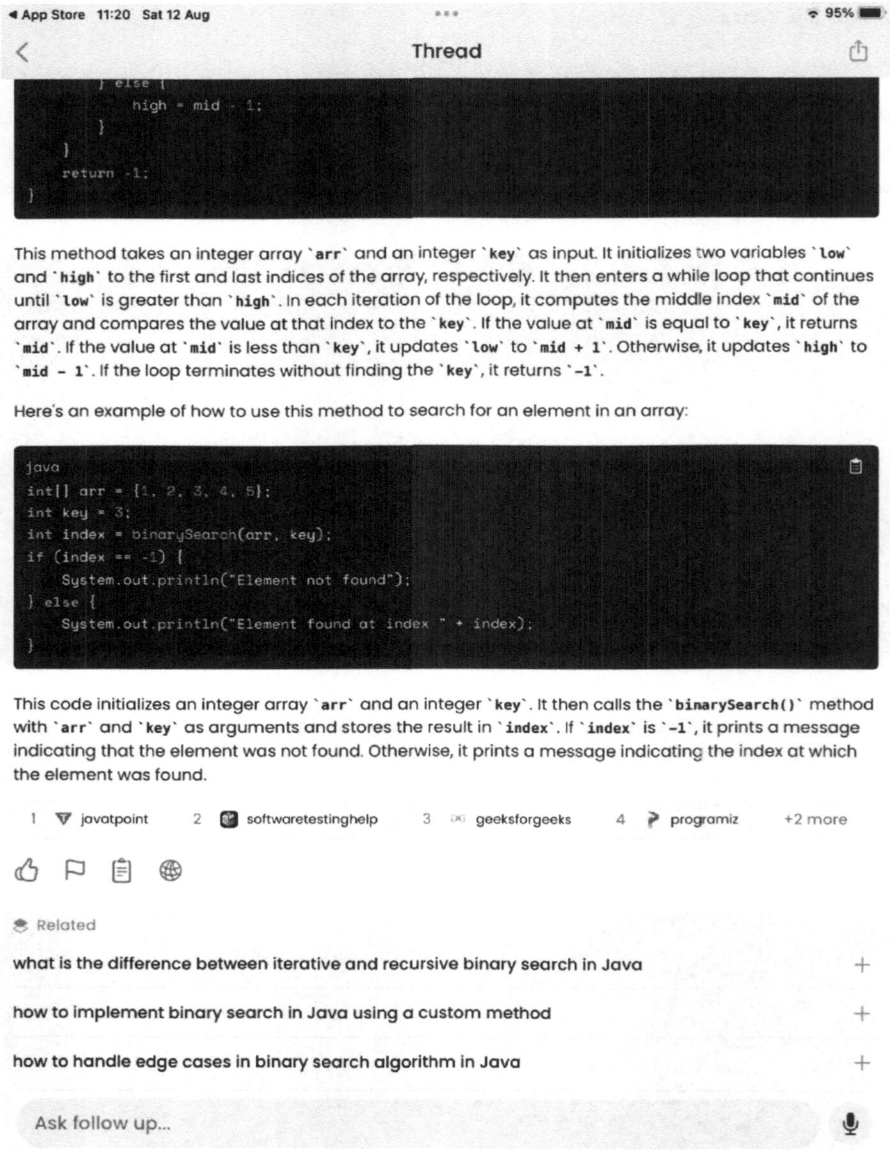

***Figure 5.19**: The list of resources available is shown in the AI response on scrolling down*

Clicking on the **+2 more** button, as shown on the right-hand side in *Figure* 5.19, we get a list of sources and their details in the pop-up window, as shown in *Figure* 5.20.

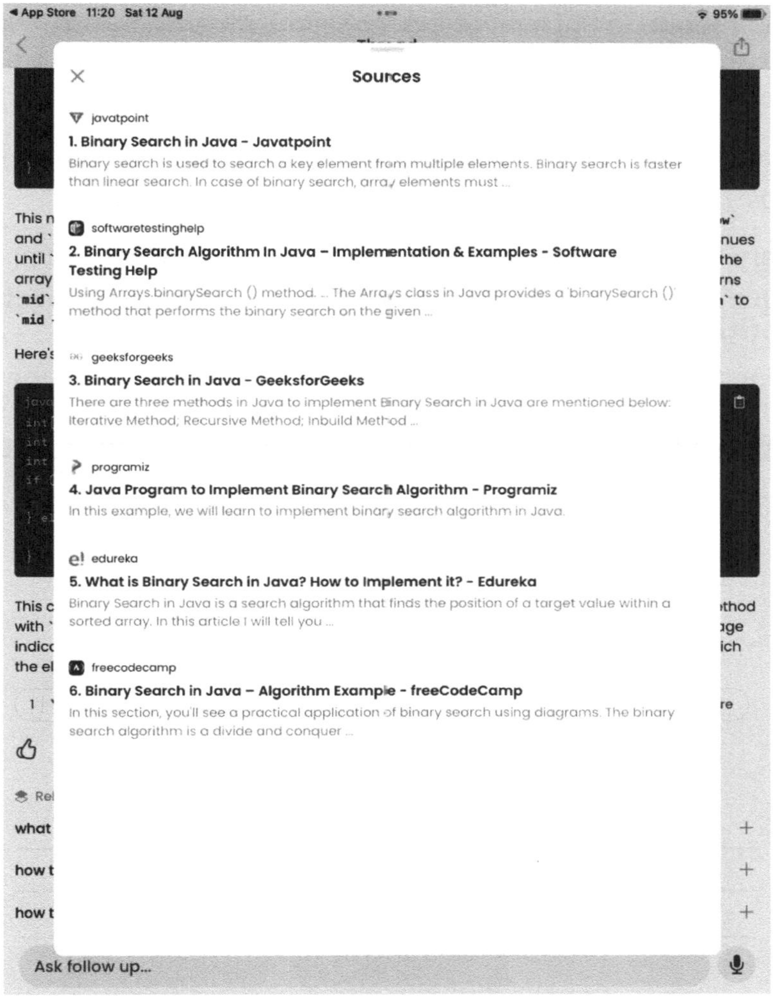

Figure 5.20: *The list of links to further details on the* ***Binary Search*** *algorithm on the internet*

The links, displayed in *Figure* 5.20, can be followed as expanded below:

1. Binary Search in Java – Javatpoint:
   https://www.javatpoint.com/binary-search-in-java
2. Binary Search Algorithm in Java – Implementation & Examples – Software Testing Help:
   https://www.softwaretestinghelp.com/binary-search-in-java/
3. Binary Search in Java – GeeksforGeeks:
   https://www.geeksforgeeks.org/binary-search-in-java/

4. Java Program to Implement Binary Search Algorithm – Programiz:

   https://www.programiz.com/java-programming/examples/binary-search

5. What is Binary Search in Java? How to Implement it? – Edureka:

   https://www.edureka.co/blog/binary-search-in-java/

6. Binary Search in Java – Algorithm Example – freeCodeCamp:

   https://www.freecodecamp.org/news/binary-search-in-java-algorithm-example/

On importing the code created by **Perplexity**, we can run it as shown in *Figure 5.21*.

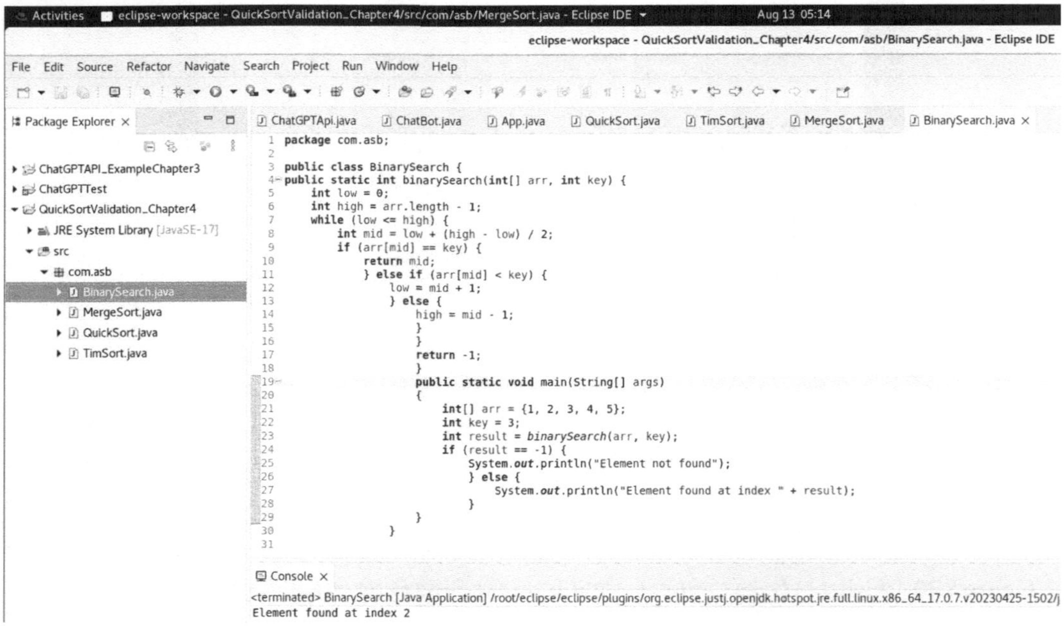

***Figure 5.21**: The Binary Search algorithm is initially validated*

In the next section, we will show how the installed **Eclipse IDE** was used to create this initial **Binary Search** program validation, as shown in *Figure 5.21*, using a step-by-step procedure.

Creating the Java BinarySearch class

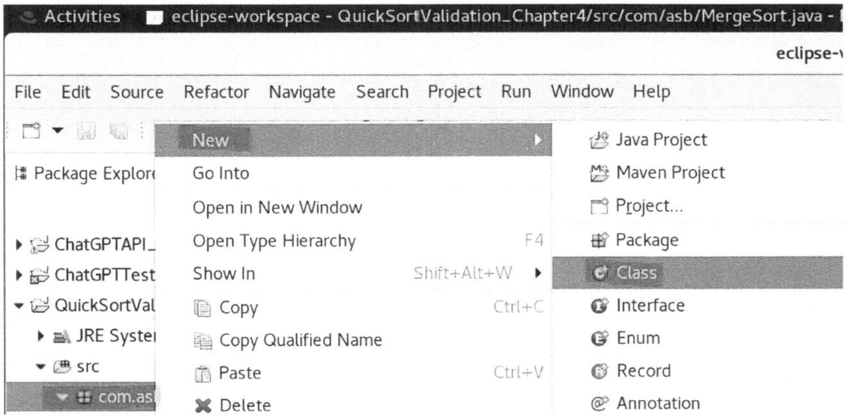

*Figure 5.22: The existing **com.asb** package is right-clicked for the **New-> Class** menu*

The **BinarySearch** class is created under the **com.asb** package after entering the class name, as shown in *Figure 5.23*.

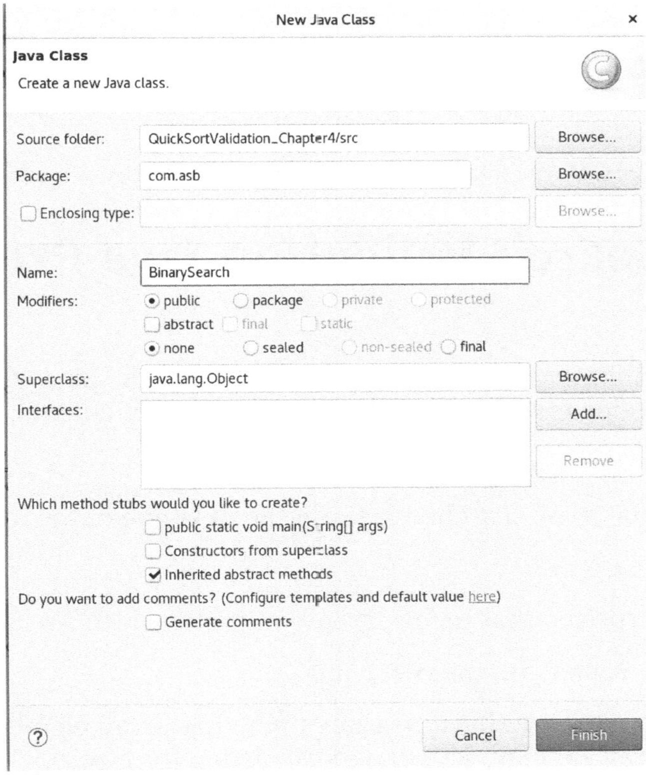

*Figure 5.23: The **BinarySearch** Java Class is created by selecting the **Finish** button*

Running the Eclipse Java Program

After pasting the code copied from the **Perplexity App** into the **Eclipse Java IDE,** we need to test run the application, as shown in *Figure 5.24*. The result of this test is shown in *Figure 5.21*: (*The Binary Search algorithm is initially validated*)

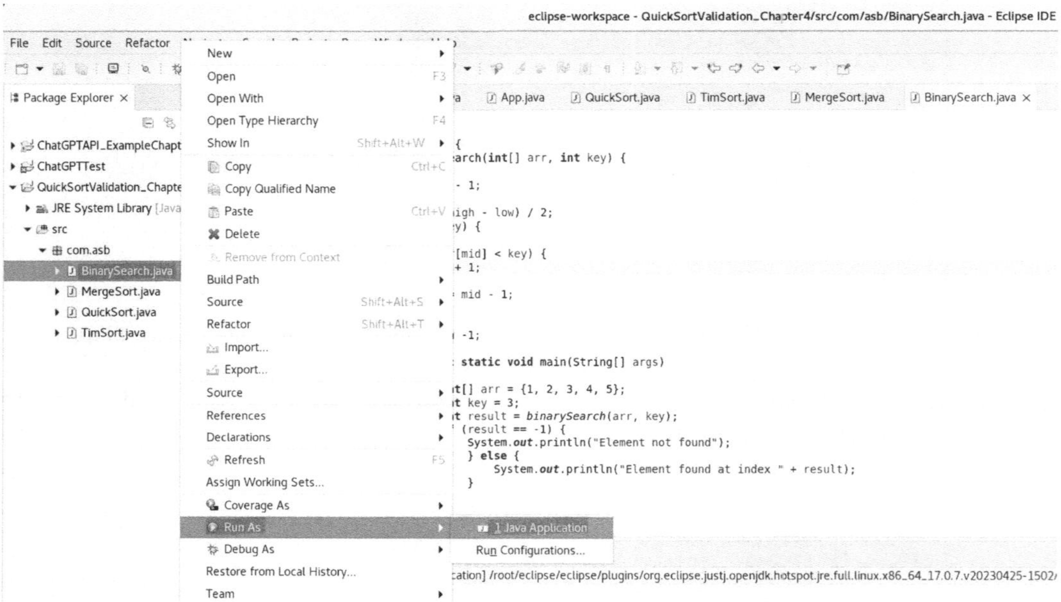

***Figure 5.24**: The initial run of the **BinarySearch** validation program*

Binary Search Validation Java Program Output

We can provide improvements to the initial output of the BinarySearch program. First, you will notice that the original array had just 5 elements:

```
int[] arr = {1, 2, 3, 4, 5};
```

The element value to be searched is set in the next line of the main program:

```
int key = 3;
```

You might be surprised that the program's output is given as:

```
Element found at index 2:
```

In the **Java** language, you have to remember that array elements are indexed with the first array element with an index starting from zero.

We asked the additional question using the **Perplexity AI App** to see if it can provide additional **Java** code to supply a more challenging example for testing to augment our **MergeSort** code, which can then be used to feed the **BinarySearch** for a more robust validation:

Have you an example of a Java program which will populate an integer array with numbers obtained from a random function generator?

This provided the following Java code example

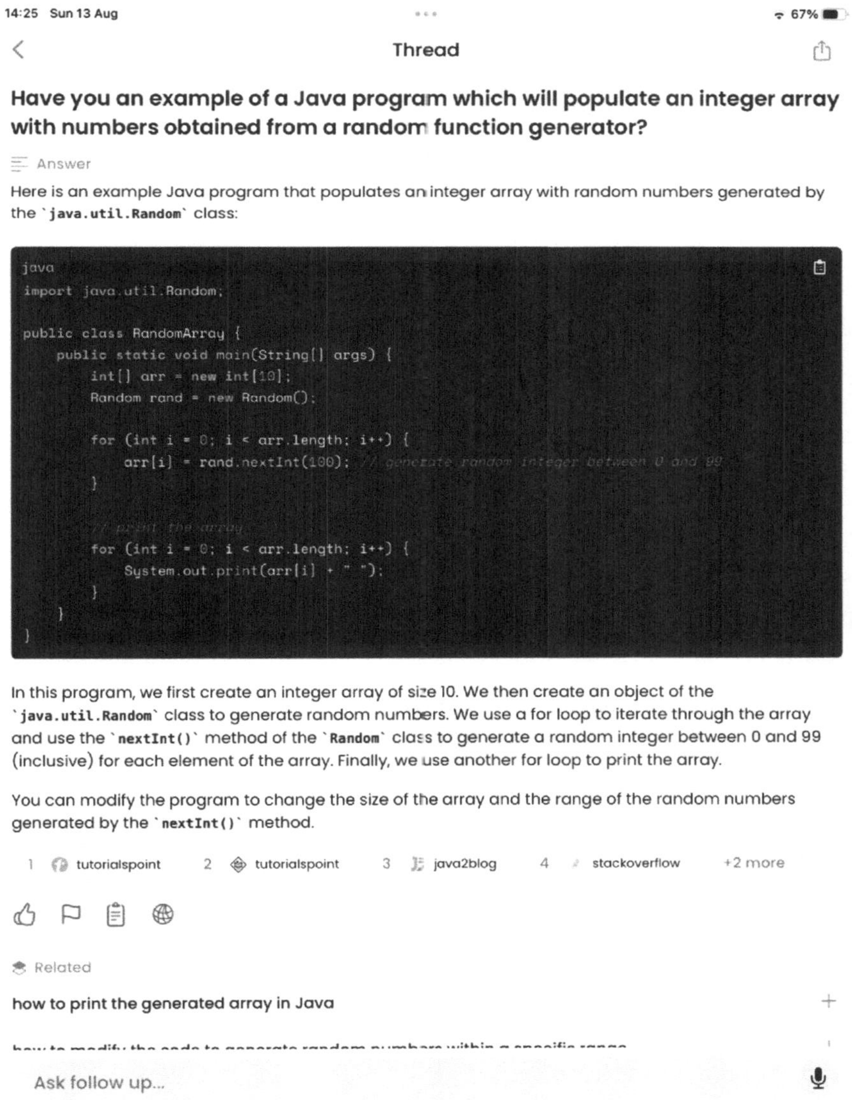

Figure 5.25: *The* **RandomArray** *class Java code that we asked from Perplexity*

The text of the **Java** code generated by **Perplexity**, as shown in *Figure* 5.25, is displayed as follows:

```
package com.asb;

import java.util.Random;

public class RandomArray {

    public static void main(String[] args) {
        int[] arr = new int[10];
        Random rand = new Random();

        for (int i = 0; i < arr.length; i++) {
            arr[i] = rand.nextInt(100); // generate random integer
between 0 and 99
        }

        // print the array
        for (int i = 0; i < arr.length; i++) {
            System.out.print(arr[i] + " ");
        }
    }
}
```

The additional code was then manually updated from the original **BinarySearch** code as follows:

- The **RandomArray** code was incorporated into the **BinarySearch** main program to generate the test array to be sorted using a new **BinarySearchValidation** class.
- The **MergeSort** code was called to sort the array created by the **RandomArray** code.
- The original **BinarySearch** function was called from the **BinarySearch** main program.

```
package com.asb;
import java.util.Arrays;
import java.util.Random;                    //ASB New Import from
the RandomArray code example
import com.asb.MergeSort;            //ASB New Import from the
```

```
MergeSort class created in Chapter 4
public class BinarySearchValidatiion {
//     public class BinarySearch {                //ASB Original
Class name changed: 13-08-2023
public static int binarySearchValidation(int[] arr, int key) { //
ASB method changed 13-08-2023
                    int low = 0;
                    int high = arr.length - 1;
                    while (low <= high) {
                          int mid = low + (high - low) / 2;
                          if (arr[mid] == key) {
                                return mid;            // ASB
We return here if the key is found
                                } else if (arr[mid] < key) {
                                      low = mid + 1;
                                      } else {
                                      high = mid - 1;
                                }
                          }
             return -1;
       }
       public static void main(String[] args) {
       // int[] arr = {1, 2, 3, 4, 5};
// int key = 3; //ASB see below, We want to ensure we find one of
the actual elements
       // ASB -New Code added from Perplexity to populate a test
array, start time and sort it
                    long startTime = System.nanoTime(); //ASB We
log the start time
                    int[] arr = new int[10];
                    Random rand = new Random();
                    for (int i = 0; i < arr.length; i++) {
                          arr[i] = rand.nextInt(100); // generate
random integer between 0 and 99
                    }
                    // print the array
```

```
                    int key = 0; //ASB We set the key starting at
zero,
    //then we use the last Randomly generated element for the key
                    for (int i = 0; i < arr.length; i++) {
                         System.out.print(arr[i] + " ");
     key = arr[i]; //ASB this should give us the randomly
selected last element
     //as the key to be searched
                    }
                         //ASB Now we use the MergeSort we created
earlier in Chapter 4
     System.out.println("Original array: " + Arrays.
toString(arr));
     System.out.println("Search key: " + Integer.toString(key));
//ASB we also print the key to be found
                    MergeSort.mergeSort(arr, 0, arr.length - 1);
                    System.out.println("Sorted array: " + Arrays.
toString(arr));
     // ASB -New Code End
               int result = binarySearchValidation(arr, key); //ASB
Original method name changed 13-08-2023
               long endTime = System.nanoTime();
//ASB We log the end time
     System.out.println("Time taken: " + (endTime - startTime) +
" nanoseconds");  //ASB Changed to nanoseconds from milliseconds
               if (result == -1) {
                    System.out.println("Element not found");
               } else {
                    System.out.println("Element found at index "
+ result);
               }
     }
}
```

Now each run will give a different test data set, the first run results were as follows:

First run:

```
28 97 40 16 44 97 76 55 89 16 Original array: [28, 97, 40, 16, 44, 97,
76, 55, 89, 16]
Search key: 16
Sorted array: [16, 16, 28, 40, 44, 55, 76, 89, 97, 97]
Time taken: 4188251 nanoseconds
Element found at index 1
```

Note that in the first run, we have located the second value of the sorted array element (which is still correct as 16).

Second run:

```
87 68 89 90 12 86 92 99 88 75 Original array: [87, 68, 89, 90, 12, 86,
92, 99, 88, 75]
Search key: 75
Sorted array: [12, 68, 75, 86, 87, 88, 89, 90, 92, 99]
Time taken: 3934707 nanoseconds
Element found at index 2
```

This time there are no duplicate values in the randomly generated array, the index value correctly locates the Search key of 75.

Conclusion

In this chapter, we have demonstrated the download of the currently available **Eclipse IDE** and then used this to validate the **BinarySearch** algorithm. We have also introduced the **Perplexity AI App**, which can be run on an **Android** mobile phone or an **Apple iPad**.

In the next chapter, we will cover the use of **ChatGPT** to assist us to create **Java** code for the **Fourier** analysis of a sine wave.

Points to Remember

- There are several **ChatGPT**-based client Applications, and the platforms they run on are being extended so quickly that reference comparison sites such as SourceForge cannot keep pace.
- The **Perplexity AI App** has the additional feature of listing the website sources it uses for its responses and the links to their web pages.
- In the Java programming language, array elements are numbered starting from zero.

- We can combine the code snippets supplied by ChatGPT to provide additional functionality.

Multiple Choice Questions

1. **Which of the following Mirror sites would be the most appropriate for downloading Eclipse for a user based in North America?**
   a. Consortium GARR
   b. Jevin Canders
   c. Yamagata University
   d. C3SL - Federal University of Parana
2. **Which of the following commands is used to unpack the Eclipse installation file on a Linux system?**
   a. `cp /mnt/hgfs/Installs/eclipse-java-2023-06-R-linux-gtk-x86_64.tar.gz .`
   b. `tar -zxvf eclipse-java-2023-06-R-linux-gtk-x86_64.tar.gz`
   c. `./eclipse`
   d. `mkdir eclipse`
3. **The SourceForge website (12/08/2023) comparison table for Perplexity shows support for which one of the following platform lists?**
   a. Mac, Linux, iPhone, iPad
   b. SaaS/Web, iPhone, iPad, Android
   c. iPhone, SaaS/Web
   d. SaaS/Web, iPhone, iPad
4. **In the final version of the BinarySearchValidation program, which of the following Java methods is used for presorting the array to be searched?**
   a. QuickSort
   b. RandomArray
   c. TimSort
   d. MergeSort

Answers

1. **b**
2. **b**
3. **a**
4. **d**

Questions

1. List the current advantages of **Perplexity AI** over **Ask AI**.
2. How could you modify the final version of the example **BinarySearch Validation** Java program to try processing 10 different arrays in a single run of the program?

   (***Hint***: *this can be achieved by adding just two additional lines of Java code*).
3. Explain why the program output is given as "Element found at index 2:" When the Key number found is the third element of the array.

Key Terms

- ***Apple***: Short for **Apple** Computer company, established on April 1, 1976, by Steve Jobs and Steve Wozniak. They developed the **Apple Mac** desktop computer and then other company products were produced including the **iPhone** and **iPad**.
- ***iPad***: The brand name for a small tablet computer made by **Apple** with a touch-sensitive screen and built-in **Wi-Fi** connectivity, usually with just one **USB** port.
- ***Mirror***: Mirror sites or mirrors are replicas of a master website. The idea of a Mirror site is to provide a fast, geographically local server for a country network. It supplies HTTP and/or FTP services with different URL links while providing the same content for download.
- ***MergeSort***: Merge sort is a "divide-and-conquer" algorithm that was invented by John von Neumann in 1945. In the worst-case scenario, merge sort uses approximately 39% fewer comparisons than quicksort.
- ***Perplexity***: It is a mobile phone app, free to use in its default mode, which has even more useful features than the **Ask AI** mobile phone app. The **Perplexity AI** was established in August 2022 by a group of AI software engineers: Denis Yarats, Aravind Srinivas, Johnny Ho, and Andy Konwinski. The **Perplexity App** now runs on **iPhone**, **Android**, and **iPad**

and has a search interface powered by **OpenAI's GPT 3.5** and **Microsoft Bing**, which answers user questions (currently using **GPT 4**). **Perplexity** also has a **Copilot** mode.

- ***QuickSort***: Quicksort is a general-purpose sorting algorithm developed by Tony Hoare in the UK in 1959 and published in 1961.
- ***RandomArray***: This method is used in this chapter to randomly assign a range of integer numbers to an array of integer elements, after which the array is sorted as input for the **Binary Search** example code we developed in this chapter.
- ***TimSort***: TimSort is a stable sorting algorithm, derived from merge sort and insertion sort. It was first implemented by Tim Peters in 2002 for use in the **Python** programming language. (Hence, the name!)

CHAPTER 6

ChatGPT Generated Java Code for Fourier Analysis

Introduction

Performing Fourier analysis on an **MP4** music file to separate instruments and vocals is a complex task. It involves multiple steps like decoding the **MP4** file, performing signal processing, and applying source separation techniques. **ChatGPT** provided an outline guide for the steps required and suggested some libraries for each step.

We did eventually manage to successfully split an **MP3** music file using a **Java** program to call a **python** library routine called **Spleeter.** Unfortunately, the **Java** code provided by **ChatGPT** was incorrect, although it was helpful in its suggestion to use **Spleeter.**

Also, the **MP4** format is mainly used for video files (although there is an **MP4** to **MP3** convertor at **https://cloudconvert.com/mp4-to-mp3**) **ChatGPT** did not flag this as an issue.

A simpler task, which **ChatGPT** did provide the full working code for, was for the **Fourier** analysis of a sine wave using **Java** code and through **Microsoft Bing** webchat, a graphical display program (this is using the **OpenAI GPT-4.5**).

Structure

In this chapter, we will discuss the following topics:

- MP4 Fourier Analysis Java Code
    - MP4 Fourier Analysis Java Code – according to OpenAI ChatGPT
- Fourier Analysis for MP4 java code validation using an Eclipse Java Program Project
- ChatGPT generated Java code for Fourier Analysis of a Sine wave
- Sine wave Fourier Analysis Java code validation using an Eclipse Java

MP4 Fourier Analysis Java Code

Is there java code for the Fourier analysis of an MP4 music file to separate the instruments and vocals?

(This was according to Ask AI)

Performing Fourier analysis on an MP4 music file to separate instruments and vocals is a complex task. It involves multiple steps like decoding the MP4 file, performing signal processing, and applying source separation techniques. While I can't give you a full Java code solution, I can guide you through the steps and suggest some libraries for each step.

1. **Decode the MP4 file:** To read and decode MP4 music files, you can use a Java library like Xuggler (**http://www.xuggle.com/xuggler/**).
2. **Perform Fourier analysis:** Once you have the audio data, you can perform Fourier analysis on it. For this, you can use the Fast Fourier Transform (FFT) algorithm provided by the JTransforms library (**https://github.com/wendykierp/JTransforms**).
3. **Separate instruments and vocals:** This is the most challenging part. Separating instruments and vocals typically involves source separation techniques, such as Non-negative Matrix Factorization (NMF) or deep learning methods like U-Net. There may not be readily available Java libraries for this step, and you may need to implement the algorithms yourself based on research papers or use other programming languages with available libraries, like Python.

   Here's a high-level outline of how the code might look like:

```
```java
import com.xuggle.mediatool.IMediaReader;
```
```

```
import com.xuggle.mediatool.IMediaWriter;
import com.xuggle.mediatool.ToolFactory;
import com.xuggle.mediatool.event.IAudioSamplesEvent;
import com.xuggle.mediatool.event.IVideoPictureEvent;
import com.xuggle.xuggler.IContainer;

// ... other imports ...

public class MusicFileAnalyzer {
    public static void main(String[] args) {

        // Step 1: Decode MP4 file
        IMediaReader mediaReader = ToolFactory.makeReader("input.mp4");
        mediaReader.addListener(new AudioSampleListener());
        while (mediaReader.readPacket() == null) {
            // continue reading the file
        }

        // Step 2: Perform Fourier analysis using JTransforms

        // Step 3: Separate instruments and vocals using source separation techniques

    }
}

class AudioSampleListener extends MediaListenerAdapter {
    @Override
    public void onAudioSamples(IAudioSamplesEvent event) {
        // Process audio samples here
    }
}
```

Keep in mind that separating instruments and vocals can be challenging and may not produce perfect results. ***If you're open to using Python, there are more advanced libraries like Spleeter (https://github.com/deezer/spleeter) that can help you achieve better source separation results.***

The suggestion in bold from the **AI** proved to be the best (and simplest) advice given by **ChatGPT**.

MP4 Fourier Analysis Java Code – according to OpenAI ChatGPT

Next, we tried **Perplexity,** since the skeleton **Java** code given by **Ask AI** was often just a list of comments, and it responded as follows:

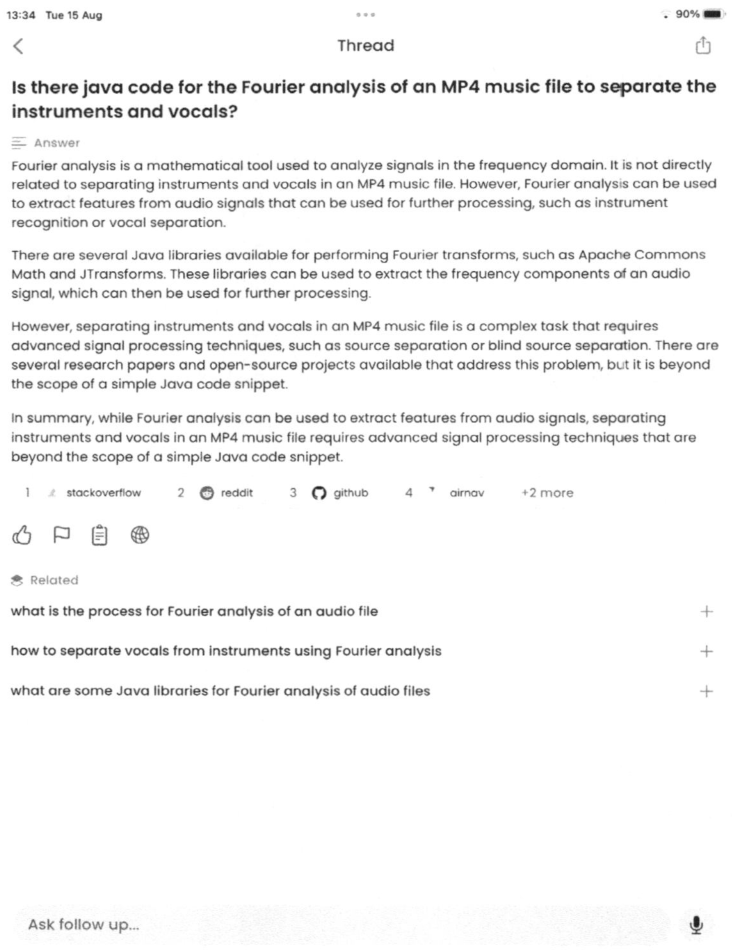

***Figure 6.1**: The Perplexity App on the iPad gives us it's advice on the question*

We then opened up the second, related thread supplied by **Perplexity**, which gave the response as shown in *Figure 6.2*:

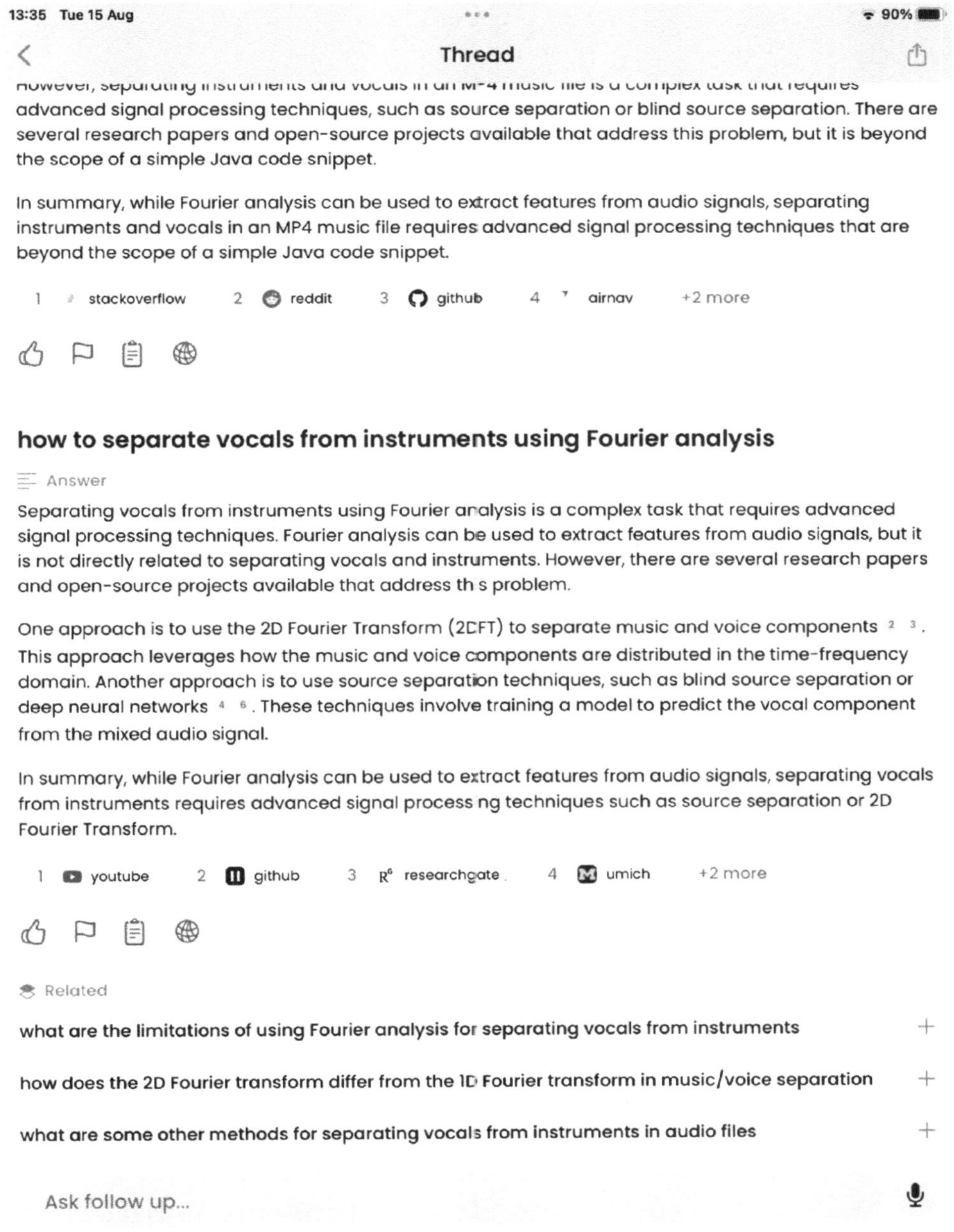

Figure 6.2: *The* **Perplexity App** *on the* **iPad** *still does not provide any code*

So, we tried the third thread as shown in *Figure 6.3*:

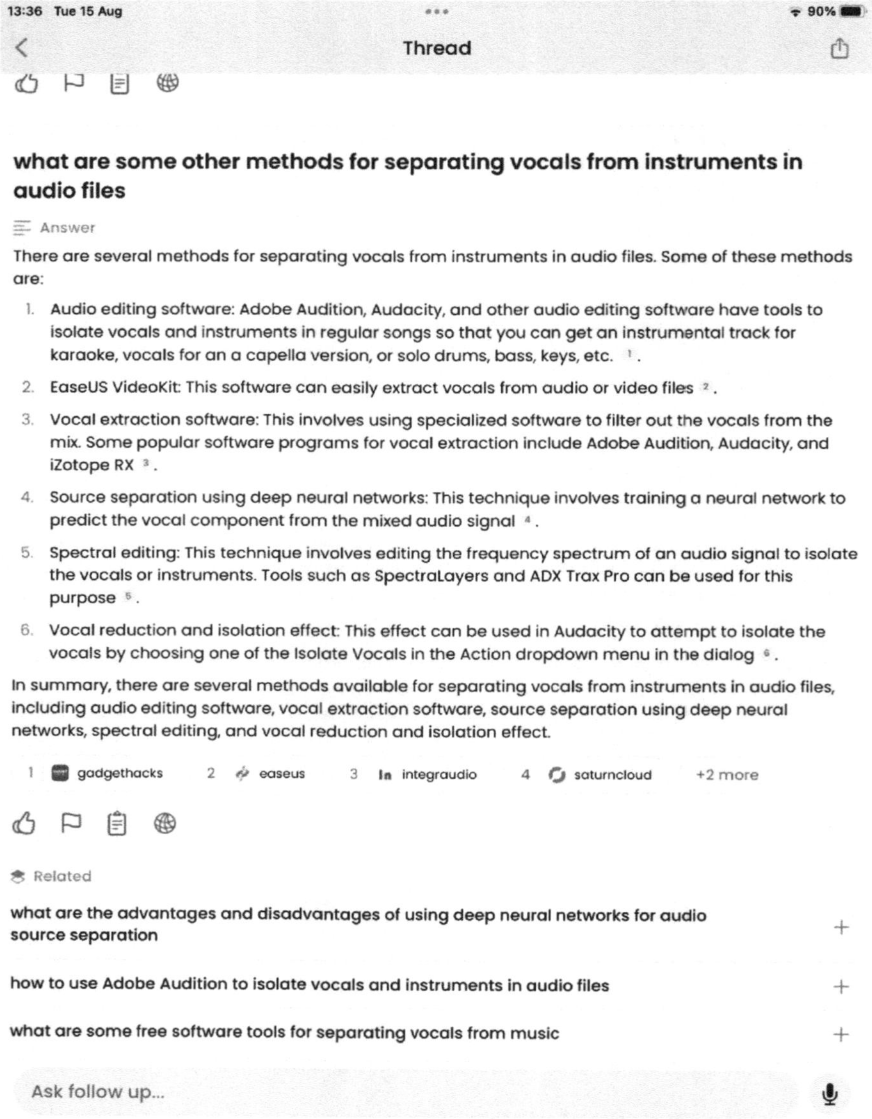

***Figure 6.3**: The **Perplexity App** on the **iPad** provides interesting links, but still no code*

We were a little disappointed that the **Ask AI** and **Perplexity Apps** didn't provide us with the full **Java** code, so we tried the OpenAI web application at **https://chat.openai.com/** as shown in *Figure 6.4*:

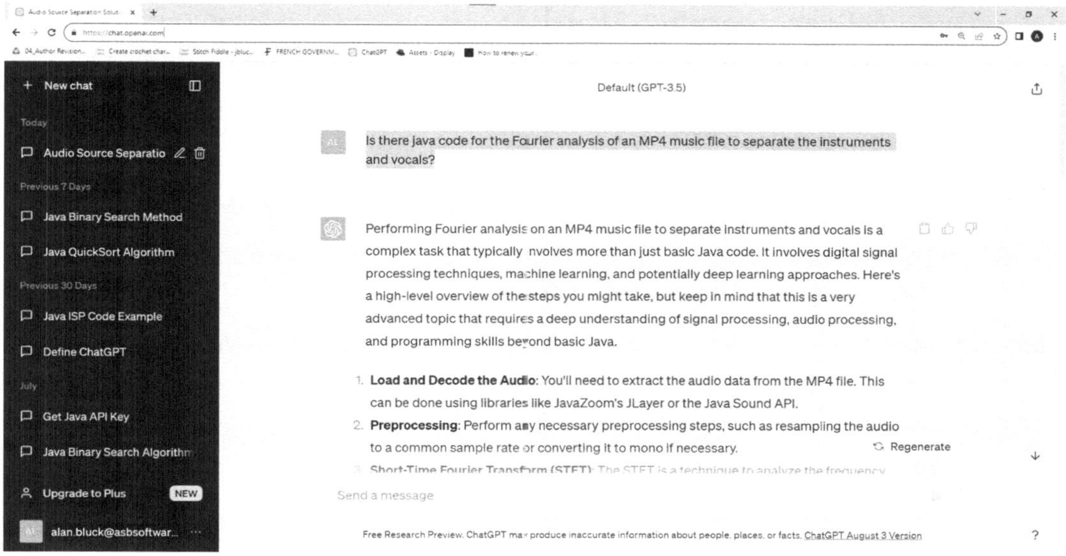

***Figure 6.4**: The OpenAI web application at* **https://chat.openai.com/ response**

The full response from **OpenAI** is shown here:

Performing Fourier analysis on an MP4 music file to separate instruments and vocals is a complex task that typically involves more than just basic Java code. It involves digital signal processing techniques, machine learning, and potentially deep learning approaches. Here's a high-level overview of the steps you might take, but keep in mind that this is a very advanced topic that requires a deep understanding of signal processing, audio processing, and programming skills beyond basic Java.

1. ****Load and Decode the Audio**:** You'll need to extract the audio data from the MP4 file. This can be done using libraries like JavaZoom's JLayer or the Java Sound API.

2. ****Preprocessing**:** Perform any necessary preprocessing steps, such as resampling the audio to a common sample rate or converting it to mono if necessary.

3. ****Short-Time Fourier Transform (STFT)**:** The STFT is a technique to analyze the frequency content of a signal over time. You'll apply the STFT to your audio signal to convert it into a time-frequency representation.

4. ****Spectral Source Separation**:** This is the heart of the process. There are different methods you can use, including:

    a. ****Non-negative Matrix Factorization (NMF)**:** NMF can be used to factorize the spectrogram into basis components (instruments/vocals) and their corresponding activations.

   b. **Deep Learning Models**: Using deep learning models like convolutional neural networks (CNNs) or recurrent neural networks (RNNs) trained on source separation tasks.

5. **Reconstruction**: Once you've separated the different sources (instruments and vocals), you need to reconstruct the audio signals from the processed spectrogram data. This involves an inverse STFT process.

6. **Post-processing**: Clean up any artifacts or imperfections introduced during separation and reconstruction.

Here's a very simplified example of how you might use the Java Sound API and JTransforms library to perform STFT:

```java
import javax.sound.sampled.*;
import org.jtransforms.fft.FloatFFT_2D;


public class AudioAnalysis {
    public static void main(String[] args) {
        try {
            AudioInputStream audioInputStream = AudioSystem.
getAudioInputStream(new File("input.mp4"));
            AudioFormat format = audioInputStream.getFormat();

            // Read and process audio data in chunks
            int chunkSize = 2048; // Adjust as needed
            byte[] audioData = new byte[chunkSize];

            FloatFFT_2D fft = new FloatFFT_2D(chunkSize, 1);

            // Process each chunk of audio data
            while (audioInputStream.read(audioData) != -1) {
                float[] audioSamples = convertBytesToFloats(audioData);

                // Apply FFT
                float[] spectrum = new float[2 * chunkSize];
                System.arraycopy(audioSamples, 0, spectrum, 0,
chunkSize);
                fft.realForwardFull(spectrum);
```

```
                // Process the spectrum data (e.g., separate sources)

                // Inverse FFT to reconstruct audio
                fft.realInverseFull(spectrum, true);

                // Process the reconstructed audio (e.g., post-processing)
            }

            audioInputStream.close();
        } catch (Exception e) {
            e.printStackTrace();
        }
    }

    private static float[] convertBytesToFloats(byte[] bytes) {
        float[] floats = new float[bytes.length / 2];
        for (int i = 0; i < floats.length; i++) {
            floats[i] = (float) ((bytes[2 * i] & 0xFF) | (bytes[2 * i + 1]
<< 8));
        }
        return floats;
    }
}
```

Please note that this example is extremely simplified and doesn't perform any actual source separation or reconstruction. Real-world source separation requires sophisticated algorithms and often deep learning models.

For a more practical and robust solution, you might want to explore existing libraries and tools specialized in audio source separation, such as Spleeter by Deezer, which is a pre-trained model for separating vocals and accompaniments in music recordings. This can be used through Python, and you can potentially integrate it with your Java application using appropriate interfacing methods like calling Python scripts from Java.

So, again the Java code only achieves the “skeleton” of a working program. Optimistically, we then asked:

Can ChatGPT input an MP4 music file and separate the instruments and vocals?

Which was responded with:

"No, ChatGPT cannot directly process or analyze audio or video files, including MP4 music files. It's a text-based language model and doesn't have the capability to handle audio or video data directly. Separating instruments and vocals from an audio file requires complex signal processing and machine learning techniques that are beyond the capabilities of a text-based model like ChatGPT.

To perform audio source separation tasks like separating instruments and vocals from an MP4 music file, you would need to use specialized tools, libraries, and software designed for audio processing and source separation. These tools often involve a combination of digital signal processing methods and machine learning algorithms. **Libraries like Spleeter, as mentioned earlier**, are examples of tools that can perform this kind of audio source separation.

Keep in mind that these tasks are quite advanced and might require some expertise in audio processing and programming to achieve meaningful results."

We have highlighted the text above since it does indicate that ChatGPT has some memory of the previous responses it gave.

So, we tried a different approach, which did appear to be more promising. We asked:

Do you have example java code to call the Spleeter python libraries for source separation of an MP4 audio file?

On posing this question, we do get some Java code, as shown in *Figure 6.5*:

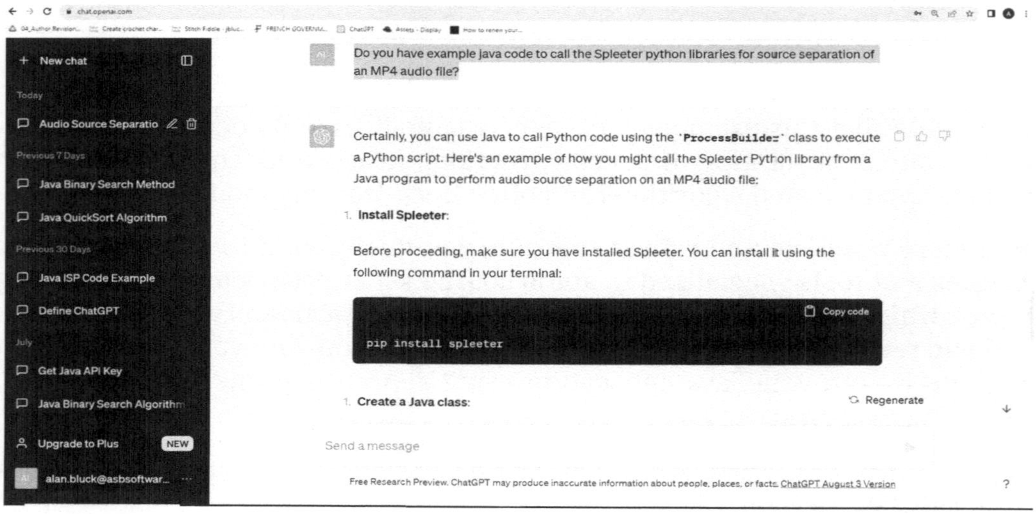

Figure 6.5: *The* **OpenAI** *web application gives us some Java code we can use at last*

This gave a full example of a method to achieve our original goal of separating the vocals from the instruments, though not directly using Fourier Analysis:

Certainly, you can use Java to call Python code using the `ProcessBuilder` class to execute a Python script. Here's an example of how you might call the Spleeter Python library from a Java program to perform audio source separation on an MP4 audio file:

1. **Install Spleeter**:

   Before proceeding, make sure you have installed Spleeter. You can install it using the following command in your terminal:

   ```
   pip install spleeter
   ```

2. **Create a Java class**:

   Create a Java class that calls a Python script. For simplicity, let's assume you have a Python script named `spleeter_separate.py` that performs the source separation using Spleeter. This script takes the input audio file path and output directory as command-line arguments.

   Here's an example of how you might structure your Java class:

   ```java
   import java.io.BufferedReader;
   import java.io.IOException;
   import java.io.InputStreamReader;

   public class SpleeterCaller {
       public static void main(String[] args) {
           try {
               String pythonScriptPath = "path/to/spleeter_separate.
   py"; // Replace with actual path
               String inputFile = "path/to/input.mp4"; // Replace
   with actual input file path
               String outputDirectory = "path/to/output/"; //
   Replace with desired output directory

               // Construct the command to execute the Python script
               String[] command = {"python", pythonScriptPath,
   inputFile, outputDirectory};
   ```

```
            ProcessBuilder processBuilder = new
ProcessBuilder(command);
            processBuilder.redirectErrorStream(true);

            Process process = processBuilder.start();

            // Read the output of the Python script
            BufferedReader reader = new BufferedReader(new
InputStreamReader(process.getInputStream()));
            String line;
            while ((line = reader.readLine()) != null) {
                System.out.println(line);
            }

            // Wait for the process to complete
            int exitCode = process.waitFor();
            System.out.println("Python script exited with code: "
+ exitCode);

        } catch (IOException | InterruptedException e) {
            e.printStackTrace();
        }
    }
}
```

3. **Python Script (`spleeter_separate.py`)**:

Create a Python script named `spleeter_separate.py` that uses the Spleeter library to perform audio source separation. Here's a simplified example of the script:

```python
import sys
from spleeter.separator import Separator

def main():
    if len(sys.argv) != 4:
        print("Usage: python spleeter_separate.py input_audio
```

```
output_directory")
        return

    input_audio = sys.argv[1]
    output_directory = sys.argv[2]

    separator = Separator('spleeter:2stems')  # Use desired
separation model
    separator.separate_to_file(input_audio, output_directory)

if __name__ == "__main__":
    main()
```

Remember to replace `'spleeter:2stems'` with the appropriate separation model depending on how many sources you want to separate. You can find more information about Spleeter and its available models in the [official Spleeter documentation] (**https://github.com/deezer/spleeter**).

Please note that this example demonstrates the basic process of calling a Python script from Java to perform source separation using Spleeter. You might need to adapt the code to your specific use case and handle error cases more robustly. Additionally, make sure that both your Java and Python environments are properly configured.

Fourier Analysis for MP4 java code validation using an Eclipse Java Program Project

So, we have several separate Java programs to validate, including **Java** calls to a **python** library.

First, as suggested by **ChatGPT**, we installed the **Spleeter python** libraries, which it referenced as:

1. ****Install Spleeter**:**

   We used the command as follows:

   `pip install Spleeter`

   We noted later, that the **Spleeter** upper-case "**S**" did not seem to cause an issue (we should have used **spleeter** with the lower-case "**s**").

This first attempt gave:

```
bash: pip: command not found...
```

So, we realized that we have to use the **Python pip** installer on our **RHEL 8.8** Linux server first, this is actually referenced as either **pip2** or **pip3**, as the major versions can co-exist on **RHEL** Linux. So, either can be used, as demonstrated below:

```
[root@ECMUKDEMO22 eclipse]# pip3 --version

pip 9.0.3 from /usr/lib/python3.6/site-packages (python 3.6)

[root@ECMUKDEMO22 eclipse]# pip2 --version

pip 9.0.3 from /usr/lib/python2.7/site-packages (python 2.7)

[root@ECMUKDEMO22 eclipse]#
```

So, then we used:

```
pip3 install Spleeter
```

This gave an error indicating there was a missing dependency called **tensorflow 2.5.0**, as shown in *Figure* 6.6:

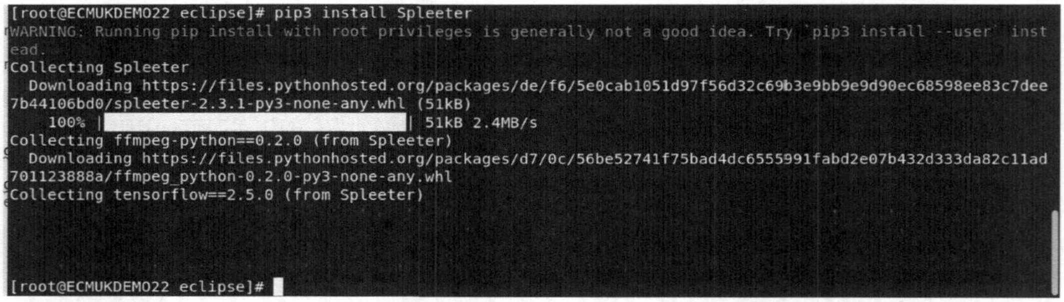

***Figure 6.6**: The first attempt at installing using pip3 gave an error on **tensorflow** 2.5.0*

So, we installed it first, using:

```
pip3 install tensorflow
```

But, this also (eventually) gave the error:

You're on RHEL/Fedora and haven't run `**yum install python3-devel**` or

`**dnf install python3-devel**` (make sure you also have **redhat-rpm-config** installed)

So, we repeated, again, using:

```
yum install redhat-rpm-config
```

```
Installed:
  annobin-10.94-1.el8.x86_64                          dwz-0.12-10.el8.x86_64
  efi-srpm-macros-3-3.el8.noarch                      gcc-plugin-annobin-8.5.0-18.el8.x86_64
  ghc-srpm-macros-1.4.2-7.el8.noarch                  go-srpm-macros-2-17.el8.noarch
  ocaml-srpm-macros-5-4.el8.noarch                    openblas-srpm-macros-2-2.el8.noarch
  perl-srpm-macros-1-25.el8.noarch                    python-rpm-macros-3-45.el8.noarch
  python-srpm-macros-3-45.el8.noarch                  python3-rpm-macros-3-45.el8.noarch
  qt5-srpm-macros-5.15.3-1.el8.noarch                 redhat-rpm-config-131-1.el8.noarch
  rust-srpm-macros-5-2.el8.noarch

Complete!
[root@ECMUKDEM022 eclipse]#
```

Figure 6.7: *The* ***redhat-rpm-config*** *is installed*

Then we need to install the **python3-devel** package as advised:

```
yum install python3-devel
```

The installation of the **`python3-devel`** libraries were successful, as shown in *Figure 6.8*:

```
Total                                                             916 kB/s | 281 kB     00:00
Running transaction check
Transaction check succeeded.
Running transaction test
Transaction test succeeded.
Running transaction
  Preparing        :                                                                        1/1
  Installing       : python3-rpm-generators-5-8.el8.noarch                                  1/3
  Installing       : platform-python-devel-3.6.8-51.el8_8.1.x86_64                          2/3
  Installing       : python36-devel-3.6.8-38.module+el8.5.0+12207+5c5719bc.x86_64           3/3
  Running scriptlet: python36-devel-3.6.8-38.module+el8.5.0+12207+5c5719bc.x86_64           3/3
  Verifying        : python36-devel-3.6.8-38.module+el8.5.0+12207+5c5719bc.x86_64           1/3
  Verifying        : python3-rpm-generators-5-8.el8.noarch                                  2/3
  Verifying        : platform-python-devel-3.6.8-51.el8_8.1.x86_64                          3/3
Installed products updated.

Installed:
  platform-python-devel-3.6.8-51.el8_8.1.x86_64            python3-rpm-generators-5-8.el8.noarch
  python36-devel-3.6.8-38.module+el8.5.0+12207+5c5719bc.x86_64

Complete!
[root@ECMUKDEM022 eclipse]#
```

Figure 6.8: *The* ***`python3-devel`*** *libraries are installed*

Now we try the missing `tensorflow` package libraries installation, as shown in *Figure 6.9*.

```
pip3 install tensorflow
```

```
  Using cached https://files.pythonhosted.org/packages/bd/df/d4a4974a3e3957fd1c1fa3082366d7fff6e428ddb55f074bf
64876f8e8ad/zipp-3.6.0-py3-none-any.whl
Installing collected packages: grpcio, cached-property, h5py, keras-applications, wheel, setuptools, dataclass
es, werkzeug, typing-extensions, zipp, importlib-metadata, markdown, tensorboard, astor, google-pasta, wrapt,
gast, keras-preprocessing, tensorflow
  Running setup.py install for grpcio ... done
Successfully installed astor-0.8.1 cached-property-1.5.2 dataclasses-0.8 gast-0.5.4 google-pasta-0.2.0 grpcio-
1.48.2 h5py-3.1.0 importlib-metadata-4.8.3 keras-applications-1.0.8 keras-preprocessing-1.1.2 markdown-3.3.7 s
etuptools-59.6.0 tensorboard-1.14.0 tensorflow-1.14.0 typing-extensions-4.1.1 werkzeug-2.0.3 wheel-0.37.1 wrap
t-1.15.0 zipp-3.6.0
[root@ECMUKDEM022 eclipse]#
```

Figure 6.9: *The* ***`pip3 install tensorflow`*** *command is used and libraries are installed*

This also installs the **`tensorflow-2.5.0`** as shown in *Figure* 6.10:

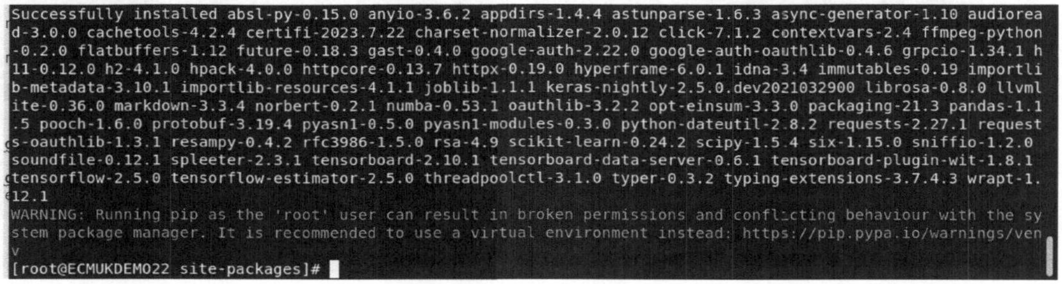

***Figure* 6.10**: *The **`tensorflow-2.5.0`** libraries are installed*

We also needed to run the pip3 upgrade:

(A link here helped; **https://qiita.com/palao/items/699f4148249481c64ad7** Although the description language used is in Japanese! The commands can still be followed as they are standard Linux.)

```
cd /usr/local/lib64/python3.6/site-packages
```

```
pip3 install --upgrade pip
```

Then we tried to run the installation for **Spleeter**, note here that we use lowercase for the **spleeter** name.

```
pip3 install spleeter
```

So, then we use the command line process to get a test MP3 as in the Japanese link to try the package out.

```
wget https://github.com/deezer/spleeter/raw/master/audio_example.mp3
```

Next, we also installed the following library, as suggested in the Japanese blog:

```
pip3 install -U urllib3
```

These installs are shown in *Figure* 6.11, with the commands as highlighted:

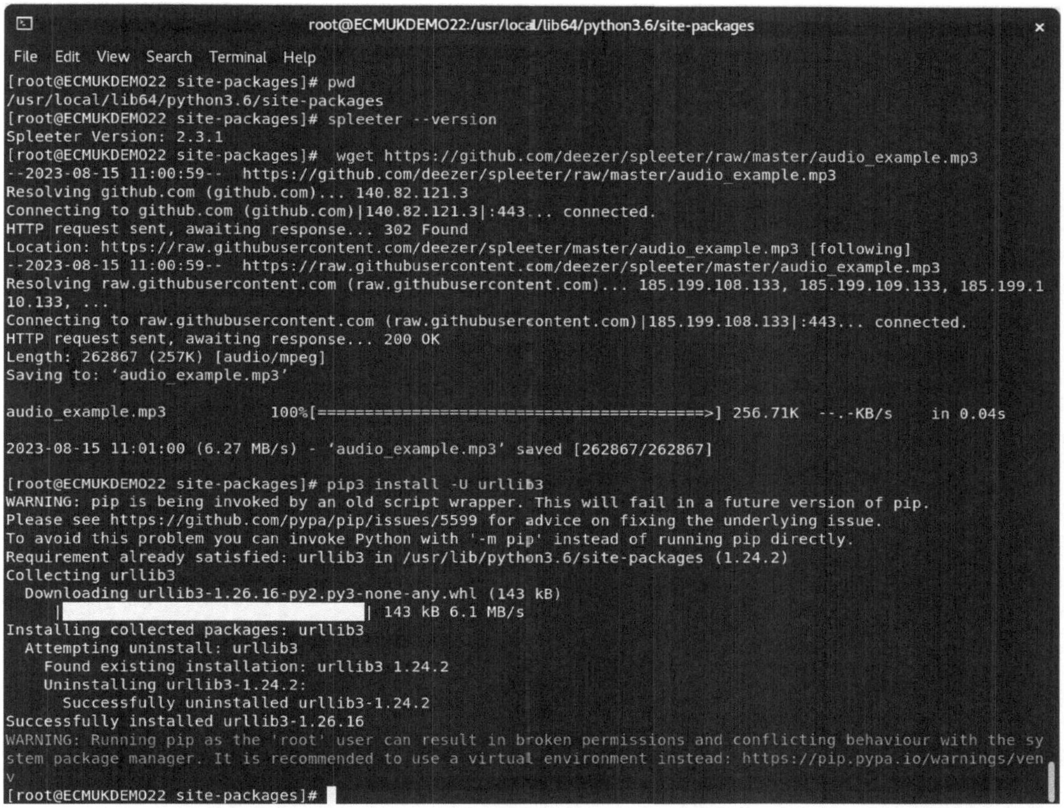

***Figure 6.11**: The audio_example.mp3 file is downloaded as the test input and the* `urllib3`

Then, we try to run the **spleeter** command from the **Linux** command window:

```
spleeter separate -p spleeter:2stems -o output audio_example.mp3
```

First, we got the error:

```
[root@ECMUKDEMO22 site-packages]# spleeter separate -p spleeter:2stems
-o output audio_example.mp3
```

`ERROR:spleeter:ffmpeg binary not found`

Searching the error in Google, we get a recommendation from the link: **https://computingforgeeks.com/how-to-install-ffmpeg-on-centos-rhel-8/**

We need to run the command as follows:

```
dnf -y install https://download.fedoraproject.org/pub/epel/epel-release-latest-8.noarch.rpm
```

So, scrolling back up the Japanese blog, I find an install for this too:

dnf install **http://rpmfind.net/linux/epel/7/x86_64/Packages/s/SDL2-2.0.14-2.el7.x86_64.rpm**

```
[root@ECMUKDEM022 site-packages]# dnf -y install https://download.fedoraproject.org/pub/epel/epel-release-late
st-8.noarch.rpm
Updating Subscription Management repositories.
Last metadata expiration check: 0:48:32 ago on Tue 15 Aug 2023 10:47:05 AM PDT.
epel-release-latest-8.noarch.rpm                                        46 kB/s |  25 kB     00:00
Dependencies resolved.
==============================================================================================================
 Package                    Architecture          Version                 Repository                     Size
==============================================================================================================
Installing:
 epel-release               noarch                8-19.el8                @commandline                   25 k

Transaction Summary
==============================================================================================================
Install  1 Package

Total size: 25 k
Installed size: 35 k
Downloading Packages:
Running transaction check
Transaction check succeeded.
Running transaction test
Transaction test succeeded.
Running transaction
  Preparing        :                                                                                      1/1
  Installing       : epel-release-8-19.el8.noarch                                                         1/1
  Running scriptlet: epel-release-8-19.el8.noarch                                                         1/1
Many EPEL packages require the CodeReady Builder (CRB) repository.
It is recommended that you run /usr/bin/crb enable to enable the CRB repository.

  Verifying        : epel-release-8-19.el8.noarch                                                         1/1
Installed products updated.

Installed:
  epel-release-8-19.el8.noarch

Complete!
[root@ECMUKDEM022 site-packages]#
```

***Figure 6.12**: We need to install the **EPEL** packages to support the **Spleeter python** program*

We run the command as follows to install the recommended CRB repository, as recommended in *Figure* 6.12.

```
subscription-manager repos --enable codeready-builder-for-rhel-8-x86_64-rpms
```

This repository is enabled as expected as shown in *Figure* 6.13:

```
[root@ECMUKDEM022 site-packages]# subscription-manager repos --enable codeready-builder-for-rhel-8-x86_64-rpms
Repository 'codeready-builder-for-rhel-8-x86_64-rpms' is enabled for this system.
[root@ECMUKDEM022 site-packages]#
```

***Figure 6.13**: We install the recommended CRB repository*

We now need to update the subscription rpm package file, using the command as follows:

dnf install -y **https://download1.rpmfusion.org/nonfree/el/rpmfusion-nonfree-release-8.noarch.rpm**

During the installation, we get prompted to import two **GPG** security keys, as shown in *Figure* 6.14

(The **GPG** security keys are used for public/private key encryption to ensure that the data is transferred securely in an encrypted format).

```
Total                                                                              4.6 MB/s |  19 MB     00:04
Extra Packages for Enterprise Linux 8 - x86_64                                     1.6 MB/s | 1.6 kB     00:00
Importing GPG key 0x2F86D6A1:
 Userid     : "Fedora EPEL (8) <epel@fedoraproject.org>"
 Fingerprint: 94E2 79EB 8D8F 25B2 1810 ADF1 21EA 45AB 2F86 D6A1
 From       : /etc/pki/rpm-gpg/RPM-GPG-KEY-EPEL-8
Is this ok [y/N]: y
Key imported successfully
RPM Fusion for EL 8 - Free - Updates                                               1.6 MB/s | 1.7 kB     00:00
Importing GPG key 0x158B3811:
 Userid     : "RPM Fusion free repository for EL (8) <rpmfusion-buildsys@lists.rpmfusion.org>"
 Fingerprint: 8379 35CD 19E1 23AA 7F8A 8E69 979F 0C69 158B 3811
 From       : /etc/pki/rpm-gpg/RPM-GPG-KEY-rpmfusion-free-el-8
Is this ok [y/N]: y
Key imported successfully
Running transaction check
Transaction check succeeded.
Running transaction test
Transaction test succeeded.
Running transaction
  Preparing        :                                                                                         1/1
  Installing       : libva-2.13.0-2.el8.x86_64                                                               1/29
  Installing       : ocl-icd-2.2.12-1.el8.x86_64                                                             2/29
```

Figure 6.14: *We confirm the use of the two* **GPG** *security keys using the highlighted lines*

The output from running this rpm package installation is shown in *Figure* 6.15:

```
root@ECMUKDEMO22:/usr/local/lib64/python3.6/site-packages
File  Edit  View  Search  Terminal  Help
  Installing       : rpmfusion-free-release-8-0.1.noarch                                     1/1
  Verifying        : rpmfusion-free-release-8-0.1.noarch                                     1/1
Installed products updated.

Installed:
  rpmfusion-free-release-8-0.1.noarch

Complete!
[root@ECMUKDEMO22 site-packages]# dnf install -y https://download1.rpmfusion.org/nonfree/el/rpmfusion-nonfree-release-8.noarch.rpm
Updating Subscription Management repositories.
RPM Fusion for EL 8 - Free - Updates                                              665 kB/s | 310 kB     00:00
rpmfusion-nonfree-release-8.noarch.rpm                                            124 kB/s |  11 kB     00:00
Dependencies resolved.
================================================================================================================
 Package                                 Architecture          Version               Repository            Size
================================================================================================================
Installing:
 rpmfusion-nonfree-release               noarch                8-0.1                 @commandline          11 k

Transaction Summary
================================================================================================================
Install  1 Package

Total size: 11 k
Installed size: 3.8 k
Downloading Packages:
Running transaction check
Transaction check succeeded.
Running transaction test
Transaction test succeeded.
Running transaction
  Preparing        :                                                                                        1/1
  Installing       : rpmfusion-nonfree-release-8-0.1.noarch                                                 1/1
  Verifying        : rpmfusion-nonfree-release-8-0.1.noarch                                                 1/1
Installed products updated.

Installed:
  rpmfusion-nonfree-release-8-0.1.noarch

Complete!
[root@ECMUKDEMO22 site-packages]#
```

Figure 6.15: *We update the subscription rpm package file, highlighted above*

Then we run the recommended `ffmpeg` and `ffmpeg-devel` package installations as shown in *Figure 6.16*:

```
yum install ffmpeg ffmpeg-devel
```

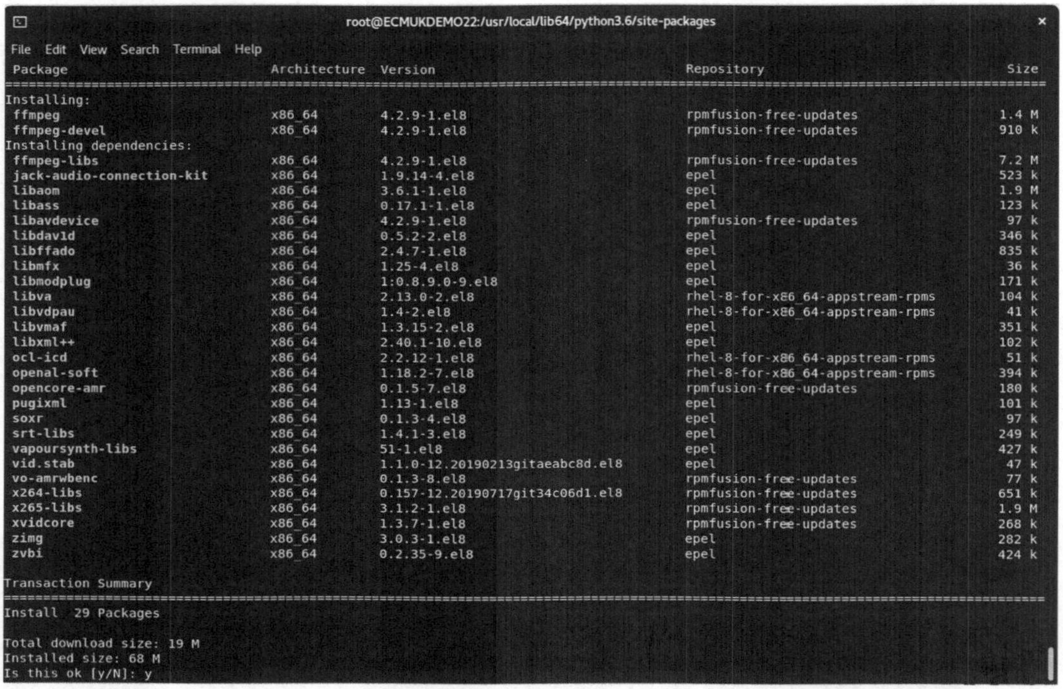

```
root@ECMUKDEMO22:/usr/local/lib64/python3.6/site-packages
File Edit View Search Terminal Help
 Package                        Architecture Version                              Repository                          Size
==========================================================================================================================
Installing:
 ffmpeg                         x86_64       4.2.9-1.el8                          rpmfusion-free-updates             1.4 M
 ffmpeg-devel                   x86_64       4.2.9-1.el8                          rpmfusion-free-updates             910 k
Installing dependencies:
 ffmpeg-libs                    x86_64       4.2.9-1.el8                          rpmfusion-free-updates             7.2 M
 jack-audio-connection-kit      x86_64       1.9.14-4.el8                         epel                               523 k
 libaom                         x86_64       3.6.1-1.el8                          epel                               1.9 M
 libass                         x86_64       0.17.1-1.el8                         epel                               123 k
 libavdevice                    x86_64       4.2.9-1.el8                          rpmfusion-free-updates              97 k
 libdav1d                       x86_64       0.5.2-2.el8                          epel                               346 k
 libffado                       x86_64       2.4.7-1.el8                          epel                               835 k
 libmfx                         x86_64       1.25-4.el8                           epel                                36 k
 libmodplug                     x86_64       1:0.8.9.0-9.el8                      epel                               171 k
 libva                          x86_64       2.13.0-2.el8                         rhel-8-for-x86_64-appstream-rpms   104 k
 libvdpau                       x86_64       1.4-2.el8                            rhel-8-for-x86_64-appstream-rpms    41 k
 libvmaf                        x86_64       1.3.15-2.el8                         epel                               351 k
 libxml++                       x86_64       2.40.1-10.el8                        epel                               102 k
 ocl-icd                        x86_64       2.2.12-1.el8                         rhel-8-for-x86_64-appstream-rpms    51 k
 openal-soft                    x86_64       1.18.2-7.el8                         rhel-8-for-x86_64-appstream-rpms   394 k
 opencore-amr                   x86_64       0.1.5-7.el8                          rpmfusion-free-updates             180 k
 pugixml                        x86_64       1.13-1.el8                           epel                               101 k
 soxr                           x86_64       0.1.3-4.el8                          epel                                97 k
 srt-libs                       x86_64       1.4.1-3.el8                          epel                               249 k
 vapoursynth-libs               x86_64       51-1.el8                             epel                               427 k
 vid.stab                       x86_64       1.1.0-12.20190213gitaeabc8d.el8      epel                                47 k
 vo-amrwbenc                    x86_64       0.1.3-8.el8                          rpmfusion-free-updates              77 k
 x264-libs                      x86_64       0.157-12.20190717git34c06d1.el8      rpmfusion-free-updates             651 k
 x265-libs                      x86_64       3.1.2-1.el8                          rpmfusion-free-updates             1.9 M
 xvidcore                       x86_64       1.3.7-1.el8                          rpmfusion-free-updates             268 k
 zimg                           x86_64       3.0.3-1.el8                          epel                               282 k
 zvbi                           x86_64       0.2.35-9.el8                         epel                               424 k

Transaction Summary
==========================================================================================================================
Install  29 Packages

Total download size: 19 M
Installed size: 68 M
Is this ok [y/N]: y
```

Figure 6.16: *We install 29 package libraries, using* `yum install ffmpeg ffmpeg-devel`

The installed **ffmpeg** packages we need are shown successfully installed as shown in *Figure 6.17*:

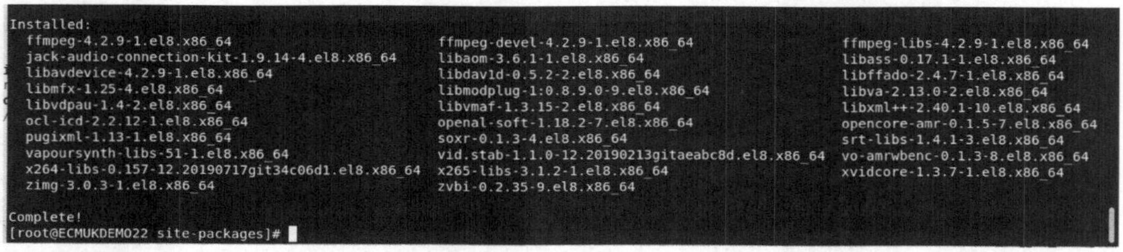

```
Installed:
  ffmpeg-4.2.9-1.el8.x86_64                                ffmpeg-devel-4.2.9-1.el8.x86_64                          ffmpeg-libs-4.2.9-1.el8.x86_64
  jack-audio-connection-kit-1.9.14-4.el8.x86_64            libaom-3.6.1-1.el8.x86_64                                libass-0.17.1-1.el8.x86_64
  libavdevice-4.2.9-1.el8.x86_64                           libdav1d-0.5.2-2.el8.x86_64                              libffado-2.4.7-1.el8.x86_64
  libmfx-1.25-4.el8.x86_64                                 libmodplug-1:0.8.9.0-9.el8.x86_64                        libva-2.13.0-2.el8.x86_64
  libvdpau-1.4-2.el8.x86_64                                libvmaf-1.3.15-2.el8.x86_64                              libxml++-2.40.1-10.el8.x86_64
  ocl-icd-2.2.12-1.el8.x86_64                              openal-soft-1.18.2-7.el8.x86_64                          opencore-amr-0.1.5-7.el8.x86_64
  pugixml-1.13-1.el8.x86_64                                soxr-0.1.3-4.el8.x86_64                                  srt-libs-1.4.1-3.el8.x86_64
  vapoursynth-libs-51-1.el8.x86_64                         vid.stab-1.1.0-12.20190213gitaeabc8d.el8.x86_64          vo-amrwbenc-0.1.3-8.el8.x86_64
  x264-libs-0.157-12.20190717git34c06d1.el8.x86_64         x265-libs-3.1.2-1.el8.x86_64                             xvidcore-1.3.7-1.el8.x86_64
  zimg-3.0.3-1.el8.x86_64                                  zvbi-0.2.35-9.el8.x86_64

Complete!
[root@ECMUKDEMO22 site-packages]#
```

Figure 6.17: *The installed **ffmpeg** packages we need are shown successfully installed*

This now installs ok and so we retry the command as shown in *Figure* 6.18:

```
spleeter separate -p spleeter:2stems -o output audio_example.mp3
```

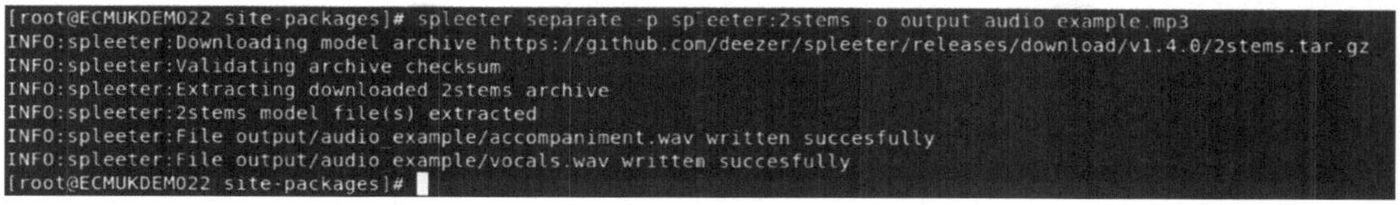

Figure 6.18: *`spleeter separate -p spleeter:2stems -o output audio_example.mp3` command*

Which now runs without any errors, as demonstrated in *Figure* 6.18.

Notice that this program uses a training model, which it downloads, as indicated by **ChatGPT**.

So, finally, we have achieved a working result, but we had to put a great deal of additional effort into achieving this result and we don't need a **Java** program to do it.

The two split files are output as `accompaniment.wav` and `vocals.wav` and listening to the original `audio_example.mp3` file and the split files that are output, it can be heard as an amazing split of the original sound, (the .wav files played are listed in *Figure* 6.19).

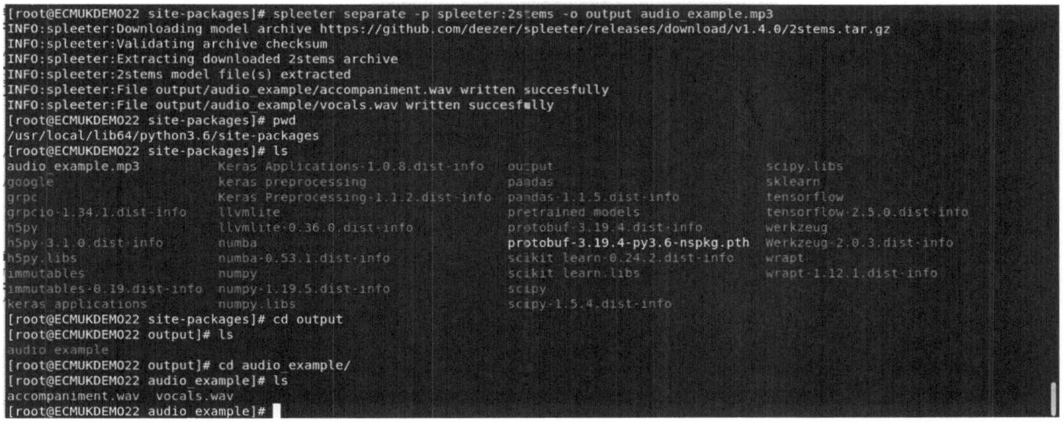

Figure 6.19: *The two split files are output as `accompaniment.wav` and `vocals.wav`.*

However, we do want to validate the **Java** program we asked **ChatGPT** to supply, so we create a new class, `SpleeterCaller` under the `com.asb` **Java** package, using the **Eclipse IDE** as shown in *Figure 6.20*:

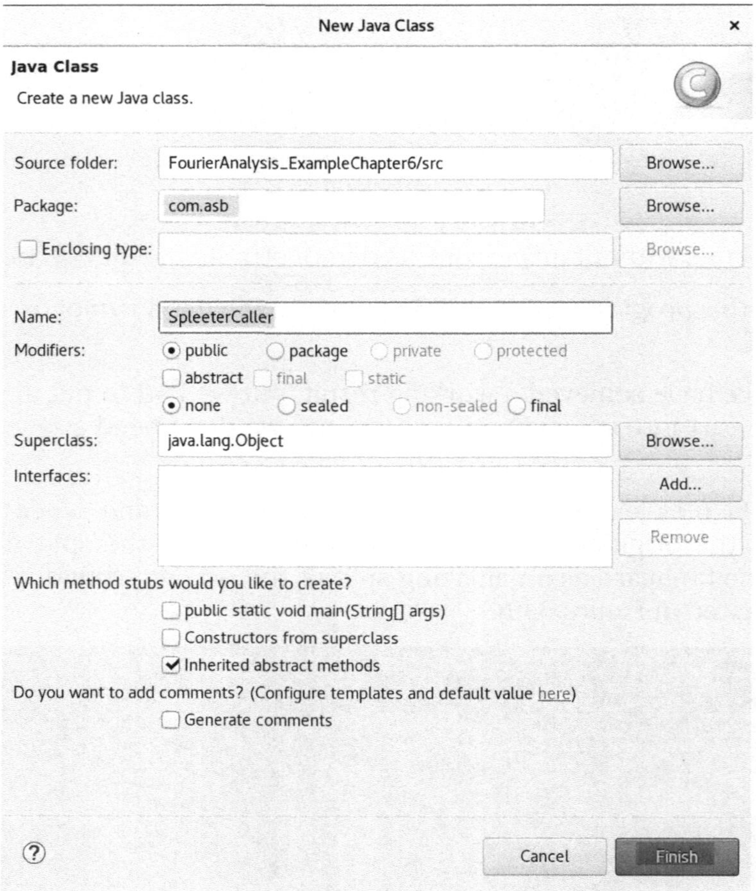

Figure 6.20: *The SpleeterCaller Java class is created under the com.asb package*

First, as advised, we created the `spleeter_separate.py` python script file as shown in *Figure 6.21*:

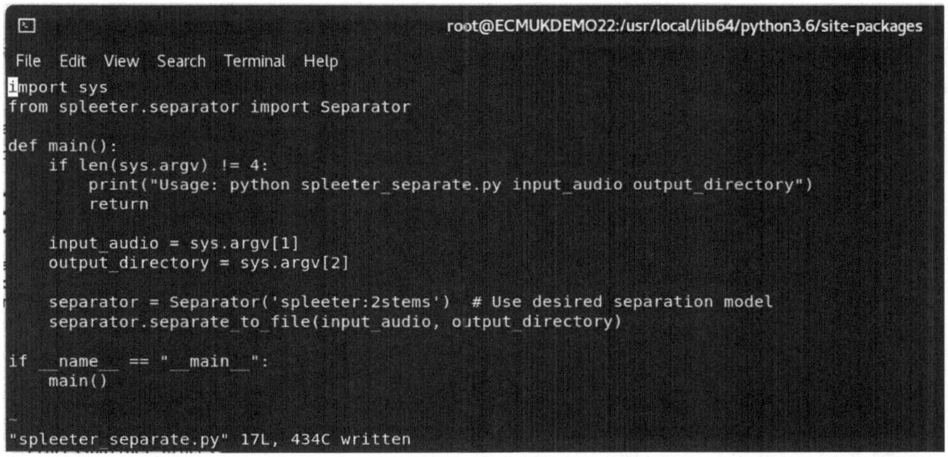

Figure 6.21: *The* `spleeter_separate.py` *python script file*

After pasting the suggested code from **ChatGPT** we save the class file, **`SpleeterCaller.java`**, and run the application main Java class as shown in *Figure 6.22*:

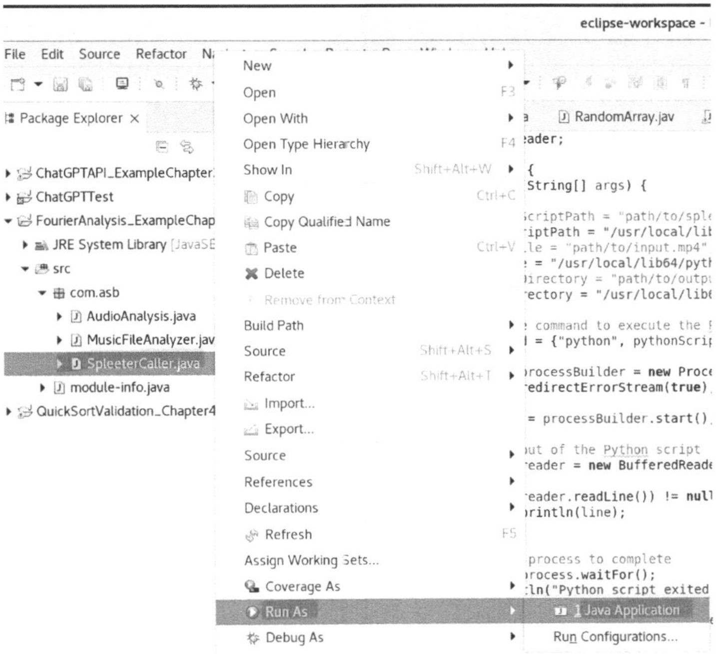

Figure 6.22: *The SpleeterCaller.java. the main Java class application is run*

At first, we get an error relating to the python which we try to fix by upgrading to the latest python version 3.9 using the `yum install python39` command, as shown in *Figure 6.23*:

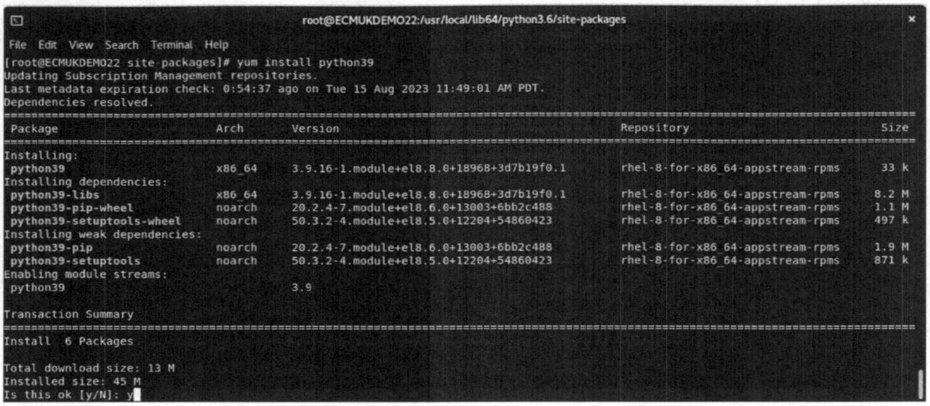

***Figure 6.23**: We try upgrading to the latest Python version 3.9 using `yum install python39` com*

We finally discovered that there were a number of issues with the code given by **ChatGPT**. The most important issue was that **ChatGPT** gave the command line code defined as a **Java String** array, which does not work (at least with the **ProcessBuilder** class used to launch the **spleeter** program **python** script). The second issue was the call to the **python** script, which we realise was not necessary at all, as the **spleeter** call could be made on the command line itself.

So, we updated the code and our first attempt ran as expected below, as shown in *Figure 6.24*:

***Figure 6.24**: The first successful run of the spleeter program from a **Java** code program*

The files are split as expected, however, in a strange directory path with a space as shown in *Figure* 6.25.

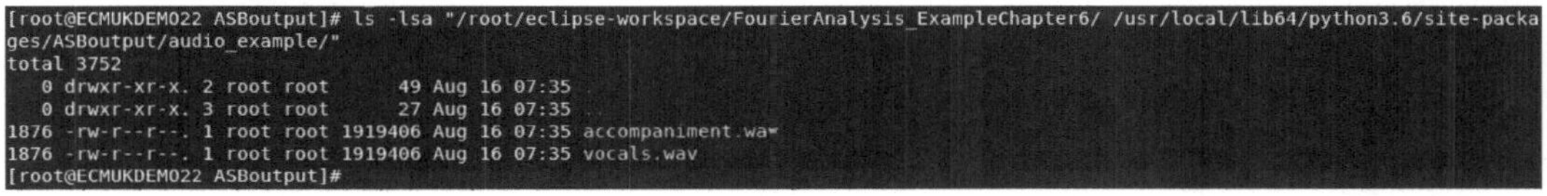

Figure 6.25: *The two wav output files are created but in an unexpected sub-folder path*

The code was updated as highlighted in *Figure* 6.26 and the program re-run:

Figure 6.26: *The program was rerun and now creates the split files in the expected path*

The files output can now be seen in the expected path, as shown in *Figure* 6.27:

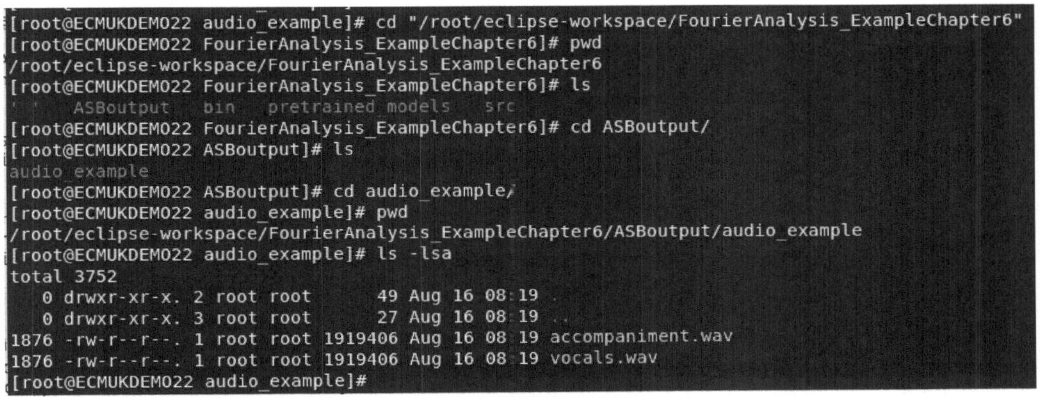

Figure 6.27: *The output files now appear as expected in the expected path*

The final working code we updated is now shown in *Figure 6.26*, which is listed as follows:

```
package com.asb;
import java.io.BufferedReader;
import java.io.IOException;
import java.io.InputStreamReader;
import java.util.ArrayList;   // ASB added for the correct call for the
Java ProcessBuilder
import java.util.List;        // ASB added for the correct call for the
Java ProcessBuilder
public class SpleeterCaller {
    public static void main(String[] args) {
        try {
            //String pythonScriptPath = "path/to/spleeter_separate.py";
// Replace with actual path
           String pythonScriptPath = "/usr/local/lib64/python3.6/site-
packages/spleeter_separate.py"; //ASB Our Path to the python script
            //String inputFile = "path/to/input.mp4"; // Replace with
actual input file path
            String inputFile = "/usr/local/lib64/python3.6/site-
packages/audio_example.mp3";           // ASB Our input file path
            //String outputDirectory = "path/to/output/"; // Replace
with desired output directory
            String outputDirectory = "ASBoutput";             // ASB our
output directory


            // Construct the command to execute the Python script
            /* ASB Software Development Limited - This section of Java
                   code, suggested by ChatGPT is incorrect
             * The String[] array is not acceptable to ProcessBuilder,
                   it requires an ArrayList
             */
            //String[] command = {"python", pythonScriptPath, inputFile,
                   outputDirectory};
            //
            //ASB We don't need the python script file suggested by
             ChatGPT, we can call spleeter directly using the command
            // spleeter separate -p spleeter:2stems -o output audio_
```

```
example.mp3

            List<String> command = new ArrayList<String>();  // ASB we
             actually need a List interface, rather than a String array
            command.add ("/usr/local/bin/spleeter");         // ASB
                   command name
            command.add ("separate");                        // ASB
                   arguments are added as separate list items
            command.add ("-p");
            command.add("spleeter:2stems");
            command.add ("-o" + outputDirectory);
            command.add (inputFile);

           ProcessBuilder processBuilder = new ProcessBuilder(command);
            processBuilder.redirectErrorStream(true);
            Process process = processBuilder.start();

            // Read the output of the Python script
            BufferedReader reader = new BufferedReader(new
                         InputStreamReader(process.getInputStream()));
            String line;
            while ((line = reader.readLine()) != null) {
                System.out.println(line);
            }

            // Wait for the process to complete
            int exitCode = process.waitFor();
            System.out.println("Python script exited with code: " +
                                          exitCode);

        } catch (IOException | InterruptedException e) {
            e.printStackTrace();
        }
    }
}
```

Just one more validation is required following the successful split of the downloaded **audio_example.mp3** supplied by **Spleeter**. We just need to be certain that the split output sound files, **vocals.wav** and **accompaniment.wav** are really processed 'live' and not just copied from a library. So, we downloaded a short mobile phone ringtone **mp3** file for the football song "**Three Lions** on the **Shirt**", using the link page:

https://www.mobiles24.co/downloads/s/641522-3-three_lions_footballs_coming_home and the download link on the web page **https://www.mobiles24.co/downloads/d/fEZsUECJgJ**

(Topical at the moment as "**The Lionesses**" have reached the World Cup Final!).

The changes were made as follows to the Java code, as shown in **Figure 6.28:**

The code line was updated as follows:

```
//String inputFile = "/usr/local/lib64/python3.6/site-packages/audio_
example.mp3";            // ASB Our input file path
```

To

```
String inputFile = "/usr/local/lib64/python3.6/site-packages/Three_
Lions_Footballs_Coming_Home-641522.mp3"; // ASB Our input file path
```

mk

```
package com.asb;
import java.io.BufferedReader;
import java.io.IOException;
import java.io.InputStreamReader;
import java.util.ArrayList;   // ASB added for the correct call for the Java ProcessBuilder
import java.util.List;        // ASB added for the correct call for the Java ProcessBuilder
public class SpleeterCaller {
    public static void main(String[] args) {
        try {
            //String pythonScriptPath = "path/to/spleeter_separate.py"; // Replace with actual path
            String pythonScriptPath = "/usr/local/lib64/python3.6/site-packages/spleeter_separate.py"; //ASB Our Path to the python script
            //String inputFile = "path/to/input.mp4"; // Replace with actual input file path
            //String inputFile = "/usr/local/lib64/python3.6/site-packages/audio_example.mp3";          // ASB Our input file path
            String inputFile = "/usr/local/lib64/python3.6/site-packages/Three_Lions_Footballs_Coming_Home-641522.mp3";          // ASB Our
```

Figure 6.28: *The code is updated for the inputFile to "The Three Lions on the Shirt" MP3 file*

The files were output as expected, as illustrated in *Figure* 6.29:

```
<terminated> SpleeterCaller [Java Application] /root/eclipse/eclipse/plugins/org.eclipse.justj.openjdk.hotspot.jre.full.linux.x86_64_17.0.7.v20230425-1502/jre/bin/java
INFO:spleeter:File ASBoutput/Three_Lions_Footballs_Coming_Home-641522/vocals.wav written succesfully
INFO:spleeter:File ASBoutput/Three_Lions_Footballs_Coming_Home-641522/accompaniment.wav written succesfully
Python script exited with code: 0
```

Figure 6.29: *The successfully split "The Three Lions on the Shirt" MP3 file output files*

So, in summary, **ChatGPT** did provide the concept of using **Spleeter**, which is a Python-based program that can be run as a standalone program on **RHEL Linux 8.8**. The **Spleeter** Java launch program requires quite a few additional supporting libraries and the actual **Java** code suggested by **ChatGPT** is incorrect as commented on in the list we created above.

ChatGPT generated Java code for Fourier Analysis of a Sine wave

So, we asked a question we hoped would be much easier for **ChatGPT** to get right:

Is *there* java code for the Fourier analysis of a sine wave?

Yes, you can perform Fourier analysis cf a sine wave using Java code. Here's an example implementation:

````
```java
import java.util.Arrays;

public class FourierAnalysis {

    public static void main(String[] args) {

        // Define the sine wave
        double[] signal = new double[1024];
        for (int i = 0; i < signal.length; i++) {
            signal[i] = Math.sin(2 * Math.PI * i / 32);
        }

        // Compute the Fourier transform
        double[] spectrum = computeSpectrum(signal);

        // Print the spectrum
        for (int i = 0; i < spectrum.length; i++) {
            System.out.println(i + "\t" + spectrum[i]);
        }
    }

    public static double[] computeSpectrum(double[] signal) {
        int n = signal.length;
        double[] spectrum = new double[n];
        for (int i = 0; i < n; i++) {
````
````

````
            double re = 0;
            double im = 0;
            for (int j = 0; j < n; j++) {
                double angle = 2 * Math.PI * i * j / n;
                re += signal[j] * Math.cos(angle);
                im -= signal[j] * Math.sin(angle);
            }
            spectrum[i] = Math.sqrt(re * re + im * im) / n;
        }
        return spectrum;
    }
}
```
````

In this code, we first define a sine wave with a frequency of 1/32 Hz and length of 1024 samples. Then, we compute the Fourier transform of the signal using the `computeSpectrum` method. The method implements the Discrete Fourier Transform (DFT) algorithm, which computes the complex Fourier coefficients and then takes the magnitude to obtain the spectrum. Finally, we print out the spectrum values for each frequency bin.

Note that this is a basic example and there are more efficient algorithms for computing the Fourier transform, such as the Fast Fourier Transform (FFT). However, the DFT algorithm is simpler to understand and can be used for educational purposes.

Sine wave Fourier Analysis java code validation using an Eclipse Java

In this section, we try again to validate the code suggested by **ChatGPT** for the **Fourier Analysis** of a **Sine** wave, and created an **Eclipse IDE** Java project as follows in *Figure* 6.30.

This project was also used for the **SpleeterCaller** class which we have already covered in the previous section, "**Fourier Analysis for MP4 java code validation using an Eclipse Java Program Project**" and the other suggested **Java** code for **MusicFileAnalyzer** and **AudioAnalysis**.
````

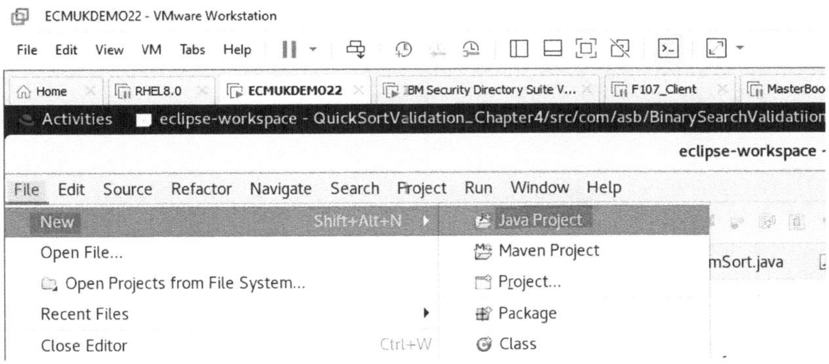

Figure 6.30: *The File-> New -> Java Project menu option is selected in the Eclipse IDE*

The project name is set to **FourierAnalysis_ExampleChapter6** as shown in *Figure 6.31*:

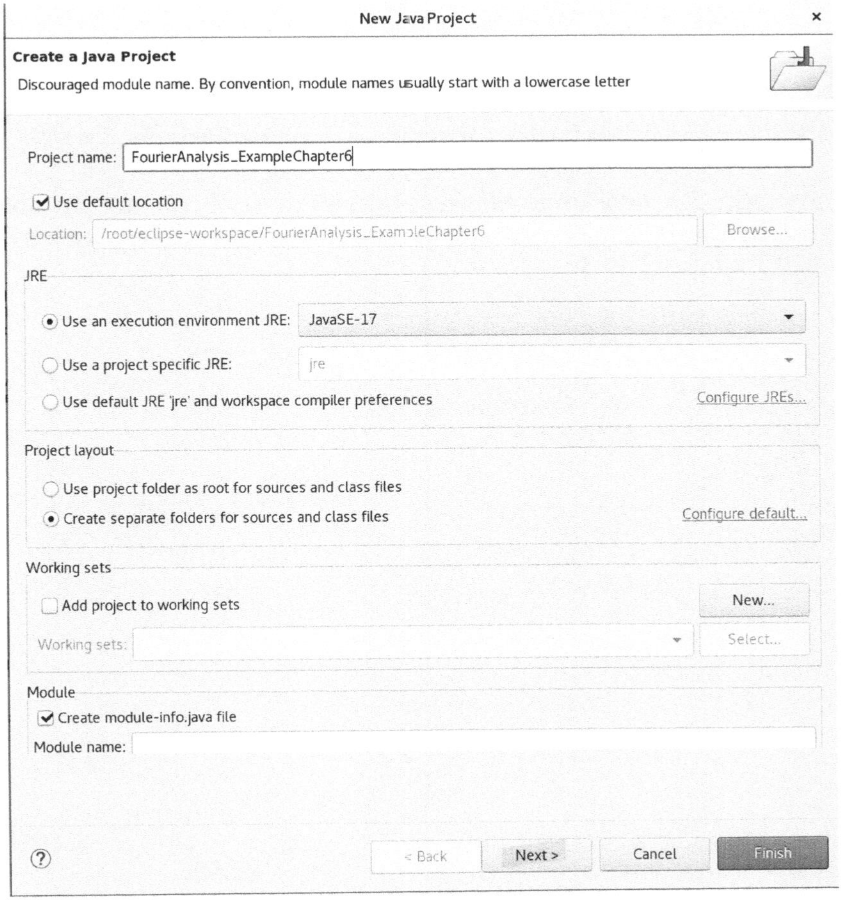

Figure 6.31: *The project name is set to* **FourierAnalysis_ExampleChapter6**

The **Next>** button is selected as highlighted in *Figure* 6.31, to display the screen in *Figure* 6.32:

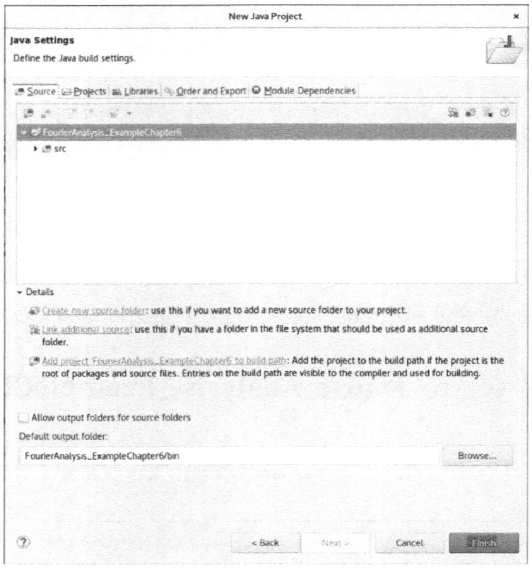

Figure 6.32: *The Finish button is clicked for the project,* ***FourierAnalysis_ExampleChapter6***

We can now add the **Java** code classes, **MusicFileAnalyzer** and **AudioAnalysis** as suggested by **ChatGPT**. The creation of the **MusicFileAnalyzer** class is shown in *Figure* 6.33.

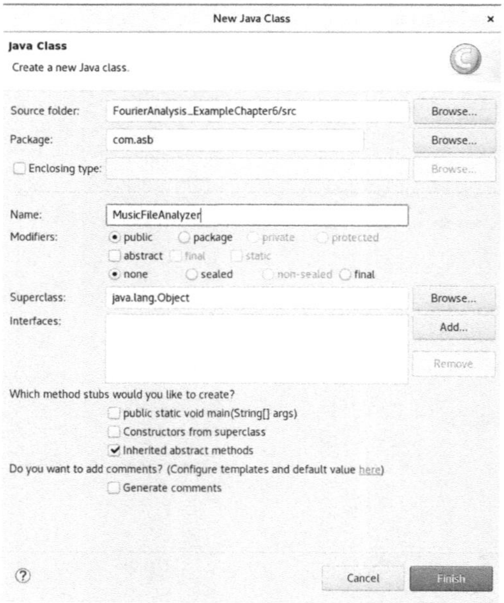

Figure 6.33: *The creation of the* **MusicFileAnalyzer** *class*

On pasting the Java code, we had to make a number of changes to allow the code to be built.

To satisfy the missing package import requirements for the software we found the Maven website as follows:

https://www.dcm4che.org/maven2/xuggle/xuggle-xuggler/5.4/

We then used the link as follows, to download the jar file we need.

https://www.dcm4che.org/maven2/xuggle/xuggle-xuggler/5.4/xuggle-xuggler-5.4.jar

The **`xuggle-xuggler-5.4.jar`** file was then copied to our **VMWare Linux** server's **Eclipse IDE** external library area, **AILibs** which we created earlier:

```
[root@ECMUKDEMO22 AILibs]# pwd
/root/eclipse/eclipse/AILibs
[root@ECMUKDEMO22 AILibs]# cp /mnt/hgfs/Installs/xuggle-xuggler-5.4.jar
.
[root@ECMUKDEMO22 AILibs]#
```

The final project library Class Path list and the Class Path updates are shown in *Figure* 6.50 through to *Figure* 6.52 at the end of this Chapter.

The updated code (still only a skeleton concept) can now be built in Eclipse:

```
package com.asb;

import com.xuggle.mediatool.IMediaListener;           //ASB This import
was required to be added
import com.xuggle.mediatool.IMediaReader;
import com.xuggle.mediatool.IMediaWriter;
import com.xuggle.mediatool.MediaListenerAdapter; //ASB This import was
required to be added
import com.xuggle.mediatool.ToolFactory;
import com.xuggle.mediatool.event.IAudioSamplesEvent;
import com.xuggle.mediatool.event.IVideoPictureEvent;
import com.xuggle.xuggler.IContainer;

// ... other imports ...

public class MusicFileAnalyzer {
```

```
    public static void main(String[] args) {
h
        // Step 1: Decode MP4 file
        IMediaReader mediaReader = ToolFactory.makeReader("input.mp4");
        mediaReader.addListener(new AudioSampleListener());
        while (mediaReader.readPacket() == null) {
            // continue reading the file
        }

        // Step 2: Perform Fourier analysis using JTransforms

        // Step 3: Separate instruments and vocals using source
separation techniques

    }
}

class AudioSampleListener extends MediaListenerAdapter implements
IMediaListener { //ASB We had to add the implements IMediaListener
interface
       //@Override //ASB We had to comment out the Override directive
    public void onAudioSamples(IAudioSamplesEvent event) {
        // Process audio samples here
    }
}
```

The creation of the **AudioAnalysis** class is shown in *Figure 6.34*.

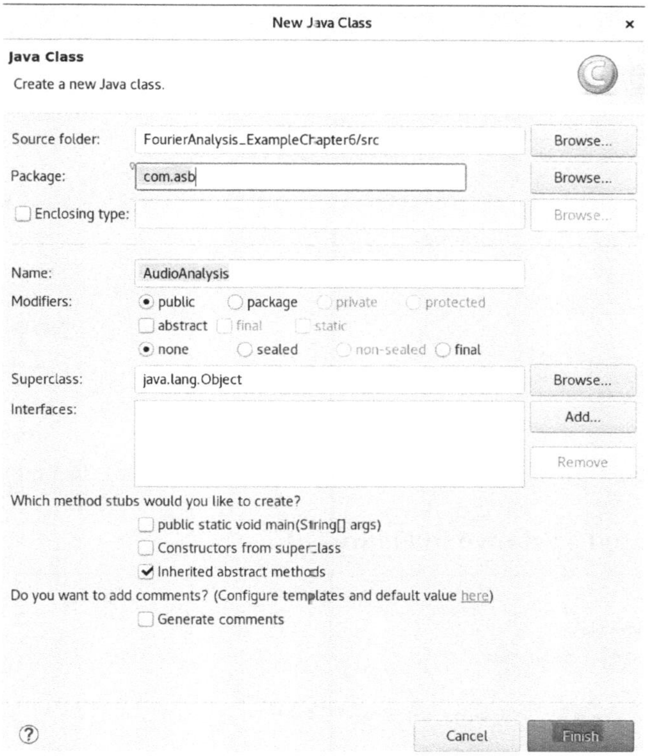

***Figure 6.34**: The creation of the **AudioAnalysis** class*

Next, we pasted the **AudioAnalysis** code into the skeleton class structure as illustrated in *Figure 6.35*:

***Figure 6.35**: The **AudioAnalysis** code pasted from the **ChatGPT** response*

Lastly as covered in the start of this section, we create the **`FourierAnalysis`** class

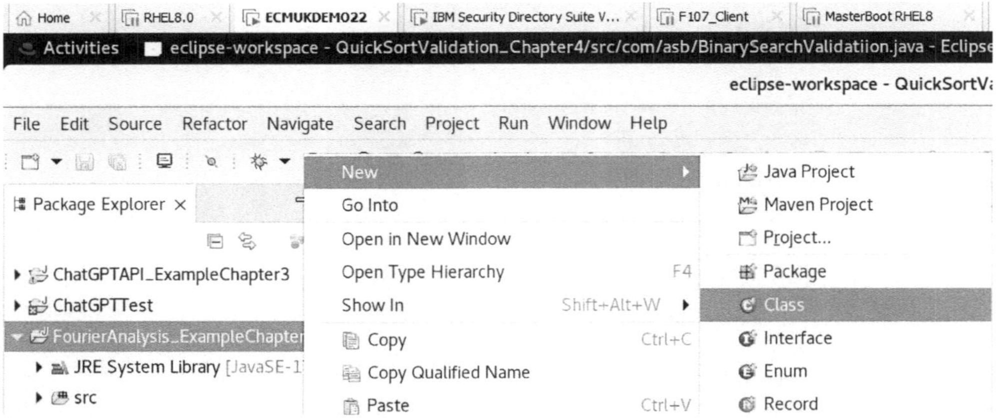

***Figure 6.36**: The New Class for **FourierAnalysis** is created using the menu shown above*

The class is created as shown in *Figure 6.37*:

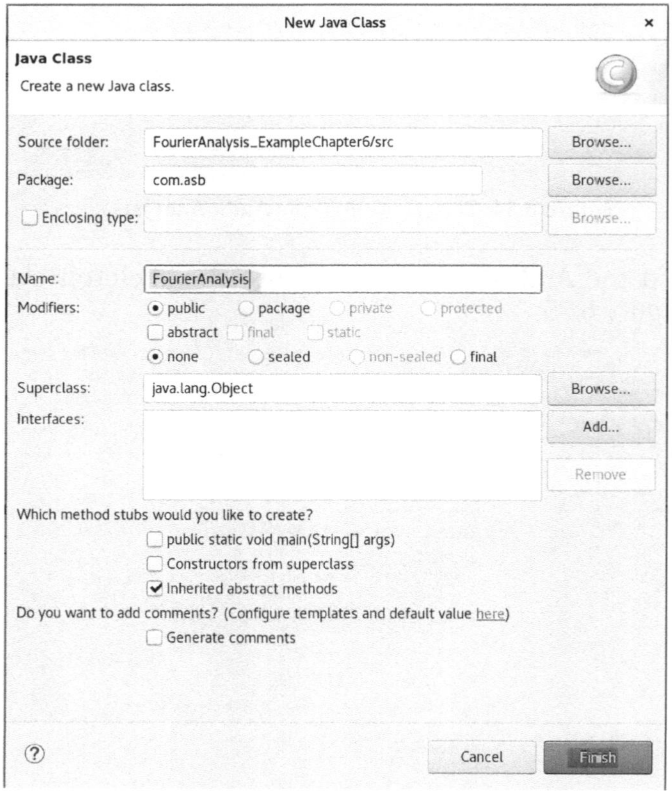

***Figure 6.37**: The **FourierAnalysis** Java class is created*

The **FourierAnalysis** code is copied from **ChatGPT**, as shown in *Figure 6.38*:

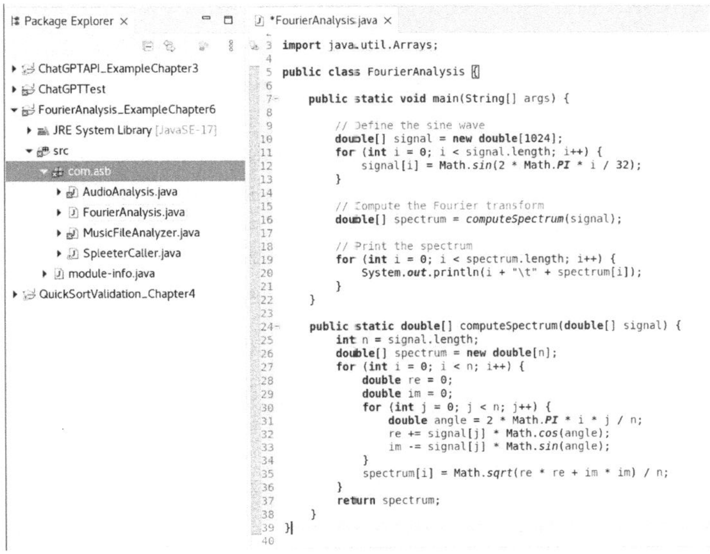

***Figure 6.38**: The **ChatGPT** `FourierAnalysis` code is pasted into the skeleton class*

The code runs unchanged and prints the 1024 elements of the **spectrum[i] double** array as shown in *Figure 6.39*:

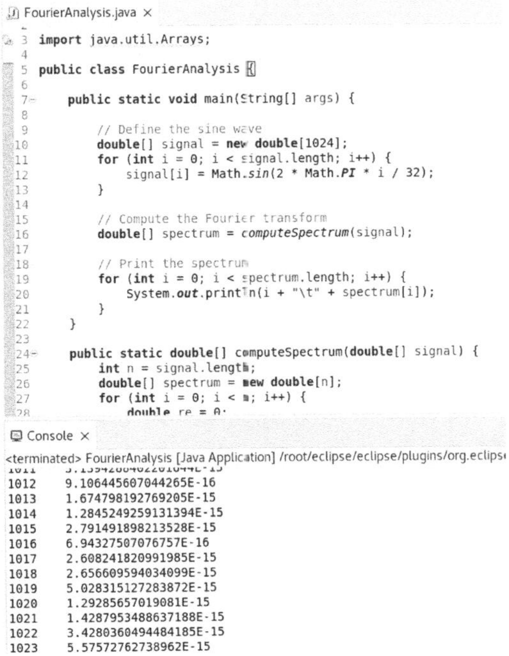

***Figure 6.39**: The **FourierAnalysis** output after running the main program*

This is great, but we would really like a more visual presentation, so we asked **Microsoft Bing Chat** (as we have discovered earlier, it's based on **ChatGPT 4.5**) the following question:

is there Java code for graphing an array of double values

https://www.bing.com/search?q=is+there+Java+code+for+graphing+an+array+of+double+values&showconv=1&sendquery=1&form=WSBQFC&qs=SW&cvid=be43c823e497494f8740fbb867baab06&pq=is+there+Java+code+for+graphing+an+array+of+double+values&cc=GB&setlang=en-US&nclid=50C9E684A994E0B58A7FD8ECD2BB1F26&ts=1692278570522&wsso=Moderate

This responded as shown in **Figure 6.40:**

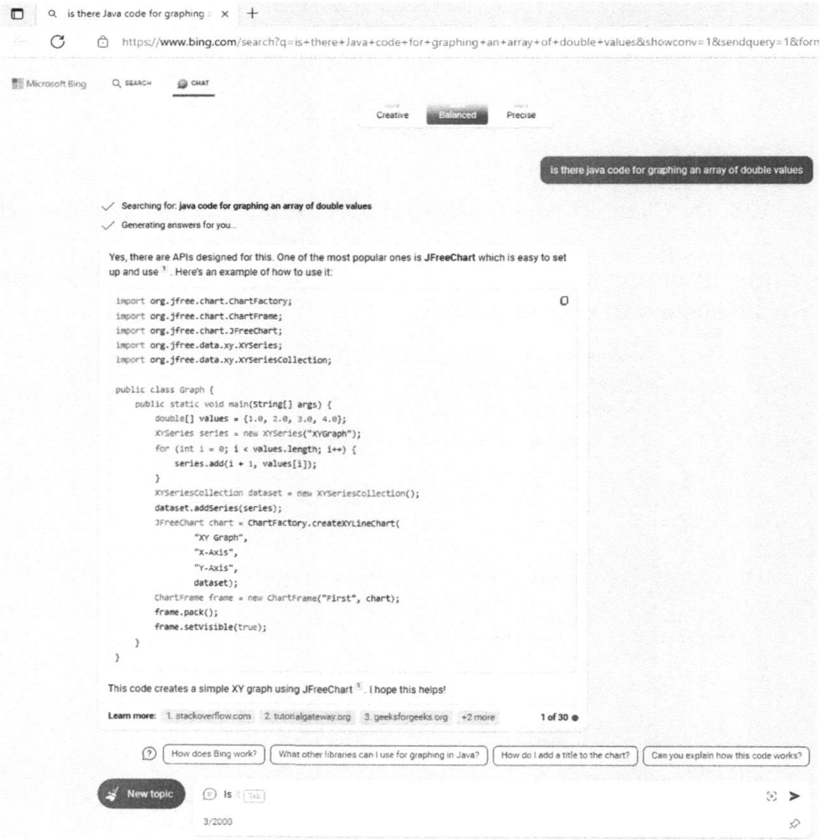

Figure 6.40**: The complete Java graph display example displayed using **Microsoft Bing Chat

We need to down load the **Jfreechart** version 1.5.3 jar file from the **maven** site to satisfy the dependencies and add the jar to the Project Classpath:

https://repo1.maven.org/maven2/org/jfree/jfreechart/1.5.3/

Then we copy the library jar file to our **AILibs** directory on the Linux server:

```
[root@ECMUKDEMO22 eclipse]# cd /root/eclipse/eclipse/AILibs/

[root@ECMUKDEMO22 AILibs]# cp /mnt/hgfs/Installs/jfreechart-1.5.3.jar .
```

Then we add the library, **`jfreechart-1.5.3.jar`,** to the **ModulePath** as shown in *Figure 6.41:*

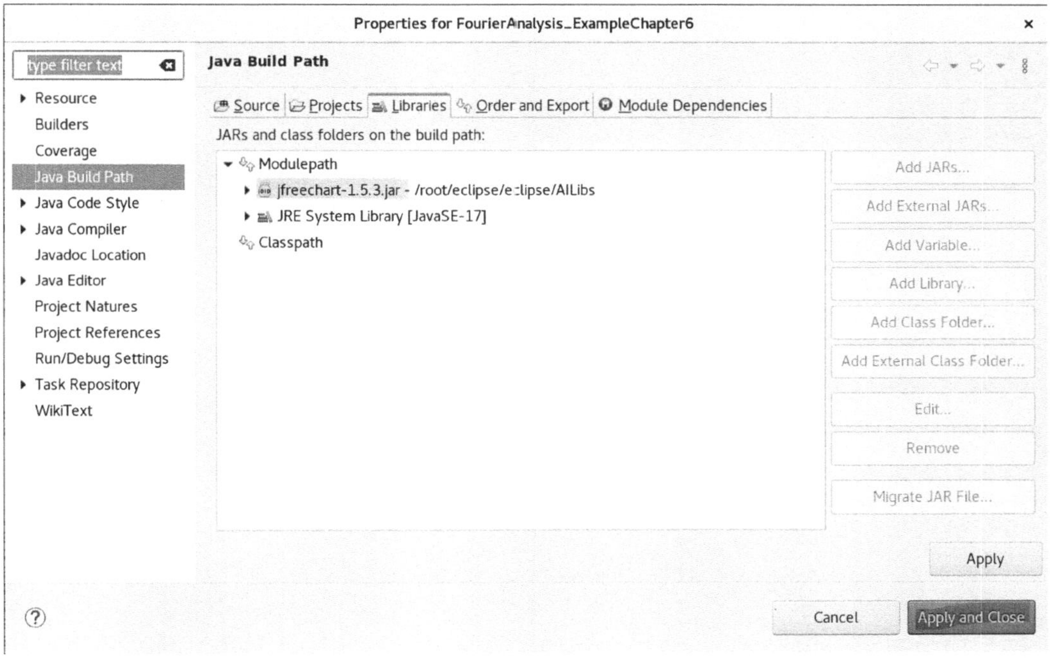

Figure 6.41: *Add the library, **`jfreechart-1.5.3.jar`,** to the **ModulePath***

After this we need to update the Java module for the project in the following code:

```
module FourierAnalysis_ExampleChapter6 {

       requires org.jfree.jfreechart;

}
```

The program then runs unchanged, with its Test Data (`double[] values = {1.0, 2.0, 3.0, 4.0};)` showing the pop-up window graph as follows, in *Figure 6.42*

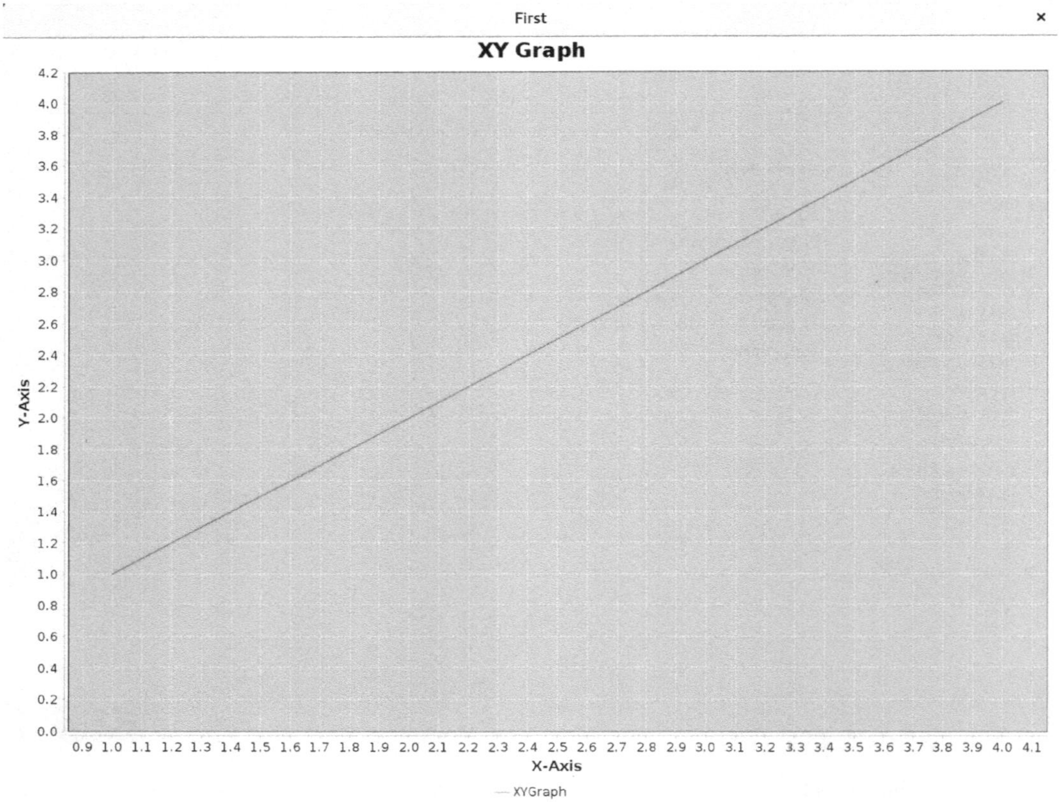

Figure 6.42: *The example graph is displayed using the code recommended by Bing*

We can now take the code example and apply it to our **Sine Curve Fourier Transform**, the signal code was added first and tested to give the output shown in *Figure* 6.43:

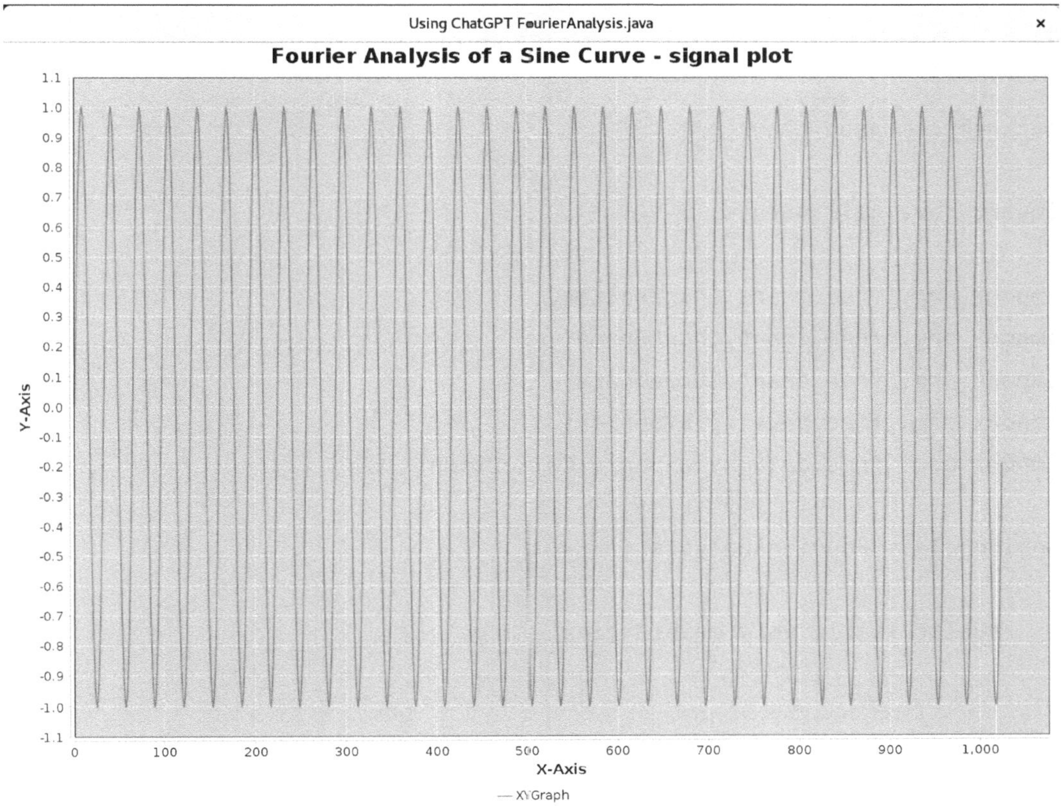

Figure 6.43: *Signal plot for the* **ChatGPT Fourier Analysis** *of a* **Sine Curve**

The Fourier transform signal output was then added to a second Chart, shown in *Figure* 6.44:

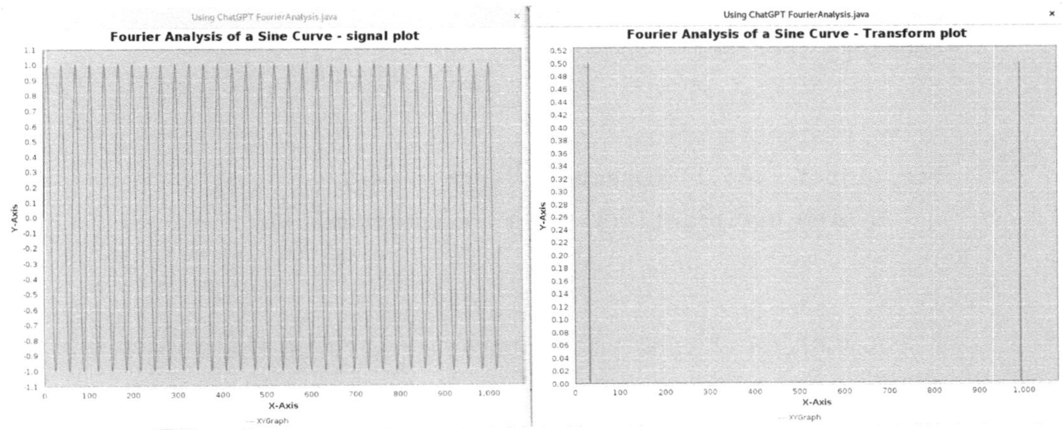

Figure 6.44: *Signal and Transform plots for the* **ChatGPT Fourier Analysis** *of a* **Sine Curve**

The final code which created the results shown in the Graphs in *Figure* 6.44 is as follows:

```
package com.asb;


import java.util.Arrays;


import org.jfree.chart.ChartFactory;
import org.jfree.chart.ChartFrame;
import org.jfree.chart.JFreeChart;
import org.jfree.data.xy.XYSeries;
import org.jfree.data.xy.XYSeriesCollection;


public class FourierAnalysis {


    public static void main(String[] args) {


        // Define the sine wave
        double[] signal = new double[1024];
        for (int i = 0; i < signal.length; i++) {
            signal[i] = Math.sin(2 * Math.PI * i / 32);
        }


        // Compute the Fourier transform
        double[] spectrum = computeSpectrum(signal);


        // Print the spectrum
        for (int i = 0; i < spectrum.length; i++) {
            System.out.println(i + "\t" + spectrum[i]);
        }
        //
        //ASB Additional code to Graph the results of the Sine Curve
Fourier Analysis
        //
```

```
        XYSeries series = new XYSeries("XYGraph");
        for (int i = 0; i < signal.length; i++) {
            series.add(i + 1, signal[i]); //
        }
        XYSeriesCollection dataset = new XYSeriesCollection();
        dataset.addSeries(series);
        JFreeChart chart = ChartFactory.createXYLineChart(
                "Fourier Analysis of a Sine Curve - signal plot",
                "X-Axis",
                "Y-Axis",
                dataset);
        ChartFrame frame = new ChartFrame("Using ChatGPT
FourierAnalysis.java", chart);
        frame.pack();
        frame.setVisible(true);
        //
        //ASB Now display the Fourier Transform array
        //
        XYSeries series2 = new XYSeries("XYGraph");
        for (int i = 0; i < spectrum.length; i++) {
            series2.add(i + 1, spectrum[i]); // The Fourier Transform
data set is added for the Graph
        }
        XYSeriesCollection dataset2 = new XYSeriesCollection();
        dataset2.addSeries(series2);
        JFreeChart chart2 = ChartFactory.createXYLineChart(
                "Fourier Analysis of a Sine Curve - Transform plot",
                "X-Axis",
                "Y-Axis",
                dataset2);
        ChartFrame frame2 = new ChartFrame("Using ChatGPT
FourierAnalysis.java", chart2);
        frame2.pack();
        frame2.setVisible(true);
```

```
    }

    public static double[] computeSpectrum(double[] signal) {
        int n = signal.length;
        double[] spectrum = new double[n];
        for (int i = 0; i < n; i++) {
            double re = 0;
            double im = 0;
            for (int j = 0; j < n; j++) {
                double angle = 2 * Math.PI * i * j / n;
                re += signal[j] * Math.cos(angle);
                im -= signal[j] * Math.sin(angle);
            }
            spectrum[i] = Math.sqrt(re * re + im * im) / n;
        }
        return spectrum;
    }
}
```

Next, although we only had an outline for some of the sections, we add the required library jar files for the ChatGPT **AudioAnalysis.java** example:

https://mvnrepository.com/artifact/clojure-interop/javax.sound/1.0.5

This has the link for the required jar:

https://clojars.org/repo/clojure-interop/javax.sound/1.0.5/javax.sound-1.0.5.jar

We downloaded using the link above and copied the jar file as follows:

```
[root@ECMUKDEMO22 AILibs]# pwd
/root/eclipse/eclipse/AILibs
[root@ECMUKDEMO22 AILibs]# cp /mnt/hgfs/Installs/javax.sound-1.0.5.jar .
```

```
[root@ECMUKDEMO22 AILibs]#
```

This is library Jar file was then added to the project as shown in *Figure 6.45*:

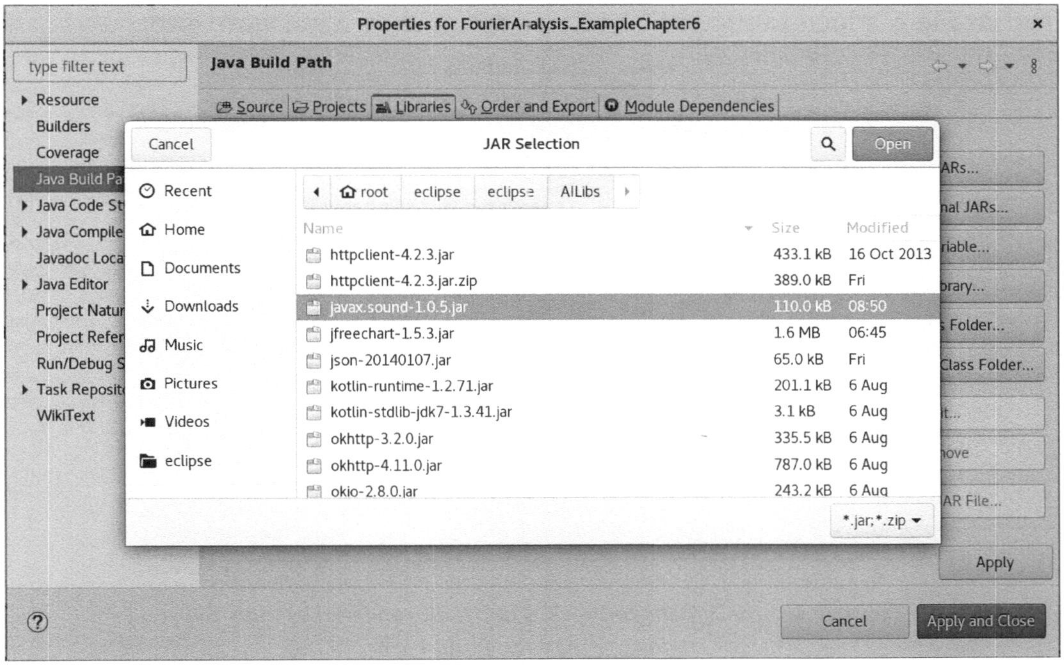

Figure 6.45: *The* ***`javax.sound-1.0.5.jar`*** *file is added to the* ***Java Build Path***

We also require the Java .jar for the **`import org.jtransforms.fft.FloatFFT_2D;`** package library

http://search.maven.org/remotecontent?filepath=com/github/wendykierp/JTransforms/3.1/JTransforms-3.1-with-dependencies.jar

The downloaded **`JTransforms-3.1-with-dependencies.jar`** jar file library is copied:

```
[root@ECMUKDEMO22 AILibs]# pwd
/root/eclipse/eclipse/AILibs
[root@ECMUKDEMO22 AILibs]# cp /mnt/hgfs/Installs/JTransforms-3.1-with-
```

```
dependencies.jar .
[root@ECMUKDEMO22 AILibs]#
```

The jar file is added to the project Class Path as shown in *Figure 6.46*:

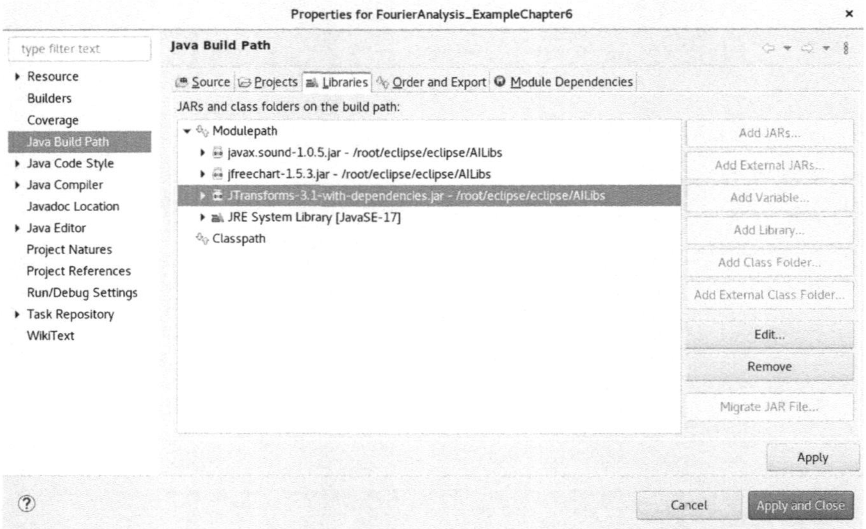

Figure 6.46**: The `JTransforms-3.1-with-dependencies.jar` file is added to the **Java Build Path

The **`module-info.java`** code for the project was updated to allow the library packages to be referenced as follows:

```
/**
 *
 */
/**
 *
 */
module FourierAnalysis_ExampleChapter6 {
       requires org.jfree.jfreechart;
       requires javax.sound;
       requires JTransforms;
       requires java.desktop;
}
```

This gives the completed **AudioAnalysis** code example as follows:

```
package com.asb;

import javax.sound.sampled.*;
import org.jtransforms.fft.FloatFFT_2D;
import java.io.*;                        // ASB This import was missing
and is required for the File("input.mp4") code line

public class AudioAnalysis {
    public static void main(String[] args) {
        try {
            AudioInputStream audioInputStream = AudioSystem.
                  getAudioInputStream(new File("input.mp4"));
            AudioFormat format = audioInputStream.getFormat();

            // Read and process audio data in chunks
            int chunkSize = 2048; // Adjust as needed
            byte[] audioData = new byte[chunkSize];

            FloatFFT_2D fft = new FloatFFT_2D(chunkSize, 1);

            // Process each chunk of audio data
            while (audioInputStream.read(audioData) != -1) {
                float[] audioSamples = convertBytesToFloats(audioData);

                // Apply FFT
                float[] spectrum = new float[2 * chunkSize];
              System.arraycopy(audioSamples, 0, spectrum, 0, chunkSize);
                fft.realForwardFull(spectrum);

                // Process the spectrum data (e.g., separate sources)

                // Inverse FFT to reconstruct audio
                fft.realInverseFull(spectrum, true);

              // Process the reconstructed audio (e.g., post-processing)
```

```
            }

            audioInputStream.close();
        } catch (Exception e) {
            e.printStackTrace();
        }
    }

    private static float[] convertBytesToFloats(byte[] bytes) {
        float[] floats = new float[bytes.length / 2];
        for (int i = 0; i < floats.length; i++) {
            floats[i] = (float) ((bytes[2 * i] & 0xFF) | (bytes[2 * i + 1]
<< 8));
        }
        return floats;
    }
}
```

We downloaded a small mp4 file to test with:

https://file-examples.com/index.php/sample-video-files/sample-mp4-files/ and used the 1.5 Mbyte example file:

https://file-examples.com/wp-content/storage/2017/04/file_example_MP4_480_1_5MG.mp4

This downloaded file was then copied for testing as follows:

```
[root@ECMUKDEMO22 site-packages]# pwd

/usr/local/lib64/python3.6/site-packages

[root@ECMUKDEMO22 site-packages]# cp /mnt/hgfs/Installs/file_example_
MP4_480_1_5MG.mp4 .

[root@ECMUKDEMO22 site-packages]#
```

Unfortunately, this mp4 file gave the error:

```
javax.sound.sampled.UnsupportedAudioFileException: File of
unsupported format at java.desktop/javax.sound.sampled.AudioSystem.
getAudioInputStream(AudioSystem.java:1066)

      at FourierAnalysis_ExampleChapter6/com.asb.AudioAnalysis.
main(AudioAnalysis.java:17)
```

Next, we get:

```
java.lang.IllegalArgumentException: rows and columns must be greater
than 1
	at JTransforms@3.1-with-dependencies/org.jtransforms.fft.
FloatFFT_2D.<init>(FloatFFT_2D.java:76)
	at FourierAnalysis_ExampleChapter6/com.asb.AudioAnalysis.
main(AudioAnalysis.java:24)
```

So, we adjusted the code line:

We found that the Java Sound Technology only supports the following:

```
Audio file formats: AIFF, AU and WAV.
Music file formats: MIDI Type 0, MIDI Type 1, and Rich Music Format (RMF)
Sound formats: 8-bit and 16-bit audio data, in mono and stereo, with
sample rates from 8 kHz to 48 kHz.
Linear, a-law, and mu-law encoded data in any of the supported audio file
formats.
```

So, we tried with the **vocals.wav** file we created earlier, but this still gave code errors later on:

```
java.lang.ArrayIndexOutOfBoundsException: Index 1024 out of bounds for
length 1024
	at JTransforms@3.1-with-dependencies/org.jtransforms.utils.
CommonUtils.cftf081(CommonUtils.java:10538)
	at JTransforms@3.1-with-dependencies/org.jtransforms.utils.
CommonUtils.cftfsub(CommonUtils.java:5924)
	at JTransforms@3.1-with-dependencies/org.jtransforms.fft.
FloatFFT_1D.realForward(FloatFFT_1D.java:537)
	at JTransforms@3.1-with-dependencies/org.jtransforms.fft.
FloatFFT_2D.realForwardFull(FloatFFT_2D.java:959)
	at FourierAnalysis_ExampleChapter6/com.asb.AudioAnalysis.
main(AudioAnalysis.java:33)
```

This was the code line throwing the above Exception error, as follows:

```
fft.realForwardFull(spectrum);
```

Next, we loaded the test class using the link as follows:

https://github.com/wendykierp/JTransforms/blob/master/src/test/java/org/jtransforms/fft/FloatFFT_2DTest.java

We tested the jar with the test set we downloaded:

We then update the project with **junit 4** for the test and download:

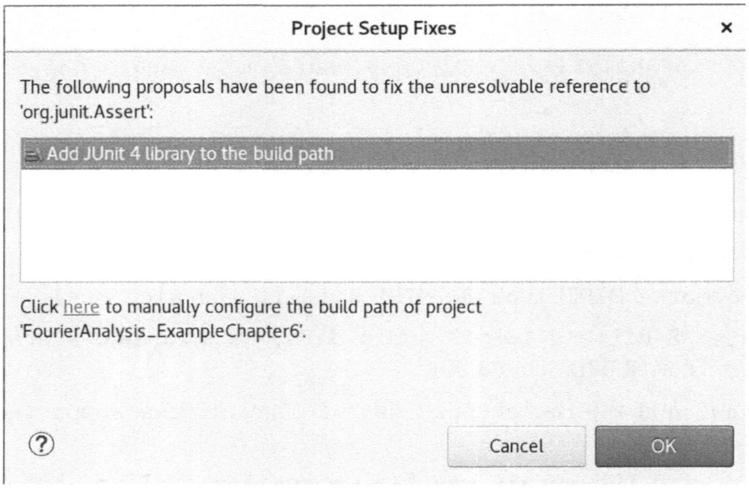

Figure 6.47: *The JUNIT 4 library is added to the project build path*

Updating the code as follows:

```
/**
 *
 */
/**
 *
 */
module FourierAnalysis_ExampleChapter6 {
        requires org.jfree.jfreechart;
        requires javax.sound;
        requires JTransforms;
        requires java.desktop;
        requires junit;
}
```

Next, we need the JTransforms source jar:

http://search.maven.org/remotecontent?filepath=com/github/wendykierp/JTransforms/3.1/JTransforms-3.1-sources.jar

We added the source jar to assist with debugging as this will load the java on clicking on the stack trace:

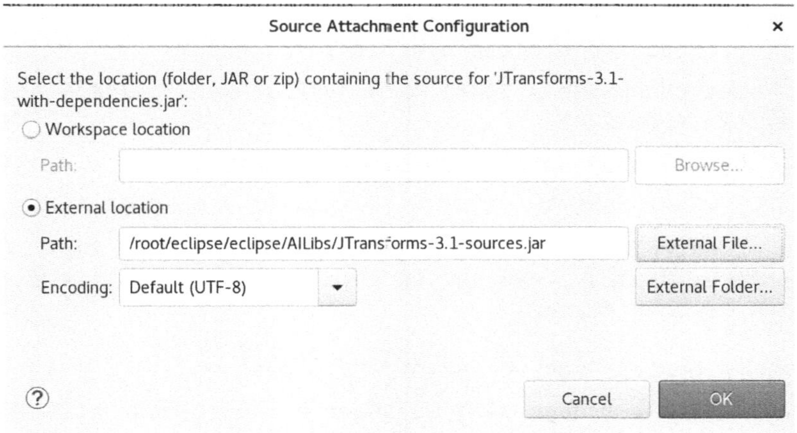

Figure 6.48: *The JTransforms source jar,* ***JTransforms-3.1-sources.jar*** *file was added*

The final code we created for the **AudioAnalysis.java**, did show that we were correctly reading the .wav file, and code was added to graph the chunks of data displaying up to five graphs with an example as in the following code list:

```
package com.asb;

import javax.sound.sampled.*;

import org.jfree.chart.ChartFactory;
import org.jfree.chart.ChartFrame;
import org.jfree.chart.JFreeChart;
import org.jfree.data.xy.XYSeries;
import org.jfree.data.xy.XYSeriesCollection;
import org.jtransforms.fft.FloatFFT_2D;
import java.io.*;                    // ASB This import was missing
and is required for the File("input.mp4") code line

public class AudioAnalysis {
    public static void main(String[] args) {
        try {
```

```
        //ASB Updated the test file from input.mp4 (which isn't supported!)
        AudioInputStream audioInputStream = AudioSystem.
getAudioInputStream(new File("/usr/local/lib64/python3.6/site-packages/
output/audio_example/vocals.wav"));
        AudioFormat format = audioInputStream.getFormat();

        // Read and process audio data in chunks
        int chunkSize = 2048; // Adjust as needed //ASB Adjusted
Chunk size down from 2048
        byte[] audioData = new byte[chunkSize];
        // final float[] actual = new float[2 * numRows * numCols];
        FloatFFT_2D fft = new FloatFFT_2D(chunkSize, 2); //ASB need
to increase the columns parameter to greater than 1 as this errors in
the FloatFFT_2D constructor!

        // Process each chunk of audio data
    Boolean nodata = true; //ASB We added a flag so that all zero
sections were ignored
        int screen_count = 0;
        //ASB We added a screen_count limit of 5 pop-up windows
        while (audioInputStream.read(audioData) != -1 & screen_count
< 5 ) {
            int bytes = audioInputStream.read(audioData);
            System.out.println("Byte size:" + bytes) ;
            float[] audioSamples = convertBytesToFloats(audioData);
            System.out.println("Array size:" + audioSamples.length) ;
            // Apply FFT
            float[] spectrum = new float[chunkSize/2]; //Changed from
2*chunksize array must be of size rows*2*columns, with only the first
rows*columns
            for (int j=0; j <  audioSamples.length; j++) {
                spectrum[j] = audioSamples[j];
                if (audioSamples[j] > 0.0f) {
                        nodata = false;
                }

            }
            //System.arraycopy(audioSamples, 0, spectrum, 0,
```

```
    chunkSize); //AS3 changed to chunkSize/2
//ASB Now display the Fourier Transform array
 if(!nodata) {
    // fft.realForwardFull(spectrum);
    //ASB Gives OutOfBounds Exception Index 1024 out of
          bounds for length 1024


    // Process the spectrum data (e.g., separate sources)


    // Inverse FFT to reconstruct audio
    // fft.realInverseFull(audioSamples, true);
    //ASB Gives OutOfBounds Exception Index 1024 out of
          bounds for length 1024


    screen_count++; //ASB Added to limit the screens to 5
    XYSeries series2 = new XYSeries("XYGraph");
    for (int i = 0; i < spectrum.length; i++) {
          series2.add(i + 1, spectrum[i]);
    // The Fourier Transform data set is added for the Graph
    }
    XYSeriesCollection dataset2 = new XYSeriesCollection();
    dataset2.addSeries(series2);
    JFreeChart chart2 = ChartFactory.createXYLineChart(
        "Fourier Analysis of an Audio .wav File - Audio
                Data plot",
        "X-Axis",
        "Y-Axis",
        dataset2);
    ChartFrame frame2 = new ChartFrame("Using ChatGPT
          AudioAnalysis.java", chart2);
    frame2.pack();
    frame2.setVisible(true);
    Thread.sleep(5000); //ASB Wait for 5 seconds to
          display the screen
// Process the reconstructed audio (e.g., post-processing)
frame2.dispose(); //ASB Drop the graph window after 5 seconds
 }
```

```
                nodata = true;//ASB Default to no data found gets set for a
                      non-zero chunk
            }

            audioInputStream.close();
        } catch (Exception e) {
            e.printStackTrace();
        }
    }

    private static float[] convertBytesToFloats(byte[] bytes) {
        float[] floats = new float[bytes.length / 2];
        for (int i = 0; i < floats.length; i++) {
            floats[i] = (float) ((bytes[2 * i] & 0xFF) | (bytes[2 * i + 1] << 8));
        }
        return floats;
    }
}
```

The 5 graph pop-up windows appear for 5 seconds each as shown in **Figure 6.49**:

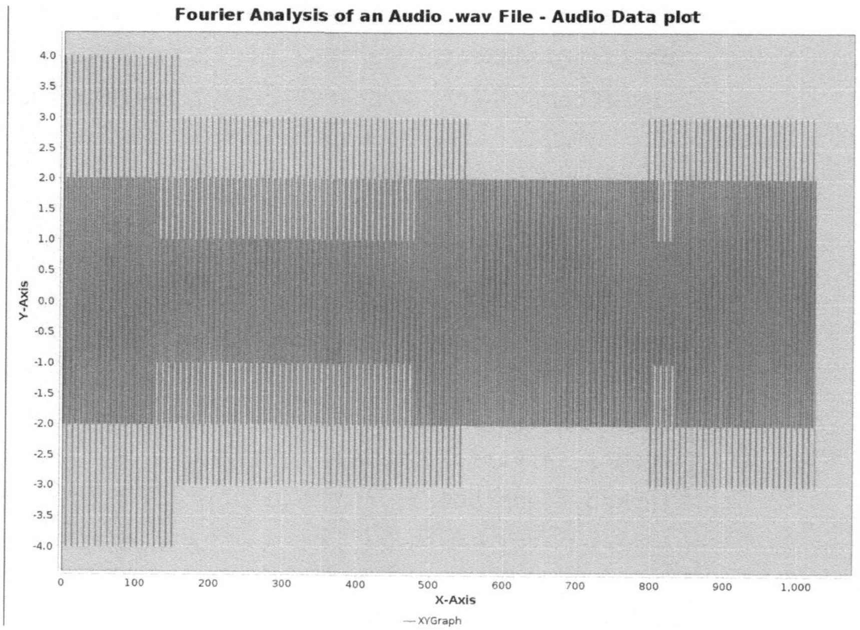

***Figure 6.49**: A section of the data loaded from the **vocals.wav** audio file*

The last updates to be made to the project were for the referenced jar file for the **MusicFileAnalyzer** class "skeleton" java code, which we listed earlier in this chapter, as shown in *Figure* 6.50.

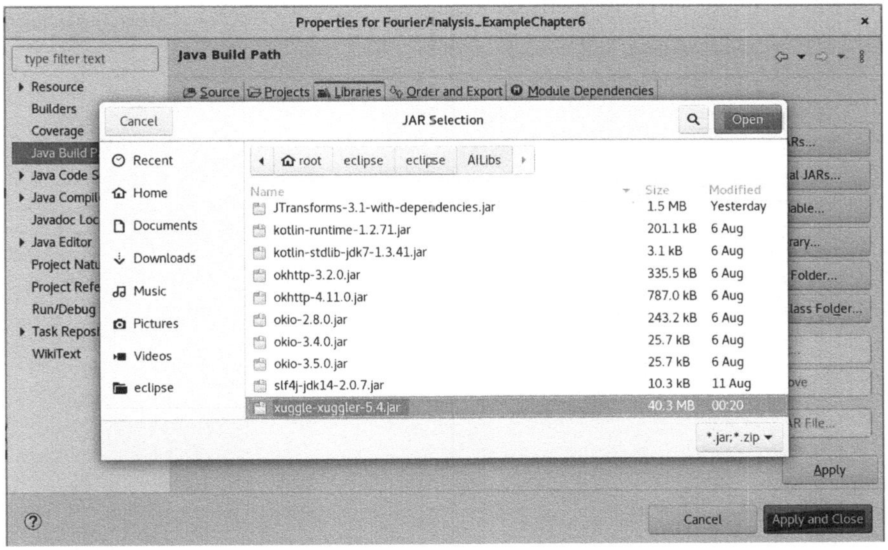

Figure 6.50: *The* ***xuggle-xuggler-5.4.jar*** *is added to the Module Path as required*

The final list of library jar files required to support the code for this chapter is shown in *Figure* 6.51:

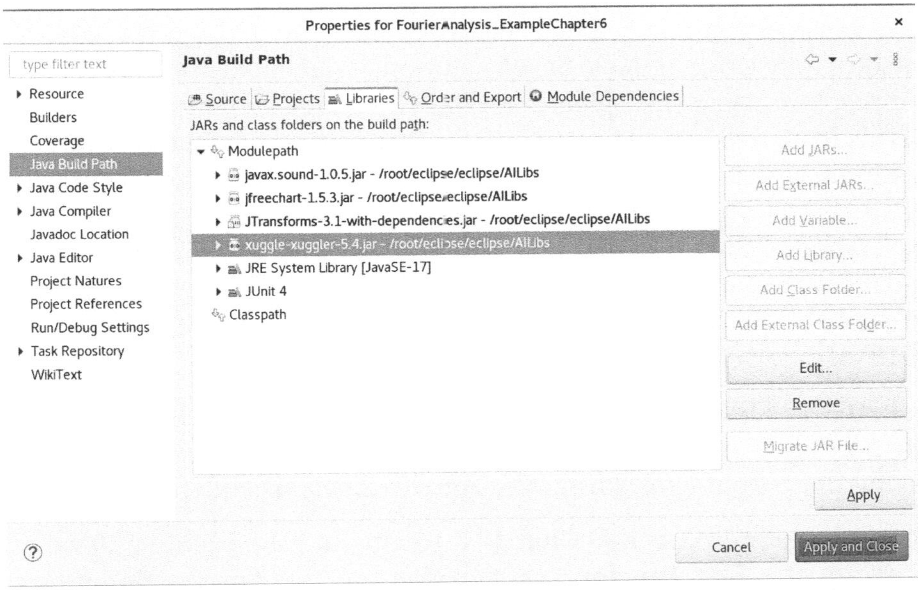

Figure 6.51: *The final list of library jar files required to support the code for this chapter*

Finally, we needed to update the reference to the library that the **MusicFileAnalyzer** class requires, so we updated the **xuggle.xuggler** package reference into the **module-info.java** file, by clicking as shown in the highlighted *Figure* 6.52, for the suggested list of fixes in the **Eclipse IDE** pop-up window.

***Figure 6.52:** The **MusicFileAnalyzer** class requires that the **xuggle.xuggler** package is added*

Conclusion

In this chapter, we explored a number of possible solutions for using **Fourier Analysis Java** code generated by the **ChatGPT AI**, and although **ChatGPT** failed to provide a fully working **Java-based** solution, it did make useful suggestions for the approach to using the **Spleeter Python** language program and we managed to call this from a modified version of the **Java** code suggested by **ChatGPT**. It is interesting to note that the code developed ab-initio, in this chapter (including the Chapter first draft with the screenshots and downloads) were created, with the assistance of the **ChatGPT AI**, between the 15th and 18th August, 2023. So, in just 4 days we created several working and tested Java programs, a task which would probably have taken a couple of weeks without the assistance of the **ChatGPT AI**.

The **ChatGPT 4.5 AI**, through the **Microsoft Bing** webchat interface, also provided a fully working graphical display **Java** program, which we adapted for displaying the output arrays from the **Fourier Analysis** code.

In the next chapter, we ask **ChatGPT** to provide an example **Java** code to demonstrate the **Fast Fourier Transform** using the **Apache Commons Math** library.

Points to remember

- Sometimes it is worth following the alternative suggestions made by the **ChatGPT AI**, even if the main response gives an outline approach. For example, **ChatGPT** did include the following recommendation in its response:

  For a more practical and robust solution, you might want to explore existing libraries and tools specialized in audio source separation, such as Spleeter by Deezer.

- You have to be prepared to add quite a number of supporting Java libraries in order to obtain functional Java code.
- Sometimes it is useful to rephrase the question posed to an AI to reach the required target response.
- Simpler questions can provide snippets of working Java code which can then be incorporated to achieve a complex requirement, as in the example question we posed to Microsoft Bing to provide the graphic representation for the Fourier Analysis output.
- If one AI App does not provide a useful response, it is often possible to get a better reply from one of the other available AI interfaces. It is also useful for obtaining a consensus.

  (Remember the LLM data models used may be different for a different AI interface.)

Multiple choice questions

1. **Which of the following list of libraries was required to build the Java launch program for Spleeter?**
   a. javax.sound-1.0.5.jar
   b. tensorflow-2.5.0
   c. Jtransforms-3.1-with-dependencies.jar
   d. xuggle-xuggler-5.4.jar
2. **Which of the following list of Java libraries was required to build the Java MusicFileAnalyzer code?**
   a. javax.sound-1.0.5.jar
   b. jfree-1.5.3.jar
   c. Jtransforms-3.1-with-dependencies.jar
   d. xuggle-xuggler-5.4.jar

3. **Which of the following sound-file types is not supported by Java Sound Technology for input?**
    a. .wav
    b. .au
    c. .mp4
    d. .AIFF
4. **Which of the following sound-file types is supported by Spleeter for input?**
    a. .wav
    b. .mp3
    c. .mp4
    d. .AIFF

Answers

1. **b**
2. **d**
3. **c**
4. **b**

Questions

1. How would you change the **SpleeterCaller** code to allow it to process a folder with a number of mp3 files? (Hint: there are some guidelines for code snippets in Chapter 8)
2. Can you describe the main functions provided by Spleeter (Hint: the links provided in this Chapter will help)?
3. Which of the AI interfaces we used in this Chapter do you think was most useful? Give your reasons for your analysis.
4. What other solutions were suggested by ChatGPT to split the vocal sounds from the accompaniment, other than Spleeter?

Key terms

- **Fourier analysis**: Fourier analysis is a mathematical analysis that is used to identify cycles in a time series of numbers and then to break down the data array by decomposing it into a series of functions such as sine waves.

- **Maven**: Maven is a build automation tool from the Apache Software Foundation, which can be set up as an Eclipse IDE project. It is used to control Java projects by assisting the build process by managing the dependencies, and maintaining these through the use of a pom.xml file.

- **MP4**: This is short for MPEG-4 Part 14, where MPEG is the abbreviation for 'Motion Picture Experts Group' a standards body defining the format of compressed video files.

  The file format is based on ISO/IEC 14496-12:2004 similar to the QuickTime player File Format but with additional features. It is mostly used to store video and audio signals.

- **Python**: Similar to **Java**, **Python** is a high-level, object-oriented programming language. It also uses code with the use of indentation which, unlike Java, is enforced since not using it can result in syntax errors.

  One important difference is that **Java** is compiled into a byte-code and then read using a **Java** virtual machine, whereas **Python** is interpreted, (like the **BASIC** language) so potentially slower to run.

  The other difference is that **Python** is dynamically typed so the type of the variable is determined only during runtime. Whereas Java is statically typed so a variable type is defined in the code.

- **Spleeter**: **Spleeter** is a free python-based program for separating a single **mp3** audio file used as input, containing a song, podcast, movie or game into a number of separate output files.

  It can extract voice and instruments from music and separate them from the rest of the file, into two, or more byte streams for output as separate "tracks".

  Spleeter can isolate vocals and accompaniments and split this again, if required, into percussion stems of the music using pretrained models. So, it uses machine-learning to automatically split the music by finding similarities across different songs for any given instrument. The full details of this program can be found at the link **https://research.deezer.com/projects/spleeter.html** . In more depth, the following link can be viewed: **https://deezer.io/releasing-spleeter-deezer-r-d-source-separation-engine-2b88985e797e**

CHAPTER 7
ChatGPT Generated Java Code for the Fast Fourier Transform

Introduction

In this chapter, **ChatGPT** was asked to provide example **Java** code to demonstrate the **Fast Fourier Transform.** Example Java code was displayed that demonstrated the **Fast Fourier Transform (FFT)** using the **Apache Commons Math** library.

Structure

In this chapter, we will discuss the following topics:

- AI Fast Fourier Transform Java code ChatGPT prompted Java Program
- Fast Fourier Transform Java code validation using an Eclipse Java Program Project

AI Fast Fourier Transform Java code ChatGPT prompted Java Program

I asked **Microsoft Bing (OpenAI GPT 4.5)** for an overview of the use of the Fast Fourier Transform, and the **AI** response provided some useful links for further reading. I asked:

Top uses of the Fast Fourier Transform

"*The **fast Fourier transform (FFT)** is an algorithm that computes the **discrete Fourier transform (DFT)** of a sequence, or its inverse (**IDFT**). It converts a signal from its original domain (often time or space) to a representation in the frequency domain and vice versa*[1].

Some of the top uses of the FFT are:

- **Signal processing:** FFTs are used for fault analysis, quality control, and condition monitoring of machines or systems[2]. They can also be used for reading sound waves, image-processing technologies, and solving various types of equations[3].
- **Engineering:** FFTs are used for applications such as digital filtering, spectral analysis, data compression, convolution, correlation, and modulation[4].
- **Mathematics:** FFTs are used for solving partial differential equations, polynomial multiplication, number theory, and cryptography[1].

You can learn more about the FFT and its applications from these sources:

[2]: Fast Fourier Transformation FFT - Basics - NTi Audio [1]: Fast Fourier transform - Wikipedia [3]: What is Fast Fourier Transform (FFT)? - Definition from Techopedia [4]: The Fast Fourier Transform and its Applications - School of Mathematics [5]: 13.2: The Fast Fourier Transform (FFT) - Engineering LibreTexts

Is there anything else you would like to know about the FFT?"

The URLs for the sources provided by Bing above, with the Hyperlinks listed, are as follows:

1. and 2 **https://en.wikipedia.org/wiki/Fast_Fourier_transform**
3. **https://www.nti-audio.com/en/support/know-how/fast-fourier-transform-fft**
4. **https://www.techopedia.com/definition/7167/fast-fourier-transform-fft**
5. **https://www.maths.ed.ac.uk/~ateckent/vacation_reports/summer_project_gillian_smith.pdf**
6. **https://eng.libretexts.org/Bookshelves/Electrical_Engineering/Signal_Processing_and_Modeling/Signals_and_Systems_%28Baraniuk_et_al.%29/13%3A_Capstone_Signal_Processing_Topics/13.02%3A_The_Fast_Fourier_Transform_%28FFT%29**

The **ChatGPT Ask AI** mobile phone App was asked for example **Java** code, which could be run to calculate using a **Fast Fourier Transform**:

1. Is there example java code you have to demonstrate the Fast Fourier transform.

   Yes, here is an example Java code that demonstrates the Fast Fourier Transform (FFT) using the Apache Commons Math library:

```
```java
import org.apache.commons.math3.complex.Complex;
import org.apache.commons.math3.transform.FastFourierTransformer;


public class FFTExample {


    public static void main(String[] args) {
        double[] input = {1.0, 2.0, 3.0, 4.0};
        FastFourierTransformer transformer = new
FastFourierTransformer();
        Complex[] output = transformer.transform(input);


        System.out.println("Input:");
        for (double d : input) {
            System.out.print(d + " ");
        }
        System.out.println("\nOutput:");
        for (Complex c : output) {
            System.out.print(c + " ");
        }
    }
}
```

This code creates an input signal of length 4 with values 1.0, 2.0, 3.0, and 4.0. It then uses the `FastFourierTransformer` class from the Apache Commons Math library to perform the FFT on the input signal. The resulting output is an array of complex numbers of the same length as the input signal.

The output of the code above will look something like this:
```

```
Input:
1.0 2.0 3.0 4.0
Output:
(10.0,0.0) (-2.0,2.0) (-2.0,0.0) (-2.0,-2.0)
```

Note that the output is in complex form, where each complex number represents the amplitude and phase of a frequency component in the original input signal. The first number in the output, (10.0,0.0), represents the DC component (i.e., the average value) of the input signal. The remaining numbers represent the frequency components of the input signal in increasing order of frequency.

Fast Fourier Transform Java code validation using an Eclipse Java Program Project

We created a new **Eclipse IDE** project to validate the **Java** code supplied by **ChatGPT,** as shown in *Figure 7.1*.

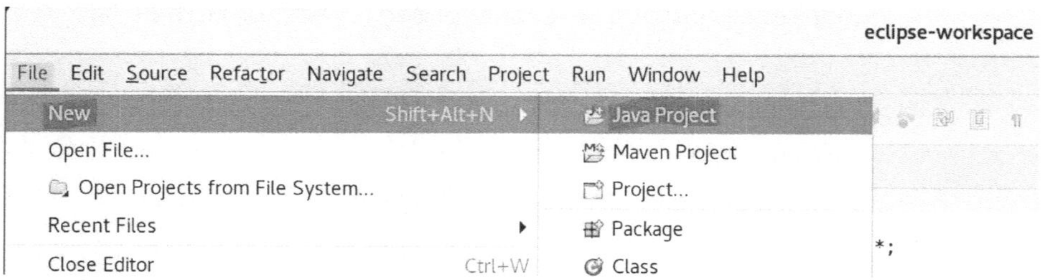

Figure 7.1: *The new* ***Eclipse IDE Java*** *project is created*

The new project name was added as **FourierTransform_ExampleChapter7.**

You may have noticed that there is a tick-box on the **Create a Java Project** pop-up window in the **Eclipse IDE** screen, as shown in *Figure 7.2*, for the option to **Create module-info.java file**.

This **module-info.java** file is used to ensure that when a jar file is declared as a named module, you will have the required **module-info.class** file, which is compiled from the **module-info.java** file.

This file declares the dependencies within the module system (using the **requires** statement, which allows this module to access public types exported in the target module) and allows the **Java** compiler and the **JVM** runtime to monitor the boundaries and detect any access violations between the modules in the application.

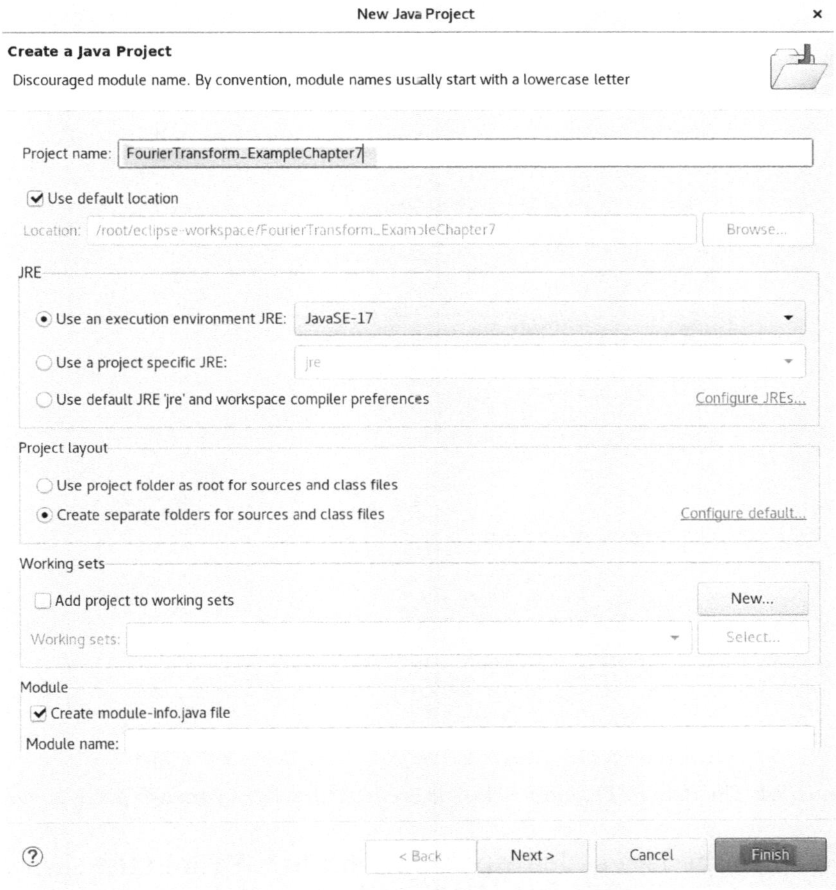

Figure 7.2**: The new **Eclipse IDE Java** project is named **FourierTransform_ExampleChapter7

We right-clicked on the **src** node of the project, as created in *Figure* 7.2, to create a new class, as shown in *Figure* 7.3.

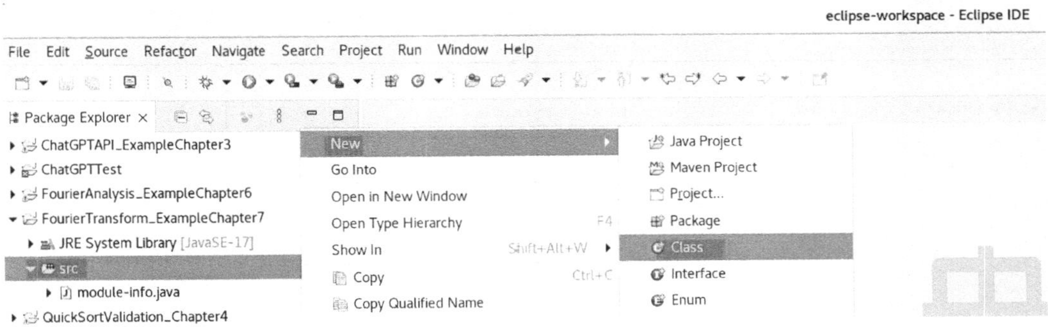

Figure 7.3**: Right- clicked on the src node to select **New-> Class

We created a new "skeleton" Java Class named **FFTExample,** as shown in *Figure* 7.4.

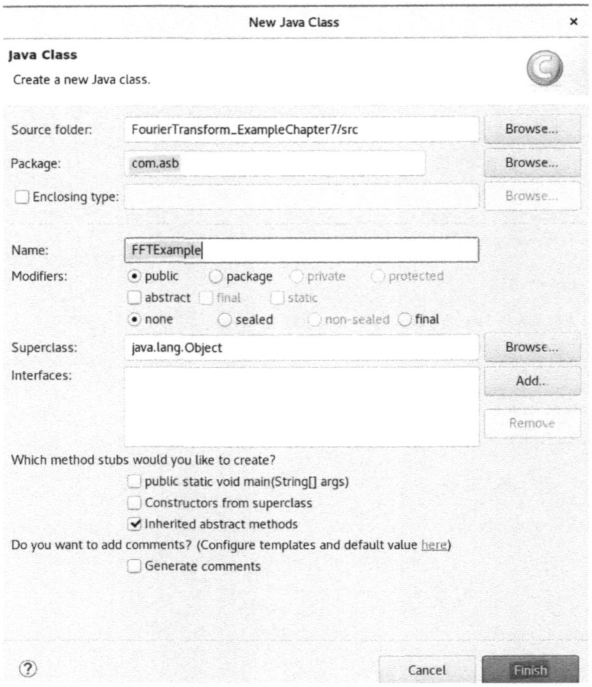

***Figure 7.4**: The new **FFTExample** class is created under the **com.asb** package name*

Next, we copied the Java code response from **ChatGPT** into the skeleton class, as shown in *Figure* 7.5, and observed that there were imports requiring a new library .jar file to be downloaded and configured as an External .jar in the **Module** Build Path.

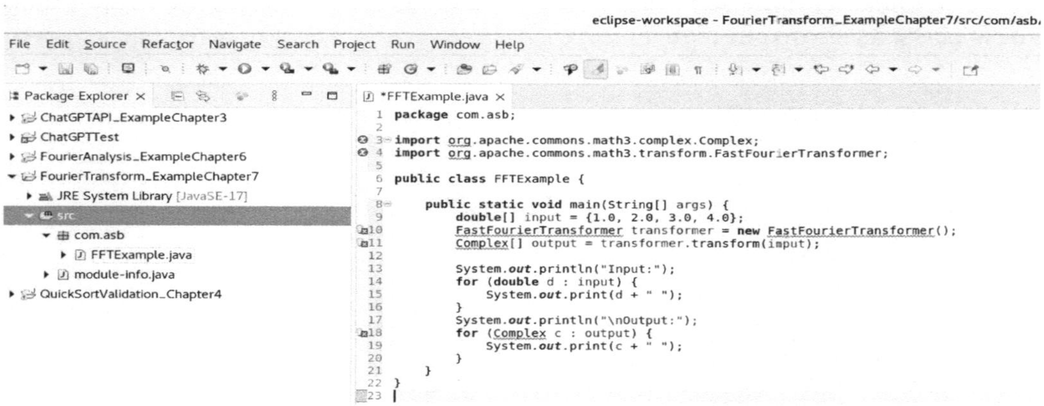

***Figure 7.5**: The **ChatGPT** Java code is added to the **FFTExample** class with flagged issues*

We searched for the Java jar to download for **org.apache.commons.math3** and used the following link:

https://mvnrepository.com/artifact/org.apache.commons/commons-math3/3.6.1

Then, we selected the jar to download using the following link:

https://repo1.maven.org/maven2/org/apache/commons/commons-math3/3.6.1/commons-math3-3.6.1.jar

The downloaded library jar, **`commons-math3-3.6.1.jar`**, is copied to the **Eclipse IDE** on the **VMware RHEL 8.8 Linux** server:`[root@ECMUKDEMO22 AILibs]# pwd`

```
/root/eclipse/eclipse/AILibs

[root@ECMUKDEMO22 AILibs]# cp /mnt/hgfs/Installs/commons-math3-3.6.1.jar
.

[root@ECMUKDEMO22 AILibs]#
```

The copied library .jar is then added to the project class path, as shown in *Figure 7.6*

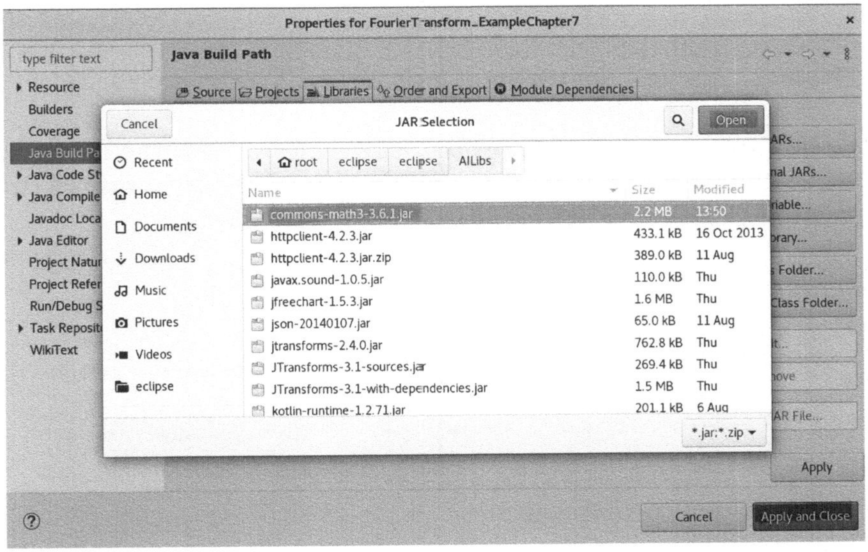

Figure 7.6: *The copied library .jar,* **commons-math3-3.6.1.jar,** *is added to the project class path*

After selecting the **Open** button, we need to select **Apply and Close,** as highlighted in *Figure 7.7*.

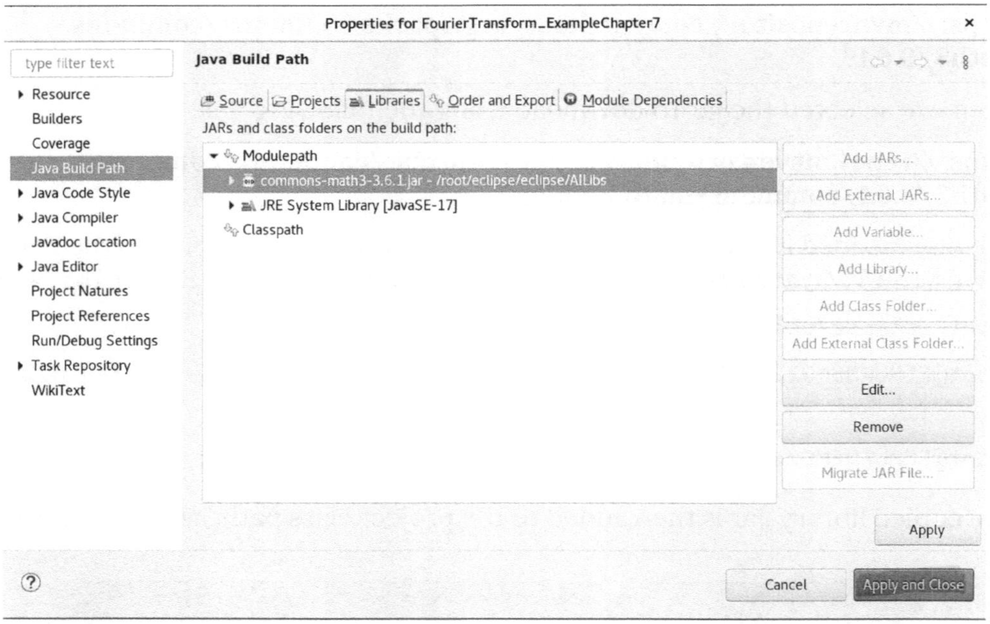

Figure 7.7: *After selecting the Open button, we need to select Apply and Close*

To fix the import error, we click on the error line to view the list of potential fixes listed by the **Eclipse IDE,** and we select the option **Add 'requires commons. math3 to module-info.java'**, as highlighted in *Figure 7.8*.

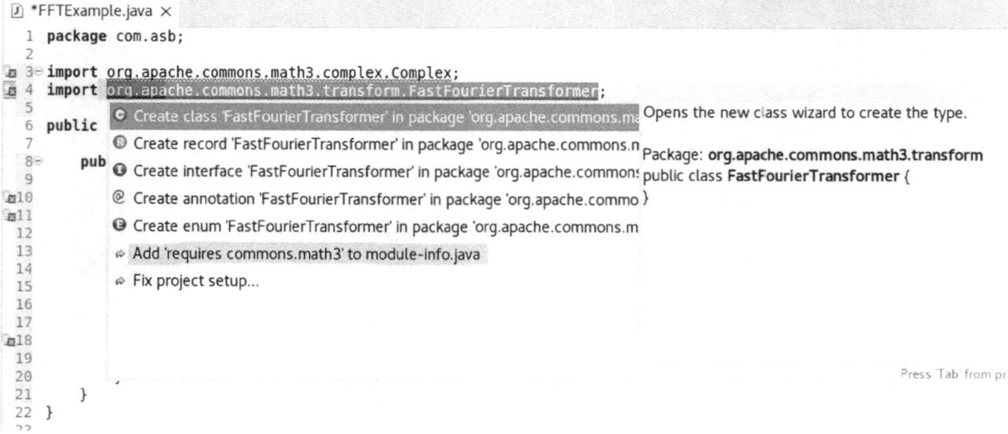

Figure 7.8: *Select the option* **Add 'requires commons.math3 to module-info.java'**

Note

We had to close, save, and re-open the code for **FFTExample.java** *and the* **module-info.java** *class code in order to clear the import error flags.*

We corrected the code supplied by **ChatGPT,** which was missing a couple of arguments on the **Fast Fourier Transform** library method calls, and found a very useful link using the Google search: "***need an example code for FastFourierTransformer transformer = new FastFourierTransformer***"

https://www.programcreek.com/java-api-examples/?api=org.apache.commons.math3.transform.FastFourierTransformer

We applied the most likely defaults, and the code ran as illustrated in *Figure* 7.9.

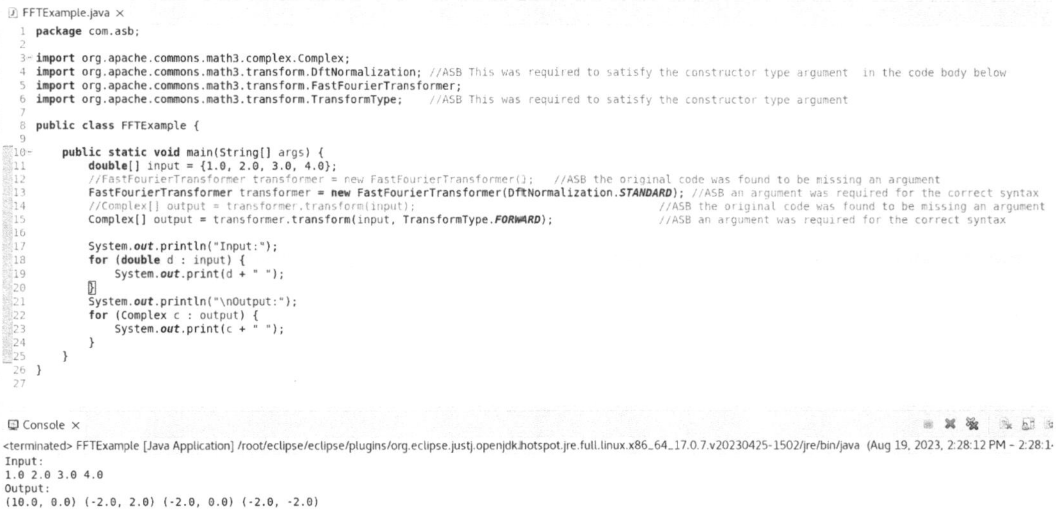

Figure 7.9: *The corrected Java code runs, giving the results expected from* **ChatGPT***'s response*

As a reminder, **ChatGPT** stated:

"The output of the code above will look something like this:

```
```

Input:

1.0 2.0 3.0 4.0

Output:

(10.0,0.0) (-2.0,2.0) (-2.0,0.0) (-2.0,-2.0)"
```
```

So, it may be that the code suggested by **ChatGPT** was based on an earlier version of the **Apache Commons Math 3** jar library (we used the latest **3.6.1** version).

The final working code, along with our commented corrections, is shown in the following **Java** code list:

```
package com.asb;

import org.apache.commons.math3.complex.Complex;
import org.apache.commons.math3.transform.DftNormalization; //ASB This
was required to satisfy the constructor type argument  in the code body
below
import org.apache.commons.math3.transform.FastFourierTransformer;
import org.apache.commons.math3.transform.TransformType;    //ASB This
was required to satisfy the constructor type argument

public class FFTExample {

    public static void main(String[] args) {
        double[] input = {1.0, 2.0, 3.0, 4.0};
        //FastFourierTransformer transformer = new
FastFourierTransformer();   //ASB the original code was found to be |
                                    missing an argument
        FastFourierTransformer transformer = new
FastFourierTransformer(DftNormalization.STANDARD); //ASB an argument was
required for the correct syntax
        //Complex[] output = transformer.transform(input);
       //ASB the original code was found to be missing an argument
        Complex[] output = transformer.transform(input, TransformType.
FORWARD);    //ASB an argument was required for the correct syntax

        System.out.println("Input:");
        for (double d : input) {
            System.out.print(d + " ");
        }
        System.out.println("\nOutput:");
        for (Complex c : output) {
            System.out.print(c + " ");
        }
    }
}
```

The **module-info.java** file was as follows:

```
/**
 *
 */
/**
 *
 */
module FourierTransform_ExampleChapter7 {
	requires commons.math3;
}
```

The first run Java build path was set, as shown in *Figure 7.10*.

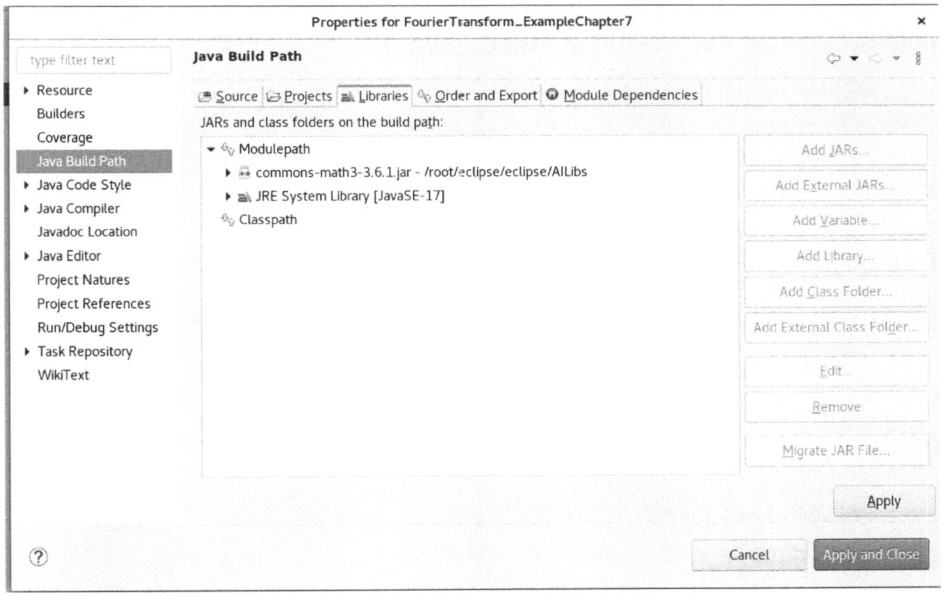

***Figure 7.10**: The first run Project **FourierTransform_ExampleChapter7** Properties **Java** build*

So, next, we wanted to process a more complex set of data, so we extended the Java code as follows:

```
package com.asb;

import org.apache.commons.math3.complex.Complex;

import org.apache.commons.math3.transform.DftNormalization; //ASB This was required to satisfy the constructor type argument in the code body
```

```
below
import org.apache.commons.math3.transform.FastFourierTransformer;
import org.apache.commons.math3.transform.TransformType;    //ASB This
was required to satisfy the constructor type argument
//ASB Added for plotting an additional example
import org.jfree.chart.ChartFactory;
import org.jfree.chart.ChartFrame;
import org.jfree.chart.JFreeChart;
import org.jfree.data.xy.XYSeries;
import org.jfree.data.xy.XYSeriesCollection;

public class FFTExample {

    public static void main(String[] args) {
        double[] input = {1.0, 2.0, 3.0, 4.0};
        //FastFourierTransformer transformer = new
FastFourierTransformer();   //ASB the original code was found to be
missing an argument
        FastFourierTransformer transformer = new
FastFourierTransformer(DftNormalization.STANDARD); //ASB an argument was
required for the correct syntax
        //Complex[] output = transformer.transform(input);
        //ASB the original code was found to be missing an argument
        Complex[] output = transformer.transform(input, TransformType.
FORWARD);    //ASB an argument was required for the correct syntax

        System.out.println("Input:");
        for (double d : input) {
            System.out.print(d + " ");
        }
        System.out.println("\nOutput:");
        for (Complex c : output) {
            System.out.print(c + " ");
        }
        /*
         * ASB Software Development Limited
         * We have developed a more interesting example based on the
```

```
following
        * w = 10*2*pi
                From t = 0 to 0.5 in steps of .001
                Sum n = 1 to 4 n* cos (n * w * t)
                See:
                https://en.wikipedia.org/wiki/Fast_Fourier_transform
                Note: Java stores the value of pi as a constant, or
                     3.141592653589793
        */
       double[] yval = new double[4096]; // ASB Note that this array
size has to be a power of two
       int j=0;
       double sum = 0.0f;
       final double PI = 3.14159265358979323846;
       double t=0.0f;
       double w = 10.0f *2.0f  *PI;
           for (int i =0 ;  i <   1000 ; i++) {
                t += 0.001; //Increment t by 1/1000 each time
                //Calculate the sum
                for (int n = 1; n < 5; n++) {
                     j++;
                     sum = sum + Math.cos(n*w*t);
                     yval[j] = sum;
                }


           }
           // ASB Plot the values using our Graph code
          XYSeries series = new XYSeries("XYGraph");
          for (int i = 0; i < yval.length; i++) {
              series.add(i + 1, yval[i]); //
          }
          XYSeriesCollection dataset = new XYSeriesCollection();
          dataset.addSeries(series);
          JFreeChart chart = ChartFactory.createXYLineChart(
                "Fourier Analysis of a Complex Sine Curve - signal
```

```
plot",
                    "X-Axis",
                    "Y-Axis",
                    dataset);
            ChartFrame frame = new ChartFrame("Using ChatGPT
                                        FourierAnalysis.java", chart);
            frame.pack();
            frame.setVisible(true);
            //ASB Set up the FFT
            FastFourierTransformer transformer2 = new
FastFourierTransformer(DftNormalization.STANDARD); //ASB an argument was
required for the correct syntax
            Complex[] output2 = transformer.transform(yval,
TransformType.FORWARD);                         //ASB an argument was
required for the correct syntax
            double[] real = new double[output2.length];
            double[] imaginary = new double[output2.length];
            //Populate our FFT results into two parts
            for(int i=0; i<real.length; ++i) {
              real[i] = output2[i].getReal();
              imaginary[i] = output2[i].getImaginary();
            }
             // ASB Plot the imaginary values using our Graph code -
                          Real plot
            XYSeries series2 = new XYSeries("XYGraph");
            for (int i = 0; i < imaginary.length; i++) {
                series2.add(i + 1, imaginary[i]); //
            }
            XYSeriesCollection dataset2 = new XYSeriesCollection();
            dataset2.addSeries(series2);
            JFreeChart chart2 = ChartFactory.createXYLineChart(
                    "Fourier Analysis of a Complex Sine Curve -
                                Imaginary part FFT plot",
```

```
                    "X-Axis",
                    "Y-Axis",
                    dataset2);
            ChartFrame frame2 = new ChartFrame("Using ChatGPT
FFTExample.java", chart2);
            frame2.pack();
            frame2.setVisible(true);
             // ASB Plot the Real values using our Graph code - Real plot
            XYSeries series3 = new XYSeries("XYGraph");
            for (int i = 0; i < real.length; i++) {
                series3.add(i + 1, real[i]); //
            }
            XYSeriesCollection dataset3 = new XYSeriesCollection();
            dataset3.addSeries(series3);
            JFreeChart chart3 = ChartFactory.createXYLineChart(
                    "Fourier Analysis of a Complex Sine Curve - Real
                                part FFT plot",
                    "X-Axis",
                    "Y-Axis",
                    dataset3);
            ChartFrame frame3 = new ChartFrame("Using ChatGPT
                                            FFTExample.java", chart3);
            frame3.pack();
            frame3.setVisible(true);
    }

}
```

The graphical output displays the arrays for the calculated multiple summed complex cosine curve signal, the **FFT Real** part of the **complex** array result, and the **FFT imaginary** part of the **complex** array result. The pop-up Graph windows were manually dragged using the mouse and adjusted to allow the three windows to be displayed side by side, as shown in *Figure 7.11*.

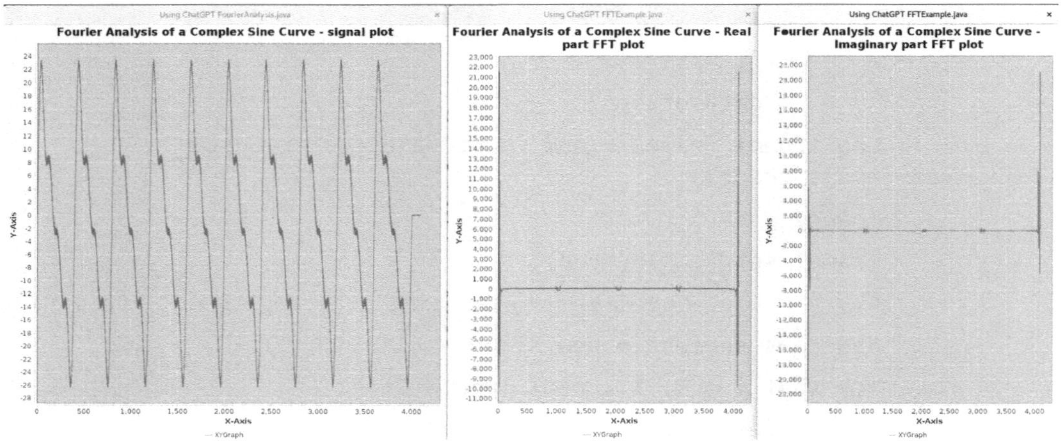

Figure 7.11: *The display of the example summed cosine curve and the FFT complex output*

You may have noticed that we use a cosine function in the code. Theoretically, a simple cosine function produces a graph that has the same shape as the graph of the sine function. The graph of sine can be obtained by translating the graph of cosine, as there is just a phase difference of 90° (π/2 radians), so, they are just out of phase with each other.

To test the effect of this with our code, we can simply replace the cos with sin in the code line:

```
sum = sum + Math.cos(n*w*t);
```

changing to:

```
sum = sum + Math.sin(n*w*t);
```

The resulting graphs look as follows:

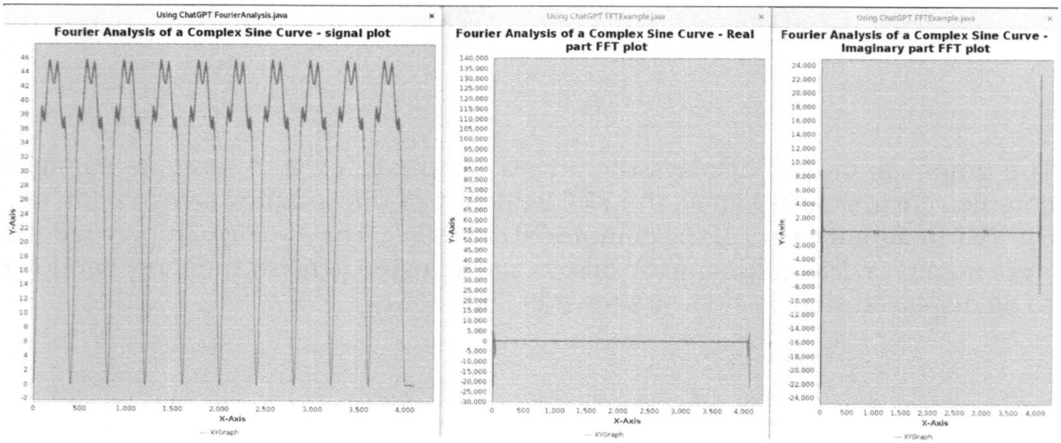

Figure 7.12: *The display of the example summed sine curve and the FFT complex array output*

Notice that although the generated signal for sine and cosine looks quite different, the generated FFT imaginary plots look very similar.

Conclusion

The example Java code suggested by the **ChatGPT 3.5, Ask AI** mobile phone App was structurally correct, but it missed a couple of import statements, which we had to add. The second argument of the two calls made to the **org.apache.commons.math3.transform** methods were missing. We think this was due to the Java code supplied by **ChatGPT** being for an earlier version of the **Apache Commons Maths** library.

We then extended the Java code example to test a more complex signal pattern. The output of the generated signal and the Real and Imaginary parts of the FFT complex number result were then plotted as a set of graphs, as displayed in *Figure* 7.11.

In the next chapter, we will analyze and validate the code provided by **ChatGPT** to create an index of documents and their associated keywords using the **Lucene** library. This code allows searching for documents based on keywords and returns the document path.

Points to Remember

- The Java code created by the **ChatGPT AI** may be specific to a particular version of a referenced supporting Maths library, so the code should always be validated and checked to compare the expected output.
- Note that the output shown in the **ChatGPT** code is in complex form, where each complex number represents the amplitude and phase of a frequency component in the original input signal. The first number in the output (Real part 10.0, Imaginary part 0.0) represents the DC component (i.e., the average value) of the input signal. The remaining complex numbers represent the frequency components of the input signal in increasing order of frequency.
- We had to close, save, and re-open the code for **FFTExample.java** and the **module-info.java** class code in order to clear the import error flags.
- Additional Java code examples for the FFT Maths library can be found using the webpage link as follows:

  https://www.programcreek.com/java-api-examples/?api=org.apache.commons.math3.transform.FastFourierTransformer

Multiple Choice Questions

1. **Which of the following imports was found to be missing for the FFT Java code supplied by ChatGPT?**
   a. `import org.apache.commons.math3.complex.Complex;`
   b. `import org.apache.commons.math3.transform.FastFourierTransformer;`
   c. `import org.apache.commons.math3.transform.DftNormalization;`
   d. `import org.jfree.data.xy.XYSeries;`
2. **When there is an import error on the FastFourierTransformer class and the project is set up with a module-info.java file, which option would you select to resolve the error?**
   a. `Create class 'FastFourierTransformer' in package org.apache.commons.math3.transform`
   b. `Create record 'FastFourierTransformer' in package org.apache.commons.math3.transform`
   c. `Add 'requires commons.math3' to module-info.java`
   d. `Create interface 'FastFourierTransformer' in package org.apache.commons.math3.transform`
3. **Which Java library jar is required to support the Fast Fourier Transform methods we used?**
   a. Jtransforms-2.4.0.jar
   b. JTransforms-3.1-sources.jar
   c. commons-math3-3.6.1.jar
   d. JTransforms-3.1-with-dependencies.jar
4. **In the extended Java program, we have used as an example, which of the following trigonometric functions is used as an example signal source?**
   a. tan
   b. cos
   c. cot
   d. sec

Answers

1. **c**
2. **c**

3. c
4. b

Question

1. What other functions (there are at least 3) would give the following graphs using the code `sum = sum + Math.???(n*w*t)` instead of `sum = sum + Math.cos(n*w*t)` (Hint: Try this by replacing the ??? with one of the other functions from the available Math list).

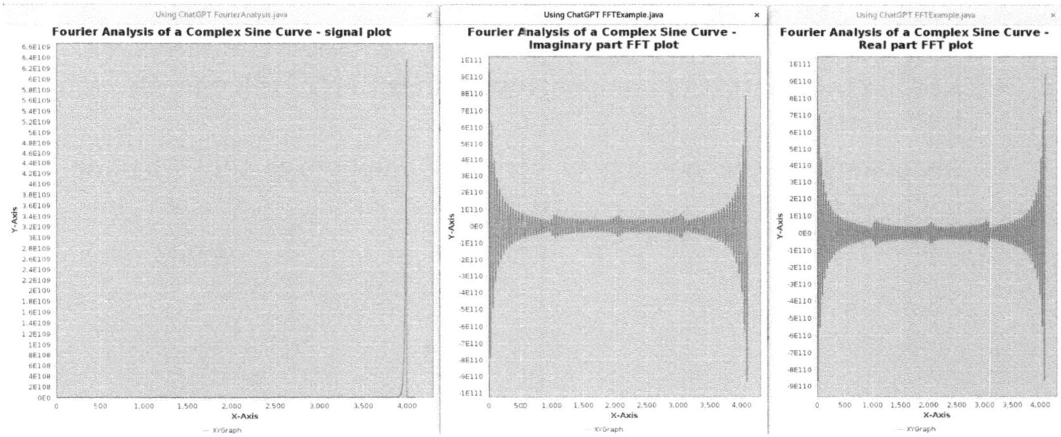

Figure 7.13: *The function we obtained by substituting* `Math.cos(n*w*t)` *function from cos*

It is interesting that, as shown in *Figure* 7.13, the resulting Real and Imaginary plots show exactly the same pattern, as shown in *Figure* 7.14.

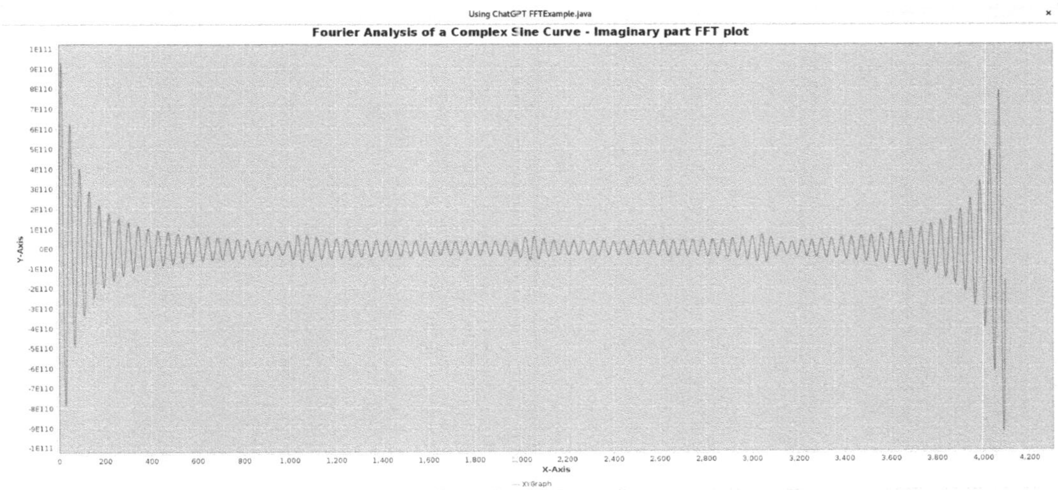

Figure 7.14: *The beautiful symmetric function obtained by substituting the cos function*

Key Terms

- **FFT**: The fast Fourier transform (FFT) is an algorithm that computes the discrete Fourier transform (DFT) of a sequence, or its inverse (IDFT). It converts a signal from its original domain (often time or space) to a representation in the frequency domain and vice versa.
- ***Complex:*** Complex numbers are expressed in the form of *a*+i*b*, where, *a*,*b* are real numbers and 'i' is an imaginary number. The value of i = (√-1).

  So, 2+3i is a complex number, where 2 is a real number and 3i is an imaginary number.
- ***Real:*** In the context of complex numbers is the "*a*" value in the complex form *a* +i*b*.
- ***Imaginary***: In the context of complex numbers is the "*b*" value in a complex form *a* +i*b*.

CHAPTER 8
ChatGPT Generated Java Code for Indexing a Document

Introduction

The **OpenAI ChatGPT** program was asked for example **Java** code for indexing a document with output of a list of keywords with the associated document page numbers.

The code provided by **ChatGPT** created an index of documents and their associated keywords using the **Lucene** library. It also allowed searching for documents based on keywords and returned the document path.

Structure

In this chapter, we will discuss the following topics:

- **ChatGPT** generated **Java** code for indexing a document giving keywords and page numbers
- Document Indexing Java code validation using an **Eclipse IDE** Java Program Project

ChatGPT generated Java code for indexing a document giving keywords and page numbers

I used the **Ask AI** mobile 'phone app the following question and the **Open AI ChatGPT 3.5** response was as listed in the quoted italics:

Is there example java code for indexing a document so listing keywords with the document page numbers.

""Yes, there is example Java code for indexing a document and listing keywords with the document page numbers. Here is an example implementation using the Apache Lucene library:

```
```java
import java.io.IOException;
import java.nio.file.Paths;
import org.apache.lucene.analysis.standard.StandardAnalyzer;
import org.apache.lucene.document.Document;
import org.apache.lucene.document.Field;
import org.apache.lucene.document.TextField;
import org.apache.lucene.index.DirectoryReader;
import org.apache.lucene.index.IndexReader;
import org.apache.lucene.index.IndexWriter;
import org.apache.lucene.index.IndexWriterConfig;
import org.apache.lucene.index.Term;
import org.apache.lucene.queryparser.classic.MultiFieldQueryParser;
import org.apache.lucene.queryparser.classic.QueryParser;
import org.apache.lucene.search.IndexSearcher;
import org.apache.lucene.search.Query;
import org.apache.lucene.search.ScoreDoc;
import org.apache.lucene.search.TopDocs;
import org.apache.lucene.store.Directory;
import org.apache.lucene.store.FSDirectory;

public class DocumentIndexer {
  private Directory indexDir;
```
```

```
  public DocumentIndexer(String indexDirectoryPath) throws IOException {
    indexDir = FSDirectory.open(Paths.get(indexDirectoryPath));
  }

  public void indexDocument(String documentPath, String[] keywords)
throws IOException {
    IndexWriterConfig indexWriterConfig = new IndexWriterConfig(new
StandardAnalyzer());

    try (IndexWriter indexWriter = new IndexWriter(indexDir,
indexWriterConfig)) {
      Document document = new Document();
      document.add(new TextField("path", documentPath, Field.Store.
YES));
      for (String keyword : keywords) {
        document.add(new TextField("keyword", keyword, Field.Store.
YES));
      }
      indexWriter.addDocument(document);
    }
  }

  public void searchDocuments(String[] keywords) throws Exception {
    IndexReader indexReader = DirectoryReader.open(indexDir);
    IndexSearcher indexSearcher = new IndexSearcher(indexReader);

    QueryParser queryParser = new MultiFieldQueryParser(new String[]
{"keyword"}, new StandardAnalyzer());
    Query query = queryParser.parse(String.join(" ", keywords));

    TopDocs topDocs = indexSearcher.search(query, 10);

    for (ScoreDoc scoreDoc : topDocs.scoreDocs) {
      Document document = indexSearcher.doc(scoreDoc.doc);
      System.out.println("Page: " + document.get("path"));
```

```
    }

    indexReader.close();
  }

  public static void main(String[] args) throws Exception {
    String indexDirectoryPath = "/path/to/index/directory";
    DocumentIndexer indexer = new DocumentIndexer(indexDirectoryPath);

    String documentPath = "/path/to/document";
    String[] keywords = {"keyword1", "keyword2", "keyword3"};
    indexer.indexDocument(documentPath, keywords);

    String[] searchDocumentssearchKeywords = {"keyword1", "keyword3"};
    indexer.(searchKeywords);
  }
}
```

This code creates an index of documents and their associated keywords using the Lucene library. It also allows searching for documents based on keywords and returns the document path. You can modify this code to suit your specific needs."

Document Indexing Java code validation using an Eclipse Java Program Project

We tried an additional approach to assist with the validation of the code by using another **AI** interface called **Phind,** which was developed and is owned by **Cognition, Inc.**, a **USA**, **Delaware** corporation.

Note

There are at least 9 other **AI** *alternatives as well as* **Phind**, *which you could try, see the link as follows for some other alternative* **AI** *systems:*

https://www.makeuseof.com/best-alternatives-chatgpt/

This can be installed on an **Android 'phone** using the **Chrome** web-browser application from the web link **https://www.phind.com** and loads a **Chrome** plugin.

(It also appears as an icon on the **Android** 'phone **Home Screen**, identifiable as a white lowercase "p" on a black background).

The **Phind AI** also functions correctly in the **Microsoft Edge** and **Firefox** browsers on a **Windows 10** operating system.

There is also a **GitHub** reference shown in the following link:

https://github.com/gptforfree/gpt4free/blob/main/phind/README.md

The **Phind** conditions of use (**https://www.phind.com/terms**) forbid the copying of any

"*....software, images, text, graphics, illustrations, logos, patents, trademarks, service marks, copyrights, photographs, audio, videos, and music...*" (hence the **Phind** logo description on the **Android** 'phone' we have given, rather than the screen-shot).

On the question of the short, quoted extract in italics above, this is allowed in USA and UK copyright law, from the US law: "**Under the fair use doctrine of the U.S. copyright statute, it is permissible to use limited portions of a work including quotes, for purposes such as commentary, criticism, news reporting, and scholarly reports**".

See **https://www.copyright.gov/help/faq/faq-fairuse.html#:~:text=Under%20the%20fair%20use%20doctrine,news%20reporting%2C%20and%20scholarly%20reports.**

And from UK law:

"Fair dealing with a work for the purpose of criticism or review, of that or another work or of a performance of a work, does not infringe any copyright in the work provided that it is accompanied by a sufficient acknowledgement [F15 (unless this would be impossible for reasons of practicality or otherwise)] [F16 and provided that the work has been made available to the public].

[F17(1ZA) Copyright in a work is not infringed by the use of a quotation from the work (whether for criticism or review or otherwise) provided that–

(a) The work has been made available to the public,

(b) The use of the quotation is fair dealing with the work,

(c) The extent of the quotation is no more than is required by the specific purpose for which it is used, and

(d) The quotation is accompanied by a sufficient acknowledgement (unless this would be impossible for reasons of practicality or otherwise).]"

See:

https://www.legislation.gov.uk/ukpga/1988/48/part/I/chapter/III

Fortunately, the **Phind** conditions of use, explicitly exclude the conditions of use restrictions on the **Phind AI** Answers from the user's questions entered.

(This exclusion was also very recently reinforced by another judgment on AI creation of copyright:

https://www.theregister.com/AMP/2023/08/21/ai_copyright_lawsuit_lost/

This article states:

"*But one thing is for sure, after a ruling by the United States District Court for the District of Columbia – AI-created works cannot be copyrighted.*")

The pdf of the full court ruling, dated August 18th, 2023 is available at:

h**ttps://storage.courtlistener.com/recap/gov.uscourts.dcd.243956/gov.uscourts.dcd.243956.24.0_2.pdf**)

We repeated the question posed to **Ask AI** to the **Phind AI** as follows:

Is there example java code for indexing a document so listing keywords with the document page numbers.

The **Phind AI's** Answer is as follows:

"To index a document and list keywords with their page numbers in Java, you need to read the document, tokenize it into words, and then store the page number for each occurrence of each word. There are several ways to do this, but one common approach is to use a `Map` where the keys are the words and the values are lists of page numbers.

Here is a simple code snippet to demonstrate this:

```
```java
import java.util.*;


public class DocumentIndexer {
    private Map<String, List<Integer>> index = new HashMap<>();


    public void indexDocument(String document, int pageNumber) {
```
```

```
        String[] words = document.toLowerCase().split("\\W+");
        for (String word : words) {
            if (!index.containsKey(word)) {
                index.put(word, new ArrayList<>());
            }
            index.get(word).add(pageNumber);
        }
    }

    public List<Integer> getPageNumbers(String word) {
        return index.get(word.toLowerCase());
    }
}
```

In this code, the `indexDocument` method takes a document (as a `String`) and a page number, splits the document into words, and adds the page number to the list of page numbers for each word. The `getPageNumbers` method then allows you to retrieve the list of page numbers for a given word [Source 1]**(https://codereview.stackexchange.com/questions/122675/program-to-index-a-book).**

This is a very basic example and may not be efficient for large documents or large numbers of documents. For more advanced use cases, you might want to consider using a search library like Apache Lucene.

Apache Lucene is a powerful Java library used for implementing full-text search on a corpus of text. With it, you can add searchable fields to your documents and then build an index of those fields. Here's a basic example of how you might do this:

```java
import org.apache.lucene.document.Document;
import org.apache.lucene.document.Field;
import org.apache.lucene.document.StringField;
import org.apache.lucene.index.IndexWriter;
import org.apache.lucene.index.IndexWriterConfig;
import org.apache.lucene.store.Directory;
import org.apache.lucene.store.RAMDirectory;
import org.apache.lucene.analysis.standard.StandardAnalyzer;
```

```
public class LuceneIndexer {
    public void indexDocument(String text, int pageNumber) throws
Exception {
        Directory indexDirectory = new RAMDirectory();
        IndexWriterConfig config = new IndexWriterConfig(new
StandardAnalyzer());
        IndexWriter writer = new IndexWriter(indexDirectory, config);

        Document document = new Document();
        document.add(new StringField("text", text, Field.Store.YES));
        document.add(new StringField("pageNumber", Integer.
toString(pageNumber), Field.Store.YES));
        writer.addDocument(document);
        writer.close();
    }
}
```

In this code, we create a `Directory` to hold the index (in this case, a `RAMDirectory` which holds the index in memory), create an `IndexWriter` to add documents to the index, create a `Document`, add fields to the document for the text and the page number, and then add the document to the index [Source 2](**https://howtodoinjava.com/lucene/lucene-index-search-examples/**).

To search the index for a particular keyword, you can use Lucene's `IndexSearcher` class:

```java
import org.apache.lucene.index.DirectoryReader;
import org.apache.lucene.index.IndexReader;
import org.apache.lucene.search.IndexSearcher;
import org.apache.lucene.search.Query;
import org.apache.lucene.search.TopDocs;
import org.apache.lucene.queryparser.classic.QueryParser;

public class LuceneSearcher {
    public TopDocs searchIndex(Directory indexDirectory, String keyword)
throws Exception {
```

```
        IndexReader reader = DirectoryReader.open(indexDirectory);
        IndexSearcher searcher = new IndexSearcher(reader);
        QueryParser parser = new QueryParser("text", new
StandardAnalyzer());
        Query query = parser.parse(keyword);
        TopDocs results = searcher.search(query, 10);
        return results;
    }
}
```

In this code, we create an **IndexReader** to read the index, create an **IndexSearcher** to search the index, create a **QueryParser** to parse the search query, create a **Query** from the keyword, and then use the searcher to search the index for the query [Source 2](**https://howtodoinjava.com/lucene/lucene-index-search-examples/**)."

So, we now have two slightly different proposals for the Java code we are looking for.

The approach **Phind AI** has taken is to provide a simpler snippet of code, then it also recommends the **Apache Lucene Java** jar libraries in a similar example of code to the code supplied by **Ask AI**, but it also shows the source web pages it has used to base its answers on.

We also tried the more appropriate sounding example link:

https://codereview.stackexchange.com/questions/122675/program-to-index-a-book

(Phind source [1])

Licensed with **https://www.apache.org/licenses/LICENSE-2.0** which allows us to use the code and describe it:

"Grant of Copyright License. Subject to the terms and conditions of this License, each Contributor hereby grants to You a perpetual, worldwide, non-exclusive, no-charge, royalty-free, irrevocable copyright license to reproduce, prepare Derivative Works of, publicly display, publicly perform, sublicense, and distribute the Work and such Derivative Works in Source or Object form."

https://lucene.apache.org/core/downloads.html

So, let's create an **Eclipse IDE Java** project to test the **AI Java** code we have copied.

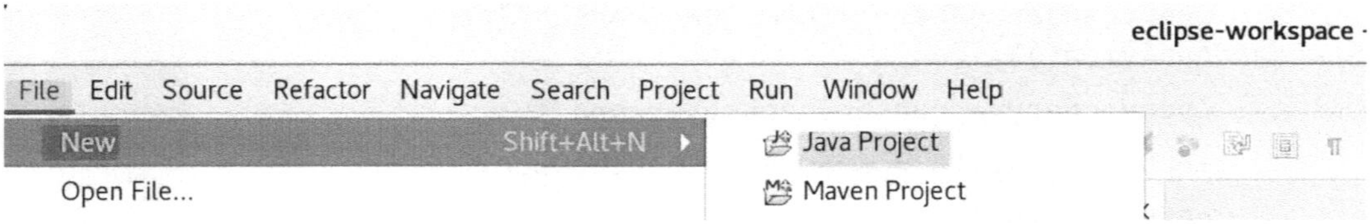

Figure 8.1**: The **New -> Java Project** menu item is selected in the **Eclipse IDE

The name of the new **Java** project is given as **IndexingDocuments_ExamplesChapter8**, as shown in *Figure 8.2*:

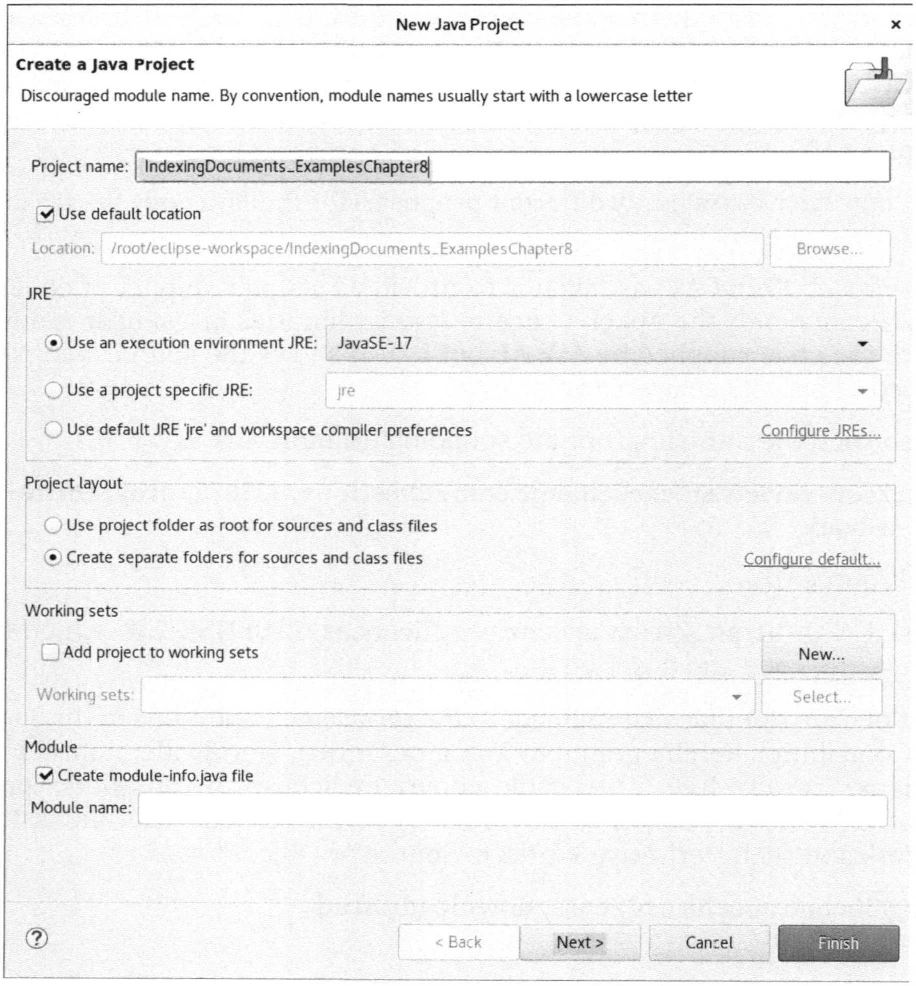

Figure 8.2**: The name of the new **Java** project is given as **IndexingDocuments_ExamplesChapter8

The project is viewed and created using the **Finish** button, as shown in *Figure 8.3*:

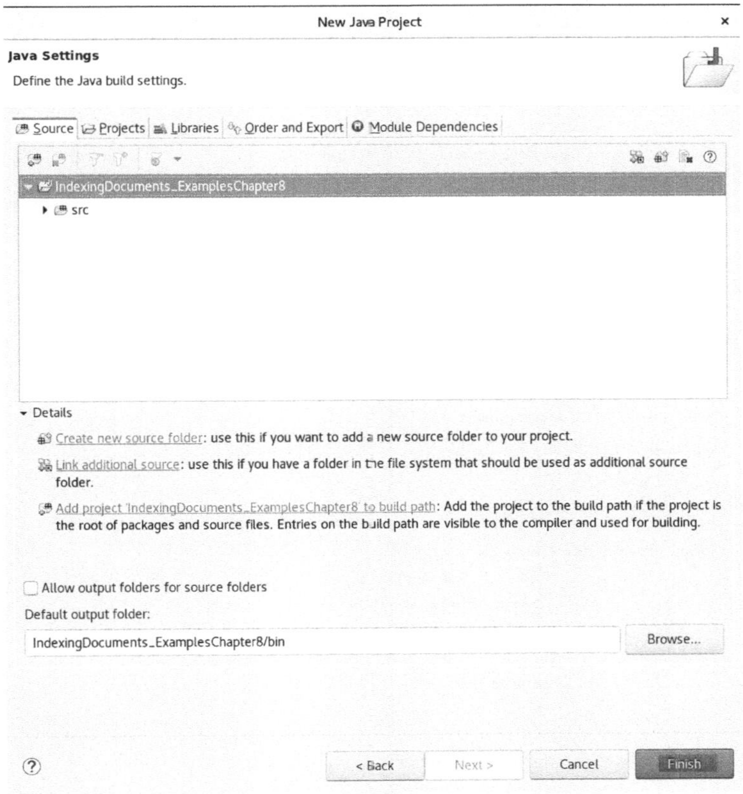

***Figure 8.3**: The project is viewed and created using the **Finish** button*

The **Java Class** to be validated is added using a right-mouse click on the **src** node of the new project, as shown in *Figure 8.4*:

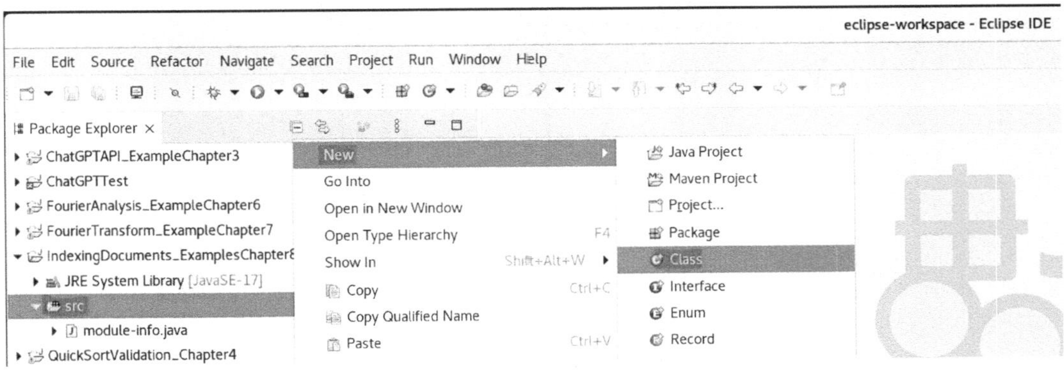

***Figure 8.4**: The **Java Class** is added using a right-mouse click on the **src** node of the project*

The **Class** name is set as **DocumentIndexer** under a new package for the project of **com.asb**, as shown in *Figure 8.5*:

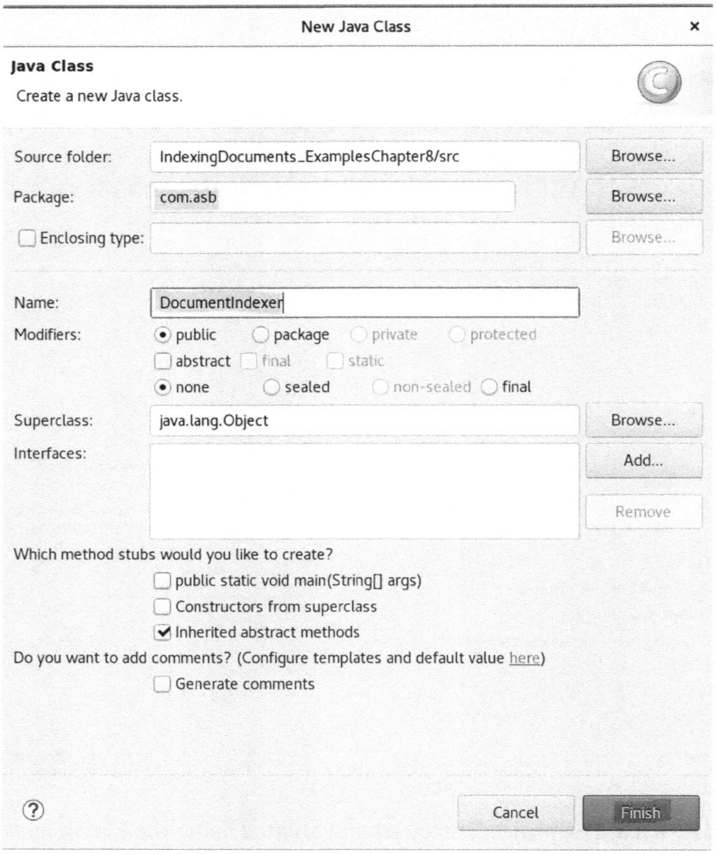

***Figure 8.5**: The **Finish** button is clicked to create the skeleton **DocumentIndexer** class*

The **Ask AI** mobile 'phone app code given for the **DocumentIndexer** is pasted into our new skeleton class, as shown in *Figure 8.6*:

Figure 8.6: *The* **Ask AI** *mobile 'phone app code given for the* **DocumentIndexer** *is pasted*

From the pasted code in the project, shown in *Figure* 8.6, it can be seen that the imports for the **org.apache.lucene** packages are missing, so we need to search for and download the **Apache Java Lucene** jar library.

The binary release (Binary releases: lucene-8.11.2.tgz [PGP] [SHA512] / lucene-8.11.2.zip [PGP] [SHA512]) is selected from our **Google** search, which has the link, **https://lucene.apache.org/core/downloads.html**, which then lists the latest release for download as **Lucene 9.7.0**, as shown in *Figure* 8.7:

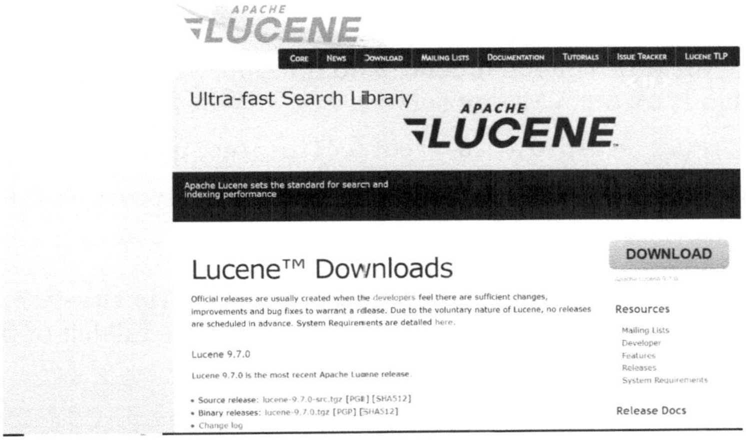

Figure 8.7: *The* **Download** *button is clicked for the current* **Apache Lucene 9.7.0** *version*

Click on the highlighted **lucene-9.7.0.tgz** file link as shown in *Figure* 8.8.

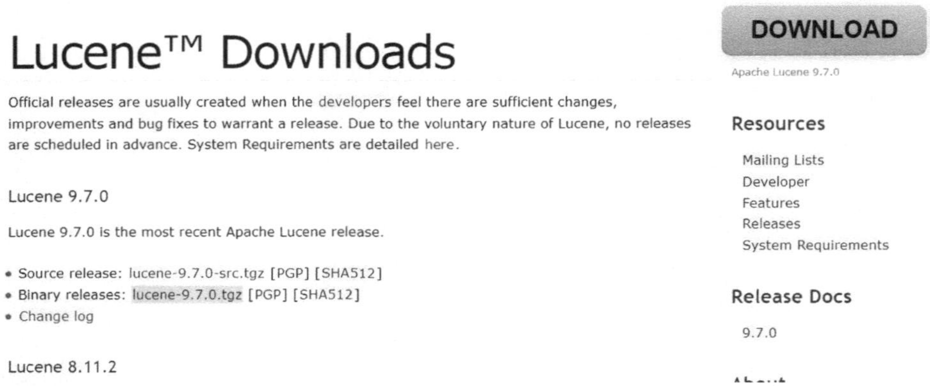

***Figure 8.8**: The **Download** for **Linux** is found by selecting the highlighted **lucene-9.7.0.tgz** link*

It redirects to the site:

https://www.apache.org/dyn/closer.lua/lucene/java/9.7.0/lucene-9.7.0.tgz

which has the recommended download site:

https://dlcdn.apache.org/lucene/java/9.7.0/lucene-9.7.0.tgz

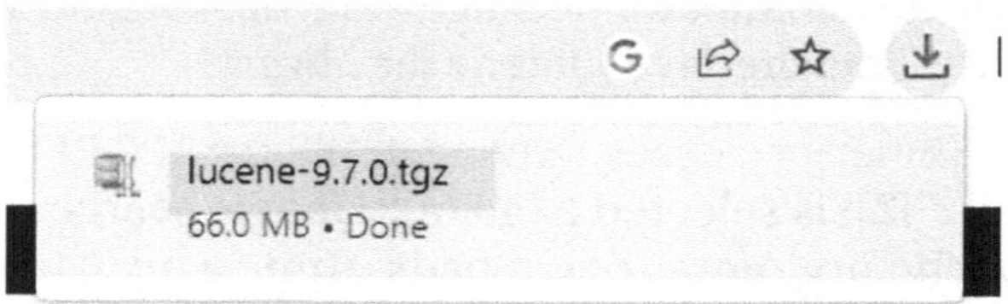

Figure 8.9**: The downloaded **lucene-9.7.0.tgz** library file is shown with a size of **66 Mbytes

We unpacked the downloaded **lucene-9.7.0.tgz** zipped tar file using the following Linux commands on our VMware server:

```
[root@ECMUKDEMO22 eclipse]# cd /root/eclipse/eclipse/AILibs
[root@ECMUKDEMO22 AILibs]# cp /mnt/hgfs/Installs/lucene-9.7.0.tgz .
[root@ECMUKDEMO22 AILibs]# tar -zxvf lucene-9.7.0.tgz
```

The unpacked path, **`/root/eclipse/eclipse/AILibs/lucene-9.7.0/modules,`** for the library jar files, are shown in *Figure* 8.10 with the full list of files:

***Figure 8.10**: The list of the unpacked **Lucene 9.7.0 Java** library Jar files*

These were copied as required to the **Eclipse IDE** Java Project **AILibs** folder and then added to the properties of the project **Module Build path**, as shown in *Figure 8.11*:

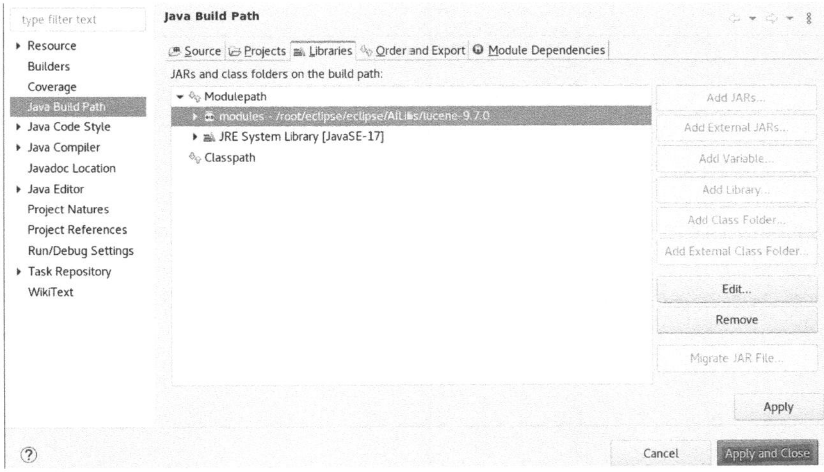

***Figure 8.11**: The **lucene-9.7.0.jar** file is added to the **Modulepath** of the Java Build path*

In order to fix the import errors shown by the **Eclipse IDE** we clicked on the first error line in the **IDE** Java code window, and then selected the **Add 'requires org. apache.lucene.core' to module-info.java** option as highlighted in *Figure 8.12*:

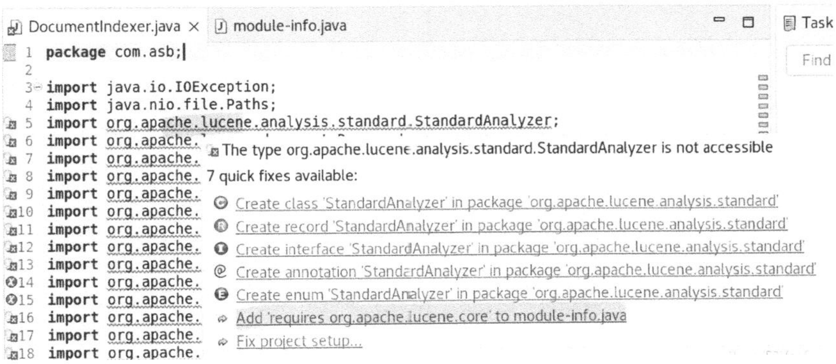

***Figure 8.12**: The **Add 'requires org.apache.lucene.core' to module-info.java** option is clicked*

The resulting **DocumentIndexer.java** and **module-info.java** code windows are closed and re-selected to re-open them to show that this has corrected all but two of the import statements, as highlighted in *Figure 8.13*:

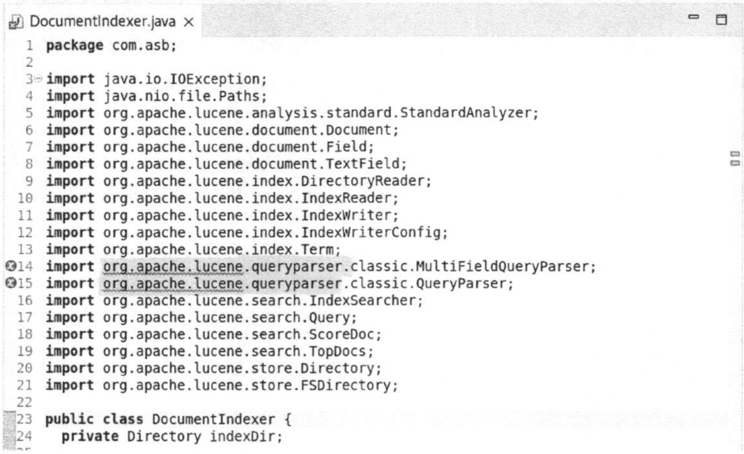

Figure 8.13: *The remaining* ***org.apache.queryparser*** *imports are required to be fixed*

Once more, we select the required external **Lucene 9.7.0** library, as shown in *Figure 8.14*:

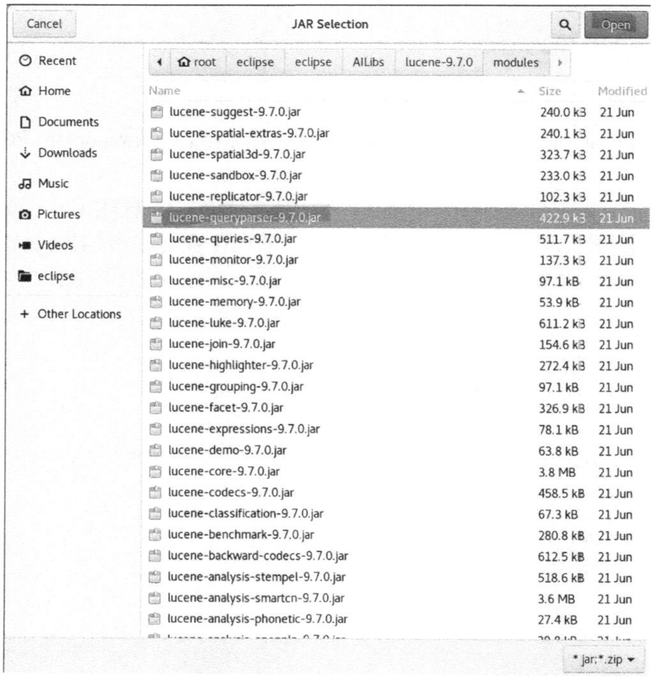

Figure 8.14: *The* ***lucene-queryparser-9.7.0.jar*** *file is selected as highlighted*

The Open button is selected, as highlighted in *Figure* 8.14, and then the **Apply and Close** button is clicked as illustrated in *Figure* 8.15, to add the **lucene-queryparser-9.7.0.jar** file to the **Modulepath** of the project.

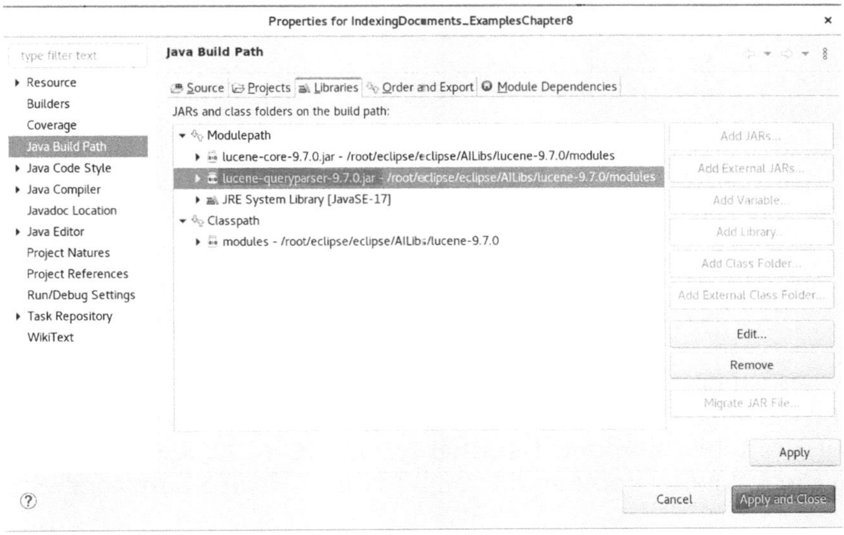

***Figure* 8.15**: *The* **lucene-queryparser-9.7.0.jar** *file is added to the* **Modulepath**

We can now repeat the process we followed earlier, to correct the remaining two Java package **import** errors, by selecting the highlighted **Eclipse IDE** fix list suggestion, **Add 'requires org.apache.lucene.queryparser' to module-info.java**, as shown highlighted in *Figure* 8.16:

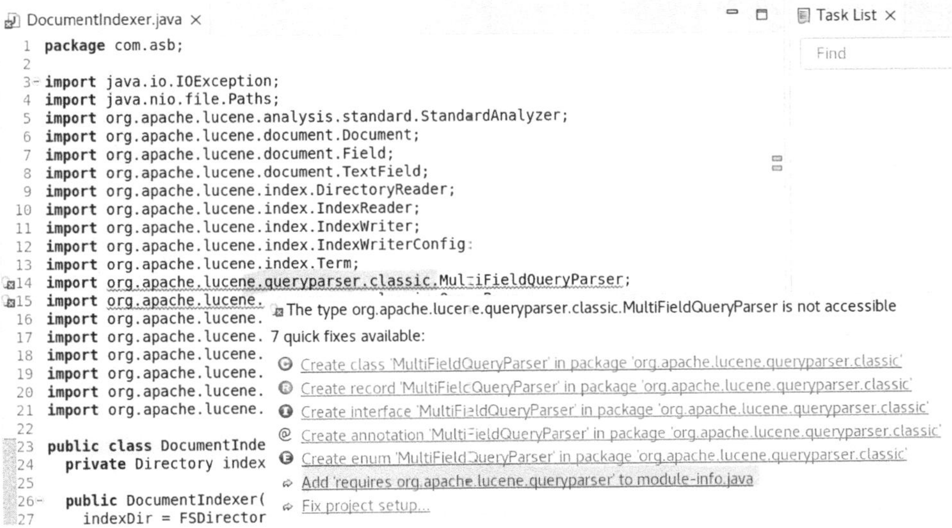

***Figure* 8.16**: *The* **Add 'requires org.apache.lucene.queryparser' to module-info.java** *is selected*

The resulting **module-info.java** code is shown in *Figure 8.17*:

DocumentIndexer.java | module-info.java

```
/**
 *
 */
/**
 *
 */
module IndexingDocuments_ExamplesChapter8 {
    requires org.apache.lucene.core;
    requires org.apache.lucene.queryparser;
}
```

***Figure 8.17**: The resulting **module-info.java** code is shown*

Now we can validate the program we have configured by setting up the test data for processing. The first document we use as test data is the first **MS Word** document draft of this book for Chapter 1, **`136_6_PD_ASB.docx,`** copied as shown in the following command listing, to our **VMware Linux** server:

```
[root@ECMUKDEMO22 AILibs]# cd /opt

[root@ECMUKDEMO22 opt]# mkdir AVA

[root@ECMUKDEMO22 opt]# cd AVA

[root@ECMUKDEMO22 AVA]# mkdir index

[root@ECMUKDEMO22 AVA]# mkdir Chapter6

[root@ECMUKDEMO22 AVA]# cd index

[root@ECMUKDEMO22 index]# mkdir directory

[root@ECMUKDEMO22 index]# cd ../Chapter6

[root@ECMUKDEMO22 Chapter6]# cp /mnt/hgfs/Installs/136_6_PD_ASB.docx .

The first run of the program gave the error:

Error occurred during initialization of boot layer

java.lang.module.FindException: Module org.apache.lucene.queries not
found, required by org.apache.lucene.queryparser
```

So, we add another library jar file, as shown in *Figure* 8.18:

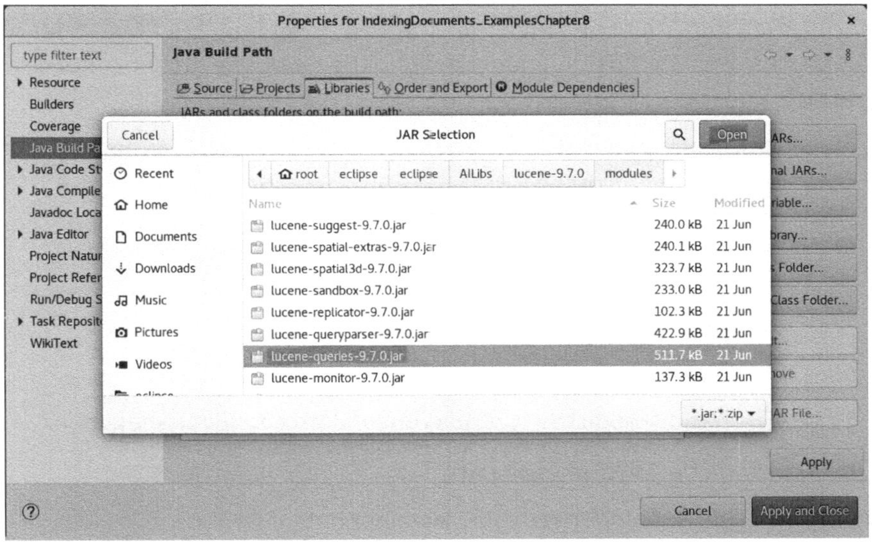

Figure 8.18**: The **lucene-queries-9.7.0.jar** file is added to the project **Modulepath

The **module-info.java** file is updated as highlighted to correct the run-time error we saw, as shown in *Figure* 8.19:

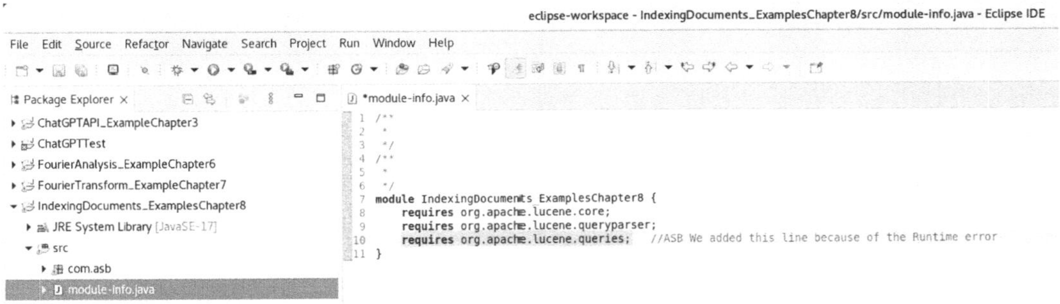

***Figure 8.19**: The **module-info.java** file is updated as highlighted*

Then, we have made progress, but we get another run-time error:

```
Error occurred during initialization of boot layer
java.lang.module.FindException: Module org.apache.lucene.sandbox not
found, required by org.apache.lucene.queryparser
```

so, we repeat the addition of the library jar file, **lucene-queries-9.7.0.jar** for the **lucene-sandbox-9.7.0.jar**.

We then get:

```
org.apache.lucene.store.MappedByteBufferIndexInputProvider <init>
WARNING: Unmapping is not supported, because Lucene cannot read 'jdk.
unsupported' module
[please add 'jdk.unsupported' to modular application either by command
line or its module descriptor]
```

We searched for the error on **Google** and found the following:

```
+    // Lucene needs two optional modules at runtime, which we want to
enforce for testing
+   // (if the runner JVM does not support them, it will fail tests):
+      jvmArgs '--add-modules', 'jdk.unsupported,jdk.management'
```

So, we then added the **JVM arguments:**

`--add-modules 'jdk.unsupported,jdk.management'`

as illustrated in *Figure 8.20,* to our project on the **Eclipse IDE**.

The **OK** button is selected as shown, highlighted in *Figure* 8.20.

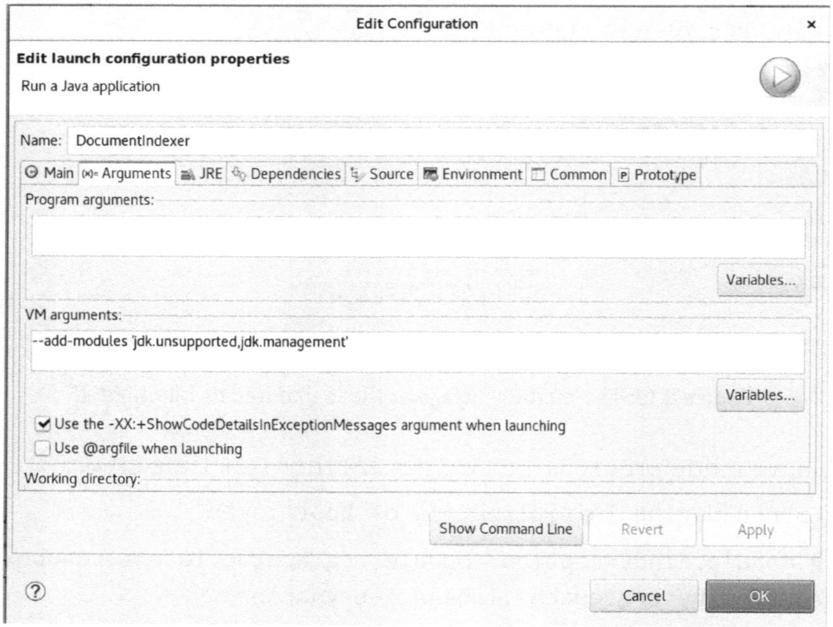

Figure 8.20: The **JVM arguments** *--add-modules 'jdk.unsupported,jdk.management'*

The update, as shown in the Project Run launch configuration properties, now gives the output for the two keywords as follows (without any runtime errors), as shown in *Figure 8.21*:

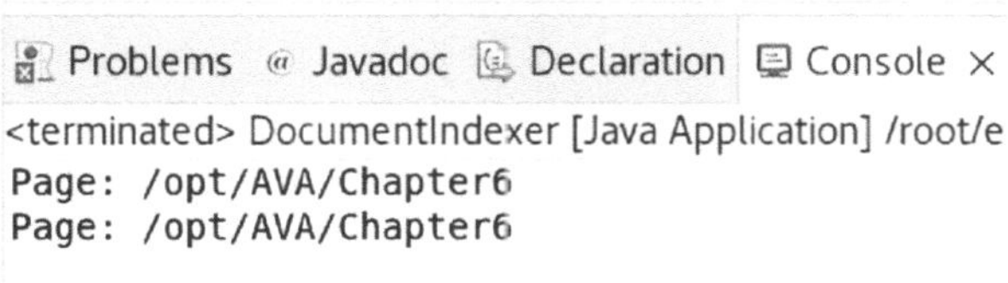

***Figure 8.21**: The output is shown for the keywords*

This is as expected, given the code:

```
for (ScoreDoc scoreDoc : topDocs.scoreDocs) {
  Document document = indexSearcher.doc(scoreDoc.doc);
  System.out.println("Page: " + document.get("path"));
}
```

But it isn't very useful to us!

We can also see that we have the following **Lucene** indexing files created in the index directory, as shown in *Figure 8.22*:

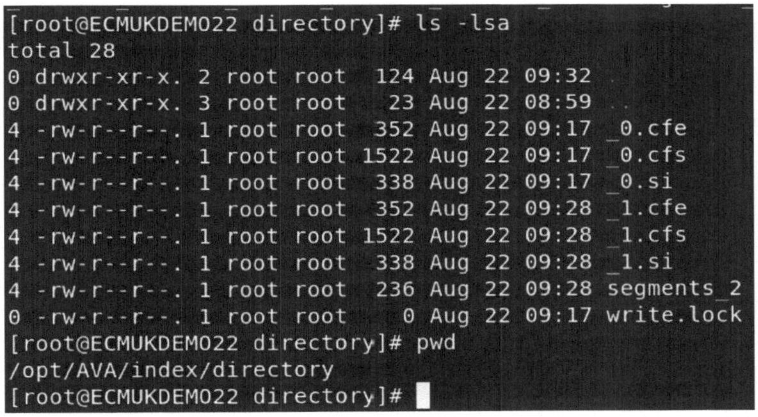

***Figure 8.22**: The **Lucene** index files are generated by the **DocumentIndexer Java** program*

The **LuceneSearcher** code also had the **JVM** arguments added as highlighted in *Figure 8.23*:

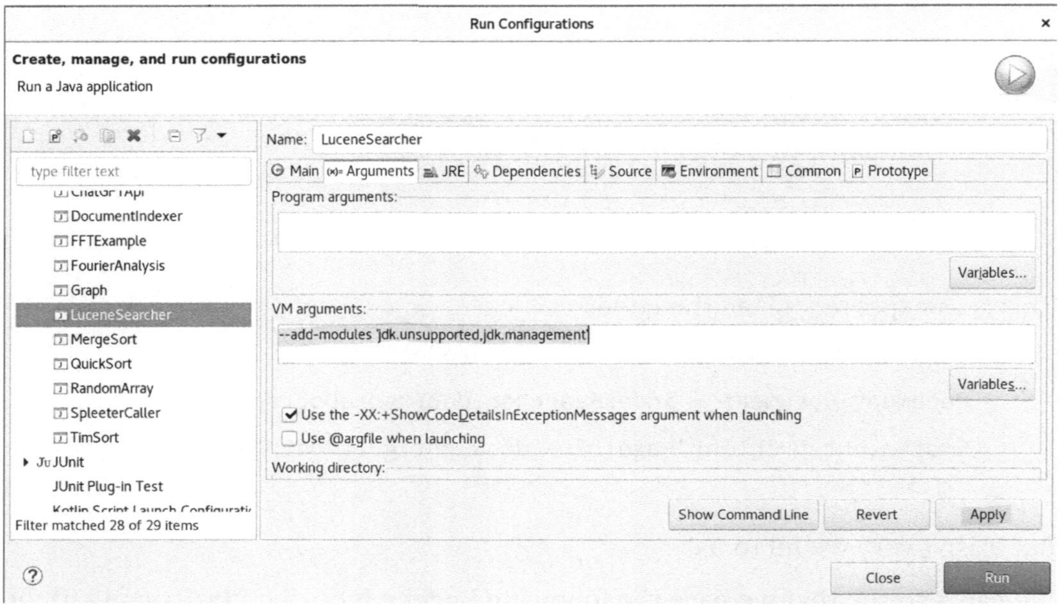

***Figure 8.23**: The LuceneSearcher code also had the JVM arguments added as highlighted*

We decided to add another set of documents to enhance the test data set:

```
[root@ECMUKDEMO22 Chapter6]# cp /mnt/hgfs/Installs/136_01_Accepted_ASB.docx .
[root@ECMUKDEMO22 Chapter6]# cp /mnt/hgfs/Installs/136_02_Accepted_SB.docx .
[root@ECMUKDEMO22 Chapter6]# cp /mnt/hgfs/Installs/136_03_Accepted_SG.docx .
[root@ECMUKDEMO22 Chapter6]# cp /mnt/hgfs/Installs/136_04_Accepted_SB.docx .
Then, we also reconfigured the process directories as follows:
[root@ECMUKDEMO22 AVA]# mv Chapter6 Chapters
[root@ECMUKDEMO22 AVA]# pwd
/opt/AVA
[root@ECMUKDEMO22 AVA]# cd Chapters
[root@ECMUKDEMO22 Chapters]# ls
136_01_Accepted_ASB.docx  136_02_Accepted_SB.docx  136_03_Accepted_SG.docx
136_04_Accepted_SB.docx  136_6_PD_ASB.docx
[root@ECMUKDEMO22 Chapters]# mkdir chapter1
[root@ECMUKDEMO22 Chapters]# mkdir chapter2
[root@ECMUKDEMO22 Chapters]# mkdir chapter3
```

```
[root@ECMUKDEMO22 Chapters]# mkdir chapter4
[root@ECMUKDEMO22 Chapters]# mkdir chapter6
[root@ECMUKDEMO22 Chapters]# mv 136_01_Accepted_ASB.docx ./chapter1/
[root@ECMUKDEMO22 Chapters]# mv 136_02_Accepted_SB.docx ./chapter2/
[root@ECMUKDEMO22 Chapters]# mv 136_03_Accepted_SG.docx ./chapter3/
[root@ECMUKDEMO22 Chapters]# mv 136_04_Accepted_SB.docx ./chapter4/
[root@ECMUKDEMO22 Chapters]# mv 136_6_PD_ASB.docx ./chapter6/
```

These additional documents just gave the following output:

```
Page: /opt/AVA/Chapter6
Page: /opt/AVA/Chapter6
Page: /opt/AVA/Chapter6
Page: /opt/AVA/Chapter6
Page: /opt/AVA/Chapters
Page: /opt/AVA/Chapters/chapter1
Page: /opt/AVA/Chapters/chapter1
```

We then changed the code to add the following line, which appends the index output:

```
config.setOpenMode(IndexWriterConfig.OpenMode.CREATE_OR_APPEND);
```

Finally, we realized the code (**LuceneSearcher** class) for the Lucene Search Index directory was using **text**, but we had stored **keywords**, so we changed from the original example code line:

```
QueryParser parser = new QueryParser("text", new StandardAnalyzer());
```

Which gave us:

```
Number of documents in the Index = 14
Query =text:mp3
Results =0
```

To the code:

```
QueryParser parser = new QueryParser("keyword", new StandardAnalyzer());
//ASB (Changed from text to keyword) and now we get:
Number of documents in the Index = 14
Query =keyword:mp3
Results =10
```

```
0.  doc=0 score=0.015409794 shardIndex=-1
1.  doc=1 score=0.015409794 shardIndex=-1
2.  doc=2 score=0.015409794 shardIndex=-1
3.  doc=3 score=0.015409794 shardIndex=-1
4.  doc=4 score=0.015409794 shardIndex=-1
5.  doc=5 score=0.015409794 shardIndex=-1
6.  doc=6 score=0.015409794 shardIndex=-1
7.  doc=7 score=0.015409794 shardIndex=-1
8.  doc=8 score=0.015409794 shardIndex=-1
9.  doc=9 score=0.015409794 shardIndex=-1
```

We then repeated the run using **xuggler** as the **keyword** to search, rather than the **mp3** value:

```
Number of documents in the Index = 14
Query =keyword:xuggler
Results =10
0.  doc=0 score=0.015409794 shardIndex=-1
1.  doc=1 score=0.015409794 shardIndex=-1
2.  doc=2 score=0.015409794 shardIndex=-1
3.  doc=3 score=0.015409794 shardIndex=-1
4.  doc=4 score=0.015409794 shardIndex=-1
5.  doc=5 score=0.015409794 shardIndex=-1
6.  doc=6 score=0.015409794 shardIndex=-1
7.  doc=7 score=0.015409794 shardIndex=-1
8.  doc=8 score=0.015409794 shardIndex=-1
9.  doc=9 score=0.015409794 shardIndex=-1
```

Using **jfreechart** as the **keyword** to search, rather than the **xuggler** value we get:

```
Number of documents in the Index = 14
Query =keyword:jfreechart
Results =10
0.  doc=0 score=0.015409794 shardIndex=-1
```

```
1.  doc=1 score=0.015409794 shardIndex=-1
2.  doc=2 score=0.015409794 shardIndex=-1
3.  doc=3 score=0.015409794 shardIndex=-1
4.  doc=4 score=0.015409794 shardIndex=-1
5.  doc=5 score=0.015409794 shardIndex=-1
6.  doc=6 score=0.015409794 shardIndex=-1
7.  doc=7 score=0.015409794 shardIndex=-1
8.  doc=8 score=0.015409794 shardIndex=-1
9.  doc=9 score=0.015409794 shardIndex=-1
```

Finally, using **commons** as the **keyword** to search, rather than the **jfreechart** value we get:

```
Number of documents in the Index = 14
Query =keyword:commons
Results =0
```

The preceding **commons** keyword example, just proved that only the stored keywords gave results.

Then, we tried the **BookIndexer.java** (From the **Phind** referenced link, described earlier:

https://codereview.stackexchange.com/questions/122675/program-to-index-a-book)_which gave the initial output of text from a section of the MS Word **.docx** file, as shown in *Figure* 8.24:

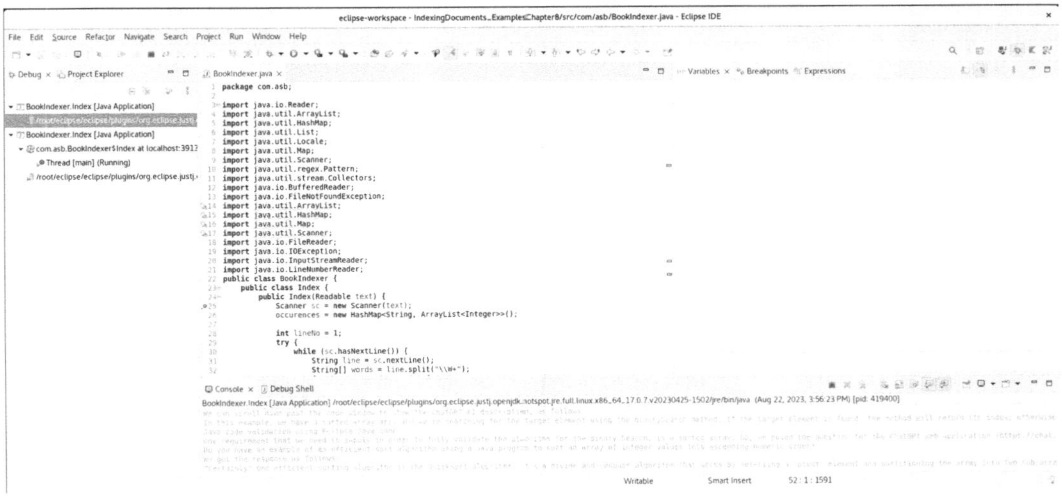

Figure 8.24: *The result using the original MS Word example file*

Next, we decided to use a simpler, text file extract, edited and then copied the text file as follows in *Figure 8.25*:

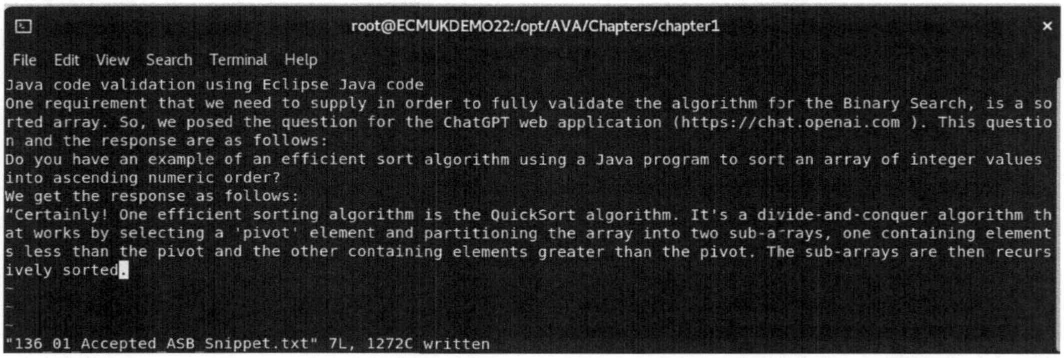

***Figure 8.25**: The Text data created for a second run of the **BookIndexer** program*

We entered the path for the new text data into the **Program arguments** of the Eclipse IDE as shown in *Figure 8.26*:

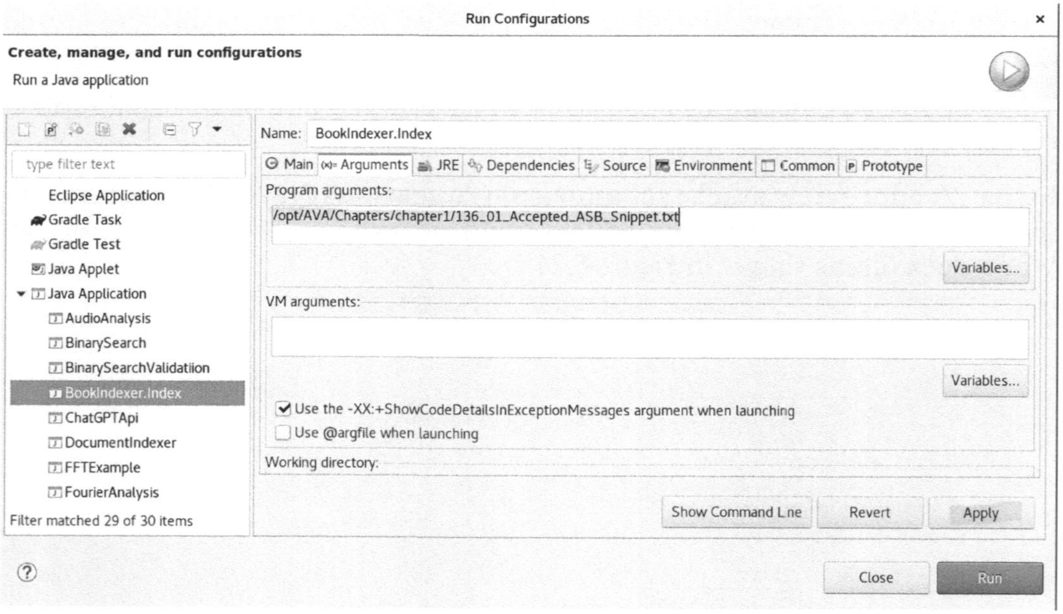

Figure 8.26**: The Text file, **`136_01_Accepted_ASB_Snippet.txt`**, and its path set for **BookIndexer

The security for the **`136_01_Accepted_ASB_Snippet.txt`** file is set as shown in the following commands:

```
[root@ECMUKDEMO22 chapter1]# chmod 775 136_01_Accepted_ASB_Snippet.txt
[root@ECMUKDEMO22 chapter1]# ls -lsa
total 14864
    0 drwxr-xr-x. 2 root root       77 Aug 23 04:06 .
    0 drwxr-xr-x. 7 root root       86 Aug 22 11:37 ..
14860 -rwxr-xr-x. 1 root root 15214049 Aug 22 10:40 136_01_Accepted_ASB.
docx
    4 -rwxrwxr-x. 1 root root     1272 Aug 23 04:05 136_01_Accepted_ASB_
Snippet.txt
[root@ECMUKDEMO22 chapter1]#
```

Running the **BookIndexer** program then gave the results as shown in *Figure 8.27*:

Figure 8.27: The Run of the **BookIndexer** *program and the* **Eclipse IDE** *Console log result*

The results from running the program were listed as follows:

```
{program=[5], supply=[4], java=[3, 3, 5], pivot=[7], greater=[7],
if=[2], you=[5], fully=[4], validation=[3], algorithm=[4, 5, 7,
7], order=[4], element=[2, 2, 2, 7], using=[2, 3, 5], method=[2,
2, 2], ).=[4], in=[2, 2, 4], containing=[7, 7], past=[1], ai=[1],
scroll=[1], is=[2, 2, 4, 7], then=[7], it=[2], an=[5, 5, 5], pivot.=[7],
sorted=[2, 4], as=[1, 4, 6], binary=[4], algorithm.=[7], 'pivot'=[7],
sorted.=[7], other=[7], works=[7], two=[7], example=[5], into=[5, 7],
so,=[4], how=[2], are=[4, 7], web=[4], by=[7], get=[6], have=[2, 5],
indicate=[2], chatgpt=[1, 4], valicate=[4], a=[2, 2, 4, 5, 7, 7],
question=[4, 4], efficient=[5, 7], follows:=[1, 4, 6], one=[4, 7, 7],
```

```
ascending=[5], sample=[2], order?=[5], the=[1, 1, 2, 2, 2, 2, 2, 2, 2,
2, 4, 4, 4, 4, 4, 6, 7, 7, 7, 7, 7, 7], elements=[7, 7], to=[1, 2, 2, 4,
4, 5], return=[2, 2], example,=[2], use=[2], otherwise,=[2], main=[2],
integer=[5], do=[5], found,=[2], down=[1], that=[2, 4, 7], sub-
arrays=[7], than=[7, 7], method.=[2], quicksort=[7], demonstrates=[2],
-1=[2], need=[4], it's=[7], divide-and-conquer=[7], this=[2, 4],
its=[2], less=[7], sort=[5, 5], posed=[4], eclipse=[3], "certainly!=[7],
binarysearch=[2, 2], we're=[2], present=[2], index;=[2], code=[1, 3,
3], arr,=[2], values=[5], provided=[2], searching=[2], for=[2, 4, 4],
show=[1], numeric=[5], description,=[1], recursively=[7], (https://chat.
openai.com=[4], we=[1, 2, 4, 4, 6], can=[1], not=[2], array=[2, 5, 7],
search,=[4], and=[2, 4, 7, 7], sorting=[7], of=[5, 5], selecting=[7],
will=[2, 2], sub-arrays,=[7], requirement=[4], target=[2, 2], with=[2],
application=[4], array.=[2, 2, 4], response=[4, 6], partitioning=[7],
window=[1]}
```

The number(s) in brackets indicate the **CR/LF** count of the line endings in the text file where the word is found. If the word is found twice on one line the line number is repeated for each occurrence. So, for example, **code[1, 3, 3]** indicates that the word "**code**" is on the first line and then appears twice on the third line. This can be clearly seen using the **notepad++** editor program with the "**show end-of-line**" **View** option selected and the **Find** search used for the "**code**" word in the text, as illustrated in *Figure* 8.28:

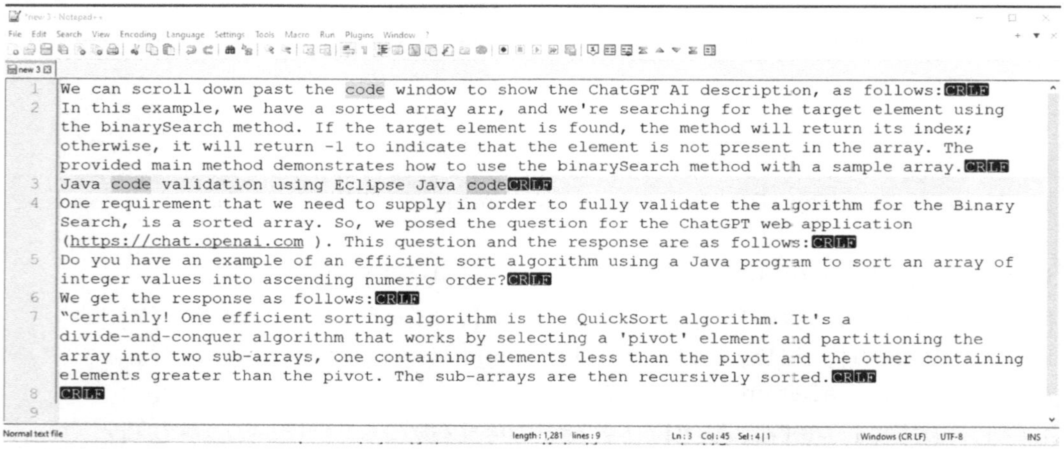

Figure 8.28**: The "**code**" word is highlighted to illustrate the program output of* ***code[1, 3, 3]

Conclusion

In this chapter, we attempted to use the **Ask AI** and **Phind AI** for **Java** code examples to index a Document. The results were a little disappointing, although we did finally get the examples running, the **BookIndexer** code came the closest but still would require a good deal of additional code to approach the output we imagined we could get, for example, with page numbers on a full **Microsoft Word** document rather than just a list at the **CR/LF** end-of-line delimiter count on a text file, that we had with the last **BookIndexer** Java code.

Of course, **Microsoft Word** has an Indexing feature built-in, see:

https://support.microsoft.com/en-us/office/create-and-update-an-index-cc502c71-a605-41fd-9a02-cda9d14bf073?ns=winword&version=16&ui=en-us&rs=en-us&ad=us

But that is still a very manual process, as you can verify by following the preceding link.

It looks like **AI** solutions have a way to go yet, to suggest Java code to provide a completely satisfactory solution.

It was interesting to search using **Google** and find that there is even an **American Society of Indexing** with a web page link **https://www.asindexing.org/reference-shelf/software/**.

Points to remember

- As mentioned previously, it is useful to try different **AI** programs to cross-check the responses to a question.
- The code provided is almost always only functional after the addition of a number of library Jar files, and some of these dependencies only become apparent after an attempt is made to run the code.
- An **AI** can also supply incorrect code, as we found when we had to replace the **text** search with the **keyword** search in the **LuceneSearcher** example, supplied by the **Phind AI**:

  ```
  QueryParser parser = new QueryParser("keyword", new StandardAnalyzer());
  ```

- Don't ignore the reference links given, some may have a better code solution like the **BookIndexer.java** we found. Also, the link sources may give an indication of any copyright limitations that are in place.

Multiple choice questions

1. **Which of the following Linux commands is used to unpack the downloaded lucene-9.7.0.tgz file?**
    a. `cp /mnt/hgfs/Installs/lucene-9.7.0.tgz .`
    b. `tar -zxvf lucene-9.7.0.tgz`
    c. `cd /root/eclipse/eclipse/AILibs`
    d. `pwd`
2. **Which of the following Lucene library jar files was not required by the `DocumentIndexer.java` program code?**
    a. `lucene-core-9.7.0.jar`
    b. `lucene-queryparser-9.7.0.jar`
    c. `lucene-misc-9.7.0.jar`
    d. `lucene-sandbox-9.7.0.jar`
3. **Which of the Eclipse IDE "Fix suggestions" was selected to correct the import error on the import `org.apache.lucene.queryparser.classic.MultiFieldQueryParser;` package?**
    a. Create class 'MultiFieldQueryParser' in package 'org.apache. lucene. queryparser.classic'
    b. Add 'requires org.apache.lucene.queryparser' to module-info.java
    c. Create interface 'MultiFieldQueryParser' in package 'org.apache. lucene. queryparser.classic'
    d. Fix project setup...
4. **In the java code for the LuceneSearcher class, `QueryParser parser = new QueryParser("text", new StandardAnalyzer());` which of the following replaced the `"text"` used, in order to obtain the correct output?**
    a. `"search"`
    b. `"xuggler"`
    c. `"mp3"`
    d. `"keyword"`
5. **The order of commands to create the Linux test directory path `/opt/AVA/index/directory/` is which one of the following?**
    a. `cd /opt then mkdir AVA then cd AVA then mkdir Chapter6 then mkdir directory`

b. `cd /opt then mkdir AVA then mkdir directory then cd directory then mkdir index`

c. `cd /opt then mkdir AVA then cd AVA then mkdir index then cd index then mkdir directory`

d. `cd /opt then mkdir directory then cd directory then mkdir AVA then cd AVA then mkdir index`

Answers

1. **b**
2. **c**
3. **b**
4. **d**
5. **c**

Questions

1. What other **AI** programs can you name besides **Ask AI** and **Phind AI**?
2. What are the main issues you can encounter when using Java code provided by an **AI** system?
3. What else could you do to enhance the output provided by the **BookIndexer** program?
4. What other examples are available using **Apache Lucene** other than keyword searching?
5. What procedure would you follow to correct an import package error in **Java** code in the **Eclipse IDE**?

Key terms

- **Apache Lucene**: Apache Lucene is a trademark of the Apache Software Foundation which provides support for open-source software projects. The Apache Lucene project consists of a set of Java Libraries supplying indexing and search features, as well as spellchecking, search word hit highlighting and advanced analysis and tokenization functions. This project, and other Apache projects, are supported by a group of software development engineers dedicated to providing software with a free-to-use software license and wishing to create high-quality software. Other projects supported are Apache Solr, Apache PyLucene and the Apache Open Relevance Project.

- **Firefox**: The **Firefox** web browser is a free, open-source program running on Windows and Linux operating systems, which was developed by the **Mozilla Foundation** and its subsidiary, the **Mozilla Corporation**. It uses the **Gecko** rendering engine to display web pages. **Gecko** was designed by **Mozilla** to support open Internet standards and is used by different applications to display web pages, including **Mozilla**'s **Thunderbird** email client program.
- **GitHub**: **GitHub** is a "cloud-based" system of servers used for the version control of software code, where a team of programmers can get access to work on large software development projects. It supports tracking and managing changes to the software code, so a team of developers can work on a Git repository and track their changes. So, every team member can access the GitHub server database simultaneously to access their previous code versions.
- **Java import package**: The **Java** language **import** keyword is used to define the access to a **package** and its classes in the **Java** program. The **import** statement gives access to the Java library class, and user-defined **packages** in the **Java** source code file so that the class defined can refer to a class that is in another **package** using the other **package** name. (In the **Eclipse IDE**, the **package** names are used to define the folder path to the **Eclipse Project** source code files. For example, the **Linux** path: **`/root/eclipse-workspace/ChatGPTAPI_ExampleChapter3/src/com/asb`** defines the **`com.asb`** **package** which has the **`ChatGPTApi.java`** source code file in the **Eclipse IDE** **`ChatGPTAPI_ExampleChapter3`** project). By convention, **package** names are given a corporation or company reversed Internet domain name to begin their package names as for example, **`com.ibm`**. (I used **`com.asb`**, my website is **`https://asb-software.com`**, but **`com.asb`** was shorter than using the full **`com.asb-software`** for the book examples)
- **Java Jar**: **JAR** stands for **J**ava **AR**chive. It's a compressed file format like the **ZIP** file format used for the compression of separate **JVM** byte-coded and source **Java** files into one file, which can then be more easily incorporated into the class path for access by a **JVM** (Java Virtual Machine) used to run the programs.
- **Microsoft Edge**: Microsoft Edge is the default browser for the Windows 10 operating system, providing similar functions to Firefox and Chrome web browsers.
- **Phind**: We asked the AI for the definition: "**What is Phind**" was asked:

"Phind is an AI-powered search engine designed specifically for developers and to handle technical questions. It's been described as an intelligent assistant for programmers, that can provide answers to queries within seconds, potentially saving hours of manual searching [Source 2](**https://www.ycombinator.com/companies/phind**).

It uses large AI language models to generate answers based on information from the internet, but it differentiates itself by using multiple sources. This allows Phind to determine what information is useful and to present relevant snippets to assist the user [Source 3](**https://medium.com/codex/what-is-phind-ae78b8977351**).

The technology behind Phind is reportedly smart enough to proactively ask users questions to clarify its assumptions and to browse the web (or your codebase) when it needs additional context [Source 2](**https://www.ycombinator.com/companies/phind**). This makes it a potentially powerful tool for debugging code and troubleshooting programming issues.

As an example, consider a scenario where you're facing an error in your code. You can input your error message into Phind, and it will attempt to find the most relevant solutions from various sources. If the initial results are not helpful, you can provide more specific information or code snippets, and Phind will refine its search accordingly [Source 3](**https://medium.com/codex/what-is-phind-ae78b8977351**).

In essence, Phind aims to be a more intuitive and efficient alternative to traditional search engines when it comes to coding and programming queries. It's an interesting development in the field of AI and could prove to be a valuable asset for developers."

CHAPTER 9

ChatGPT-generated Java Code for Saltikov Particle Distribution

Introduction

ChatGPT was prompted to provide **Java** code for the **Saltikov** determination of the size distribution of particles in an opaque material from a measurement of the size distribution of their sections.

This code generated by **ChatGPT** prompted the user to input the number of sections measured, the size of each section, and the area under the curve. It then calculated the particle size distribution using the **Saltikov** determination and printed the results.

Structure

In this chapter, we will discuss the following topics:

- **ChatGPT-**generated Java code for the **Saltikov** determination of the size distribution of particles
- **Saltikov** determination of the particle's size distribution - Java code validation using a new Eclipse IDE Project.

ChatGPT-generated Java code for the Saltikov determination of the size distribution of particles

We asked the mobile 'phone, **Ask AI app** a question that assists with the analysis of freeze-dried particles measured using microscopes by examining slide sections.

See: **https://link.springer.com/chapter/10.1007/978-3-642-88260-9_31**

Saltikov, S.A. (1967). The Determination of the Size Distribution of Particles in an Opaque Material from a Measurement of the Size Distribution of Their Sections. In: Elias, H. (eds) Stereology. Springer, Berlin, Heidelberg. **https://doi.org/10.1007/978-3-642-88260-9_31**

There is also a detailed article discussing this and other techniques, which can be read online, or also available as a free downloadable PDF, by clicking on the pdf icon at the top of the page:

https://onlinelibrary.wiley.com/doi/full/10.1111/maps.12812

("**Recovering 3D particle size distributions from 2D sections**" by Jeffrey N. CUZZI, and Daniel M. OLSON)

Note

In the article above, by **JN Cuzzi** and **DM Olson**, they spell **Saltikov** as **Saltykov**.:

The question we asked the mobile 'phone app, **Ask AI**, was as follows:

Do you have java code for the analysis of the Saltikov determination of the size distribution of particles in an opaque material from a measurement of the size distribution of their sections?

"Yes, I can provide you with a Java code for the Saltikov determination of the size distribution of particles in an opaque material from a measurement of the size distribution of their sections. Please note that this code is provided for educational purposes only and should be used at your own risk.

Here's the Java code:

```
```java
import java.util.Scanner;


public class Saltikov {


    public static void main(String[] args) {
```
```

```
        Scanner scanner = new Scanner(System.in);

        // Get the number of sections measured
        System.out.print("Enter the number of sections measured: ");
        int n = scanner.nextInt();

        // Get the section size measurements
        double[] sizes = new double[n];
        for (int i = 0; i < n; i++) {
            System.out.print("Enter the size of section " + (i+1) + " in
                    micrometers: ");
            sizes[i] = scanner.nextDouble();
        }

        // Get the area under the curve
        System.out.print("Enter the area under the curve: ");
        double area = scanner.nextDouble();

        // Calculate the particle size distribution
        double[] distribution = new double[n];
        for (int i = 0; i < n; i++) {
            double x = sizes[i];
            double y = area / sizes[i];
            distribution[i] = y * Math.exp(-2 * y * x);
        }

        // Print the particle size distribution
        System.out.println("\nParticle size distribution:");
        for (int i = 0; i < n; i++) {
            System.out.println(String.format("%.2f", sizes[i]) + " um: "
                        + String.format("%.2f", distribution[i]));
        }
    }
}
```

This code prompts the user to input the number of sections measured, the size of each section, and the area under the curve. It then calculates the particle size distribution using the Saltikov determination and prints the results.

Note that this code assumes that the size measurements are in micrometers and that the area under the curve is in square micrometers. If your inputs are in different units, you will need to modify the code accordingly."

Analyzing this first **Java** code listing that was provided, we noticed the following:

1. There was a minor issue, in that the scanner I/O had no close method called at the end of the code, so we added the following line as the last Java statement:

```
            //ASB We correct the warning by closing the scanner input
            scanner.close();
        }
    }
```

2. Looking at the section of code which calculates the distribution of the particles:

   We added the comments shown in *Figure 9.1*:

```
// Calculate the particle size distribution
double[] distribution = new double[n];
for (int i = 0; i < n; i++) {
    double x = sizes[i];
    double y = area / sizes[i];           //ASB This makes 2 * x * y which is used later a constant value of 2 * area
    double z = 2.0f * y * x;              //ASB Which makes the calculated distribution a constant value independent of
                                          //ASB each of the section particle sizes.
                                          //ASB The distribution is therefore a constant value just dependent on the area entered
    System.out.println("y =" + y + ", x=" + x + " 2.0f * y * x =" +z ); //ASB Debug added here
    distribution[i] = Math.exp(-2.0f * y * x);
}
```

***Figure 9.1**: The comments and debug code line added for analysis*

This can be seen to calculate a value for the distribution of the particles which is independent of the actual slices added and effectively proportional to Exp (2 * the area entered).

The response was updated a month later, by repeating the same question to Ask AI, as follows:

"Certainly! Below is an example of Java code for analyzing the Saltikov determination of the size distribution of particles in an opaque material from a measurement of the size distribution of their sections. Please note that this code provides a basic implementation and may require customization based on your specific requirements and input data format.

```
```java
import java.util.ArrayList;
```
```

```
import java.util.List;

public class SaltikovParticleSizeAnalysis {

    public static void main(String[] args) {
        // Example input data - section size distribution
        List<Double> sectionSizes = new ArrayList<>();
        sectionSizes.add(0.5);
        sectionSizes.add(1.0);
        sectionSizes.add(1.5);
        sectionSizes.add(2.0);
        sectionSizes.add(2.5);
        sectionSizes.add(3.0);

        // Parameters for Saltikov determination
        double thickness = 0.1; // Thickness of the material
        double shapeFactor = 0.9; // Shape factor for the particles

        // Perform Saltikov determination
        List<Double> particleSizes =
calculateParticleSizes(sectionSizes, thickness, shapeFactor);

        // Output the results
        System.out.println("Particle Size Distribution:");
        for (double size : particleSizes) {
            System.out.println(size);
        }
    }

    /**
     * Calculates the particle size distribution based on the Saltikov
determination.
     *
     * @param sectionSizes   List of section sizes
     * @param thickness      Thickness of the material
```

```
     * @param shapeFactor    Shape factor for the particles
     * @return List of particle sizes
     */
    public static List<Double> calculateParticleSizes(List<Double>
sectionSizes, double thickness, double shapeFactor) {
        List<Double> particleSizes = new ArrayList<>();

        for (double sectionSize : sectionSizes) {
            // Calculate the particle size using the Saltikov
determination formula
            double particleSize = Math.sqrt((8 * thickness *
sectionSize) / (Math.PI * shapeFactor));
            particleSizes.add(particleSize);
        }

        return particleSizes;
    }
}"
```

This was an improvement on the first response, since it does include the section thickness and the particle shape factors and supplies some example test data to use. However, from having written a real-world application in **Fortran,** we were aware that a triangular matrix inversion of the polynomial coefficients was required to obtain a solution, so we asked **Ask AI** the following question in the same thread:

Does the Java program code suggested include a matrix inversion to obtain the particle size distribution?

This additional question prompted **Ask AI** to extend the code given with the response:

"Apologies for the confusion. The Java program code provided in the previous response does not include a matrix inversion step. It simply calculates the particle sizes based on the Saltikov determination formula.

If you need to perform matrix inversion as part of your particle size distribution analysis, you would need to incorporate additional code to handle the matrix inversion operation. Java does not have a built-in matrix inversion method in its standard library, so you would either need to implement the matrix inversion algorithm yourself or use a third-party library that provides matrix manipulation capabilities.

Here's an example of how you could modify the code to include a matrix inversion step using the Apache Commons Math library:

```
```java
import org.apache.commons.math3.linear.Array2DRowRealMatrix;
import org.apache.commons.math3.linear.MatrixUtils;
import org.apache.commons.math3.linear.RealMatrix;
import org.apache.commons.math3.linear.SingularMatrixException;

import java.util.ArrayList;
import java.util.List;

public class SaltikovParticleSizeAnalysis {

    public static void main(String[] args) {
        // Example input data - section size distribution
        List<Double> sectionSizes = new ArrayList<>();
        sectionSizes.add(0.5);
        sectionSizes.add(1.0);
        sectionSizes.add(1.5);
        sectionSizes.add(2.0);
        sectionSizes.add(2.5);
        sectionSizes.add(3.0);

        // Parameters for Saltikov determination
        double thickness = 0.1; // Thickness of the material
        double shapeFactor = 0.9; // Shape factor for the particles

        // Perform Saltikov determination
        List<Double> particleSizes =
calculateParticleSizes(sectionSizes, thickness, shapeFactor);

        // Output the results
        System.out.println("Particle Size Distribution:");
        for (double size : particleSizes) {
            System.out.println(size);
```
```

```
        }
    }

    /**
     * Calculates the particle size distribution based on the Saltikov
determination.
     *
     * @param sectionSizes List of section sizes
     * @param thickness Thickness of the material
     * @param shapeFactor Shape factor for the particles
     * @return List of particle sizes
     */
    public static List<Double> calculateParticleSizes(List<Double>
sectionSizes, double thickness, double shapeFactor) {
        int n = sectionSizes.size();

        // Create the matrix A
        double[][] aData = new double[n][n];
        for (int i = 0; i < n; i++) {
            for (int j = 0; j < n; j++) {
                aData[i][j] = Math.pow(sectionSizes.get(i), 2 * j + 1);
            }
        }
        RealMatrix aMatrix = new Array2DRowRealMatrix(aData);

        // Create the vector b
        double[] bData = new double[n];
        for (int i = 0; i < n; i++) {
            bData[i] = Math.pow(sectionSizes.get(i), 2 * n + 1);
        }
        RealMatrix bVector = MatrixUtils.createColumnRealMatrix(bData);

        try {
            // Perform matrix inversion to solve for x
            RealMatrix xMatrix = MatrixUtils.inverse(aMatrix).
```

```
multiply(bVector);

            // Extract the particle sizes from the solution vector x
            double[] x
```

This is all very impressive, but unfortunately the **Java** code was clearly truncated, so we guessed that we had reached a cut-off of the free tokens available.

We then tried the question as follows:

> **The code stopped just after the comment**
>
> **//Extract the particle sizes from the solution vector X**
>
> **Is there any more**

Which, unfortunately, was the fourth question for the day, so we got the response as shown in *Figure* 9.2:

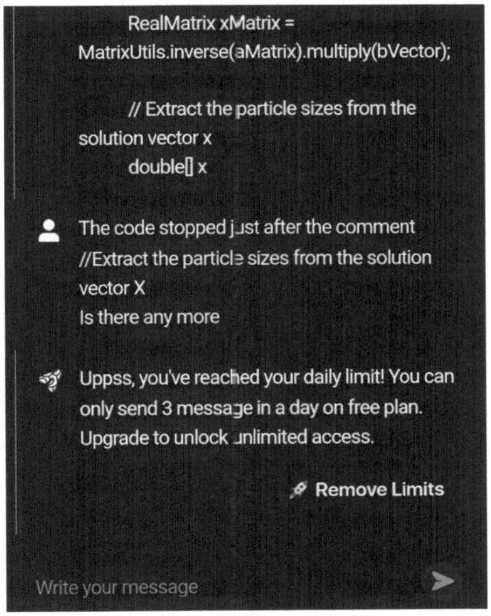

***Figure* 9.2**: *The response after the 3rd question from our free version of* **Ask AI**

Fortunately, **Ask AI** keeps a list of the previous conversation threads, so the next day, the first question of the previous day's response was selected and we just asked the previous day's fourth question again and we were rewarded with the rest of the missing **Java** code, as in the following dialogue:

> **The code stopped just after the comment**
>
> **//Extract the particle sizes from the solution vector X**
>
> **Is there any more**

Apologies for the incomplete response. Here's the complete code snippet, including the extraction of particle sizes from the solution vector `xMatrix`:

````
```java
            // Extract the particle sizes from the solution vector x
            double[] xData = xMatrix.getColumn(0);
            List<Double> particleSizes = new ArrayList<>();
            for (double value : xData) {
                double particleSize = Math.sqrt((8 * thickness * value)
/ (Math.PI * shapeFactor));
                particleSizes.add(particleSize);
            }

            return particleSizes;
        } catch (SingularMatrixException e) {
            // Matrix inversion failed due to a singular matrix
            System.out.println("Matrix inversion failed. The section
sizes may not be suitable for analysis.");
            return null;
        }
    }
}
````

Next, we logged into our **ChatGPT** account (**https://chat.openai.com/**) and repeated the question, as shown in *Figure* 9.3:

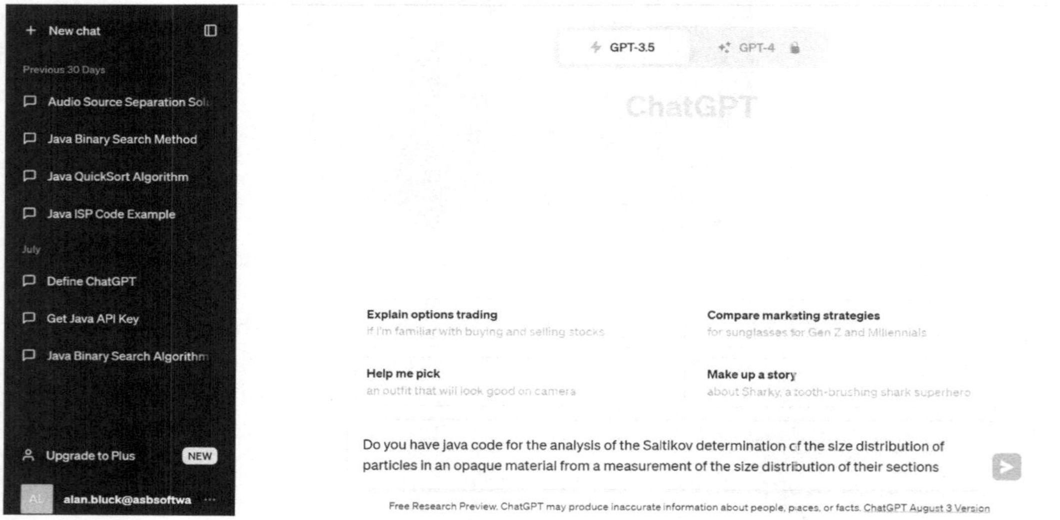

Figure 9.3**: The **Saltikov** determination for particle-size distribution **Java** code is asked of **ChatGPT 3.5
````

Using the **ChatGPT 3.5 AI**-trained version we had a much more detailed response illustrated as follows in *Figure* 9.4:

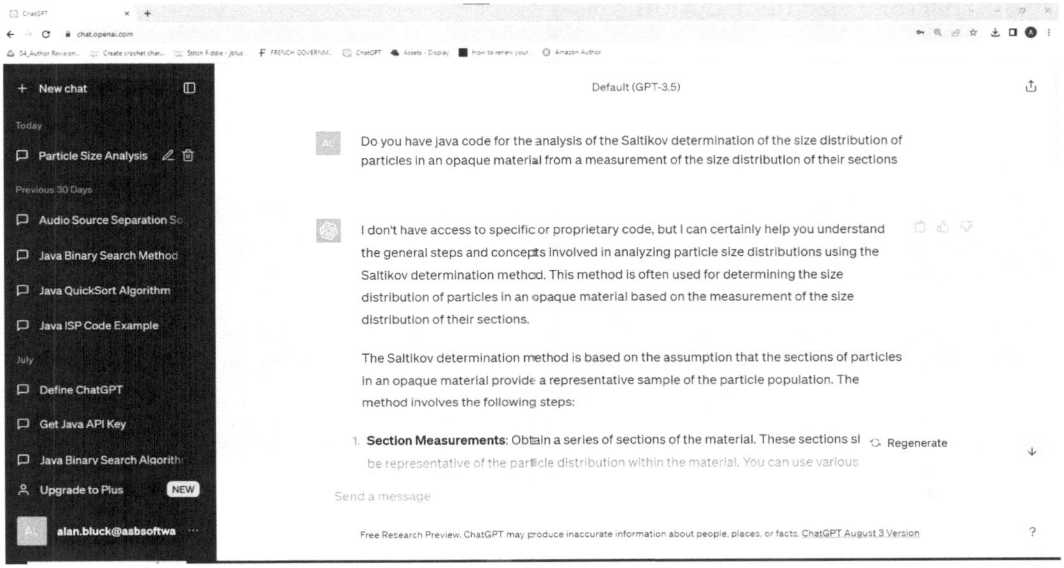

***Figure* 9.4**: *The **Saltikov** determination for particle-size distribution **Java**, with the **ChatGPT** response*

"I don't have access to specific or proprietary code, but I can certainly help you understand the general steps and concepts involved in analyzing particle size distributions using the Saltikov determination method. This method is often used for determining the size distribution of particles in an opaque material based on the measurement of the size distribution of their sections.

The Saltikov determination method is based on the assumption that the sections of particles in an opaque material provide a representative sample of the particle population. The method involves the following steps:

1. **Section Measurements:** Obtain a series of sections of the material. These sections should be representative of the particle distribution within the material. You can use various imaging techniques such as microscopy or imaging software to measure the sizes of these sections.

2. **Size Distribution Calculation:** Calculate the size distribution of the sections. This involves creating a histogram or frequency distribution of the measured section sizes. This distribution represents the observed sizes of the particle sections.

3. **Statistical Corrections:** Due to the projection effect (larger particles are more likely to be intersected by the section plane), the observed section

sizes do not directly correspond to the actual particle sizes. Statistical corrections are applied to the observed distribution to estimate the true particle size distribution.

4. **Inversion:** The observed section size distribution is then mathematically inverted to obtain an estimate of the true particle size distribution. This inversion process typically involves solving an integral equation.
5. **Normalization:** Ensure that the obtained particle size distribution is properly normalized so that the integral of the distribution over all sizes is equal to one. This step is necessary to ensure that the distribution accurately represents the particle population.
6. **Interpretation:** Analyze the resulting particle size distribution to extract information about the material's particle population, such as the mean particle size, standard deviation, and other relevant parameters.

Here's a simplified example of how you might approach this concept in Java:

````
```java
import java.util.ArrayList;
import java.util.List;

public class ParticleSizeAnalysis {
    public static void main(String[] args) {
        // Simulated observed section sizes
        List<Double> observedSectionSizes = new ArrayList<>();
        observedSectionSizes.add(10.0);
        observedSectionSizes.add(15.0);
        observedSectionSizes.add(20.0);
        // ... Add more observed section sizes

        // Calculate the observed section size distribution (histogram)
        int[] observedDistribution =
calculateHistogram(observedSectionSizes);

        // Apply statistical corrections and inversion
        double[] trueParticleSizeDistribution =
applyCorrectionAndInversion(observedDistribution);

        // Normalize the true particle size distribution
````
````

```
        normalizeDistribution(trueParticleSizeDistribution);

        // Print or analyze the results
        for (int i = 0; i < trueParticleSizeDistribution.length; i++) {
            System.out.println("Particle Size: " + i + ", Distribution:
" + trueParticleSizeDistribution[i]);
        }
    }

    // Simplified histogram calculation
    private static int[] calculateHistogram(List<Double> sizes) {
        int[] histogram = new int[100];
        for (Double size : sizes) {
            int index = (int) (size / 1.0); // Adjust bin size as needed
            histogram[index]++;
        }
        return histogram;
    }

    // Simplified statistical correction and inversion
    private static double[] applyCorrectionAndInversion(int[]
observedDistribution) {
        // Apply statistical corrections and inversion algorithm
        double[] trueDistribution = new double[100];
        // ... Apply corrections and inversion logic
        return trueDistribution;
    }

    // Simplified normalization
    private static void normalizeDistribution(double[] distribution) {
        double total = 0;
        for (double value : distribution) {
            total += value;
        }
        for (int i = 0; i < distribution.length; i++) {
```

~~~
                distribution[i] /= total;
            }
        }
    }
```
~~~

Please note that this example is highly simplified and doesn't include the actual correction and inversion algorithms, as they can be quite complex. The code also assumes a fixed number of bins for the histogram and doesn't handle potential edge cases or errors that might arise in a real-world scenario. In practice, you would likely need to use specialized libraries for numerical computations and potentially consult research papers or experts in the field for more accurate algorithms and methods."

Although it appears to be more code, and the second explanation is more verbose, the **Java** supplied by the **OpenAI ChatGPT** web application, is not as useful as the **Ask AI** code, which does seem to provide a working program.

Next, I asked the **Phind AI** we have used earlier, the same initial question, which also gave a detailed response, but with no useful **Java** code:

"Based on the search results, I couldn't find any specific Java code for the analysis of the Saltikov determination of the size distribution of particles in an opaque material from a measurement of the size distribution of their sections. However, I can provide you with an outline of the steps involved in this analysis and some relevant information that can help you implement the code:

1. Understand the Saltikov Determination Method:

   - The Saltikov determination method is based on the principle that the distribution of random cross-sectional areas of any body depends only on its shape[^3^].

   - The method is applicable to both spherical and non-spherical particles[^3^].

   - The proposed method is simple and less elaborate compared to other procedures[^3^].

2. Obtain the size distribution of the sections:

   - You need to measure the size distribution of the sections of the particles in the opaque material.

   - This can be done using imaging techniques such as microscopy or other measurement methods.

   - Store the size distribution data in a suitable format, such as an array or a list.

3. Implement the Saltikov determination algorithm:

   - Use the size distribution of the sections to determine the size distribution of the particles.

   - The exact algorithm will depend on the specific details of the Saltikov method, which are not available in the search results.

   - However, you can refer to the research papers listed in the search results, such as the paper by Saltikov[^2^], for more details on the algorithm.

4. Write the Java code:

   - Based on your understanding of the Saltikov determination method, implement the algorithm in Java.

   - Use appropriate data structures and algorithms to process the size distribution data and calculate the particle size distribution.

   - You may need to use statistical methods or mathematical calculations to analyze the data.

Here's an example of how the code structure might look like:

```java
public class SaltikovParticleSizeAnalysis {
    public static void main(String[] args) {
        // Step 2: Obtain the size distribution of the sections
        double[] sectionSizes = { /* Array of section sizes */ };

        // Step 3: Implement the Saltikov determination algorithm
        double[] particleSizes = calculateParticleSizes(sectionSizes);

        // Print the particle size distribution
        for (double size : particleSizes) {
            System.out.println(size);
        }
    }

    private static double[] calculateParticleSizes(double[]
sectionSizes) {
        // Implement the Saltikov determination algorithm here
        // Use the sectionSizes array to calculate the particle size
```

```
distribution
        // Return the particle size distribution as an array
    }
}
```

Please note that the above code is just a basic outline and you will need to fill in the details of the Saltikov determination algorithm based on the specific requirements of your analysis."

Microsoft Bing didn't even attempt to give us any **Java** code, as shown in **Figure 9.5:**

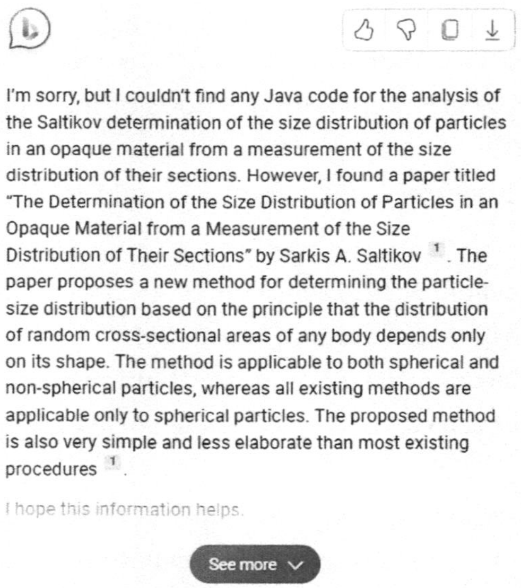

***Figure 9.5**: The response from Microsoft Bing was a little disappointing!*

"I'm sorry, but I couldn't find any Java code for the analysis of the Saltikov determination of the size distribution of particles in an opaque material from a measurement of the size distribution of their sections. However, I found a paper titled "The Determination of the Size Distribution of Particles in an Opaque Material from a Measurement of the Size Distribution of Their Sections" by Sarkis A. **Saltikov** [1]. The paper proposes a new method for determining the particle-size distribution based on the principle that the distribution of random cross-sectional areas of any body depends only on its shape. The method is applicable to both spherical and non-spherical particles, whereas all existing methods are applicable only to spherical particles. **The proposed method is also very simple and less elaborate than most existing procedures** [1].

I hope this information helps."

To be fair, this response did give us the link marked with superscript[1] above, which we have referenced at the beginning of the chapter **(https://link.springer.com/chapter/10.1007/978-3-642-88260-9_31).**

Saltikov determination of the particle's size distribution - Java code validation using a new Eclipse IDE Project

The next step is to validate the responses and select the most accurate **Java** code from the various responses supplied by the **ChatGPT AI** client platforms. A new **Eclipse IDE** chapter project is created using the **File -> New-> Java Project** menu as highlighted in *Figure 9.6*:

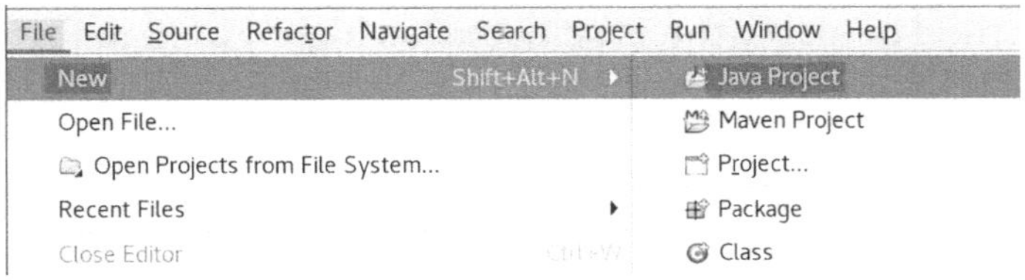

Figure 9.6**: A new **Java Project** is created using the **Eclipse IDE

The **SaltikovParticleDistribution_ExamplesChapter9** project name is entered and the **Finish** button is selected as shown in *Figure 9.7*:

***Figure 9.7**: The **SaltikovParticleDistribution_ExamplesChapter9** project name is entered*

A new class is created by right-mouse clicking the new project node and selecting the pop-up menu items with **New-> Class**, as shown in *Figure 9.8*:

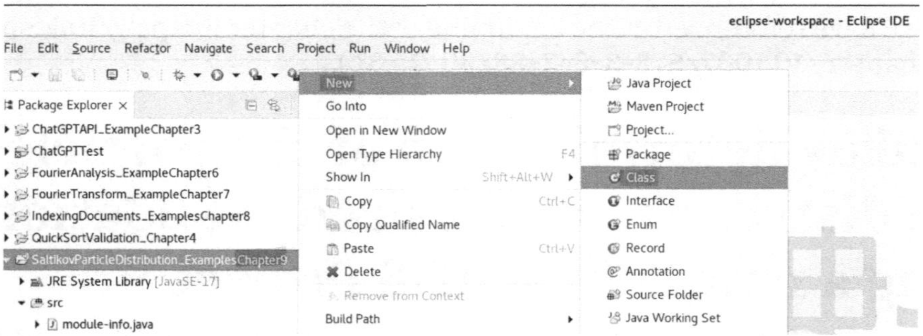

Figure 9.8**: A new class is created by right-mouse clicking the new project node and selecting the pop-up menu items with **New-> Class

The package name, **com.asb**, and the class name of **Saltikov** are added for the new class and the **Finish** button is selected, as highlighted in *Figure 9.9*:

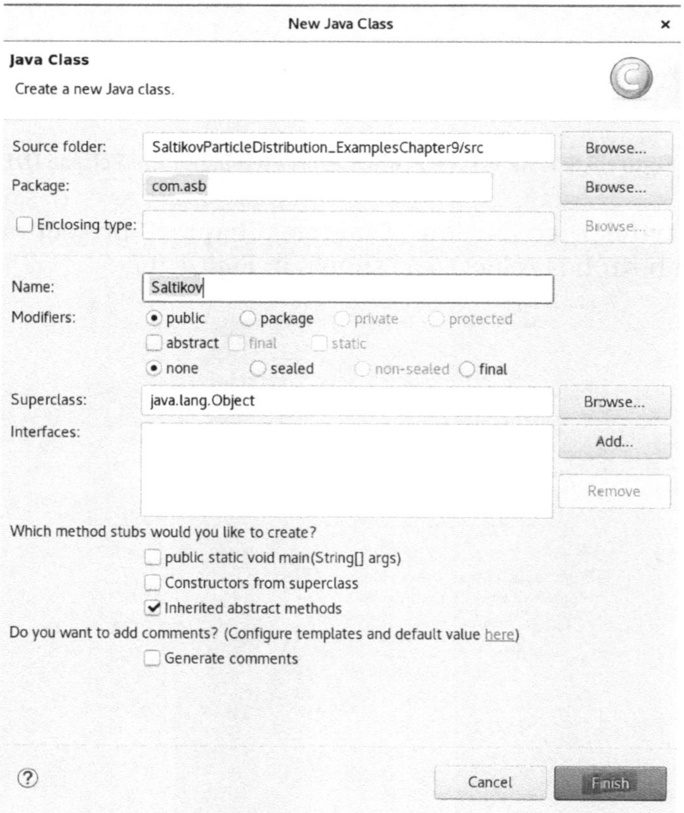

***Figure 9.9**: The package name, **com.asb**, and the class name of **Saltikov** are added*

The Java code is pasted from the first listing presented by **Ask AI,** as shown in *Figure 9.10.*

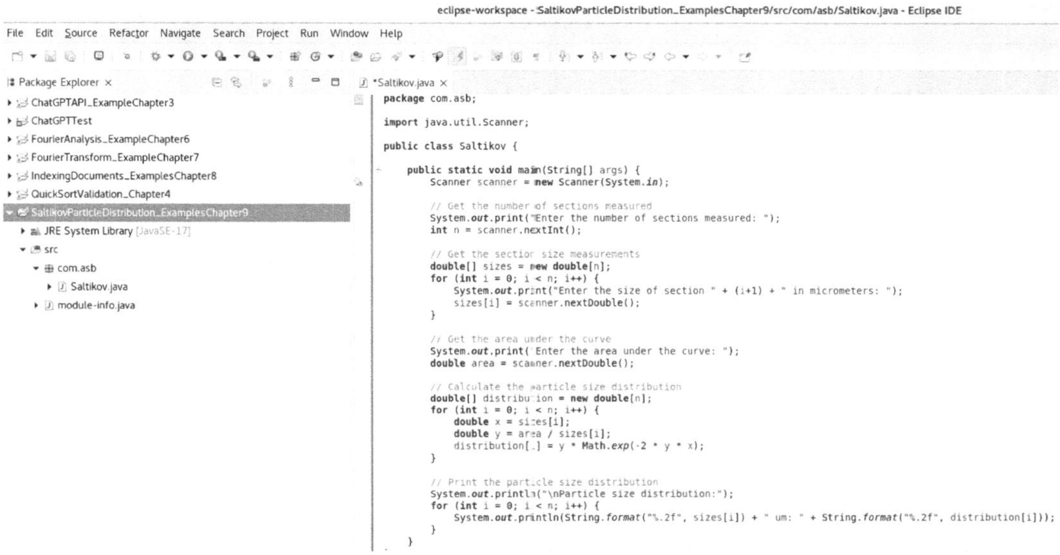

Figure 9.10: *The* ***Ask AI*** *Java code is pasted into the Skeleton class structure*

We notice a warning on the Scanner object used to read values from the IDE console input stream, as shown in *Figure 9.11*:

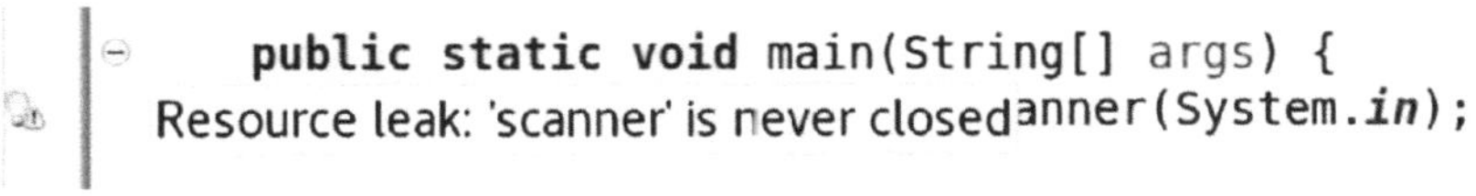

Figure 9.11: *The Scanner object has a warning flag from the* ***Java*** *compiler*

The final code we used for the first code validation is listed as follows:

```
package com.asb;
import java.util.Scanner;


public class Saltikov {


    public static void main(String[] args) {
        Scanner scanner = new Scanner(System.in);


        // Get the number of sections measured
```

```
        System.out.print("Enter the number of sections measured: ");
        int n = scanner.nextInt();

        // Get the section size measurements
        double[] sizes = new double[n];
        for (int i = 0; i < n; i++) {
            System.out.print("Enter the size of section " + (i+1) + " in
micrometers: ");
            sizes[i] = scanner.nextDouble();
        }

        // Get the area under the curve
        System.out.print("Enter the area under the curve: ");
        double area = scanner.nextDouble();
        System.out.println("Enter the area under the curve: =" + area);
        // Calculate the particle size distribution
        double[] distribution = new double[n];
        for (int i = 0; i < n; i++) {
            double x = sizes[i];
            double y = area / sizes[i];           //ASB This makes 2 * x
* y which is used later a constant value of 2 * area
            double z = 2.0f * y * x;              //ASB Which makes the
calculated distribution a constant value independent of
                                                  //ASB each of the
section particle sizes.
                                                  //ASB The distribution
is therefore a constant value just dependent on the area entered
            System.out.println("y =" + y + ", x=" + x + " 2.0f * y * x
=" +z ); //ASB Debug added here
            distribution[i] = Math.exp(-2.0f * y * x);
        }

        // Print the particle size distribution
        System.out.println("\nParticle size distribution:");
        for (int i = 0; i < n; i++) {
            System.out.println(String.format("%.2f", sizes[i]) + " um: "
```

```
+ String.format("%.8f", distribution[i]));
        }
        //ASB We correct the warning by closing the scanner input
        scanner.close();
    }
}
```

We tested the code above by entering the values as follows, highlighted in green:

```
Enter the number of sections measured: 6
Enter the size of section 1 in micrometers: 0.5
Enter the size of section 2 in micrometers: 1.0
Enter the size of section 3 in micrometers: 1.5
Enter the size of section 4 in micrometers: 2.0
Enter the size of section 5 in micrometers: 2.5
Enter the size of section 6 in micrometers: 3.0
Enter the area under the curve: 0.001
Enter the area under the curve: =0.001
y =0.002, x=0.5 2.0f * y * x =0.002
y =0.001, x=1.0 2.0f * y * x =0.002
y =6.666666666666666E-4, x=1.5 2.0f * y * x =0.002
y =5.0E-4, x=2.0 2.0f * y * x =0.002
y =4.0E-4, x=2.5 2.0f * y * x =0.002
y =3.333333333333333E-4, x=3.0 2.0f * y * x =0.002

Particle size distribution:
0.50 um: 0.99800200
1.00 um: 0.99800200
1.50 um: 0.99800200
2.00 um: 0.99800200
2.50 um: 0.99800200
3.00 um: 0.99800200
```

We repeated the **Eclipse IDE** class creation for the second **Java** code example given, as shown in *Figure* 9.8 through to *Figure* 9.11, for the **`SaltikovParticleSizeAnalysis`** class.

This second Java example code ran without any errors, giving the output of the particle size distribution from input values as follows:

```
// Example input data - section size distribution
List<Double> sectionSizes = new ArrayList<>();
sectionSizes.add(0.5);
sectionSizes.add(1.0);
sectionSizes.add(1.5);
sectionSizes.add(2.0);
sectionSizes.add(2.5);
sectionSizes.add(3.0);

// Parameters for Saltikov determination
double thickness = 0.1; // Thickness of the material
double shapeFactor = 0.9; // Shape factor for the particles
```

Particle Size Distribution:

0.37612638903183754

0.5319230405352436

0.65147001587056

0.7522527780636751

0.84104417400672

0.9213177319235614

We then tried the final code example (renamed from **SaltikovParticleSizeAnalysis** to **SaltikovParticleSizeAnalysisV2**) that **Ask AI** suggested, which we asked it to include with the matrix inversion.

For this **Java** code to compile, we need to add the external library, **commons-math3-3.6.1.jar**, which we also used earlier in the book, to use for the **Apache Commons** math matrix manipulation code, added to the **Eclipse IDE** Project properties, as shown in *Figure* 9.12.

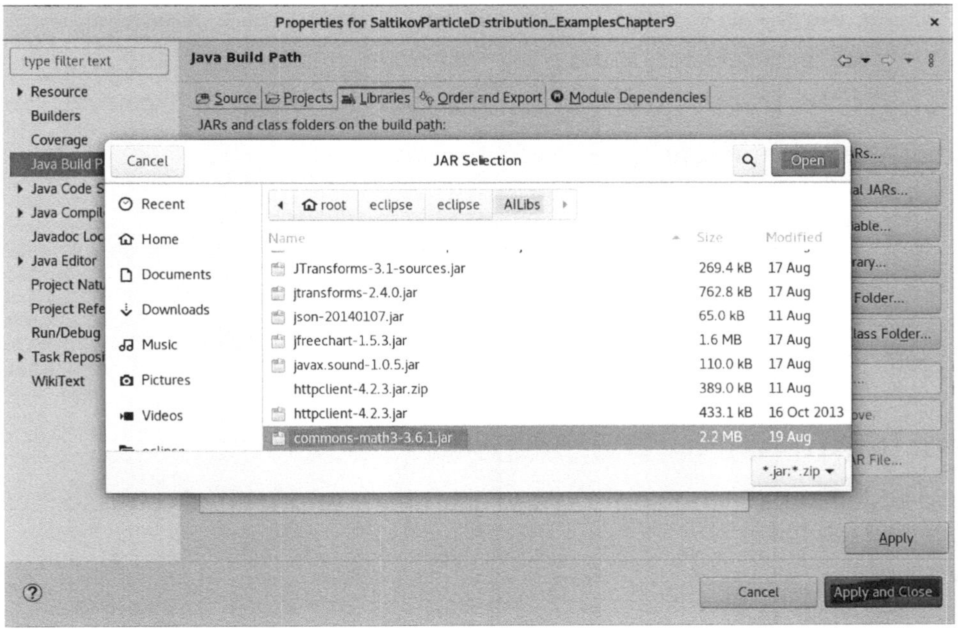

***Figure 9.12**: The **commons-math3-3.6.1.jar** Apache Commons library is added*

Then, we also needed to update the **SaltikovParticleSizeAnalysisV2.java** code import error by modifying the project **module-info.java** code as shown highlighted in **Figure 9.13**:

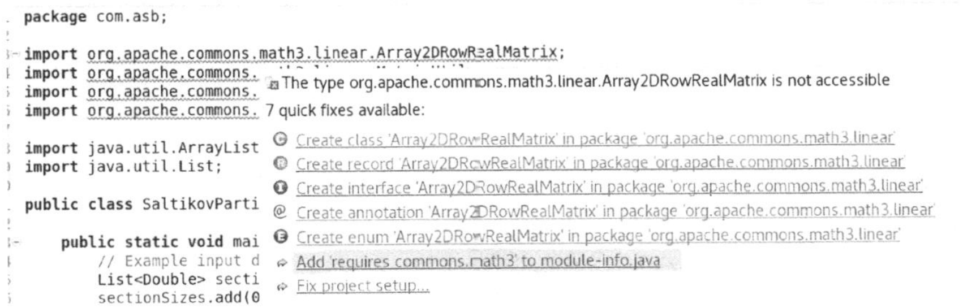

***Figure 9.13**: The code import statements are corrected*

From the same input values as before:

```
sectionSizes.add(0.5);
sectionSizes.add(1.0);
sectionSizes.add(1.5);
sectionSizes.add(2.0);
sectionSizes.add(2.5);
sectionSizes.add(3.0);
```

```
        // Parameters for Saltikov determination
        double thickness = 0.1; // Thickness of the material
        double shapeFactor = 0.9; // Shape factor for the particles
```

Running this the first time gave the following output:

```
Particle Size Distribution:
NaN
14.615940693851403
NaN
14.0219052677269
NaN
2.5371112025176443
```

So, we added some debug print out which I have reformatted to make it easier to view, which gave:

```
A Matrix:
Array2DRowRealMa-
trix{{0.5,0.125,0.03125,0.0078125,0.001953125,0.0004882812},
 {1.0,  1.0,    1.0,      1.0,          1.0,           1.0},
 {1.5, 3.375,7.59375,17.0859375,38.443359375,86.4975585938},
 {2.0, 8.0,      32.0,    128.0,        512.0,       2048.0},
 {2.5,15.625, 97.65625,610.3515625,3814.697265625,23841.8579101562},
 {3.0,27.0,     243.0,     2187.0,           19683.0, 177147.0}}
B Vector Matrix:
Array2DRowRealMa
rix{{0.0001220703},{1.0},{194.6195068359},{8192.0},{149011.6119384766},
{1594323.0}}
Inverse Matrix:BlockRealMatrix
{{-126.5625000004},{755.0156250038},{-
1157.4062500032},{694.890625001},{-187.6875000001},{22.75}}

Particle Size Distribution:
NaN
14.615940693851403
NaN
14.0219052677269
NaN
2.5371112025176443
```

The A Matrix is built up from **`Math.pow(sectionSizes.get(i), 2 * j + 1);`**

which returns the value of each of the section values, raised to the power of (2* the position in the array).

Which is calculated using the code:

```
double[][] aData = new double[n][n];
for (int i = 0; i < n; i++) {
    for (int j = 0; j < n; j++) {
        aData[i][j] = Math.pow(sectionSizes.get(i), 2 * j + 1);
    }
}
```

This can be seen most easily from the A matrix line for section element 4, with the value 2.0:

Where the powers are calculated as 1, 3, 5, 7, 9 and 11:

So, 2.0^1, 2.0^3, 2.0^5, 2.0^7, 2.0^9, 2.0^{11}, giving:

```
{2.0, 8.0,     32.0,   128.0,     512.0,     2048.0},
```

We analyzed the code and made some final changes as required to avoid the **NaN** values.

We also added code to graph the particle distribution. The final code used was as follows:

```
package com.asb;

import org.apache.commons.math3.linear.Array2DRowRealMatrix;
import org.apache.commons.math3.linear.MatrixUtils;
import org.apache.commons.math3.linear.RealMatrix;
import org.apache.commons.math3.linear.SingularMatrixException;
//ASB Added Graph Imports
import org.jfree.chart.ChartFactory;
import org.jfree.chart.ChartFrame;
import org.jfree.chart.JFreeChart;
import org.jfree.data.xy.XYSeries;
import org.jfree.data.xy.XYSeriesCollection;
//ASB
```

```
import java.util.ArrayList;
import java.util.List;

public class SaltikovParticleSizeAnalysisV2 {

    public static void main(String[] args) {
        // Example input data - section size distribution
        List<Double> sectionSizes = new ArrayList<>();
        sectionSizes.add(0.5);
        sectionSizes.add(1.0);
        sectionSizes.add(1.5);
        sectionSizes.add(2.0);
        sectionSizes.add(2.5);
        sectionSizes.add(3.0);

        // Parameters for Saltikov determination
        double thickness = 0.1; // Thickness of the material
        double shapeFactor = 0.9; // Shape factor for the particles

        // Perform Saltikov determination
        List<Double> particleSizes = 
calculateParticleSizes(sectionSizes, thickness, shapeFactor);

        // Output the results
        System.out.println("Particle Size Distribution:");
        for (double size : particleSizes) {
            System.out.println(size);
        }
        //ASB Now display the Particle Distribution array
        XYSeries series = new XYSeries("XYGraph");
        for (int i = 0; i < particleSizes.size(); i++) {
            series.add(i + 1, particleSizes.get(i)); // The Saltikov 
data set is added for the Graph
        }
        XYSeriesCollection dataset = new XYSeriesCollection();
        dataset.addSeries(series);
```

```
        JFreeChart chart = ChartFactory.createXYLineChart(
                "Saltikov Particle Distribution - Using Matrix Calculation",
                "X-Axis - Size in µmetres",
                "Y-Axis - Number of particles",
                dataset);
        ChartFrame frame = new ChartFrame("Using ChatGPT
SaltykovParticleAnalysisV2.java", chart);
        frame.pack();
        frame.setVisible(true);


    }


    /**
     * Calculates the particle size distribution based on the Saltikov
determination.
     *
     * @param sectionSizes List of section sizes
     * @param thickness Thickness of the material
     * @param shapeFactor Shape factor for the particles
     * @return List of particle sizes
     */
    public static List<Double> calculateParticleSizes(List<Double>
sectionSizes, double thickness, double shapeFactor) {
        int n = sectionSizes.size();

        // Create the matrix A
        double[][] aData = new double[n][n];
        for (int i = 0; i < n; i++) {
            for (int j = 0; j < n; j++) {
             int ipower= 2 * j + 1 ;
                aData[i][j] = Math.pow(sectionSizes.get(i), 2 * j + 1);
            }
        }
        RealMatrix aMatrix = new Array2DRowRealMatrix(aData);
        System.out.println("A Matrix:" + aMatrix.toString()); //ASB
Added to debug the final results given
```

```
        // Create the vector b
        double[] bData = new double[n];
        for (int i = 0; i < n; i++) {
            bData[i] = Math.pow(sectionSizes.get(i), 2 * i + 1);//
ASB Changed from n to i otherwise, n is a static 13, which would make
nonsense of the other calculations given in the code
        }
        RealMatrix bVector = MatrixUtils.createColumnRealMatrix(bData);
        System.out.println("B Vector Matrix:" + bVector.toString()); //
ASB Added to debug the final results given
        try {
            // Perform matrix inversion to solve for x
            RealMatrix xMatrix = MatrixUtils.inverse(aMatrix).
multiply(bVector);
            System.out.println("Inverse Matrix:" + xMatrix.toString());
//ASB Added to debug the final results given

            // Extract the particle sizes from the solution vector x
            double[] xData = xMatrix.getColumn(0);
            List<Double> particleSizes = new ArrayList<>();
            for (double value : xData) {
                //ASB Use the ABs function to see the impact of
calculated values (otherwise we are using some negatives which give NaN)
             //ASB This affects 0.5, 1.5, and 2.5 which give NaN without
this line of code
             value = Math.abs(value);
                double particleSize = Math.sqrt((8 * thickness * value)
/ (Math.PI * shapeFactor));
                particleSizes.add(particleSize);
            }

            return particleSizes;
        } catch (SingularMatrixException e) {
            // Matrix inversion failed due to a singular matrix
            System.out.println("Matrix inversion failed. The section
sizes may not be suitable for analysis.");
```

```
            return null;
        }
    }
}
```

This gave the printed output as follows:

```
Matrix{{0.5,0.125,0.03125,0.0078125,0.001953125,0.0004882812},
{1.0,1.0, 1.0,1.0,1.0,1.0},{1.5,3.375,7.59375,17.0859375,
38.443359375,86.4975585938},{2.0,8.0,32.0,128.0,512.0,2048.0},{2.5,15.62
5,97.65625,610.3515625,3814.697265625,23841.8579101562},{3.0,27.0,243.0,
2187.0,19683.0,177147.0}}

B Vector Matrix:Array2DRowRealMatrix{{0.5},{1.0},{7.59375},
{128.0},{3814.697265625},{177147.0}}

Inverse Matrix:BlockRealMatrix{{-94.2677556822},{559.0709784242},
{-816.7561549286},{442.895164931},{-97.3250496032},{7.3828168591}}

Particle Size Distribution:

5.164525025551897

12.577151046803674

15.201799855871627

11.194360069667129

5.247604783732639

1.4453061479996012
```

The graph created is shown in *Figure* 9.14, as follows:

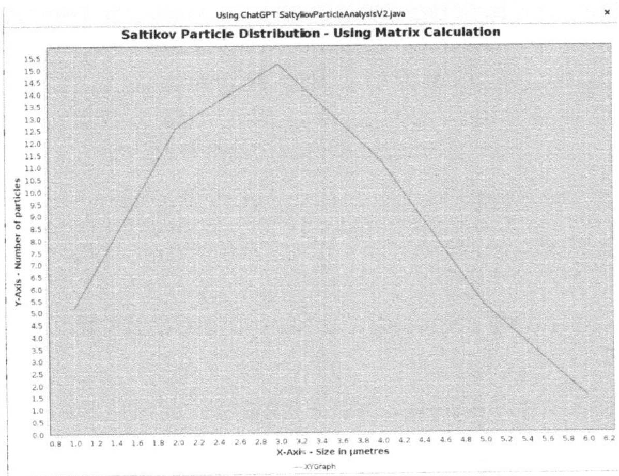

Figure 9.14: *The Saltikov Particle Distribution - Using Matrix Calculation*

Conclusion

It was difficult to find **Java** code that **ChatGPT**, could provide, which would provide code that could satisfactorily calculate the **Saltikov Particle Distribution** algorithm. The **Ask AI** mobile 'phone **App** provided the best code option but required additional changes to give viable output. The final graph produced, which is shown in **Figure 9.14**, does give a fair distribution, which was checked against the best example we could find, given in the most recent literature, as shown in *Figure* 9.15:

The **MatrixUtils** class was recommended and used by **Ask AI** for the matrix inversion after we asked it to include this in the **Java** code. This is part of the **Apache Commons Math** library which we used earlier, in Chapter 7, "**ChatGPT generated Java code for the Fast Fourier Transform**".

In the next chapter, **ChatGPT** is prompted for an example Java program with code to invert a triangular matrix to obtain the coefficients of a polynomial as the result of a set of polynomial equations.

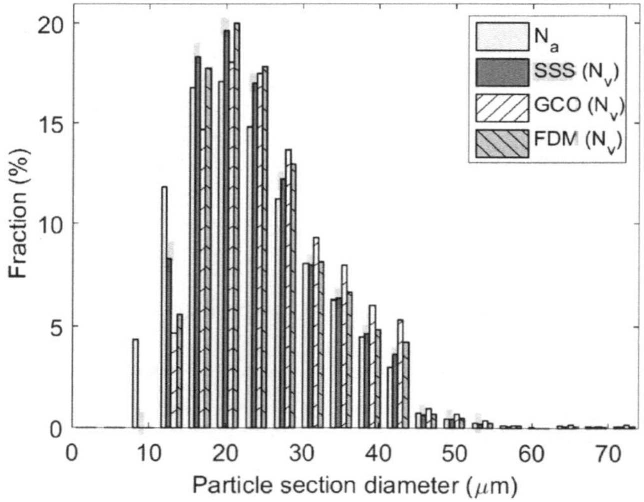

Fig. 4. Comparison of apparent 2D section size distribution to 3D particle size distribution after stereological correction using the Scheil-Schwartz-Saltykov (SSS) method, the Goldsmith and Cruz-Orive (GCO) method and the finite difference method (FDM).

See: **Page 6** (This is free of copyright under the **CC BY license**, with the details below)

https://doi.org/10.1016/j.powtec.2023.118873

Received 31 May 2023; Received in revised form 21 July 2023; **Accepted 5 August 2023**

Available online **7 August 2023**

There is also some example **Fortran** code from another open-source article publicly available at:

https://onlinelibrary.wiley.com/action/downloadSupplement?doi=10.1111%2Fmaps.12812&file=maps12812-sup-0001-DataS1.zip

Points to remember

- Sometimes, it is not possible to obtain the full Java code if this exceeds the 'free' token limit of the **AI**, as we discovered using the **Ask AI** mobile 'phone app.
- The **Ask AI** mobile 'phone app keeps the full questions and responses of previous threads which have been used, and these can be re-selected to continue the conversation, since the **AI** 'remembers' the previous responses.
- The **Java** code we eventually selected, assumes that the size measurements are in micrometers and that the area under the curve is in square micrometers.
- The free version of the **Ask AI** mobile 'phone app only allows 3 questions per day.

Multiple choice questions

1. **Which of the following acronyms is used as a shorthand for the Scheil-Schwartz-Saltykov method?**
   a. N
   b. FDM
   c. GCO
   d. SSS
2. **How many questions can you ask the free version of the Ask AI mobile 'phone App?**
   a. 21 questions per week
   b. 28 questions per week
   c. 35 questions per week
   d. 15 questions per week

3. **What line of code is required to resolve the NaN issue found in the output of the matrix inversion version of the ChatGPT Java code supplied by Ask AI?**
    a. RealMatrix xMatrix = MatrixUtils.inverse(aMatrix).multiply(bVector);
    b. value = Math.abs(value);
    c. particleSizes.add(particleSize);
    d. List<Double> particleSizes = new ArrayList<>();
4. **Which AI have we not used in this chapter, to ask the question for displaying the Java code for the Saltikov determination of the size distribution of particles?**
    a. Ask AI
    b. OpenAI ChatGPT with GPT-3.5
    c. Perplexity AI
    d. Phind AI
5. **Which AI did not provide any Java code when asked the question for displaying the Java code for the Saltikov determination of the size distribution of particles??**
    a. Ask AI
    b. OpenAI ChatGPT with GPT-3.5
    c. Microsoft Bing
    d. Phind AI

Answers

1. d
2. a
3. b
4. c
5. c

Questions

1. **What are the main techniques available for calculating the determination of the size distribution of particles in an opaque material from a measurement of the size distribution of their sections and which one is considered to give the most accurate result? (Hint: We have given a link to the full article which discusses this.)**

2. **What other computer language could you use to calculate the size distribution of particles in an opaque material from a measurement of the size distribution of their sections using the matrix inversion method?**
3. **Which AI provided the most useful Java code and which AI provided the most useful link for further investigation?**
4. **How could you extend the final Java code supplied, to compare its results directly with the graph shown in Figure 9.15? (Hint: It would be useful to use the la**st link supplied in this chapter.)

Key terms

- **Fortran**: FORTRAN, Short for Formula Translation, was originally developed by IBMs John Backus in 1957. See **https://en.wikipedia.org/wiki/Fortran** for further details: "*Since August 2021, Fortran has ranked among the top fifteen languages in the* TIOBE *index, a measure of the popularity of programming languages.*"
- **Matrix**: Matrices are two-dimensional sets of numbers held in a rectangular-shaped set of columns and rows, used for defining systems of linear or differential equations and polynomial functions, as well as representing a linear application.
- **Phind AI**: Phind is a similar search engine to **ChatGPT** designed for developers. It is a web-based system using generative **AI** to give answers including code examples, and links to its sources.
- **Saltikov**: Wrote the original paper:" The Determination of the Size Distribution of Particles in an Opaque Material from a Measurement of the Size Distribution of Their Sections", by Sarkis A. Saltikov, a conference paper in the Stereology Journal, found on pages, 163–173.
- There is a DOI link: for Saltikov, S.A. (1967). "The Determination of the Size Distribution of Particles in an Opaque Material from a Measurement of the Size Distribution of Their Sections. In: Elias, H. (eds) Stereology. Springer, Berlin, Heidelberg". **https://doi.org/10.1007/978-3-642-88260-9_31**
- **Vector**: Is a special type of matrix that has only one row (called a row vector) or only one column.

CHAPTER 10
ChatGPT-generated Java Code to Invert a Triangular Matrix

Introduction

In this chapter, **ChatGPT** was prompted for an example Java program with code to invert a triangular matrix to obtain the coefficients of a polynomial as the result of a set of polynomial equations.

The **Java** code created prompted the user to input the degree of the polynomial and the coefficients of a set of polynomial equations. It then used **Gaussian** elimination to invert the resulting matrix and obtain the coefficients of the polynomial. Finally, it printed the coefficients of the polynomial.

Structure

In this chapter, we will discuss the following topics:

- **ChatGPT** generated Java code to invert a triangular matrix to obtain the coefficients of a polynomial
- Triangular matrix inversion to obtain the coefficients of a polynomial - Java code validation using an **Eclipse IDE** Java Program Project
    - MagicSquare example

ChatGPT-generated Java code to invert a triangular matrix to obtain the coefficients of a polynomial

There is a good description of some of the mathematical techniques we employ in this section of the chapter at the link: **https://en.wikipedia.org/wiki/Gaussian_elimination**

We asked the **Ask AI** mobile phone application the following question:

Do you have example Java code to invert a triangular matrix to obtain the coefficients of a polynomial as the result of a set of polynomial equations?

The response from the **Ask AI, ChatGPT 3.5 OpenAI** interface, was as follows (in quoted Italics):

"Yes, I can provide you with an example Java program code to invert a triangular matrix to obtain the coefficients of a polynomial as the result of a set of polynomial equations. Please note that this code is provided for educational purposes only and should be used at your own risk.

Here's the Java code:

```
```java
import java.util.Scanner;

public class PolynomialSolver {

    public static void main(String[] args) {
        Scanner scanner = new Scanner(System.in);

        // Get the degree of the polynomial
        System.out.print("Enter the degree of the polynomial: ");
        int n = scanner.nextInt();

        // Create the matrix of coefficients
        double[][] matrix = new double[n+1][n+2];
        for (int i = 0; i <= n; i++) {
            for (int j = 0; j <= n; j++) {
                System.out.print("Enter the coefficient of x^" + (n-j) + "
```
```

```
in equation " + (i+1) + ": ");
                    matrix[i][j] = scanner.nextDouble();
                }
                System.out.print("Enter the result of equation " + (i+1) +
": ");
                matrix[i][n+1] = scanner.nextDouble();
            }

            // Invert the matrix
            for (int i = n; i >= 0; i--) {
                double divisor = matrix[i][i];
                for (int j = 0; j <= n+1; j++) {
                    matrix[i][j] /= divisor;
                }
                for (int j = i-1; j >= 0; j--) {
                    double factor = matrix[j][i];
                    for (int k = 0; k <= n+1; k++) {
                        matrix[j][k] -= factor * matrix[i][k];
                    }
                }
            }

            // Print the solution
            System.out.println("\nPolynomial coefficients:");
            for (int i = 0; i <= n; i++) {
                System.out.println("x^" + (n-i) + " = " + String.
format("%.2f", matrix[i][n+1]));
            }
        }
}
```

This code prompts the user to input the degree of the polynomial and the coefficients of a set of polynomial equations. It then uses Gaussian elimination to invert the resulting matrix and obtain the coefficients of the polynomial. Finally, it prints the coefficients of the polynomial.

Note:

that this code assumes that the polynomial is of the form `a_n*x^n + a_{n-1}*x^{n-1} + ... + a_0`, where `n` is the degree of the polynomial and `a_n`, `a_{n-1}`, ..., `a_0` are the coefficients of the polynomial. If your polynomial has a different form, you will need to modify the code accordingly."

Next, we asked the **Perplexity AI** mobile phone App the same question and received the following response, as illustrated in *Figure 10.1*:

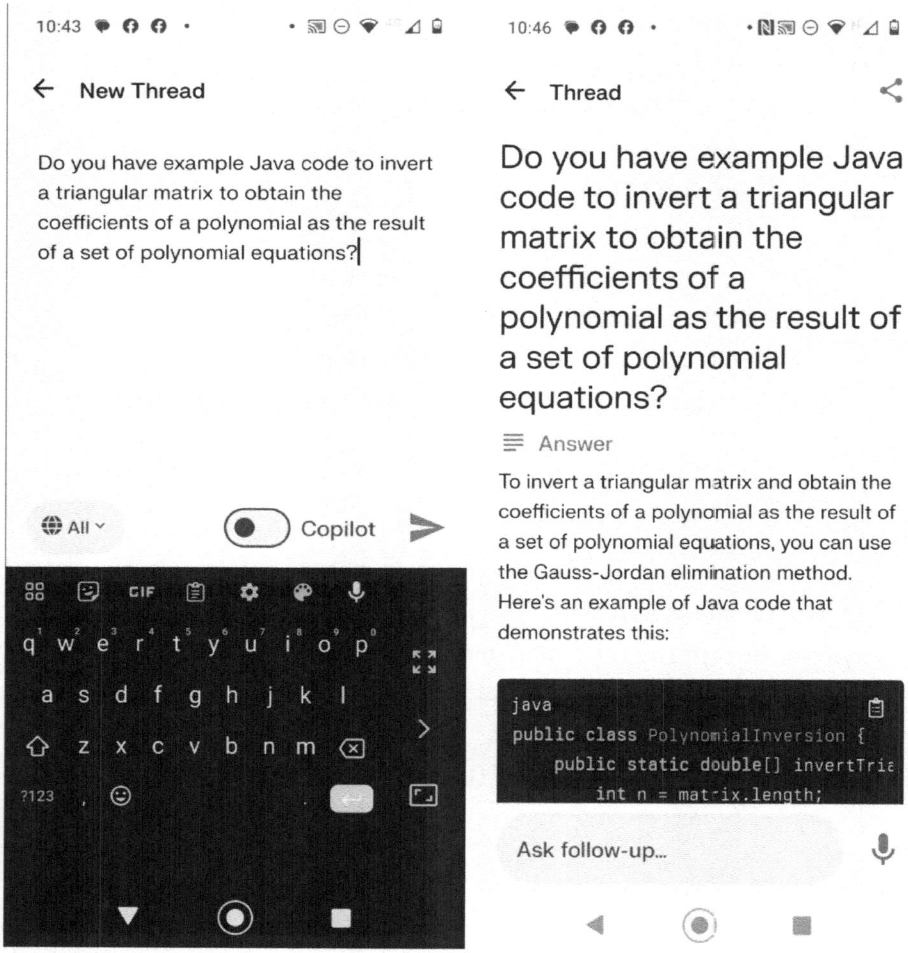

Figure 10.1: *(a) The question for Perplexity AI* *(b) The answer and Java Code from the AI*

Do you have example Java code to invert a triangular matrix to obtain the coefficients of a polynomial as the result of a set of polynomial equations?

"java

```
public class PolynomialInversion {
    public static double[] invertTriangularMatrix(double[][] matrix) {
        int n = matrix.length;
        double[] coefficients = new double[n];
        for (int i = n - 1; i >= 0; i--) {
            double sum = 0;
            for (int j = i + 1; j < n; j++) {
                sum += matrix[i][j] * coefficients[j];
            }
            coefficients[i] = (matrix[i][n] - sum) / matrix[i][i];
        }
        return coefficients;
    }
    public static void main(String[] args) {
        double[][] matrix = {
            {1, 0, 0, 1},
            {0, 1, 0, 2},
            {0, 0, 1, 3}
        };
        double[] coefficients = invertTriangularMatrix(matrix);
        System.out.println("Coefficients of the polynomial:");
        for (int i = 0; i < coefficients.length; i++) {
            System.out.println("x^" + i + ": " + coefficients[i]);
        }
    }
}
```

In this example, the invertTriangularMatrix method takes a triangular matrix as input and returns an array of coefficients for the polynomial. The main method demonstrates how to use this method with a sample triangular matrix. The resulting coefficients are then printed. Please note that this code assumes that the triangular matrix is already in upper triangular form, where the main diagonal elements are non-zero. If your matrix is not in this form, you may need to perform additional steps to convert it to upper triangular form before using the inversion method.

Scrolling down in the **Perplexity AI App**, we can view the code window, which was copied, and the source links, which can be clicked in turn to browse the internet, still within the App control, as shown in *Figure 10.2*:

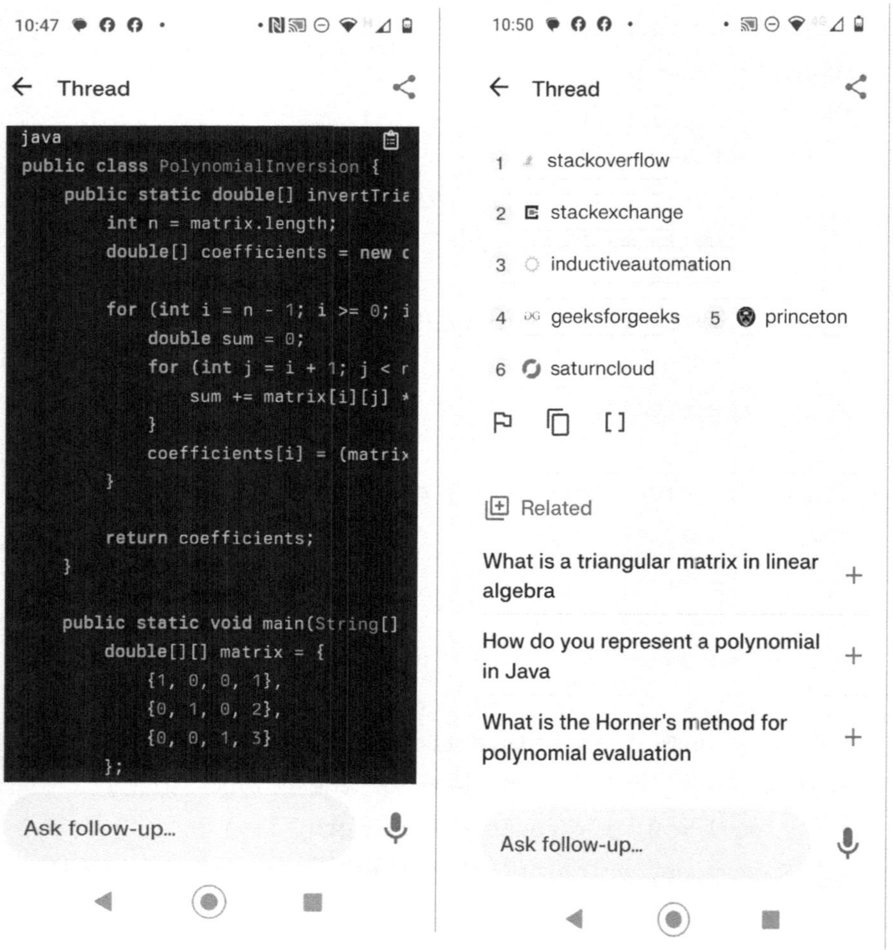

***Figure 10.2**: (a) The full **Java** code window (b) The **Perplexity AI** links to the sources used*

The provided links were as follows:

1. **https://stackoverflow.com/questions/32844417/java-parsing-a-polynomial-with-complex-coefficients-with-regex**
2. **https://crypto.stackexchange.com/questions/78200/how-to-find-the-inverse-of-a-polynomial-in-ntru-pkcs**
3. **https://forum.inductiveautomation.com/t/matrix-based-regression-calculations-for-polynomial-coefficients/24857**

4. **https://www.geeksforgeeks.org/horners-method-polynomial-evaluation/**
5. **https://introcs.cs.princeton.edu/95linear**
6. **https://saturncloud.io/blog/algorithm-for-computing-the-inverse-of-a-polynomial/**

Triangular matrix inversion to obtain the coefficients of a polynomial - Java code validation using an Eclipse Java Program Project

The example Java code provided by the two mobile phone **AI** Apps is quite different, so it will be interesting to compare their efficiency and accuracy in this validation section.

In terms of lines of code, the **Perplexity AI** Java code is almost half the length of the **Ask AI** Java code example.

So, first, we create a new **Eclipse IDE Java** project for the validation of the **AI** code, as shown in *Figure* 10.3:

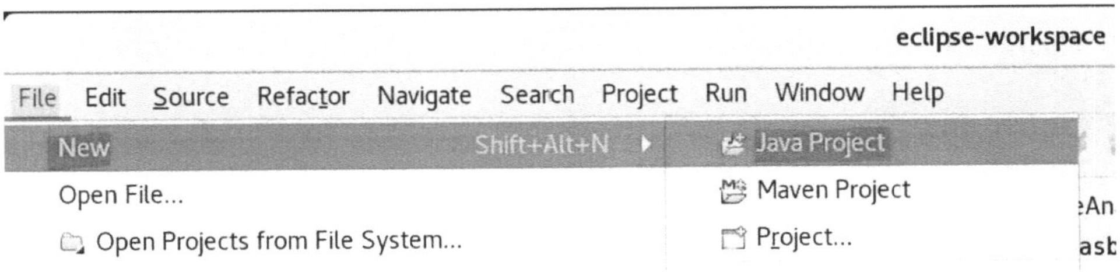

***Figure 10.3**: We create a new Eclipse IDE Java project for the validation of the AI code*

The **Eclipse IDE Java** Project name is entered as **TriangularMatrixInversion_Chapter10** for the chapter, as shown in *Figure* 10.4, and then the Next button is selected:

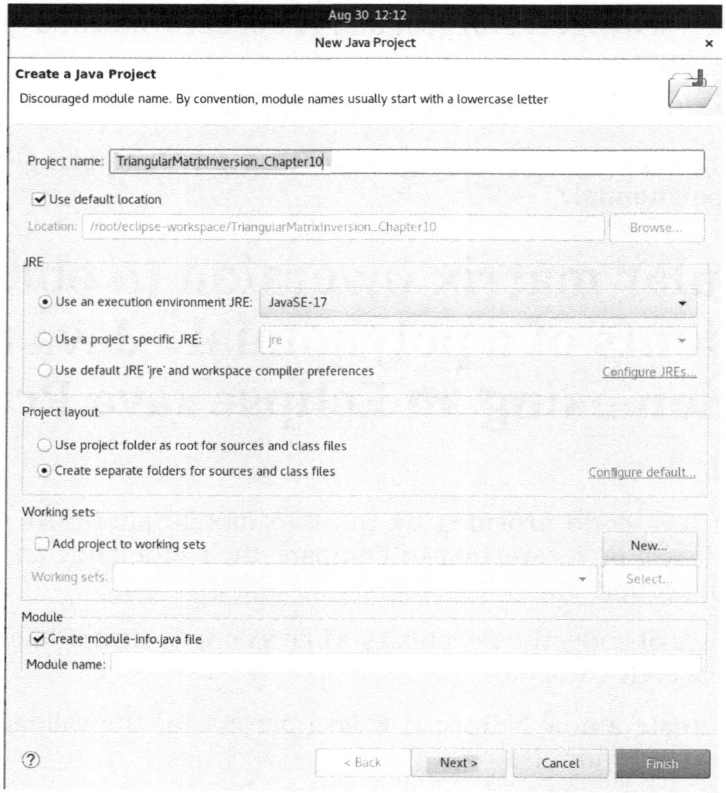

Figure 10.4: *The Project name is entered as* ***TriangularMatrixInversion_Chapter10***

The **Finish** button is selected to create the **TriangularMatrixInversion_Chapter10** Java project with the settings, as illustrated in *Figure* 10.5. Notice that there are a number of **Tabs** that can be selected, which can be used to customize the project properties from left to right as follows:

- **Projects**

  A Java project can have a list of other Java projects added as dependencies, which can then be referenced. This allows the use of classes from the project added as the dependency. This is a feature of the **Eclipse IDE**, which can be used to develop several related Java projects and will then facilitate the export of all the project JAR files together.

- **Libraries**

  We have already covered the addition of several library jar files to the **Module** and **Class Build** Paths. This feature is required when the code has import package statements, which require the reference to external supporting jar files.

- **Order and Export**

  The order and export tab allows the library definitions, including the version of the **Java JVM** compiler, to be defined. This is necessary in cases where several external jar files are used, and there is a conflict between two classes with the same package name and class name, where one may be a much older version. The first class referenced in the **Class path** is always selected, so that a non-working class can be excluded by placing the jar file later in the class path list, while still allowing other dependent classes to be used.

- **Module Dependencies**

  The module dependencies tab was added in the June 2019 release of the **Eclipse IDE**, version **4.12.** We have previously covered its detailed usage earlier in this book. The concept of **Modules** was added in **Java 9**. From **Eclipse IDE** version **4.12** onwards, the **Module Dependencies** tab was made available for configuring dependencies between modules.

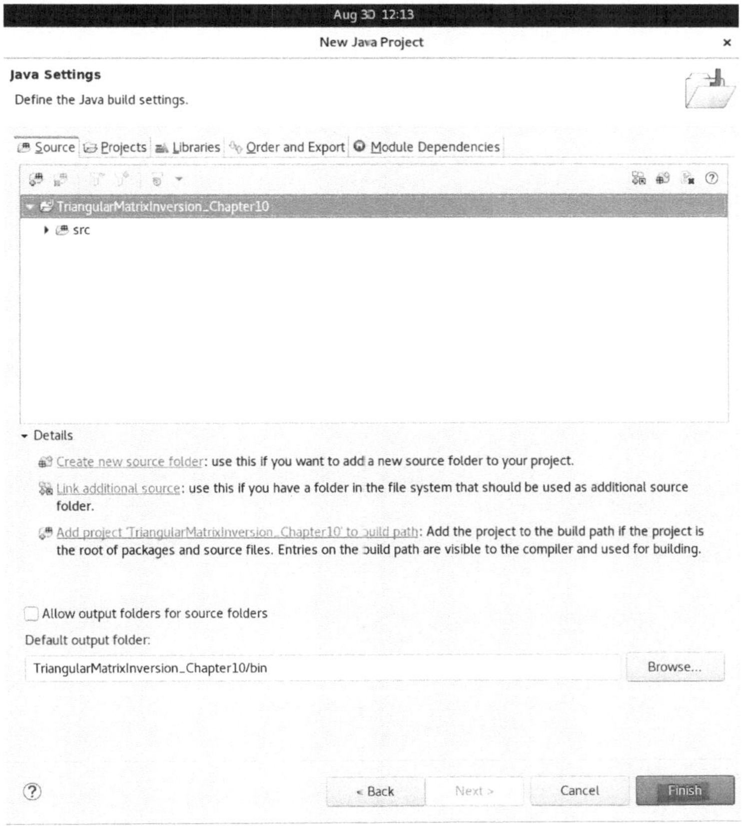

***Figure 10.5**: The **TriangularMatrixInversion_Chapter10** Java project with the settings*

Next, we create a **Java** class, **PolynomialSolver**, by right-clicking the Project node and then selecting the **New -> Class** menu item, as highlighted in *Figure 10.6:*

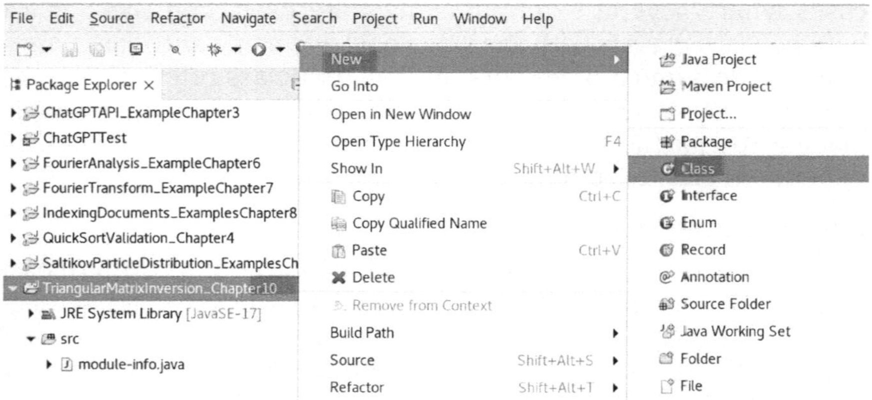

Figure 10.6: *The* ***New -> Class*** *menu item is selected for the new* ***PolynomialSolver*** *Class*

The **com.asb** package name and the **PolynomialSolver** Java class name (used from the Java code class name, suggested by **Ask AI**) is entered, as shown highlighted in *Figure 10.7:*

Figure 10.7: *The* ***com.asb*** *package name and* ***PolynomialSolver*** *Java class name are entered.*

We can now paste the code suggested by **Ask AI** into the skeleton class created by the **Eclipse IDE**, as shown in *Figure* 10.8:

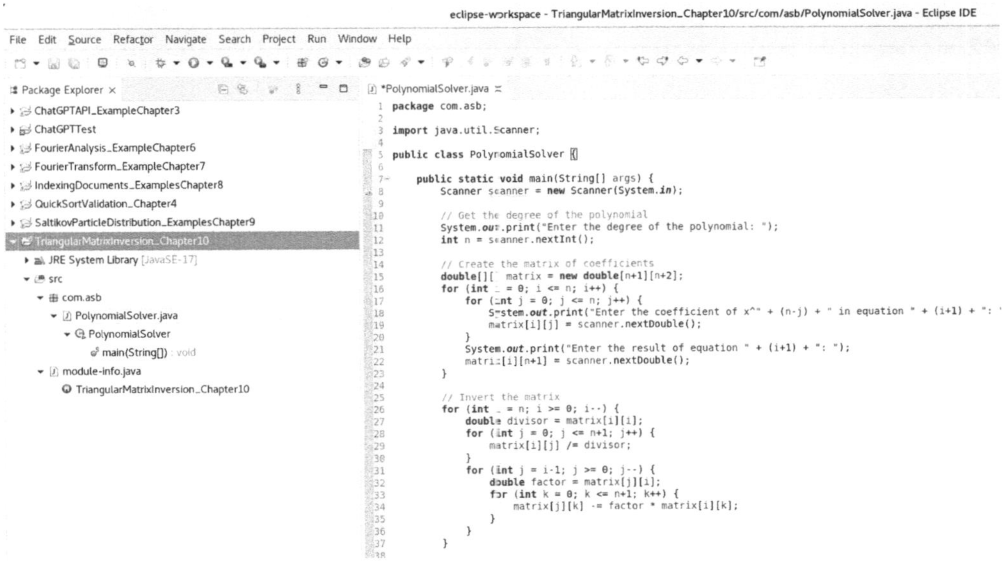

***Figure* 10.8**: *The* **Ask AI** *Java code is pasted into the* **Eclipse IDE PolynomialSolver.java** *file*

The pasted **Ask AI** Java code has just one warning, as shown in *Figure* 10.9, where the **Eclipse Java IDE** has identified that there is no **scanner.close()** call to close the console **I/O** stream. This can cause unnecessary orphaned **byte-code** to be left running in a **JVM** thread:

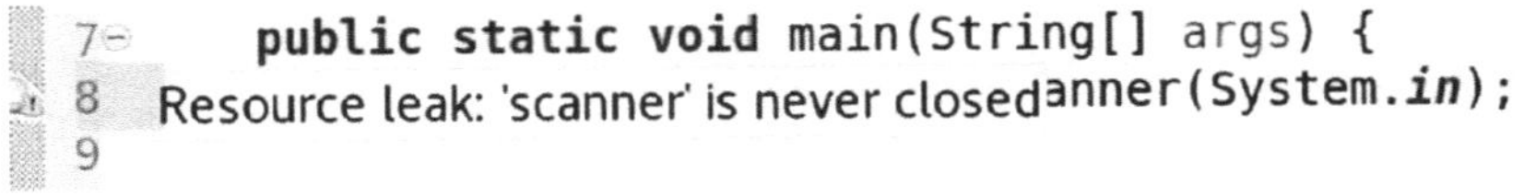

***Figure* 10.9**: *The warning of a* **Resource leak** *is identified on code line 8 by the* **Eclipse IDE**

So, before running the code, we add the **scanner.close()** statement, as highlighted and commented in *Figure* 10.10:

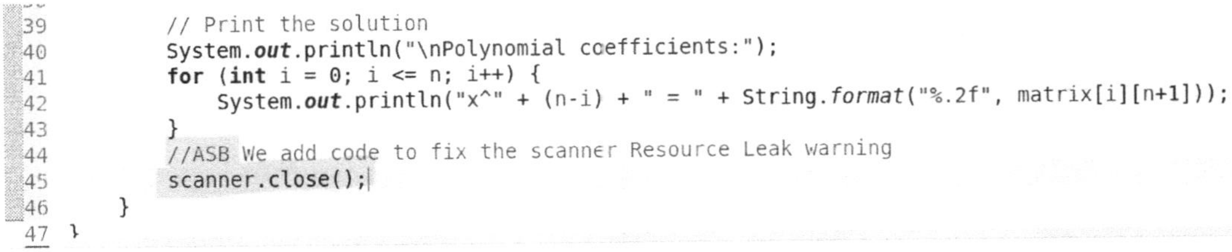

***Figure* 10.10**: *The* **scanner.close()** *statement is added as the last statement of the code*

Now, we are ready to run the code we were looking for, with an expected solution of 9, 3, 1 for the linear equations as follows:

```
2x^2 +   x + 1  = 22
5x^2 +  3x + 2  = 56
 x^2  + 5x + 8  = 32
```

First, we tried using the test data on the first **PolynomialSolver** Java code created by **Ask AI**.

Validation Test 1

We entered the prompts from the **PolynomialSolver Java** program, as follows:

```
Enter the degree of the polynomial: 2
Enter the coefficient of x^2 in equation 1: 2
Enter the coefficient of x^1 in equation 1: 1
Enter the coefficient of x^0 in equation 1: 1
Enter the result of equation 1: 22
Enter the coefficient of x^2 in equation 2: 5
Enter the coefficient of x^1 in equation 2: 3
Enter the coefficient of x^0 in equation 2: 2
Enter the result of equation 2: 56
Enter the coefficient of x^2 in equation 3: 1
Enter the coefficient of x^1 in equation 3: 5
Enter the coefficient of x^0 in equation 3: 8
Enter the result of equation 3: 32
```

The following results were then printed by the **PolynomialSolver Java** program:

```
Polynomial coefficients:
x^2 = 9.00   (As expected.)
x^1 = 27.43  (Should be 3?)
x^0 = 4.00   (Should always be 1?)
```

So, the first result made sense since we had set x=3 for the equation values we then entered.

The other outputs were unexpected. Perhaps, we have misunderstood the way the program works and what it is displaying here.

Clearly, if x^2 is 9, as we thought was correctly calculated, then x^1 may be assuming a different form for the equations.

So, we wondered if this might be:

```
2x^2 +  y +   z   = 22
5x^2 + 3y + 2z  = 56
  x^2 + 5y + 8z  = 32
```

Where `x^2 = x and x^1 = y and x^0 = z`

However, the values are still incorrect when substituting the printed numbers back in.

So, let's show what should have been calculated:

$$\begin{pmatrix} 2 & 1 & 1 \\ 5 & 3 & 2 \\ 1 & 5 & 8 \end{pmatrix}^{(-1)} = \begin{pmatrix} 1.17 & -0.25 & -0.08 \\ -3.17 & 1.25 & 0.08 \\ 1.8\overline{3} & -0.75 & 0.08 \end{pmatrix} \cdot \begin{pmatrix} 22 \\ 56 \\ 32 \end{pmatrix} = \begin{pmatrix} 9 \\ 3 \\ 1 \end{pmatrix}$$

Figure 10.11: *The validated matrix calculations from our calculator*

So, in *Figure* 10.11, we first calculate the inverse of the matrix. Then, we use matrix multiplication, using the inverse of the matrix multiplied by the Vector of the results (22,56,32). This gives us our solution Vector (9,3,1).

Next, we test the second Java code program, the response from the **Perplexity AI**, called **`PolynomialInversion,`** which was created using the **Java** class and compiled in the file **`PolynomialInversion.java.`** We entered it by right-clicking on the project node and then selecting the **New-> Class** menu item, as highlighted in *Figure 10.12*:

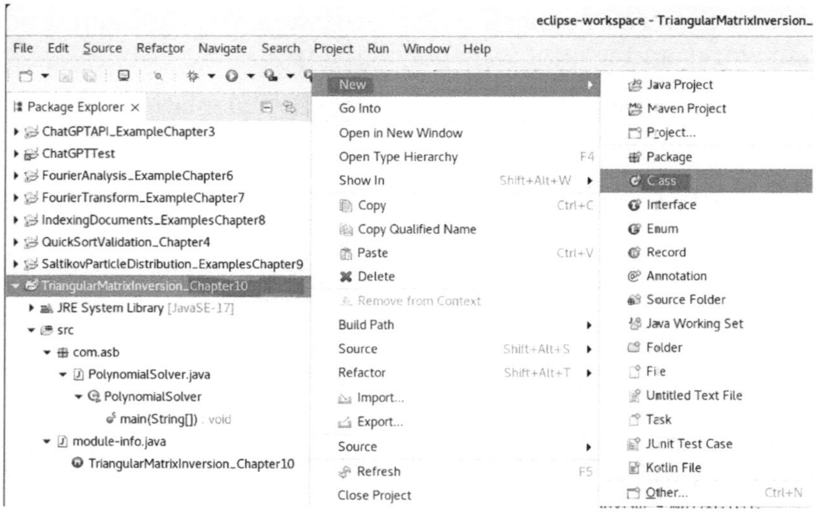

***Figure 10.12**: The highlighted **New-> Class** menu item is selected*

The highlighted **PolynomialInversion** class name is entered in the **New Java Class** pop-up window, and then the **Finish** button is selected, as shown in *Figure 10.13*:

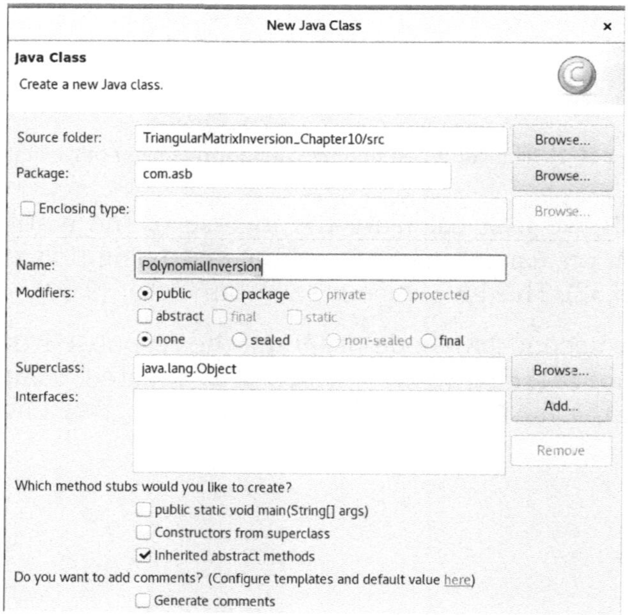

***Figure 10.13**: The highlighted **PolynomialInversion** class name is entered*

The **PolynomialInversion** Java code is pasted into the skeleton class created by the **Eclipse IDE**, as illustrated in *Figure 10.14*:

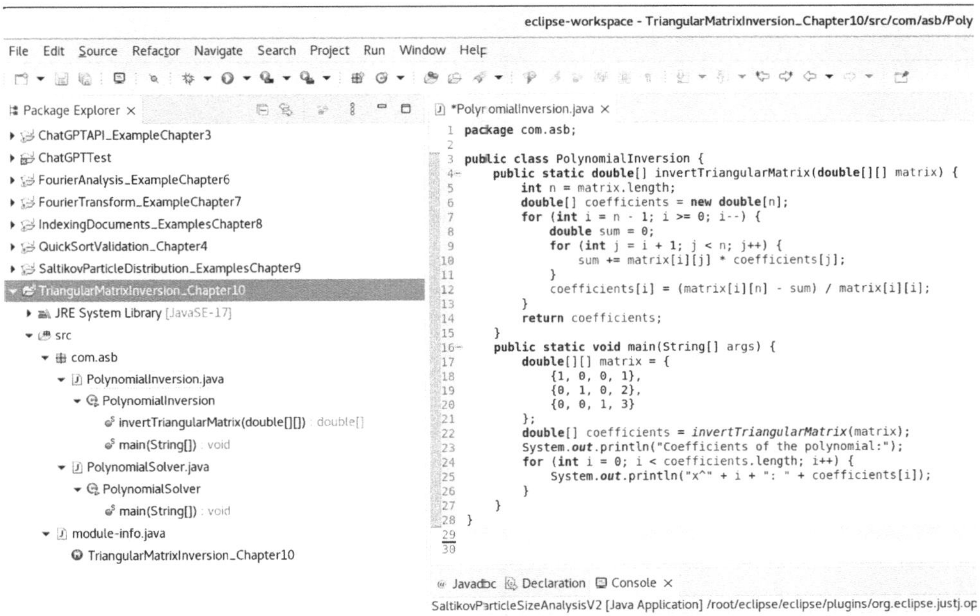

Figure 10.14: *The Perplexity AI Java code given*

Validation Test 2

First, we run the program, **PolynomialInversion,** using the embedded test data supplied by the **Perplexity AI**, which gives the output as follows:

```
Coefficients of the polynomial:
x^0: 1.0
x^1: 2.0
x^2: 3.0
```

This is not really surprising as the matrix is mostly just a diagonal, much like an identity matrix, except for the values in the last column, which contains the values that correspond to the output we see.

Note:

An identity matrix is a square matrix of any order, which contains on its main diagonal elements with one, and the other matrix elements are populated with zero.

So, we replaced the **AI** test matrix with the following matrix (already inverted):

```
1      0      0       2
0      1      0       3
0      0      1      -1
```

This is the final representation of our original test equations, as shown in the link:

https://en.wikipedia.org/wiki/Gaussian_elimination for the equations listed here

```
-3x -y + 2x = -11
-2x +y + 2z =  -3
 2x +y -  z =   8
```

This printed out:

```
Coefficients of the polynomial:
x^0: 2.0
x^1: 3.0
x^2: -1.0
```

Compared to the values provided in Wikipedia, for the solution of z = –1, y = 3, and x = 2, it prints the expected numbers. However, it doesn't really do much more than you can work out just by viewing the matrix. This is clearly because the code expects to use the already inverted matrix as input!

Also, you will notice that the code uses the syntax **x^n** to really stand for the nth row, numbered from zero, down, of the matrix. So, **x^0** translates to **x** in our test equation, **x^1** is **y**, and **x^2** is **z**.

If we wanted to see the printout reflecting our **x,y,z** values as identified in our printed output, we would need to change the Java code.

There are other Polynomial Java examples available on the internet, as follows:

1. The link: **http://introcs.cs.princeton.edu/java/92symbolic/Polynomial.java.html**

   (This code is copyright "Copyright © 2000–2022, Robert Sedgewick and Kevin Wayne.
   Last updated: Sat Nov 19 08:38:44 EST 2022.")

   However, on their website, it states:

"For teachers:

- *This online content.* Everything on these pages is freely available. We ask only that you adhere to normal academic traditions of attribution if you adapt this content in your own course. One best practice is to just provide links to our pages."

  The code is publicly available and can be compiled and run, error-free, on the **Eclipse IDE** with just one change to all the occurrences of:

  ```
  StdOut.println
  ```

  to

  ```
  System.out.println
  ```

2. Another example of Java code for matrix manipulations was found using the **Google** search text as follows:

   "free example java code for matrix solving equations"

You need to check carefully the access allowed for the resulting links and ensure that the code is open source/copyright-free when using the Google results.

For example, one site looked promising, but the code is strongly copyrighted:

https://www.sanfoundry.com/java-program-represent-linear-equations-matrix-form/

While scrolling down the Google search page results, we noticed the following, as illustrated in *Figure 10.15*:

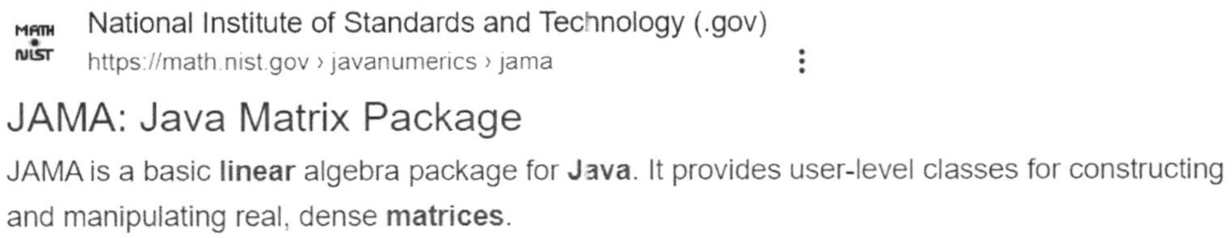

***Figure 10.15**: The Google search gives a promising link to useful Java code*

Government sites (often funded by the taxpayer) are more likely to wish to promote the use of developed software, since government organizations are more likely to be assisted with government grants.

The website page we are interested in is as follows:

https://math.nist.gov/javanumerics/jama/

It provides an example that looked like the kind of code we were looking for.

Example of Use: The following simple example solves a 3x3 linear system Ax=b and computes the norm of the residual:

```
double[][] array = {{1.,2.,3},{4.,5.,6.},{7.,8.,10.}};
Matrix A = new Matrix(array);
Matrix b = Matrix.random(3,1);
Matrix x = A.solve(b);
Matrix Residual = A.times(x).minus(b);
double rnorm = Residual.normInf();
```

The Java source and Jar libraries can be downloaded from the following links:

https://math.nist.gov/javanumerics/jama/Jama-1.0.3.tar.gz

https://math.nist.gov/javanumerics/jama/Jama-1.0.3.zip

https://math.nist.gov/javanumerics/jama/Jama-1.0.3.jar

The Javadocs documentation is also available from:

https://math.nist.gov/javanumerics/jama/doc/

There is also a code example at:

https://math.nist.gov/javanumerics/jama/examples/MagicSquareExample.java

We are obliged to display Copyright and Author acknowledgments on publication. The specific Copyright statement for the aforementioned particular software development link is as follows:

"Copyright Notice This software is a cooperative product of The MathWorks and the National Institute of Standards and Technology (NIST) which has been released to the public domain.

Neither The MathWorks nor NIST assumes any responsibility whatsoever for its use by other parties, and makes no guarantees, expressed or implied, about its quality, reliability, or any other characteristic."

Also from the main link is as follows:

https://www.nist.gov/open/copyright-fair-use-and-licensing-statements-srd-data-software-and-technical-series-publications

"To the extent NIST may assert rights outside of the United States, the public is granted the non-exclusive, perpetual, paid-up, royalty-free, worldwide right to reprint works in all formats including print, electronically, and online, and in all subsequent editions, and derivative works."

Please use the recommended citation format below, followed by "**Republished courtesy of the National Institute of Standards and Technology.**"

(Some works published by NIST may have been written by third parties and may be subject to copyright protection).

The last bracketed notice is already satisfied as public domain, as indicated by the specific copyright text on the Matrix software webpage we cited earlier.

Authors

"JAMA's *initial design, as well as this reference implementation, was developed by*

Joe Hicklin

Cleve Moler

Peter Webb ... from ***The MathWorks***

Ronald F. Boisvert

Bruce Miller

Roldan Pozo

Karin Remington ... from ***NIST***"

MagicSquare example

We downloaded the **Jama-1.0.3.jar** matrix library and then copied it, as shown in *Figure* 10.16:

```
[root@ECMUKDEM022 eclipse]# cd AILibs/
[root@ECMUKDEM022 AILibs]# cp /mnt/hgfs/Installs/Jama-1.0.3.jar .
[root@ECMUKDEM022 AILibs]# pwd
/root/eclipse/eclipse/AILibs
[root@ECMUKDEM022 AILibs]#
```

Figure 10.16: *The* ***Jama-1.0.3.jar*** *matrix library is copied to our* **RedHat RHEL 8 Linux** *server*

Next, we created a **`MagicSquareExample.java`** java source file in the **TriangularMatrixInversion_Chapter10, Eclipse IDE** project. We added the copied **Jama-1.0.3.jar** matrix library to the project properties, as shown in *Figure 10.17*:

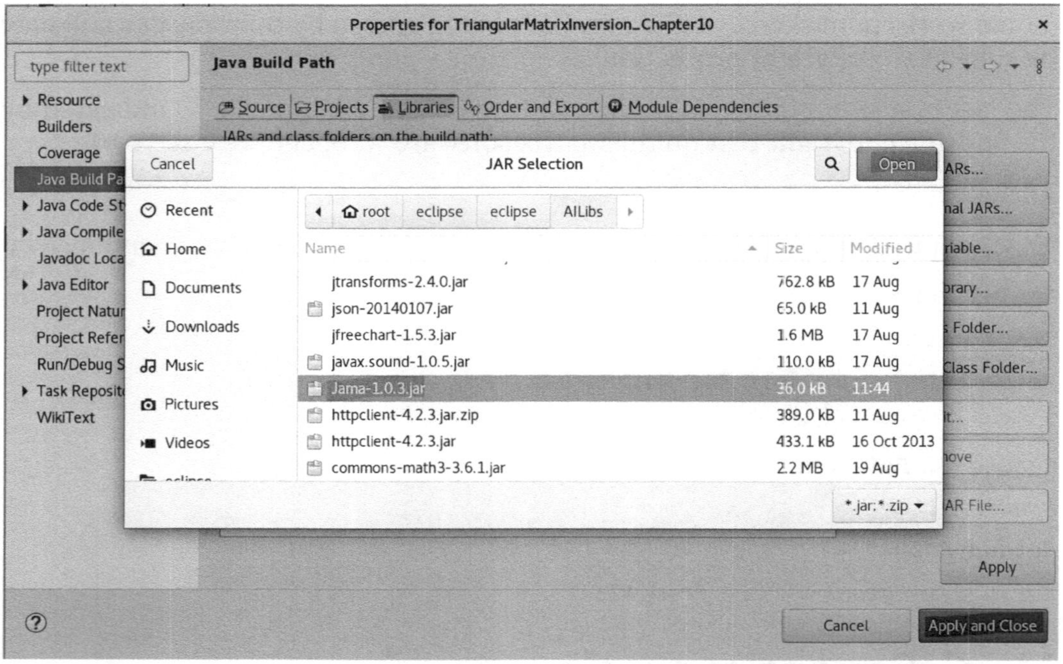

***Figure 10.17**: The copied **Jama-1.0.3.jar** matrix library is added to the project properties*

We then referenced the Matrix class from the jar file in the pasted code from the downloaded Java code from the webpage link: **https://math.nist.gov/javanumerics/jama/examples/MagicSquareExample.java,**

as shown in *Figure 10.18*:

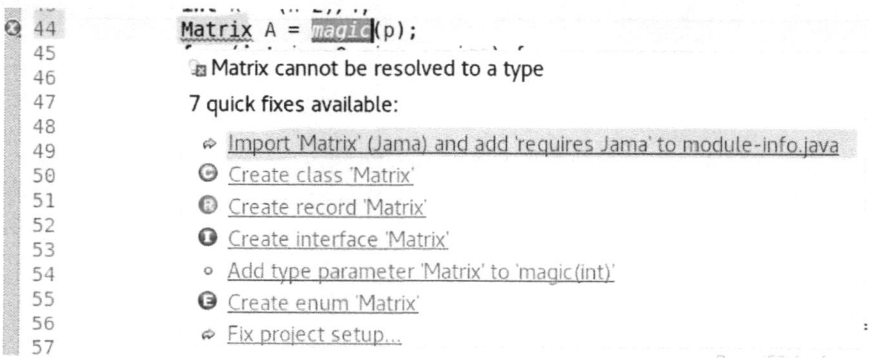

***Figure 10.18**: The highlighted Eclipse IDE fix was selected to clear the import error*

This gave the following Java code in the project's **module-info.java** file:

```
/**
 *
 */
/**
 *
 */
module TriangularMatrixInversion_Chapter10 {
      requires Jama;
}
```

Running the **MagicSquare** program gave the following output, as described in the Java comments:

```
  /*
    | Tests LU, QR, SVD and symmetric Eig decompositions.
    |
    |   n       = order of magic square.
    |   trace   = diagonal sum, should be the magic sum, (n^3 + n)/2.
    |   max_eig = maximum eigenvalue of (A + A')/2, should equal trace.
    |   rank    = linear algebraic rank,
    |             should equal n if n is odd, be less than n if n is even.
    |   cond    = L_2 condition number, ratio of singular values.
    |   lu_res  = test of LU factorization, norm1(L*U-A(p,:))/(n*eps).
    |   qr_res  = test of QR factorization, norm1(Q*R-A)/(n*eps).
    */
```

The console output is as follows:

```
   Test of Matrix Class, using magic squares.
    See MagicSquareExample.main() for an explanation.
      n      trace       max_eig   rank        cond      lu_res  qr_res
      3         15        15.000      3       4.330       0.000  11.333
      4         34        34.000      3         Inf       0.000  13.500
      5         65        65.000      5       5.462       0.000  14.400
      6        111       111.000      5         Inf       5.333  16.000
      7        175       175.000      7       7.111       2.286  37.714
```

```
        8       260       260.000     3        Inf      0.000  59.000
        9       369       369.000     9      9.102      7.111   53.333
       10       505       505.000     7        Inf      3.200  159.200
       11       671       671.000    11     11.102      2.909  215.273
       12       870       870.000     3        Inf      0.000  185.333
       13      1105      1105.000    13     13.060      4.923  313.846
       14      1379      1379.000     9        Inf      4.571  540.571
       15      1695      1695.000    15     15.062      4.267  242.133
       16      2056      2056.000     3        Inf      0.000  488.500
       17      2465      2465.000    17     17.042      7.529  267.294
       18      2925      2925.000    11        Inf      7.111  520.889
       19      3439      3439.000    19     19.048     16.842  387.368
       20      4010      4010.000     3        Inf     14.400  584.800
       21      4641      4641.000    21     21.035      6.095 1158.095
       22      5335      5335.000    13        Inf      6.545 1132.364
       23      6095      6095.000    23     23.037     11.130 1268.870
       24      6924      6924.000     3        Inf     10.667 827.500
       25      7825      7825.000    25     25.029     35.840 1190.400
       26      8801      8801.000    15        Inf      4.923 1859.077
       27      9855      9855.000    27     27.032     37.926 1365.333
       28     10990     10990.000     3        Inf     34.286 1365.714
       29     12209     12209.000    29     29.025     30.897 1647.448
       30     13515     13515.000    17        Inf      8.533 2571.733
       31     14911     14911.000    31     31.027     33.032 1426.581
       32     16400     16400.000     3        Inf      0.000 1600.125

Elapsed Time =          0.137 seconds Adios
```

So, now, having found the copyright-free Java library of matrix calculations, we then asked the **OpenAI ChatGPT 3.5** (**https://chat.openai.com/**) the following question:

Do you have a Java code example for code to invert a triangular matrix to obtain the coefficients of a polynomial as the result of a set of polynomial equations based on the code libraries available from https://math.nist.gov/javanumerics/jama/?

This showed the following response from **ChatGPT 3.5**, as shown in *Figure 10.19*:

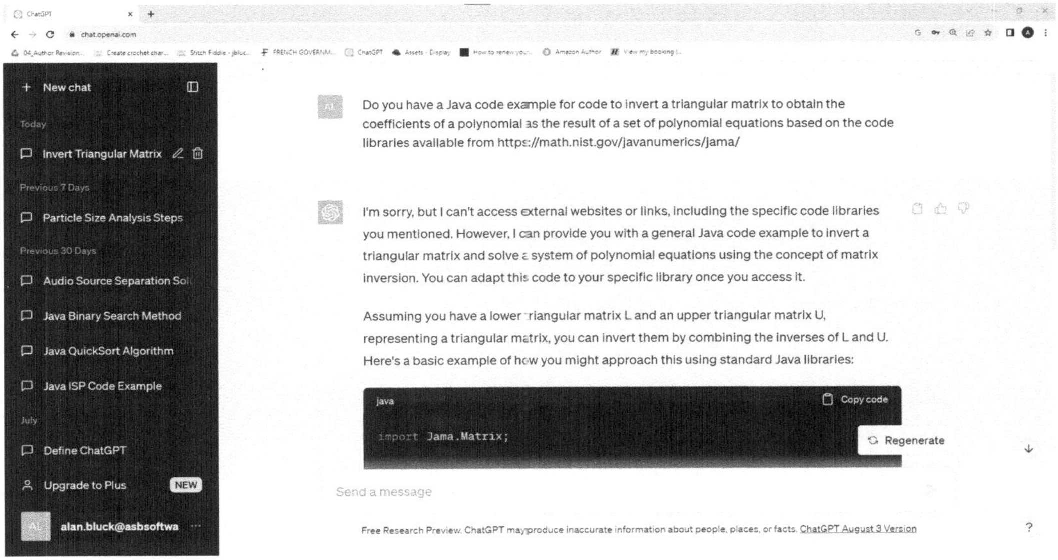

***Figure 10.19**: The response from **ChatGPT 3.5** showing that it is using the **Jama.Matrix** code*

So, although the **OpenAI ChatGPT 3.5** trained **AI** confirms that it has no internet access, it clearly has scraped the internet before for our website we found, in order to use the import statement, it displays.

The full response from **ChatGPT 3.5** is as follows:

"*I'm sorry, but* **I can't access external websites or links**, *including the specific code libraries* you mentioned. However, I can provide you with a general Java code example to invert a triangular matrix and solve a system of polynomial equations using the concept of matrix inversion. You can adapt this code to your specific library once you access it.

Assuming you have a lower triangular matrix L and an upper triangular matrix U, representing a triangular matrix, you can invert them by combining the inverses of L and U. Here's a basic example of how you might approach this using standard Java libraries:

```
```java
import Jama.Matrix;


public class TriangularMatrixInversionExample {
    public static void main(String[] args) {
        // Define your coefficients matrix A here (lower triangular part)
```
```

```
        double[][] coefficients = {
            {1.0, 0.0, 0.0},
            {2.0, 3.0, 0.0},
            {4.0, 5.0, 6.0}
        };

        // Create a matrix from the coefficients
        Matrix A = new Matrix(coefficients);

        // Calculate the inverse of the lower triangular matrix
        Matrix LInverse = A.inverse();
        // Define your polynomial equation result vector B here (upper 
triangular part)
        double[][] polynomialResults = {
            {10.0},
            {20.0},
            {30.0}
        };
        // Create a matrix from the polynomial results
        Matrix B = new Matrix(polynomialResults);
        // Solve for the coefficients using the inverted lower triangular 
matrix
        Matrix coefficientsVector = LInverse.times(B);
        // Print the resulting coefficients vector
        coefficientsVector.print(5, 2);
    }
}
```

Keep in mind that this is a simplified example and might need adjustments based on the actual structure of your code library and the triangular matrices you're working with. Make sure to consult the documentation of the library you're using for the exact syntax and methods related to matrix inversion and multiplication."

This example was compiled and run without any changes, or errors, giving the output, as follows:

```
10.00
 0.00
-1.67
```

We can validate this result using the online matrix calculator available at **https://matrixcalc.org/**

So, we enter the first Java code matrix, as shown in *Figure* 10.20, based on the Java code supplied, and then select the **Inverse** button as highlighted:

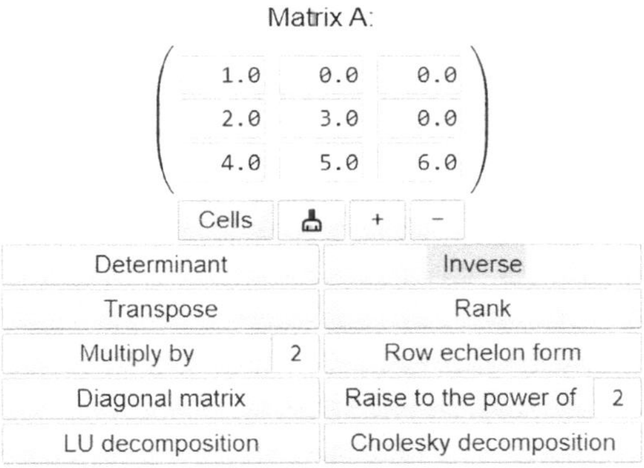

***Figure* 10.20**: *The Matrix A boxes are filled with the values as set in the Java code*

The inverse result is shown in the lower panel of the calculator giving the following, as shown in *Figure* 10.21:

$$\begin{pmatrix} 1.0 & 0.0 & 0.0 \\ 2.0 & 3.0 & 0.0 \\ 4.0 & 5.0 & 6.0 \end{pmatrix}^{(-1)} = \begin{pmatrix} 1 & 0 & 0 \\ \frac{-2}{3} & \frac{1}{3} & 0 \\ \frac{-1}{9} & \frac{-5}{18} & \frac{1}{6} \end{pmatrix}$$

***Figure* 10.21**: *The Result of the inverse calculation of the matrix*

Next, we enter the Vector values we are multiplying by using the Java code example values, as shown in *Figure 10.22*, and multiply the inverse matrix and the vector together:

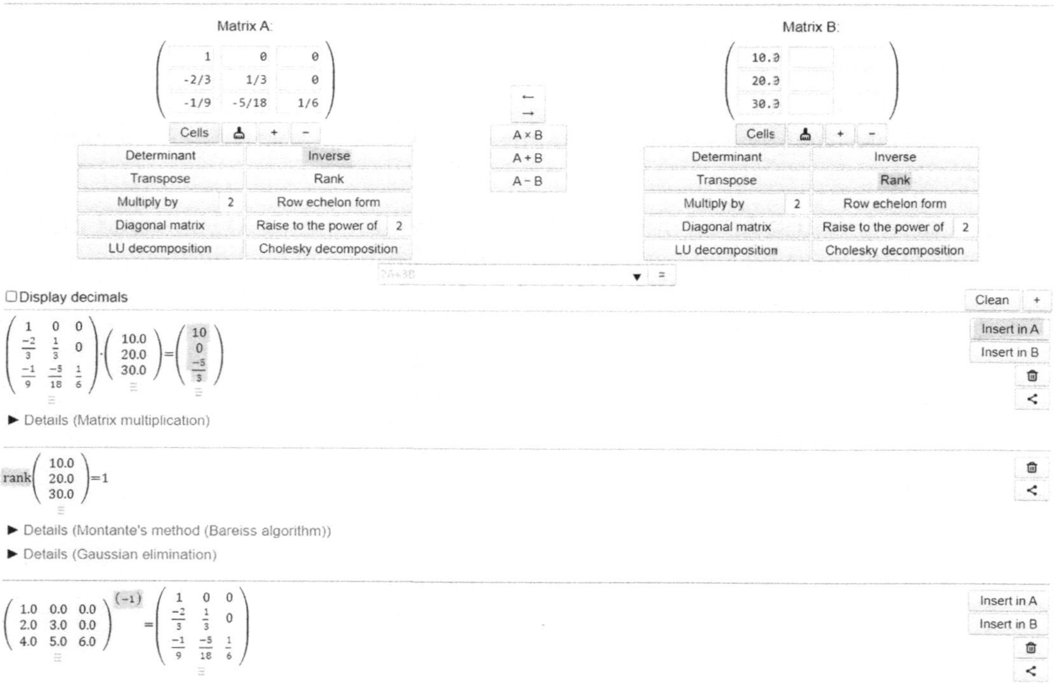

***Figure 10.22**: The final result is highlighted*

In *Figure 10.23*, after we entered the **Inverse** button, we used the **Insert in A** button to load the inverse result into the **Matrix A** box ready for the next calculation.

We then entered the **Vector** values into the **Matrix B** box and clicked the **Rank** button (which confirms this as a **rank** of 1). Next, we clicked the **A x B**, top button in the middle, which gave us our result, highlighted in *Figure 10.22*, as 10, 0, and -5/3.

Finally, we clicked the **Display decimals** tick box and clicked the **A x B** button again, as shown in *Figure 10.23:*

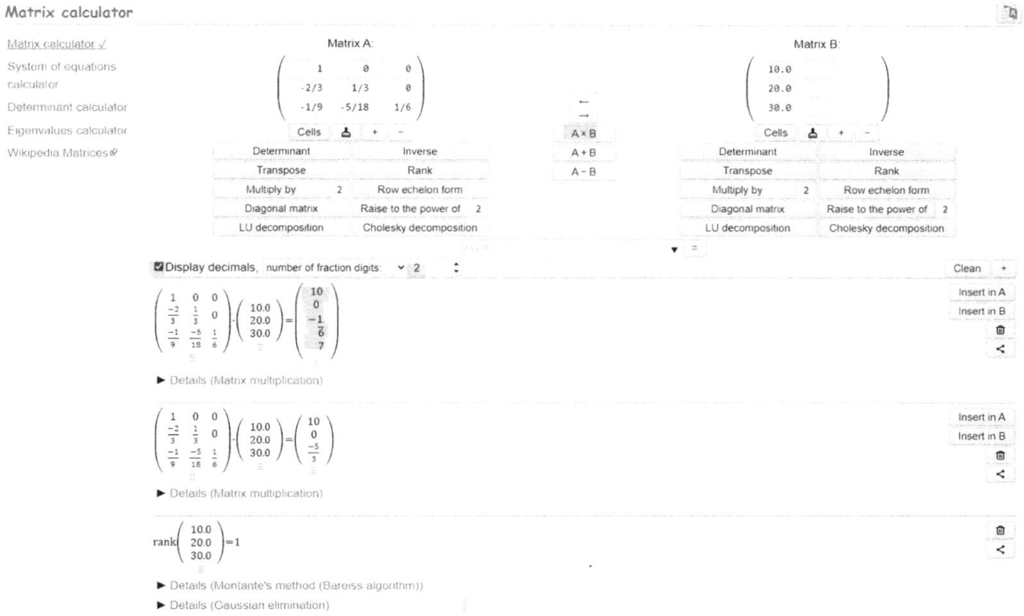

Figure 10.23: *The final decimalized highlighted results for the* **Matrix** *calculator validation*

The final result can be seen in detail in *Figure* 10.23, as shown when zoomed in *Figure 10.24*:

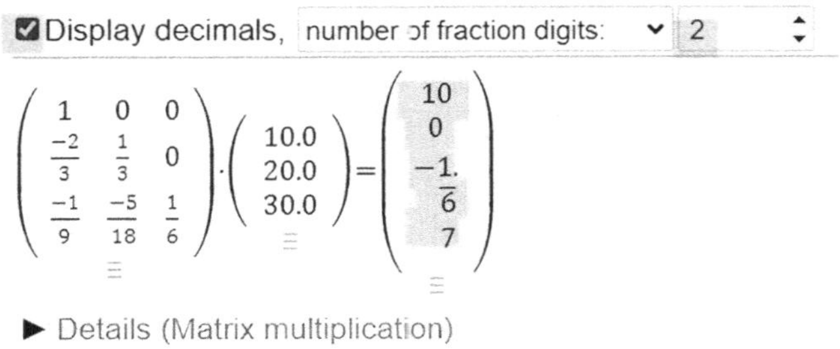

Figure 10.24: *The final decimalized highlighted results for the Matrix calculator*

The results can be seen to match the **ChatGPT 3.5** Java code output:

```
10.00
 0.00
-1.67
```

The **Matrix** calculation details can be seen by clicking the "**Details (Matrix multiplication)**" opener, as shown in *Figure* 10.24, to display the calculations, as shown in *Figure* 10.25:

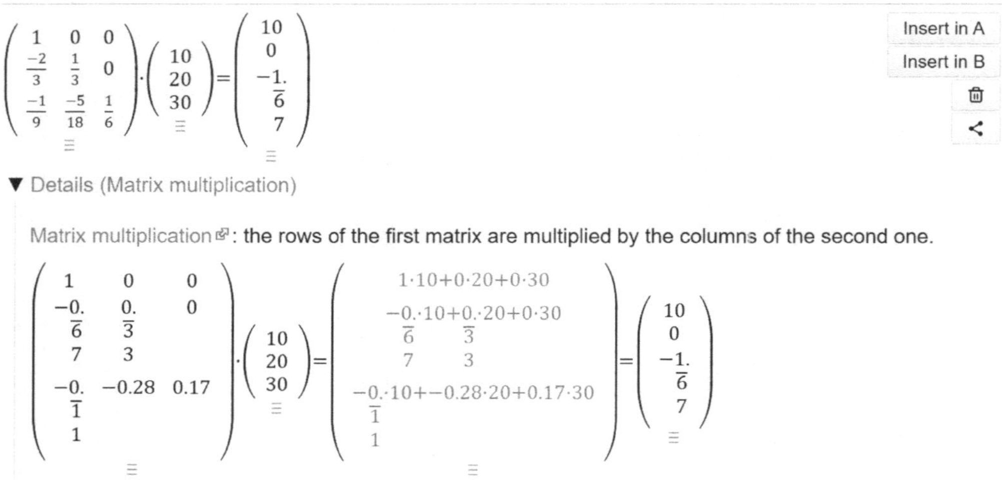

Figure* 10.25**: *The "Details (Matrix multiplication)***" opener, for* **https://matrixcalc.org/**

Conclusion

We asked three different AI systems: the **Ask AI** mobile phone app, the **Perplexity AI** mobile phone App, and the **OpenAI ChatGPT 3.5** web-chat app, to provide Java code examples to invert a triangular matrix to obtain the coefficients of a polynomial as the result of a set of polynomial equations.

Then, we asked the **OpenAI ChatGPT 3.5 (https://chat.openai.com/**) an additional follow-up question to supply the Java code to invert a triangular matrix to obtain the coefficients of a polynomial as the result of a set of polynomial equations based on the code libraries available from **https://math.nist.gov/javanumerics/jama/.**

This last question was based on the additional research we conducted using the Google search text: '**free example java code for matrix solving equations**".

This finally produced fully working Java example code, which we then tested using an excellent (and free-to-use) **Matrix calculator**.

So, the first **Ask AI** Java code example contained some errors and didn't correctly display the expected results. In addition, the **Perplexity AI** Java code required the matrix embedded in the code to be already inverted.

The final Java code example from **OpenAI ChatGPT 3.5** (with the help from the **Jama-1.0.3.jar** matrix library we had already found) gave us Java code that produced the results as expected.

In the next chapter, we will describe and validate code, generated by ChatGPT, which is the response to provide a Java program to use the **IBM FileNet Document manager** Java **API** calls to create a new document, set the document properties, add content to it, save the document, and then file it in a specified **Object Store** folder.

Points to Remember

- The Java code results from an AI may appear to run and display results, but the code should always be validated using an independent process.
- Using a Google search can sometimes produce better results, but if you are going to use the Java code obtained from the link results for a commercial application or a publication, make absolutely sure that you have identified the copyright limitations.
- Java code for matrix calculations can be tested using the internet web-based Matrix calculator, available at **https://matrixcalc.org/**

Multiple Choice Questions

1. **Which AI finally gave working, validated Java code?**
    a. Perplexity AI
    b. OpenAI ChatGPT 3.5
    c. Ask AI
    d. Phind AI
2. **What is the degree of our test polynomial, 2x^2 + x + 1 = 22?**
    a. 1
    b. 2
    c. 3
    d. 4

3. **Which of the following matrix equations gives us the correct result for the Vector coefficients of the matrix representing the input test polynomials we used?**

   (where A is our polynomial matrix, B is the result vector of the polynomials, and C is the coefficient results)

   a. $A^{-1}\ B = C$
   b. $A\ B^{-1} = C$
   c. $A^{-1}\ B^{-1} = C$
   d. $A^{-1} = B\ C$

4. **Which of the following Eclipse IDE Project property tabs allows the version of the Java JRE system to be selected?**

   a. Projects
   b. Libraries
   c. Order and Export
   d. Module Dependencies

Answers

1. **b**
2. **b**
3. **a**
4. **b**

Questions

1. What internet websites would you view to get a background knowledge of some of the mathematical techniques used for matrix calculations?
2. What website would you use to validate a Java program matrix calculation to ensure the results given were mathematically correct?
3. What other question could we have asked the AI to help us validate the matrix calculations? (Hint: we are looking for an online, website matrix calculator).
4. There is another Apache Java library for mathematical functions we used in Chapter 7, can you write a short list of the Java methods from this library, which we could use to solve the polynomial we have used as test data?

Key Terms

- **Cholesky decomposition**: Cholesky decomposition can be used to solve systems of linear equations; it is a decomposition of a Hermitian, positive-definite matrix into the product of a lower triangular matrix and its conjugate transpose.
- **Conjugate Transpose Matrix:** The conjugate transpose of a matrix interchanges the row and column index for each element of the matrix, effectively reflecting the elements across the main diagonal.
- **Gaussian Elimination**: This is the process of adding multiples of one equation to the other equations in order to eliminate a variable and then this process is repeated until only one variable is left. Once this final variable is found, the value is substituted back into the other equations in order to calculate the remaining unknowns.
- **Hermitian**: A square matrix is described as a **Hermitian** matrix if it is equal to its conjugate transpose matrix. A complex square matrix $A_{n \times n} = [a_{ij}]$ is said to be a Hermitian matrix if $A = A^H$, where A^H is the conjugate transpose of matrix A.
- **Matrix**: It is a set of numbers arranged in rows and columns to form a rectangular array. Each number in the array is called an element.
- **Identity Matrix**: An identity matrix is a square matrix having "1" value elements on the main diagonal, and "0" value elements everywhere else.

  These are called identity matrices because when they are multiplied with another compatible matrix, you get the first compatible matrix, unchanged again.
- **Inverse Matrix**: An inverse matrix of matrix A (written as A^{-1}) is a matrix that when multiplied with the original matrix A gives the identity matrix. This inverse matrix calculation is shown as $A^{-1} A = I$, where A is a square matrix and I is the identity matrix.
- **Matrix Inversion**: As for the Inverse Matrix, the product between a square matrix and its inverse is equal to the identity matrix.
- **Polynomial**: A polynomial defines a mathematical expression that contains unknown variables, constants, and exponents combined with add, subtract, multiply, and divide operators.
- **Rank**: The maximum number of linearly independent columns of a matrix.
- **Row Echelon**: A matrix is in echelon form if it has the shape resulting from a Gaussian elimination.

- **Triangular Matrix:** This defines an upper triangular matrix, sometimes denoted as U, which is a square matrix where all of the elements below the principal diagonal are zeros, or a lower triangular matrix, sometimes denoted as L, which is a square matrix where all of the elements above the principal diagonal are zeros.
- **Vector:** A vector is the special case of a matrix, where there is only one row or column.

CHAPTER 11

ChatGPT Generated Java Code to Store a Document in the IBM FileNet System

Introduction

In this chapter, the **Ask AI ChatGPT 3.5,** mobile phone **App,** was asked if there was any example **Java** code to store a document in the latest **IBM FileNet Document Management** system using the **FileNet Java API**.

The code, generated by the **ChatGPT AI**, established a connection to the **FileNet** server, created a new document, set the document properties, added content to it, saved the document, and then filed it in the specified **IBM FileNet Object Store** folder.

Structure

In this chapter, we will discuss the following topics:

- **ChatGPT** generated **Java** code to store a document in the latest **IBM FileNet Document Management** system
- Store a document in the latest **IBM FileNet Document Management** system – **Java** code validation using an **Eclipse IDE** Java Program Project

ChatGPT generated Java code to store a document in the latest IBM FileNet Document Management system

The **IBM FileNet Document Management** system provides an extensive set of **Java** and **C#** language libraries (using the **.NET API**) to support the **FileNet API** for program development to enhance the standard system, enabling the automatic upload, maintenance, and distribution of documents in a server for storage with both database and file storage facilities supported. The **IBM FileNet API** transparently supports a number of commercially available Database systems, such as **IBM DB2** 11.x, **Oracle** 12c, and **Microsoft SQL*Server**.

The **Ask AI** Mobile phone App was asked the following question:

Is there example Java code to store a document in the latest IBM FileNet Document Management system, using the FileNet Java API?

The **Ask AI** app responded as follows:

"Certainly! Here's an example of Java code that demonstrates how to store a document in IBM FileNet using the FileNet Java API:

````
```java
import com.filenet.api.collection.ContentElementList;
import com.filenet.api.core.Connection;
import com.filenet.api.core.ContentTransfer;
import com.filenet.api.core.Document;
import com.filenet.api.core.Factory;
import com.filenet.api.core.Folder;
import com.filenet.api.core.ObjectStore;
import com.filenet.api.util.UserContext;
import com.ibm.filenet.api.util.CEConnection;

public class FileNetDocumentStorageExample {

    public static void main(String[] args) {
        // Connection parameters
        String uri = "http://localhost:9080/wsi/FNCEWS40MTOM/";
        String username = "your_username";
````
````

```
String password = "your_password";

// Document properties
String documentPath = "/Folder/Subfolder/";
String documentName = "example_document.txt";
String documentContent = "This is the content of the document.";

// Establish connection to FileNet
Connection connection = CEConnection.getCEConnection(uri);
UserContext.get().pushSubject(UserContext.
    createSubject(connection, username, password, null));

try {
    // Get the Object Store
    ObjectStore objectStore = Factory.ObjectStore.
     fetchInstance(connection, "your_object_store", null);

    // Get the target folder
    Folder targetFolder = Factory.Folder.
          fetchInstance(objectStore, documentPath, null);

    // Create a new document
    Document document = Factory.Document.
          createInstance(objectStore, null);

    // Set document properties
    document.getProperties().putValue("DocumentTitle",
          documentName);
    document.set_MimeType("text/plain");

    // Create a content element list
    ContentElementList contentList = Factory.ContentElement.
          createList();

    // Create a content transfer object
    ContentTransfer contentTransfer = Factory.ContentTransfer.
```

```
createInstance();

            // Set the content of the document
            contentTransfer.setCaptureSource(documentContent);
            contentTransfer.set_ContentType("text/plain");
            contentTransfer.set_RetrievalName(documentName);
            contentList.add(contentTransfer);

            // Set the content of the document
            document.set_ContentElements(contentList);

            // Save the document
            document.save(RefreshMode.REFRESH);

            // File the document in the target folder
            document.file(targetFolder, null, null, null);

            System.out.println("Document stored successfully.");
        } catch (Exception e) {
            e.printStackTrace();
        } finally {
            // Disconnect from FileNet
            UserContext.get().popSubject();
        }
    }
} ```
```

This code establishes a connection to the FileNet server, creates a new document, sets its properties, adds content to it, saves the document, and then files it in the specified folder. Make sure to replace the connection parameters (`uri`, `username`, `password`) and document properties (`documentPath`, `documentName`, `documentContent`) with your own values.

Note that you'll need to have the FileNet Java API and its dependencies included in your project for this code to work."

In the preceding Note, the **Ask AI** app acknowledged that we will need to provide the **FileNet Java API** libraries, which will require downloading and then some configuration for the **Eclipse IDE Java** project property, **Class path**.

I also asked the **OpenAI ChaGPT 3.5 (https://chat.openai.com/)** the same question as for **Ask AI**, but the Java code produced was not viable, with many import statements, such as:

```
import com.ibm.ecm.util.p8.P8Connection;
import com.ibm.ecm.util.p8.P8Domain;
import com.ibm.ecm.util.p8.P8Session;
import com.ibm.ecm.util.p8.ce.*;
import com.ibm.ecm.util.p8.pe.P8Processor;
import com.ibm.ecm.util.p8.pe.P8ProcessItem;
import com.ibm.ecm.util.p8.pe.P8Queue;
import com.ibm.ecm.util.p8.pe.P8QueueItem;
import com.ibm.ecm.util.p8.pe.P8QueueProcessor;
```

On asking the **OpenAI ChatGPT**:

**"where can I download the Java Library for the package com.ibm.ecm.util.p8.P8Connection"**

The response was as follows:

"As of my last knowledge update in September 2021, the package com.ibm.ecm.util.p8.P8Connection does not appear to be part of the standard IBM

FileNet libraries provided by IBM. It's possible that this package is specific to a custom utility or framework developed for a particular project or organization.

If you are looking for a Java library related to IBM Enterprise Content Management (ECM), you should generally rely on the official IBM FileNet libraries and APIs, which are provided by IBM as part of the FileNet installation or SDK. These libraries include the com.filenet.api package for interacting with FileNet Content Manager."

(Along with further impressive but useless waffle.)

It is also necessary to install a **FileNet** system to use for testing the program code. There is a complete description of the step-by-step procedure to build an **IBM FileNet** document management system on our **RedHat Linux** server available for free download from **ResearchGate** using the **DOI URL** link: **http://dx.doi.org/10.13140/RG.2.2.21170.76480,**

Visit the download web page and then select the **Download file PDF** button, as shown in *Figure* 11.1:

***Figure 11.1**: The **Download file PDF** button is selected for the free **ContentFoundation5.5.3InstallationonRHEL8.0_V2.docx** MS Word document*

The latest available version of the **IBM FileNet** system is currently version **5.5.11.**

**Note:**

The version 5.5.11 of IBM FileNet was released on 23rd June 2023, but some IBM Knowledge base document links still have the 5.5.10 version as the latest link.

(At the time of writing, September 2023.)

The part numbers for this new IBM FileNet version 5.5.11 are listed at the following URL:

**https://www.ibm.com/support/pages/download-ibm-filenet-content-manager-version-5511**

With release notes at:

**https://www.ibm.com/docs/en/filenet-p8-platform/5.5.11?topic=welcome-release-notes**

There is also a new link for the website for logging into the **IBM** system for downloads:

**https://www.ibm.com/software/passportadvantage/pao_download_software.html**

# Store a document in the latest IBM FileNet Document Management system – Java code validation using an Eclipse Java Program Project

First, we need to download the **Java IBM FileNet API** jar libraries. These can be downloaded from the **IBM FileNet** server system **ACCE** web application, IBM **A**dministration **C**onsole for **C**ontent platform **E**ngine, as outlined in the following procedure:

> **Note**
>
> This is the best practice procedure for using the IBM API libraries since there are Java objects serialized that can change with the FileNet API version. This procedure avoids the possibility of using deprecated methods or invalid objects. The **IBM FileNet API** supports two types of **Java API**: **EJB** services and the **MTOM** (Message Transmission Optimization Mechanism) protocol web **SOAP** services.

1. On our system, we can use the URL, **http://ecmukdemo22:9080/acce/**, to display the login window as follows:

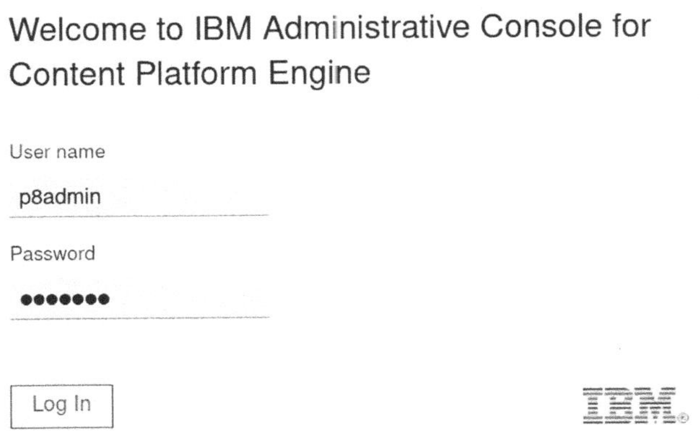


***Figure 11.2**: Log in to the **ACCE IBM Administrative Console for Content Engine***

2. Then, in the **ACCE** administration console, from the domain navigation pane, click the **Client API Download** folder, as shown in *Figure 11.3*:

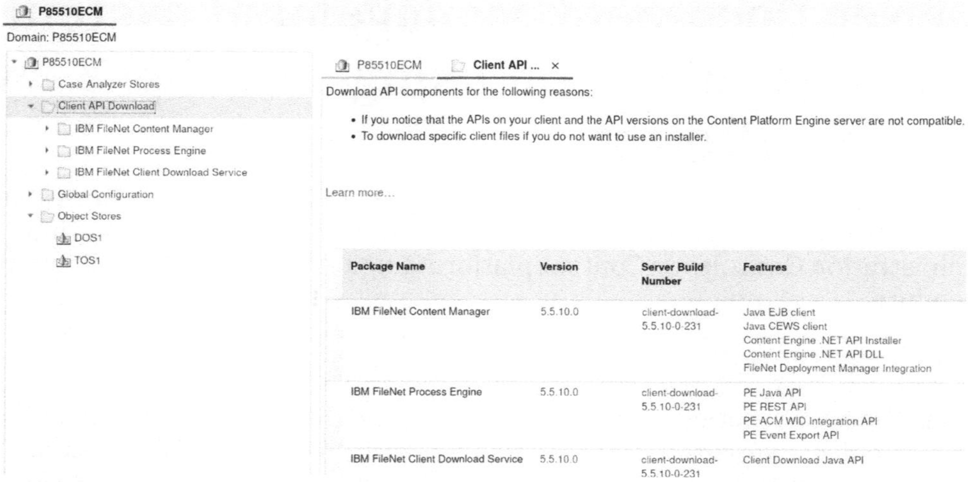

***Figure 11.3**: The **Client API Download** folder is opened for the sub-folder Client Jar sets*

3. Locate the client files that you want to download by selecting the **IBM FileNet Content Manager** sub-folder. Then, right-click on the **Java CEWS client** and select the **Download Feature Set**, as shown in *Figure 11.4*:

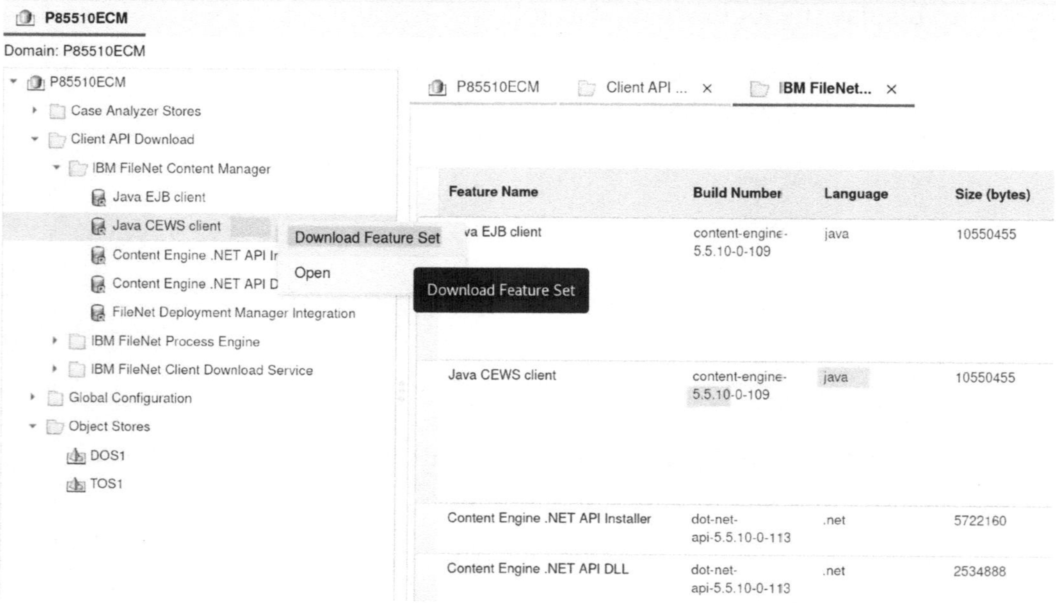

***Figure 11.4**: Right-click on the **Java CEWS client** for the Download Feature Set option*

4. The jar files are downloaded from the Document management server object store as a **JavaCEWSclient.zip** file, as shown in *Figure 11.5*:

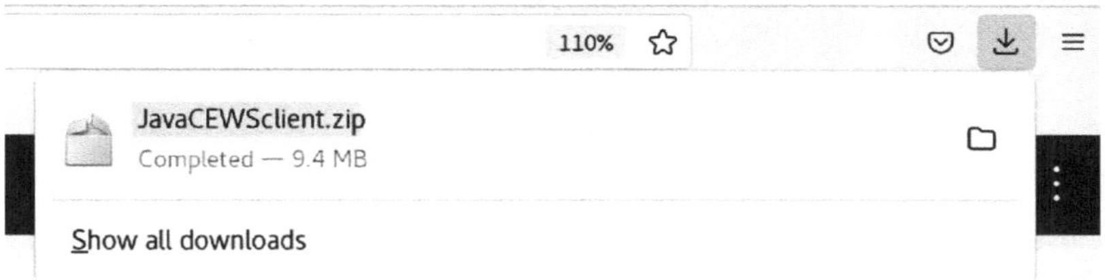


***Figure 11.5***: *The* ***JavaCEWSclient.zip*** *file is downloaded for use*

5. The **Folder icon** was selected to open the **Linux File Manager**, and the right button was clicked on the zip file icon to select the **Extract to...** menu item, as shown in *Figure 11.6:*

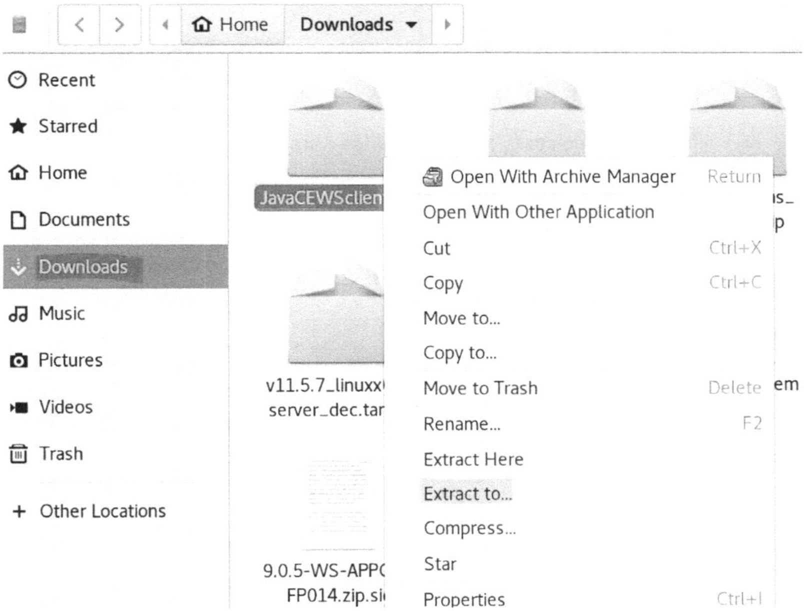


***Figure 11.6***: *The* ***Extract to...*** *option is selected*

6. The **Select** button is clicked after choosing the destination extraction subfolder, **/root/eclipse/eclipse/AILibs,** as shown in *Figure 11.7*:

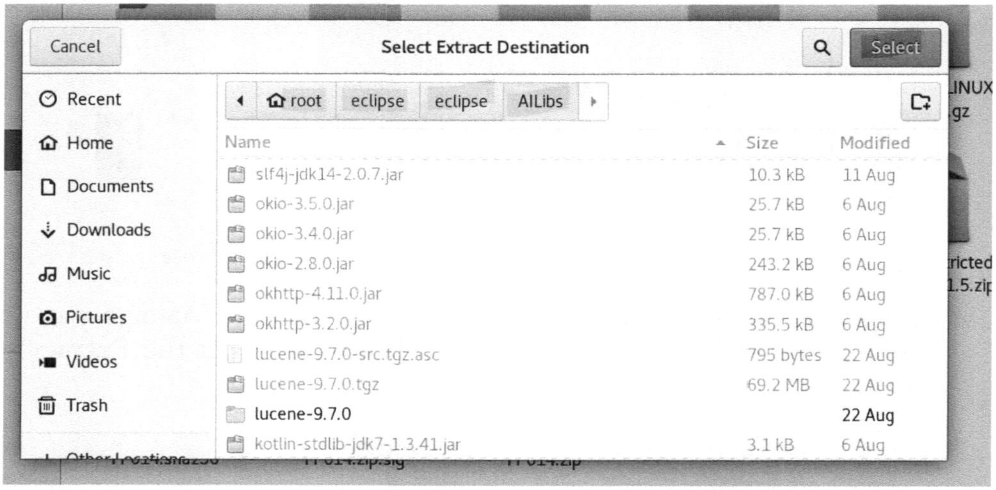

***Figure 11.7**: The **Select** button is selected to extract jar files to **/root/eclipse/eclipse/AILibs/JavaCEWSclient***

Next, we need to create the **Eclipse IDE** Java project and the package and class files, as shown in *Figure 11.8*:

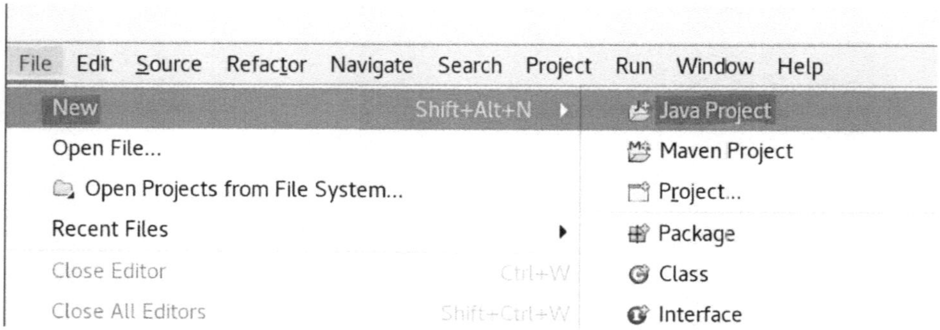

***Figure 11.8**: Create the **Eclipse IDE** Java project and the package and class files*

The project name is entered as **IBMFileNetDocuments_Chapter11** in the highlighted **Project name** field, as shown in *Figure 11.9*:

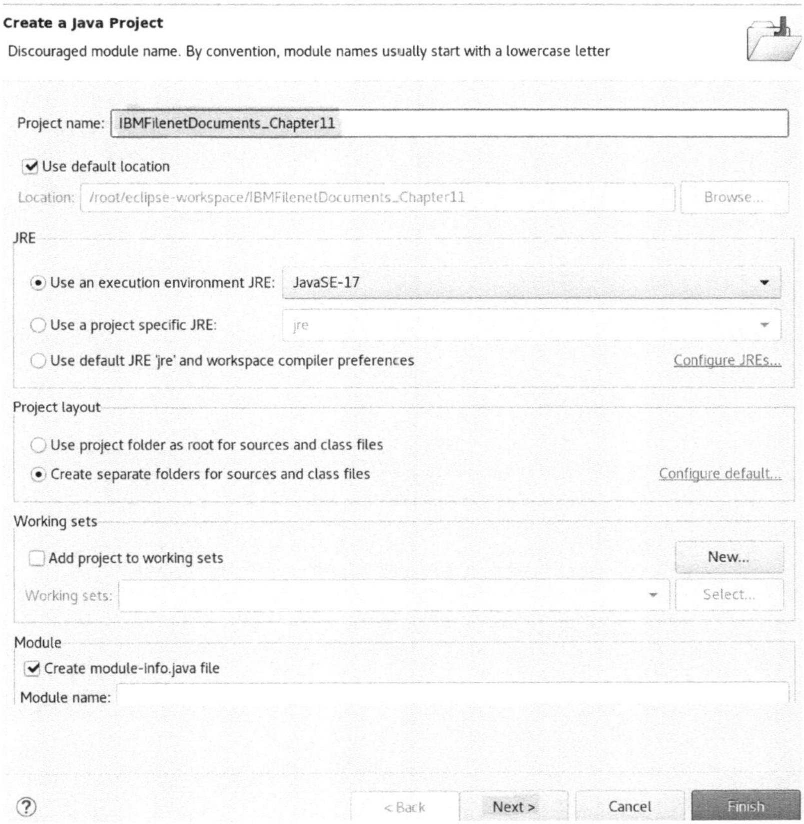


***Figure 11.9**: The project name is entered as **IBMFileNetDocuments_Chapter11***

The **Next>** button is then clicked, as shown in *Figure 11.10*, to display the Java settings.

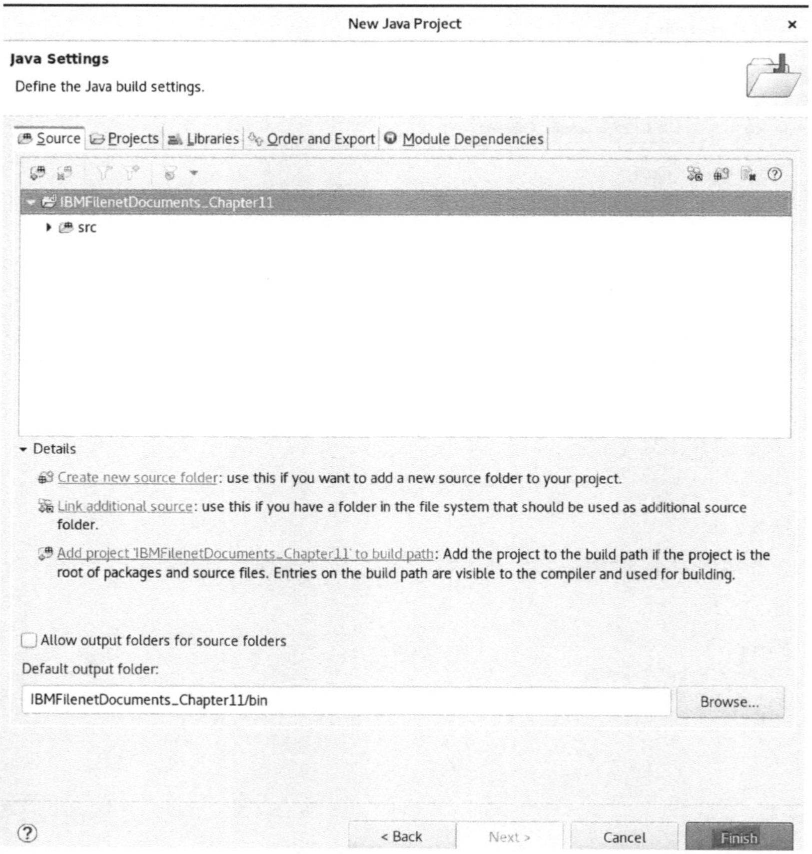


***Figure 11.10*: IBMFileNetDocuments_Chapter11** *Project Java settings are displayed*

After the **Finish** button is clicked, as shown in *Figure 11.10*, the **New ->Class** menu is selected by right-clicking on the **Project name** node, as highlighted in *Figure 11.11:*

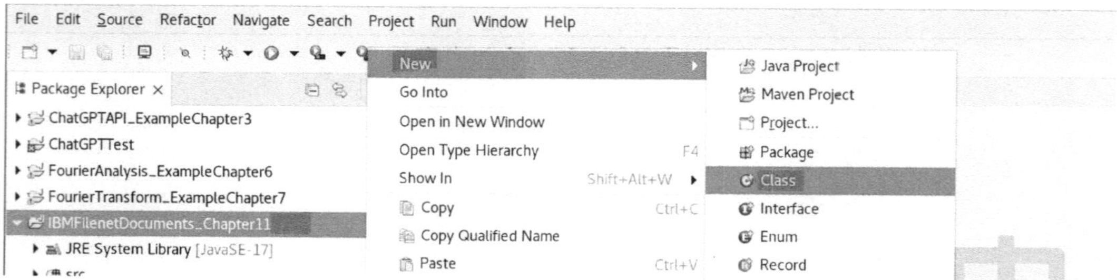


***Figure 11.11***: *The project* **New-> Class** *menu item is selected, as highlighted*

The new **FileNetDocumentStorageExample** class name, suggested by the **Ask AI**, **ChatGPT 3.5** system, was entered into the **Eclipse IDE "New Java Class"** window, as shown in *Figure 11.12*:

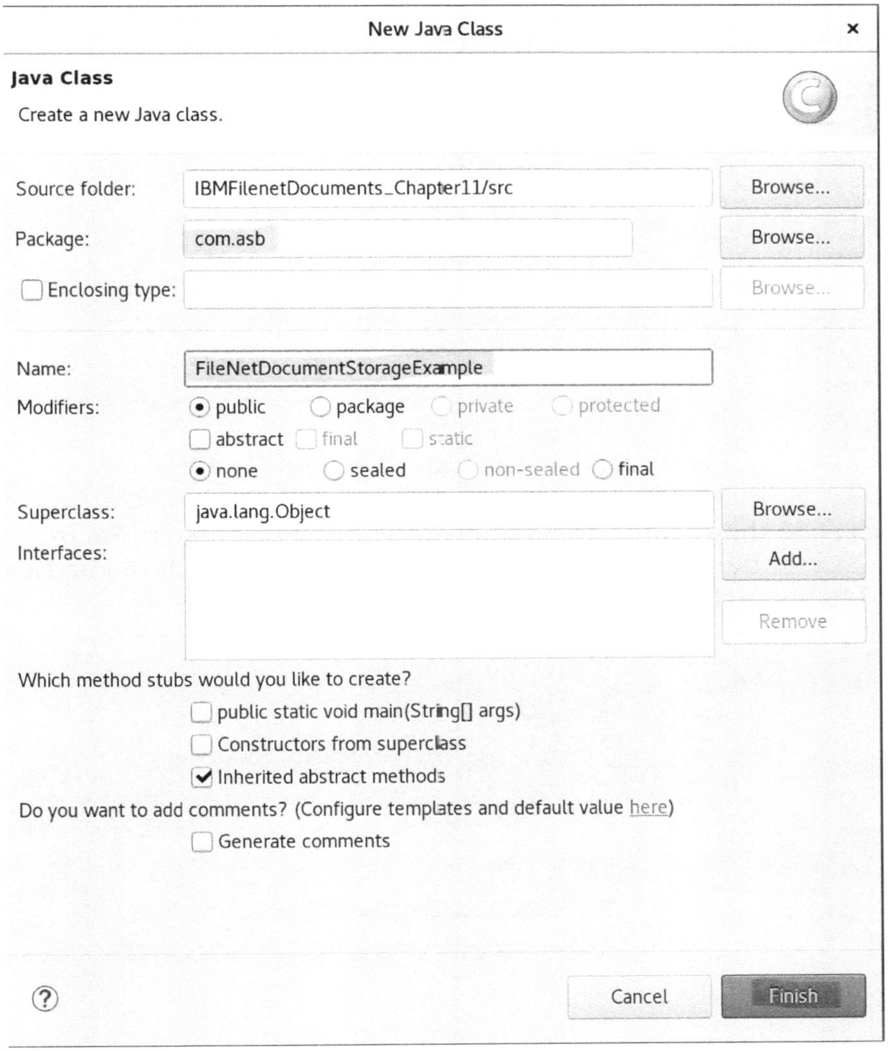


**Figure 11.12**: *The* **FileNetDocumentStorageExample** *class name was entered*

The initial **Java** code suggested by **Ask AI** was pasted into the skeleton **FileNetDocumentStorageExample.java,** as shown in *Figure 11.13:*

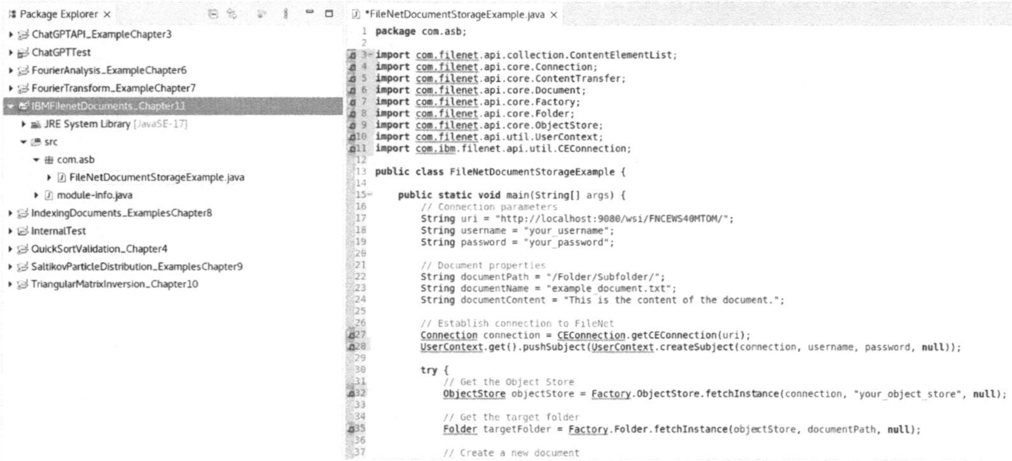

***Figure 11.13**: The initial **Java** code suggested by **Ask AI***

This **Java** code shows there are **import** errors, as highlighted in *Figure* 11.13, that we can correct by adding the **p8ce10n.jar** and the **Jace.jar Java** libraries to the project **Modulepath** node, as shown in *Figure 11.14:*

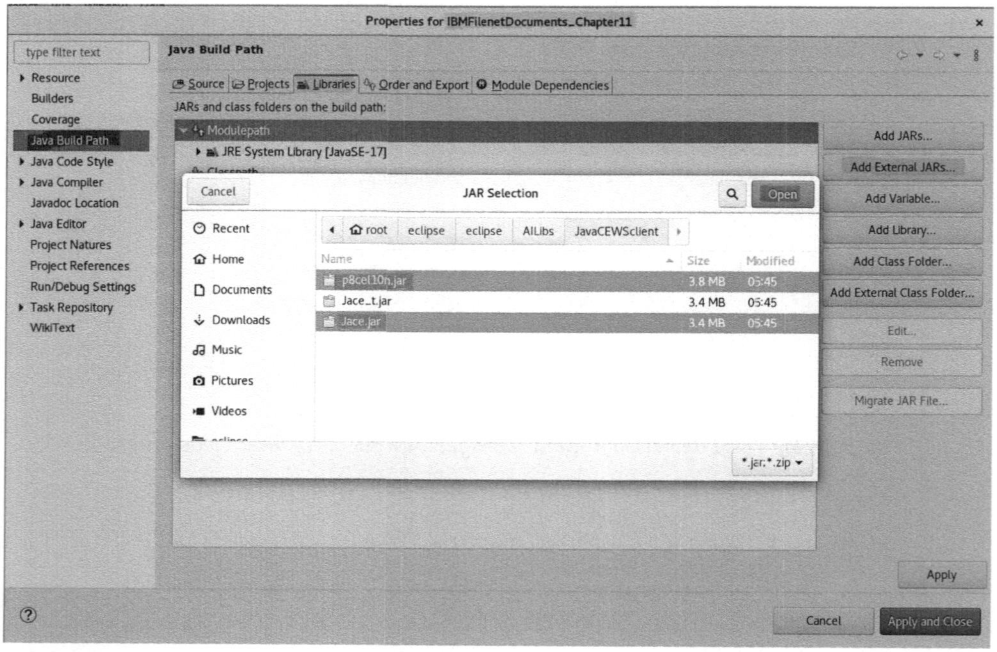

***Figure 11.14**: The **p8ce10n.jar** and the **Jace.jar Java** libraries are added to the **Modulepath***

After adding the **p8ce10n.jar** and the **Jace.jar Java** libraries, we still have to update the **module-info.java** file, which we can let the **Eclipse IDE** change for us by clicking on **Fix,** as highlighted in *Figure 11.15*:

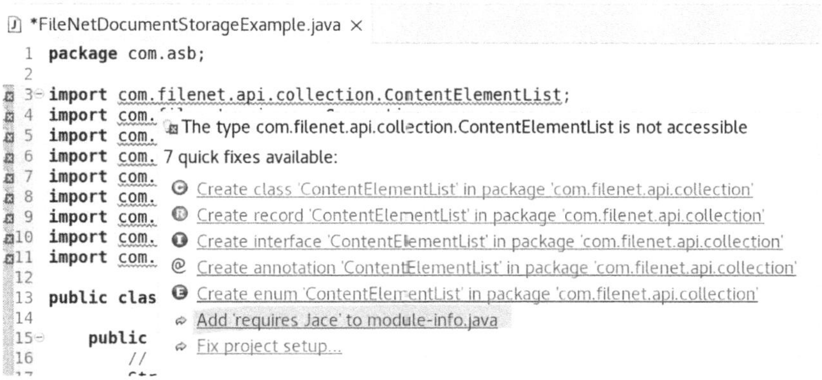


***Figure 11.15**: The **Add 'requires Jace' to module-info.java** is selected, as highlighted in the Fix list*

This still leaves a few errors. The first in the code is the line for connection, as follows:

```
Connection connection = CEConnection.getCEConnection(uri);
```

This **`CEConnection`** `class` is from a whole helper **Java** source class that is missing, usually provided by downloading the **IBM FileNet** supporting, **DemoJava.zip** file, It is available for download at the following link:

**https://www.ibm.com/support/pages/filenet-content-engine-java-api-demo-sample-code**

The **DemoJava.zip** file usage is covered for use in the **ResearchGate** documentation, which can be accessed via the following link:

*https://doi.org/10.13140/RG.2.2.20160.69129*

(This document, entitled "***IBM FileNet P8 Java Development on ECM Cloud Private Container P8 Examples***", is available as a free download.)

The initial **CEConnection** class code from the **DemoJava.zip** file is listed as follows:

```
package com.asb;


/**
IBM grants you a nonexclusive copyright license to use all programming
code
```

```
examples from which you can generate similar function tailored to your
own
specific needs.

All sample code is provided by IBM for illustrative purposes only.
These examples have not been thoroughly tested under all conditions.
IBM,
therefore cannot guarantee or imply reliability, serviceability, or
function of
these programs.

All Programs or code component contained herein are provided to you "AS
IS "
without any warranties of any kind.
The implied warranties of non-infringement, merchantability and fitness
for a
particular purpose are expressly disclaimed.

© Copyright IBM Corporation 2007, ALL RIGHTS RESERVED.
*/

import java.util.Iterator;
import java.util.Vector;
import javax.security.auth.Subject;
import com.filenet.api.collection.ObjectStoreSet;
import com.filenet.api.core.Connection;
import com.filenet.api.core.Domain;
import com.filenet.api.core.Factory;
import com.filenet.api.core.ObjectStore;
import com.filenet.api.util.UserContext;

/**
* This object represents the connection with
* the Content Engine. Once connection is established
* it initializes Domain and ObjectStoreSet with
* available Domain and ObjectStoreSet.
```

```
*
*/
public class CEConnection
{
private Connection con;
private Domain dom;
private String domainName;
private ObjectStoreSet ost;
private Vector osnames;
private boolean isConnected;
private UserContext uc;

/*
 * constructor
 */
public CEConnection()
{
        con = null;
        uc = UserContext.get();
        dom = null;
        domainName = null;
        ost = null;
        osnames = new Vector();
        isConnected = false;
}

/*
 * Establishes connection with Content Engine using
 * supplied username, password, JAAS stanza and CE Uri.
 */
public void establishConnection(String userName, String password, String
stanza, String uri)
{
    con = Factory.Connection.getConnection(uri);
    Subject sub = UserContext.
```

```
createSubject(con,userName,password,stanza);
    uc.pushSubject(sub);
    dom = fetchDomain();
    domainName = dom.get_Name();
    ost = getOSSet();
    isConnected = true;
    return con; //ASB we added this for use with the AI code

}

/*
 * Returns Domain object.
 */
public Domain fetchDomain()
{
    dom = Factory.Domain.fetchInstance(con, null, null);
    return dom;
}

/*
 * Returns ObjectStoreSet from Domain
 */
public ObjectStoreSet getOSSet()
{
    ost = dom.get_ObjectStores();
    return ost;
}

/*
 * Returns vector containing ObjectStore
 * names from object stores available in
 * ObjectStoreSet.
 */
public Vector getOSNames()
```

```
{
        if(osnames.isEmpty())
        {
                Iterator it = ost.iterator();
                while(it.hasNext())
                {
                        ObjectStore os = (ObjectStore) it.next();
                        osnames.add(os.get_DisplayName());
                }
        }
     return osnames;
}

/*
 * Checks whether connection has established
 * with the Content Engine or not.
 */
public boolean isConnected()
{
        return isConnected;
}

/*
 * Returns ObjectStore object for supplied
 * object store name.
 */
public ObjectStore fetchOS(String name)
{
     ObjectStore os = Factory.ObjectStore.fetchInstance(dom, name, null);
     return os;
}

/*
 * Returns the domain name.
```

```
 */
public String getDomainName()
{
    return domainName;
}
}
```

The **module-info.java** has also been updated with the **jace.jar** file reference, which has the core **IBM FileNet API** classes that we require, as shown in *Figure 11.16:*

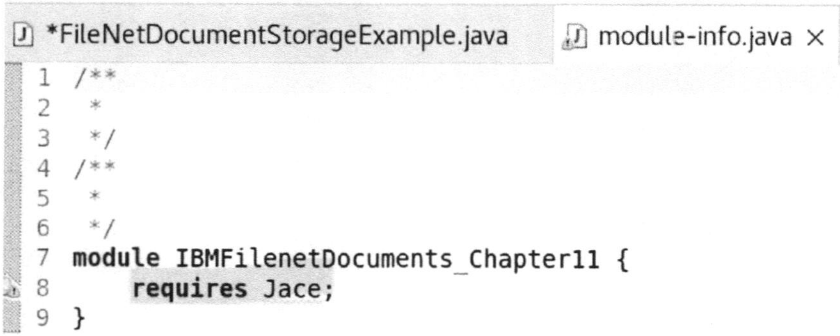


***Figure 11.16**: The **jace.jar** file reference, which has the core **IBM FileNet API** classes*

The required source code, which can be found in the folder path of the unzipped **DemoJava.zip** file, was downloaded from the link:

https://www.ibm.com/support/pages/system/files/inline-files/DemoJava.zip, and was unzipped with the path as follows:

`.../Demo/src/cesample/CEConnection.java`

This code was added to the **Eclipse IDE** project under our standard **com.asb** package, as shown in *Figure 11.17:*

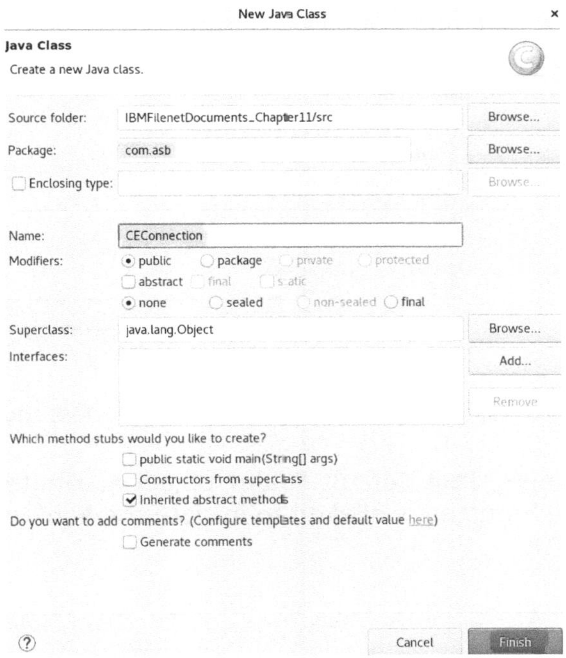


**Figure 11.17**: *The downloaded* **CEConnection Java** *class is created under* **com.asb**

Next, we need to create an **IBM FileNet Object Store Folder** object to link to our uploaded test document using the target **Object Store, TOS1,** accessed with the **ACCE** web application, as shown in *Figure 11.18*:

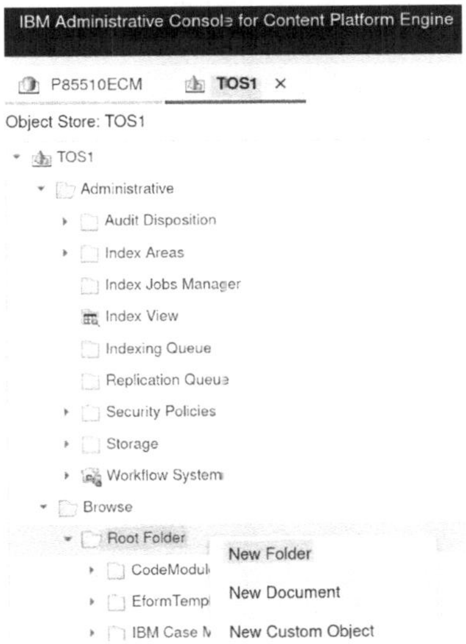


**Figure 11.18**: *The* **ACCE** *web application is used with a right-click for the* **New Folder**

We enter the test folder name as **AVA_Orange_Test** and continue selecting **Next** (taking all the defaults in the following pages) until the **Next** button is grayed out, as shown in *Figure 11.19*:

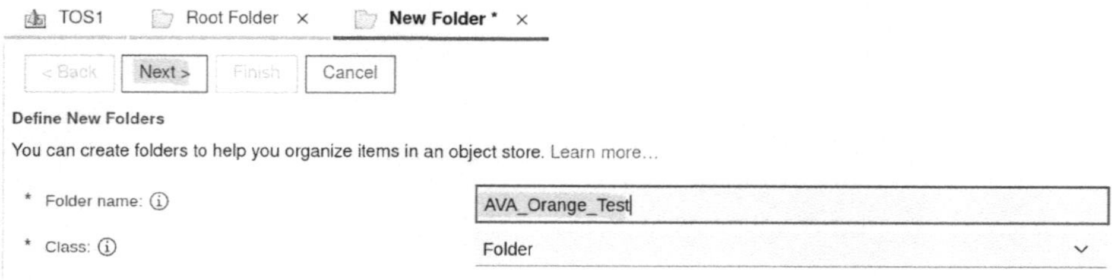


***Figure 11.19**: We enter the test folder name as **AVA_Orange_Test** and then select **Next>***

The new **AVA_Orange_Test** default **Folder** object attributes are displayed for review and the **Finish** button is clicked to initiate the **Folder** object creation, as shown in *Figure 11.20*:

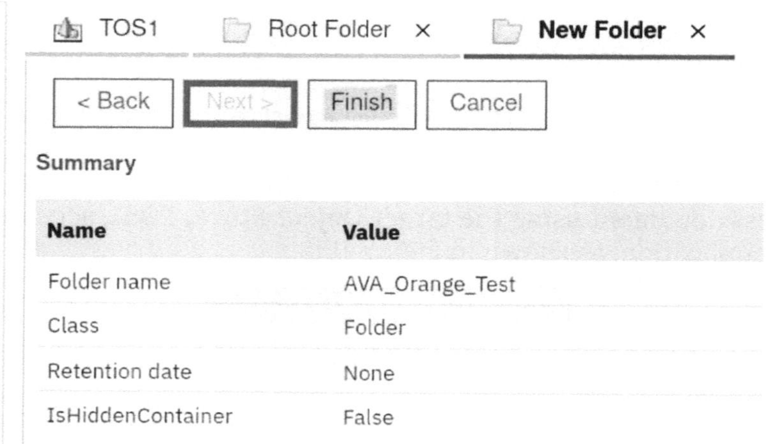


***Figure 11.20**: The new **AVA_Orange_Test Folder** object attributes are displayed for review*

The panels in the **ACCE** web application tool show that we have successfully created the **AVA_Orange_Test Folder** object, as shown in *Figure 11.21*:

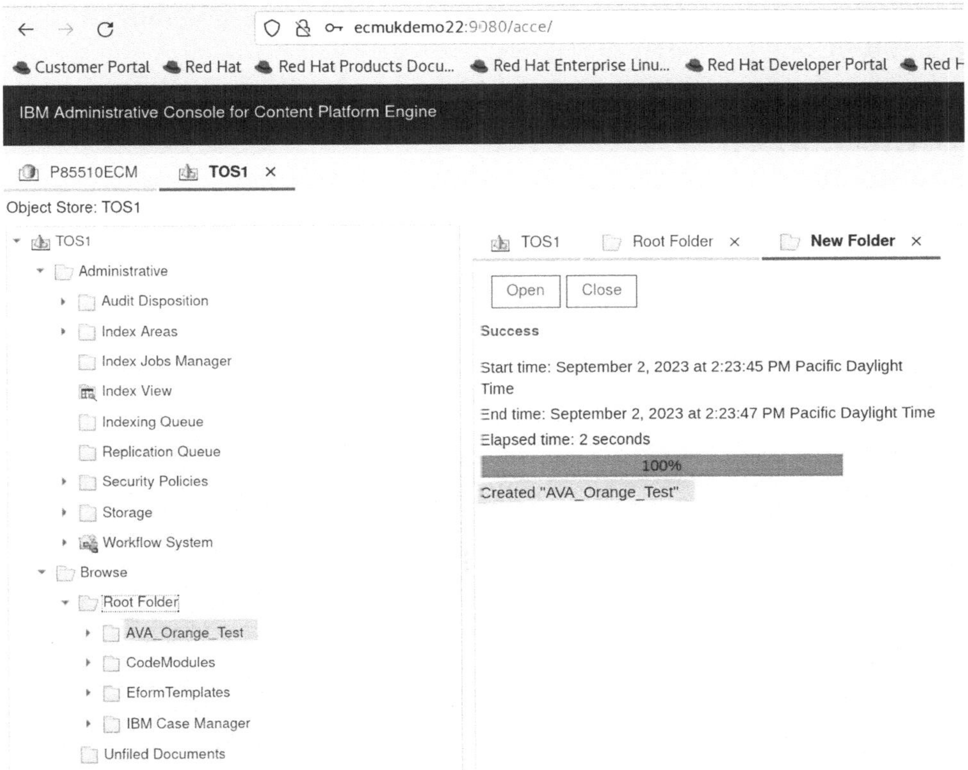


***Figure 11.21**: The **AVA_Orange_Test** folder is shown under the **Root Folder** in **TOS1***

The original code suggested by **Ask AI** requires quite a few changes. First, we have to set up the **API** configuration file for the **SOAP API** interface that the **Ask AI** app has selected.

This configuration file defines the **JAAS Web Service Interface (WSI)** protocol and is selected, as shown in *Figure 11.22*:

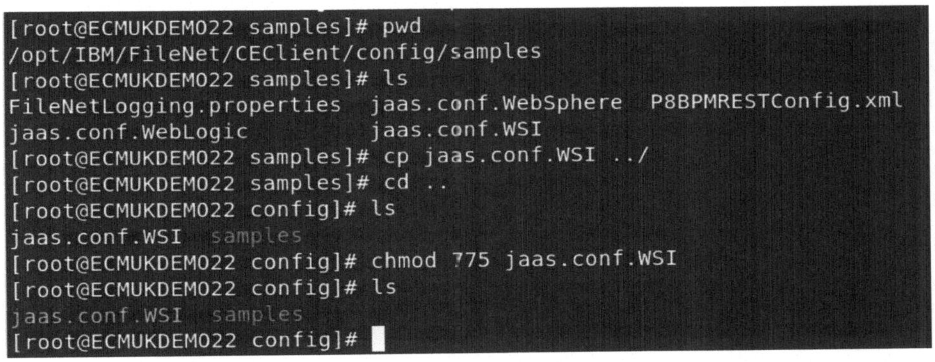


***Figure 11.22**: The **jaas.conf.WSI** file for the **JAAS WSI** protocol is selected*

The preceding commands were run to set up the **IBM FileNet** configuration file, **jaas.conf.WSI,** and are listed as follows:

```
cd /opt/IBM/FileNet/CEClient/config/samples
cp jaas.conf.WSI ../
cd ..
chmod 775 jaas.conf.WSI
```

Next, we need to create the text document we are uploading to the **TOS1** object store.

We decided to use the updated **Ask AI** Java code example for the test document text file content (in the path **/root/eclipse/eclipse**), as shown in *Figure 11.23*:

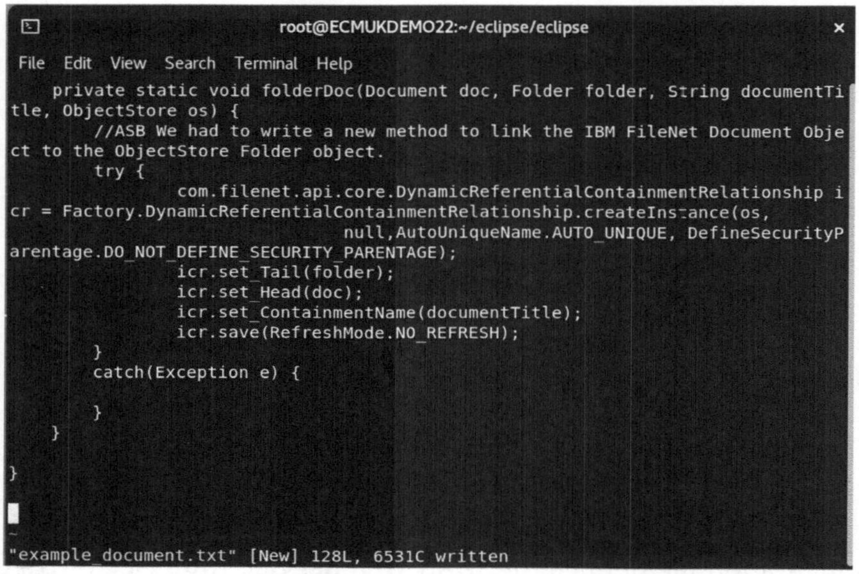


***Figure 11.23**: The test document, **example_document.txt**, is created in vi using our Java code*

Next, we reviewed all the code and made the (extensive) changes indicated in **bold/highlight** in the **Java** code lists as follows:

```
package com.asb;
//ASB There are no Java I/O classes imported which we need to have to
load a byte stream from our text document
import java.io.BufferedReader;     //ASB Added for File I/O
import java.io.File;               //ASB Added for File I/O
import java.io.FileInputStream;    //ASB Added for File I/O
import java.io.FileNotFoundException;
```

```
import java.io.FileOutputStream;  //ASB Added for File I/O
import java.io.IOException;                //ASB Added for File I/O
import java.io.InputStreamReader; //ASB Added for File I/O

import com.filenet.api.collection.ContentElementList;
import com.filenet.api.constants.AutoClassify;
import com.filenet.api.constants.AutoUniqueName;
import com.filenet.api.constants.CheckinType;
import com.filenet.api.constants.DefineSecurityParentage;
import com.filenet.api.constants.RefreshMode; //ASB Needed to add this
missing import
import com.filenet.api.core.Connection;
import com.filenet.api.core.ContentTransfer;
import com.filenet.api.core.Document;
import com.filenet.api.core.Domain;
import com.filenet.api.core.Factory;
import com.filenet.api.core.Folder;
import com.filenet.api.core.ObjectStore;
import com.filenet.api.util.UserContext;
//import com.ibm.filenet.api.util.CEConnection; //ASB we needed to change
this import
import com.filenet.api.core.Connection;

public class FileNetDocumentStorageExample {

    public static void main(String[] args) {
       Domain dom; //ASB We need this object for retrieving the Object
Store
        // Connection parameters
        String uri = "http://ecmukdemo22:9080/wsi/FNCEWS40MTOM/"; //ASB
Changed to our Server name, ecmukdemo22 from localhost
        String username = "p8admin";
//ASB your_username changed to p8admin
        String password = "filenet";
//ASB your password changed to filenet
        String stanza = "FileNetP8WSI";
//ASB Added this for the FileNet WSI connection type
        String WcmApiConfigPath = "/opt/IBM/FileNet/CEClient/config/jaas.
```

```
conf.WSI";  //ASB Added this for the FileNet WSI Path
        // Document properties
        String documentPath = "/AVA_Orange_Test";              //ASB
Changed to our TOS1 ObjectStore test folder /AVA_Orange_Test
        String documentFilePath = "/root/eclipse/eclipse";     //ASB
Added for the Linux server test document folder path
        String documentName = "example_document.txt";          //ASB
created using the vi editor
        String documentContent = "This is the content of the document.";
//ASB Not used, we use a real document here and create a byte stream

        // Establish connection to FileNet
        //ASB There is a whole helper Java source class missing, usually
provided by downloading the IBM FileNet supporting .zip file
        //ASB DenoJava.zip file Found on
        //ASB https://www.ibm.com/support/pages/filenet-content-engine-
java-api-demo-sample-code
        //ASB Also, the method is incorrect,  getCEConnection(uri) was
changed to the call
        //ASB establishConnection(userName, password, stanza, uri)
        //Connection connection = CEConnection.getCEConnection(uri); //
ASB Original AI code
        CEConnection connection = new CEConnection();
             connection.establishConnection(username, password, stanza,
uri, WcmApiConfigPath);
        //UserContext.get().pushSubject(UserContext.
createSubject(connection, username, password, null));//ASB not required
now

        try {
            // Get the Object Store
            //ObjectStore objectStore = Factory.ObjectStore.
fetchInstance(connection, "your_object_store", null); //ASB This needs
to be re-factored
             ObjectStore objectStore  =  connection.fetchOS("TOS1");//
ASB replacement code also changed the "your_object_store"

            // Get the target folder
            Folder targetFolder = Factory.Folder.
fetchInstance(objectStore, documentPath, null);
```

```
            // Create a new document
            Document document = Factory.Document.
createInstance(objectStore, null);

            // Set document properties
            document.getProperties().putValue("DocumentTitle",
documentName);
            document.set_MimeType("text/plain");

           // Create a content element list
            ContentElementList contentList = Factory.ContentElement.
createList();

            // Create a content transfer object
            ContentTransfer contentTransfer = Factory.ContentTransfer.
createInstance();
            // ASB We need to load the document file
            FileInputStream is = null;
             try {
                    is = new FileInputStream(documentFilePath + File.
separator + documentName);
             }
             catch (FileNotFoundException e){
                     e.printStackTrace();
                     }
             catch (IOException e){

             }
            // Set the content of the document
            //contentTransfer.setCaptureSource(null); // ASB Needed a
non-null value here ;
            contentTransfer.setCaptureSource(is);   // ASB This can't be
a String , so we changed documentContent to is
            contentTransfer.set_ContentType("text/plain");
           contentTransfer.set_RetrievalName(documentName);
            contentList.add(contentTransfer);

            // Set the content of the document
            document.set_ContentElements(contentList);
```

```
            document.save(RefreshMode.REFRESH);
            // File the document in the target folder
            // ASB This code doesn't work, we need another Java method
, folderDoc, to link our  FileNet Document object to the Object Store
Folder

            //document.file(targetFolder, null, null, null);//ASB
replaced with a method call
            folderDoc(document,targetFolder,documentName, objectStore);
            // Save the document
            document.checkin(AutoClassify.DO_NOT_AUTO_CLASSIFY,
CheckinType.MAJOR_VERSION);
            document.save(RefreshMode.REFRESH);

            System.out.println("Document stored successfully.");
        } catch (Exception e) {
            e.printStackTrace();
        } finally {
            // Disconnect from FileNet
            UserContext.get().popSubject();
        }
    }
    private static void folderDoc(Document doc, Folder folder, String
documentTitle, ObjectStore os) {
      //ASB We had to write a new method to link the IBM FileNet
Document Object to the ObjectStore Folder object.
      try {
            com.filenet.api.core.ReferentialContainmentRelationship rcr
= folder.file(doc,
                          AutoUniqueName.AUTO_UNIQUE, null,
DefineSecurityParentage.DO_NOT_DEFINE_SECURITY_PARENTAGE);
            rcr.set_ContainmentName(documentTitle);
            rcr.save(RefreshMode.NO_REFRESH);
      }
      catch(Exception e) {

      }
    }
```

```
}
```

And the additional modified connection code from the downloaded **DemoJava.zip** required a few changes, as highlighted:

```
package com.asb;

/**
IBM grants you a nonexclusive copyright license to use all programming code examples from which you can generate similar function tailored to your own specific needs.

All sample code is provided by IBM for illustrative purposes only.
These examples have not been thoroughly tested under all conditions. IBM, therefore cannot guarantee or imply reliability, serviceability, or function of these programs.

All Programs or code component contained herein are provided to you "AS IS "without any warranties of any kind.
The implied warranties of non-infringement, merchantability and fitness for a particular purpose are expressly disclaimed.
© Copyright IBM Corporation 2007, ALL RIGHTS RESERVED.
*/

import java.util.Iterator;
import java.util.Vector;
import javax.security.auth.Subject;
import com.filenet.api.collection.ObjectStoreSet;
import com.filenet.api.core.Connection;
import com.filenet.api.core.Domain;
import com.filenet.api.core.Factory;
import com.filenet.api.core.ObjectStore;
import com.filenet.api.util.UserContext;

/**
* This object represents the connection with
* the Content Engine. Once connection is established
* it intializes Domain and ObjectStoreSet with
* available Domain and ObjectStoreSet.
*
```

```
*/
public class CEConnection
{
private Connection con;
private Domain dom;
private String domainName;
private ObjectStoreSet ost;
private Vector osnames;
private boolean isConnected;
private UserContext uc;

/*
 * constructor
 */
public CEConnection()
{
      con = null;
      uc = UserContext.get();
      dom = null;
      domainName = null;
      ost = null;
      osnames = new Vector();
      isConnected = false;
}

/*
 * Establishes connection with Content Engine using
 * supplied username, password, JAAS stanza and CE Uri.
 */
public Connection establishConnection(String userName, String password,
String stanza, String uri, String WcmApiConfigPath)
{
      //ASB Need to set this property for the connection session
       System.setProperty("java.security.auth.login.
config",WcmApiConfigPath);
    con = Factory.Connection.getConnection(uri);
```

```
    Subject sub = UserContext.
createSubject(con,userName,password,stanza);
    uc.pushSubject(sub);
    dom = fetchDomain();
    domainName = dom.get_Name();
    ost = getOSSet();
    isConnected = true;
      return con; //ASB we added this for use with the AI code
}

/*
 * Returns Domain object.
 */
public Domain fetchDomain()
{
    dom = Factory.Domain.fetchInstance(con, null, null);
    return dom;
}

/*
 * Returns ObjectStoreSet from Domain
 */
public ObjectStoreSet getOSSet()
{
    ost = dom.get_ObjectStores();
    return ost;
}

/*
 * Returns vector containing ObjectStore
 * names from object stores available in
 * ObjectStoreSet.
 */
public Vector getOSNames()
{
```

```
        if(osnames.isEmpty())
        {
                Iterator it = ost.iterator();
                while(it.hasNext())
                {
                        ObjectStore os = (ObjectStore) it.next();
                        osnames.add(os.get_DisplayName());
                }
        }
     return osnames;
}
/*
 * Checks whether connection has established
 * with the Content Engine or not.
 */
public boolean isConnected()
{
        return isConnected;
}

/*
 * Returns ObjectStore object for supplied
 * object store name.
 */
public ObjectStore fetchOS(String name)
{
    ObjectStore os = Factory.ObjectStore.fetchInstance(dom, name, null);
    return os;
}

/*
 * Returns the domain name.
 */
public String getDomainName()
```

```
{
    return domainName;
}
}
```

Then, on running the program in the **Eclipse IDE**, we get the following in the **Console** pane, as shown in *Figure 11.24*:

```
[Perf Log] No interval found. Auditor disabled.
Document stored successfully.
```

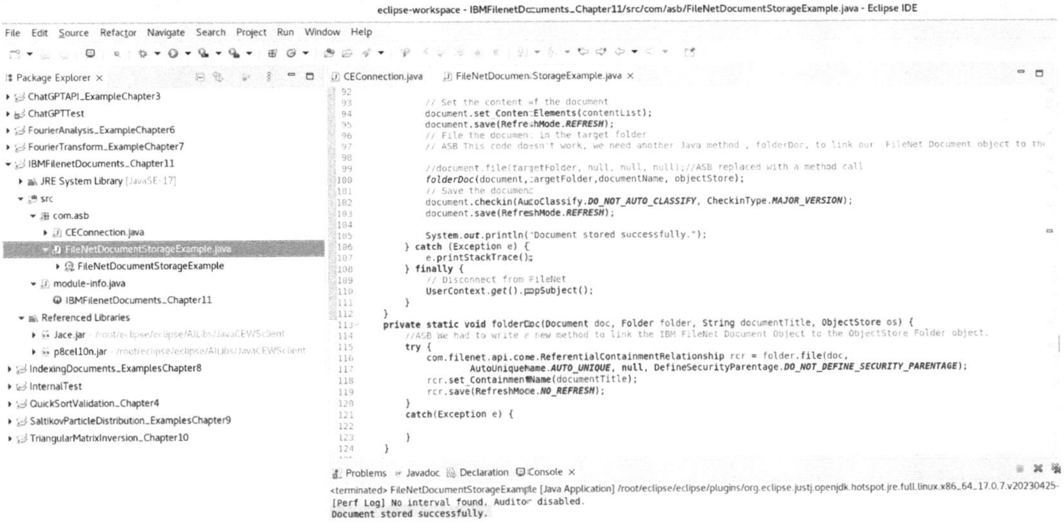

***Figure 11.24**: The test **Document** is stored successfully, as highlighted in the **Console** pane*

The document can also be seen to be stored in the **TOS1** object store using the **ACCE** IBM FileNet administration web application tool, as shown in *Figure 11.25*:

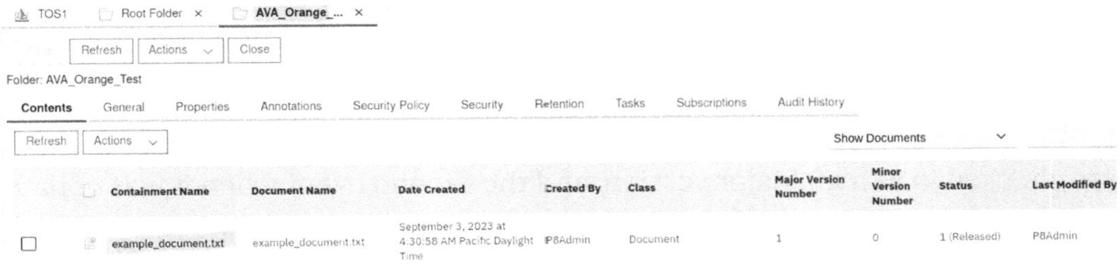

***Figure 11.25**: The **example_document.txt** file is displayed in the **AVA_Orange_Test** folder*

We can look at the new document details, as shown in *Figure 11.26*:

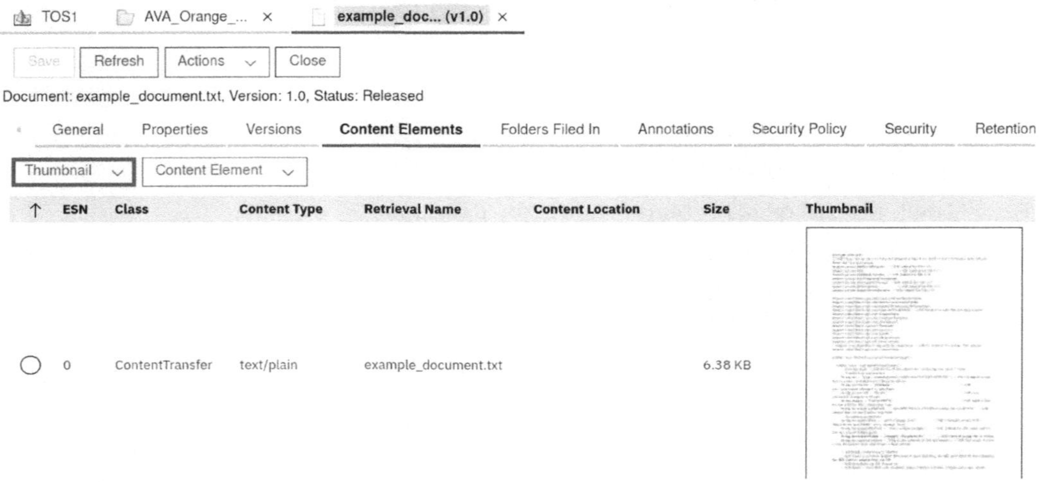


***Figure 11.26**: The Content Element tab is displayed showing our document thumbnail*

The Audit history tab shows the two main event actions: creating the document object, checking it in, and then linking it to our AVA_Orange_Test, Folder object, as shown in *Figure 11.27*:

***Figure 11.27**: The **Audit history** tab shows the details of our program transactions*

So, we can see two events: the first event when the uploaded Document object was checked in as a 1.0 Major version, and the second event when it was updated by linking it to our test **Folder** object.

# Conclusion

In this chapter, we optimistically asked the **Ask AI** system for **API Java** code to upload a document to the latest available **IBM FileNet Document Manager** system.

The **Ask AI** mobile phone app confidently supplied the required **Java** code, and did warn us that we would need to provide "*the FileNet Java* API *and its dependencies*". So, we weren't completely surprised to find that we had to provide the **Jace.jar** file. However, there were a number of important **Java** code lines missing from the code the **AI** supplied. Fortunately, having developed many similar **IBM FileNet Java** programs before, we were able to quickly fill in the gaps in the **Java** code to create a working version.

The actual outline given by **Ask AI** was not too far from the structure we eventually had working, and the **AI** did provide a framework for our development.

In the next chapter, we will discuss the main conclusions on the currently used **ChatGPT 3.5** and **ChatGPT 4.0**, as well as describe some of the most likely future extensions that are being planned for **ChatGPT 5.0** and the competitive **AI** systems available for program development.

# Points to Remember

- In many examples of the **Ask AI Java** code that we have been presented, we have had to research and provide additional Jar files to correct the class **import** statements. This chapter wasn't an exception, as we needed to have the **FileNet Java API, Jace.jar** and its dependencies included in the project for the code to work.
- For the **IBM FileNet Manager API**, there are two main supported computer language frameworks: the Microsoft **.NET API**, which supports **C#** development, and the **Java API** we covered in this chapter.
- There is also a requirement to select and set up the **API** configuration file for the **SOAP API** interface that the **Ask AI** app has selected. This defines the **JAAS Web Service Interface** (**WSI**) protocol, using the **jaas.conf.WSI** file.
- There are a number of other API configuration files available:
    - **FileNetLogging.properties**

  Starting from **IBM FileNet Document Manager**, **V5.5.6** (when the code was switched from **log4j** to the **JUL**, `java.util.logging` (j.u.l) **API** for logging), an updated logging system was used by the **Content Platform Engine**. This allowed logging settings to be defined either by using **JVM** arguments or by a combination of **JVM** arguments and the **FileNetLogging.properties** file. (The properties file takes precedence over the **JVM** arguments). Also, for Windows systems, either double backslashes or single forward slashes must be used for file paths in the properties file.

(Also see the link:

**https://www.ibm.com/docs/en/filenet-p8-platform/5.5.x?topic=logging-api** )

- **jaas.conf.WebSphere**

As might be expected, this file is used for the **IBM WebSphere** web application server configuration, set up as follows:

1. Log in to the WebSphere administrative console:

   **(https://ecmukdemo22:9043/ibm/console/logon.jsp )**

2. Navigate to the Java Virtual Machine settings at **Servers** > **Server Types** > **WebSphere application servers** >**server1**>**Java & Process Management**>**Process Definition**>**Java Virtual Machine**.

3. In the **Generic JVM arguments** field, add the following entry:

```
-Djava.security.auth.login.config=/opt/IBM/FileNet/CEClient/config/
jaas.conf.WebSphere
```

Which is added to the location as shown in *Figure 11.28*:

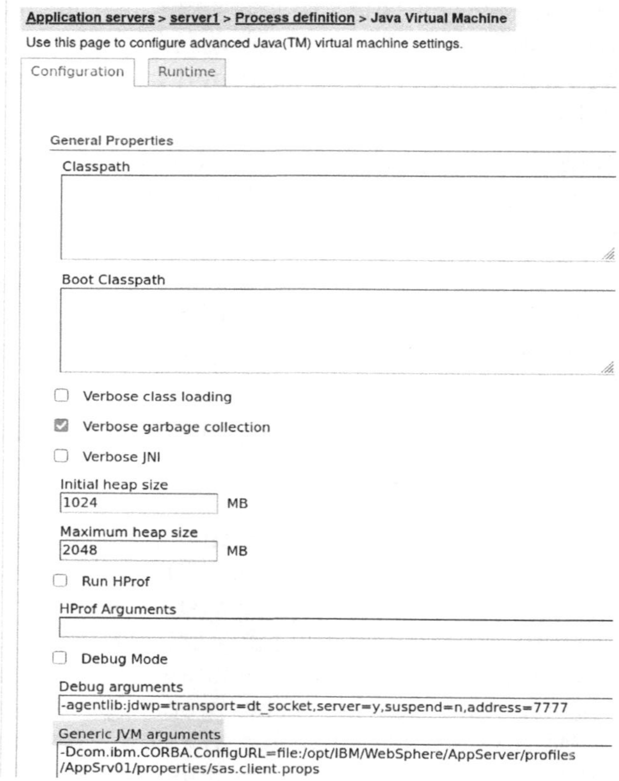


***Figure 11.28**: The **IBM WebSphere** web application server **Generic JVM arguments***

**Note**

You may have to add additional arguments space separated, if there is an existing **JVM** argument, as shown above, so in this case, each **additional** JVM argument has a space character followed by `-Dcom.ibm...etc.` `-Djava.security.auth...etc.` as shown here:

```
-Dcom.ibm.CORBA.ConfigURL=file:/opt/IBM/WebSphere/AppServer/profiles/
 AppSrv01/properties/sas.client.props -Djava.security.auth.login.
 config=/opt/IBM/FileNet/CEClient/config/jaas.conf.WebSphere
```

# Multiple Choice Questions

1. **Which additional sample file is required for the JAAS authentication to function correctly for the MTOM SOAP connection for the Eclipse IDE?**
   a. jaas.conf.WebSphere
   b. jaas.conf.WSI
   c. jaas.conf.WebLogic
   d. FileNetLogging.properties
2. **Which of the following databases are not supported by IBM FileNet 5.5.11?**
   a. IBM DB2
   b. Oracle
   c. Microsoft Access
   d. Microsoft SQL*Server
3. **Which of the following import statements is not viable for use with the IBM FileNet 5.5.10 Jace.jar?**
   a. `import com.filenet.api.core.Factory;`
   b. `import com.filenet.api.core.Connection;`
   c. `import com.ibm.ecm.util.p8.P8Connection;`
   d. `import com.filenet.api.util.UserContext;`

# Answers

1. b
2. c
3. c

# Questions

1. Which of the AI systems did we attempt to use in this chapter and why did we select the one which was then used as a working template?
2. What additional Java code could be added to load every document in a Linux folder to the IBM FileNet Document Management System TOS1 Object Store?
3. What are the main supported IBM FileNet Document Management System API development languages?
4. Why is it important to download the Jace.jar file using the IBM FileNet ACCE web application administrator tool?
5. What Java logging system change was made to the IBM FileNet API and from which version of the IBM FileNet Document Management system was this introduced?

# Key terms

- **C#:** C# is an object-oriented programming language, with some similarity to Java, developed by **Microsoft**, that enables developers to build applications that run on the Windows **.NET** platform.
- **CEWS:** This is the IBM FileNet Content Engine Web Service interface, which controls security access. The IBM FileNet Content Engine server accepts API requests using two network transport protocols: Enterprise Java Beans (EJB) and the IBM FileNet Content Engine Web Service (CEWS) transports.

  The **Content Engine Web Service** sits as an interface layer on top of the **EJB** service layer, for the **IBM FileNet Content Engine** services, as shown in the system architecture diagram at:

  **https://www.ibm.com/docs/en/filenet-p8-platform/5.5.11?topic=engine-content-services**
- **DOI:** A **DOI** (**D**igital **O**bject **I**dentifier) is a permanent ID that, when appended to **http://dx.doi.org/** in the address bar of an Internet browser, will lead to the document source. **ASB Software Development Limited** has over 30 of these document publications with DOI numbers available for free download.

- **Domain:** The FileNet P8 domain identifies a group of Object Stores and also one or more of the IBM FileNet Content Platform Engine servers that provide access to the Object Stores. There is only one domain defined for a set of Object Stores on a server.
- **DOS:** This is the Development Object Store designation for an IBM FileNet Content Manage System using the **IBM Case Manager** system.
- **EJB: E**nterprise **J**ava **B**eans is a service protocol option for the **IBM FileNet Content Manager System API**. It is a transport layer that runs in the **Java** system, **Enterprise Edition** (**Java EE**). There is an **EJB** container for the application server that hosts the IBM FileNet Content Engine Service.
- **JAAS:** The IBM FileNet Content Engine uses the Java Authentication and Authorization standard (**JAAS**) for authentication. The **JAAS** architecture is a standard Java framework that manages authentication and authorization.
- **MTOM:** The **MTOM** (Message Transmission Optimization Mechanism) protocol is a web **SOAP** service standard protocol used by the IBM FileNet Content Engine.
- **SOAP: S**imple **O**bject **A**ccess **P**rotocol is a general messaging protocol specification for a client/server transport to implement web services in computer networks.
- **TOS:** This is the Target Object Store designation for an IBM FileNet Content Manage System, which is used for the **IBM Case Manager** system.
- **WSI:** This is the **W**eb **S**ervice **I**nterface, now designated as **CEWS** (see above), but still found in the naming convention of some of the **JAAS** configuration files.

# CHAPTER 12
# Conclusions and the Future of ChatGPT for Program Development

## Introduction

The knowledge cutoff for **ChatGPT 3.5** was in September 2021. As a result, there are ongoing developments by the **OpenAI** Foundation to enhance this knowledge base, and there is rapid development of the currently released beta **ChatGPT 4.0**. Additionally, there is a ChatGPT version 5.0 in the pipeline (**https://www.youtube.com/watch?v=Bb_tIsyB9YY** ).

This version may be available sometime in December 2023 or early 2024 (according to the "leaks").

## Structure

In this chapter, we will discuss the following topics:

- Conclusions and the future of ChatGPT for program development
    - The Future of AI and ChatGPT
    - AI Bias Effects on the Responses
    - ChatGPT taking Jobs from People
    - Building a Custom ChatGPT with Your Own Additional Data

  - Using AI Transfer Learning
- IBM and Generative AI With Watsonx
- GPT4All and How It Works
- Security Threats and Privacy Concerns
- Alternative Code Assistant AI Software - ChatGPT Alternatives for Coding Programs Automatically
  - Llama 2 code AI free use
  - Setting up the Jupyter Notebook environment
  - GPT4All and How It Works
  - GitHub Copilot
  - Google Duet AI
  - Codeium
  - CodeWhisperer
  - Falcon-180B

# Conclusions and the future of ChatGPT for program development

The momentum and the potential revenues from the use of Artificial Intelligence systems for a broad range of applications, which has also been widely discussed in the world's media, mean that **ChatGPT**, or one of the many rival systems challenging its dominant position, is sure to produce significant improvements in the capabilities of the systems for software development.

The software industry is one area that has always faced a shortage of skilled labor, and the use of **AI** systems for enhancing the productivity of the development of programs and systems is already a significant factor in helping to resolve this issue. One thing that can be guaranteed is that there will be even greater use of AI systems for program and system development, driven by large corporate enterprises, such as **IBM, Microsoft, Google (Alphabet Inc.,), Amazon,** and **Meta**. The founding organizations of the **OpenAI** foundation have board members, including Sam Altman and Elon Musk, and have received funding from other investments such as **Microsoft**, **Reid Hoffman, Khosla Ventures, Andreessen Horowitz, Sequoia,** and other financial institutes.

# The future of AI and ChatGPT

We asked **Perplexity AI** the question:

**What is the future of AI and ChatGPT for enhancing Java code development?**

"*AI and ChatGPT have the potential to revolutionize the way we approach coding and make it easier and more accessible for people of all skill levels[1]. ChatGPT is a conversational model of AI that can answer follow-up questions and write code for users[3]. It can write simple webpages and applications in programming languages such as JavaScript, Python, and React, find bugs in code, and help create new programming languages[6]. However, according to experts, AI will not replace developers but rather enhance their productivity[2][6]. Developers can use AI to create basic code and enhance it according to the requirements using their own skills[2]. In 2023, we expect to see even more AI-driven resources available to assist with coding tasks[5]. With the advancement of ChatGPT, this tool could be of great help in the future[3]. The future of ChatGPT and other language models like it is likely to involve continued advancements in their capacity to comprehend and produce text that appears human-like, as well as increased use in a variety of applications like customer service, language translation, and content creation[3].*

Citations:

[1] h**ttps://neuroflash.com/blog/chatgpt-code-interpreter-future-programming/**

**[2] https://www.turing.com/blog/will-generative-ai-replace-software-developers/**

**[3] https://www.edureka.co/blog/chatgpt-for-coding-unleash-the-power-of-chatgpt/**

**[4] https://hackbrightacademy.com/blog/use-chatgpt-to-code-will-ai-replace-programmers/**

**[5] https://itnext.io/the-future-is-now-how-ai-driven-development-will-make-developers-life-easier-in-2023-f2a26a85cbbe**

**[6] https://www.techtarget.com/searchsoftwarequality/news/252528379/ChatGPT-writes-code-but-wont-replace-developers"**

See also,

**https://aicontentfy.com/en/blog/future-of-chatgpt-predictions-and-opportunities-1**

From Meta (the Code Llama developers):

**"The future of generative AI for coding**

**Code Llama** is designed to support software engineers in all sectors – including research, industry, open-source projects, NGOs, and businesses. But there are still many more use cases to support than what our base and instruct models can serve.

We hope that Code Llama will inspire others to leverage Llama 2 to create new innovative tools for research and commercial products."

For further discussions on possible AI future functionality and next-generation capabilities, you can watch the following videos:

- The next release of AI from Google, Project Gemini, is discussed in the following **YouTube** video link:

  **https://www.youtube.com/watch?v=SEhk67R4R9g**

- The following **YouTube** video link is an interview of a robot called **Sophia** created by **Hanson Robotics** (**https://www.hansonrobotics.com/**) based in **Tsuen Wan, Hong Kong**, with **Al Jazeera** interviewer, **Heidi Zhou-Castro**:

  **https://www.youtube.com/watch?v=bJjXq6Pj0_c**

# AI Bias effects on the responses

The quote from the following blog link states "*ChatGPT's odds of getting code questions correct are worse than a coin flip*"

They analyzed the ChatGPT responses as follows:

"*52 percent of ChatGPT answers are incorrect and 77 percent are verbose*"

See **https://www.theregister.com/AMP/2023/08/07/chatgpt_stack_overflow_ai/**

The preceding link also describes how the AI response language style is very convincing, making even the incorrect responses sound plausible.

The preceding article references a research paper available at the following link, which concludes:

"*These findings underscore the need for meticulous error correction in ChatGPT while also raising awareness among users about the potential risks associated with seemingly accurate answers.*"

See **https://arxiv.org/abs/2308.02312**

(Or, download the paper from **https://arxiv.org/pdf/2308.02312.pdf** )

**Note:**

We have used a number of references and free pdf downloads from **arXiv:**

*"This is a community of volunteer authors, readers, moderators, advisory board members, supporting members, donors, and third-party collaborators that are supported by staff at* ***Cornell University****."*

## ChatGPT taking Jobs from People

The following article lists the 10 jobs most likely to be replaced by AI technology:

**https://www.businessinsider.com/chatgpt-jobs-at-risk-replacement-artificial-intelligence-ai-labor-trends-2023-02?r=US&IR=T**

They stated the findings of an earlier study, in 2013, by the University of Oxford (see: **https://www.oxfordmartin.ox.ac.uk/downloads/academic/future-of-employment.pdf).**

This study found that 47% of US jobs could be eliminated by AI over the next 20 years.

This estimate appears to have been completely revised, so a more recent estimate from Goldman Sachs estimated that generative AI tools could impact 300 million full-time jobs worldwide! (see: **https://www.businessinsider.com/generative-ai-chatpgt-300-million-full-time-jobs-goldman-sachs-2023-3)**

## Building a Custom ChatGPT with Your Own Additional Data

CodeProject AI is a local server-based free Open-Source AI server for any platform and any language. It claims to be sandboxed, so does not upload any data. It is self-contained with no dependencies, running either as a Windows Service or a Docker container.

For further information, you can refer to the following sources:

**CodeProject.AI Server**: AI the easy way - CodeProject (3 Aug 2023)

Version 2.1.10. Our fast, free, self-hosted Artificial Intelligence Server for any platform and any language

**https://www.codeproject.com/Article.aspx?tag=2.NTMyMjU1NzowOjYzODI3MjY1OTkxNDgyNDcyNw&_z=534**

For a Docker container, we can run:

docker run -p 32168:32168 --name CodeProject.AI-Server -d codeproject/ai-server

Then select the last repo option, using the down arrow key and press return:

docker.io/codeproject/ai-server:latest

Using:

**http://localhost:32168**

From their website:

*"CodeProject.AI Server is a locally installed, self-hosted, fast, free and Open Source Artificial Intelligence server for any platform, any language. No off-device or out of network data transfer, no messing around with dependencies, and able to be used from any platform, any language. Runs as a Windows Service or a Docker container."*

# Using AI Transfer Learning

Transfer learning is the term used in AI machine learning to describe the process of reusing a pre-trained model on a new problem. In transfer learning, an **AI** program uses the knowledge gained from a previous **LLM** model starting point and augments it for a new and similar task to generate an improved **LLM** model.

# IBM and Generative AI With Watsonx

IBM also has collaborations with other specialist AI-based companies, and **SingleStore** is active in this area:

https://www.singlestore.com/blog/ibm-data-replication-and-singlestoredb-real-time-applications/?utm_source=thenewstack&utm_medium=website

The blog describes the use of the **IBM Data Replication CDC** (Change Data Capture) tool and

the Cloud-based **SingleStore** system **(https://docs.singlestore.com/managed-service/en/getting-started-with-singlestoredb-cloud.html)**, supported by **IBM InfoSphere** Data Replication (**https://www.ibm.com/products/data-replication**).

The SingleStore company's **About** webpage states:

"A business' ability to operate with true intelligence at speed can be the deciding factor in success or failure. SingleStore helps companies deliver value at higher velocity so they can make the most of every moment.

SingleStore handles transactions and analytics, effortlessly, at the same time. Structured, semi-structured or unstructured. Streaming and historical alike. Unified through a single-pane-of-glass experience to make timely, accurate insight accessible for every worker and every workload.

Giving you a business intelligence ecosystem to develop products and services with real-time analytics, machine learning, AI – breaking down data silos that stifle innovation. The pace of business is only accelerating."

# Security Threats and Privacy Concerns

There is a perceived (and possibly real) issue with the impact of AI systems on personal user security and the issue of fraud.

There are several publicized cases of AI systems used to simulate a video message using a celebrity (for example, Martin Lewis) to fraudulently suggest investments in spoof Financial Institutions.

- For further information, you can refer to the following links: **https://www.moneysavingexpert.com/news/2023/07/beware-terrifying-new--deepfake--martin-lewis-video-scam-promoti/**
- https://zapier.com/blog/ai-security-risks/

# Alternative Code Assistant AI Software - ChatGPT Alternatives for Coding Programs Automatically

Here are some alternative code assistant AI software options that serve as alternatives to ChatGPT for automatically coding programs:

## Llama 2 code AI free use

**Code Llama** is a programming language **AI** version of **Llama 2,** introduced by **Meta** (formerly, **Facebook** Inc., co-founded by **Mark Zuckerberg**). The **Llama 2, Code Llama** system (**https://ai.meta.com/llama/**), was created by using **Llama 2** as the starting **LLM** (large Language Model), with Meta's code-specific datasets and by training more code-based data

(**Llama 2** Version Release Date: July 18, 2023).

**Code Llama**, built on top of **Llama 2**, has enhanced coding capabilities. It generates program code and describes the code produced using an input of program code and the normal prompts (e.g., "Have you got a Java program for demonstrating the Binary Search algorithm?").

It can also be used for code syntax checking, code completion, and debugging. Some of the key features of **Code Llama** are as follows:

- Allows commercial use
- Uses a 4096 default context window (can be expanded) (Context length refers to the number of tokens a language model can process as input for a response. LLMs process text by breaking it down into tokens and average 4 characters with many words being a single token).
- Trained on 2 trillion tokens of text data
- The 70B model uses the grouped-query attention (GQA) architecture
- Available on Hugging Face Hub

---

**Note:**

**Perplexity** has both the 7B and 13B LLaMA 2 models accessible through the conversational AI demo.

**Code Llama** supports most of the common modern programming languages, including Java, Python, C++, C#, PHP, JavaScript, and Linux Bash script.

---

For more information, please refer to "Introducing Code Llama, a state-of-the-art large language model for coding (meta.com)"

**https://ai.meta.com/blog/code-llama-large-language-model-coding/**

The **Llama2 LLM** models can be downloaded locally, as shown in *Figure 12.1*:

**https://ai.meta.com/llama/**

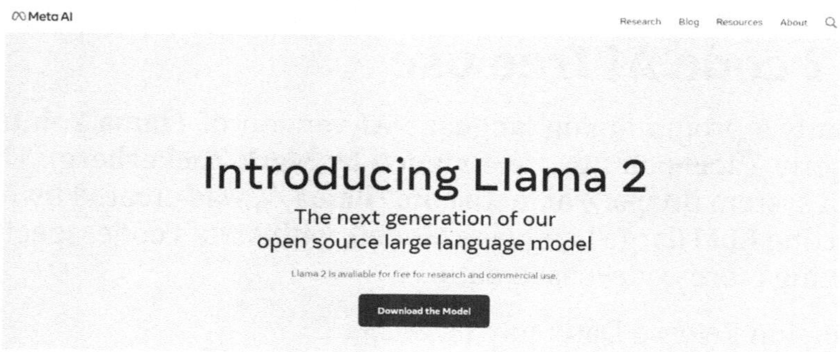


**Figure 12.1:** *Download the Model button is selected to load the Llama 2 LLM models*

The next Meta webpage displays the form to be filled to get the required access, as shown in *Figure 12.2*:

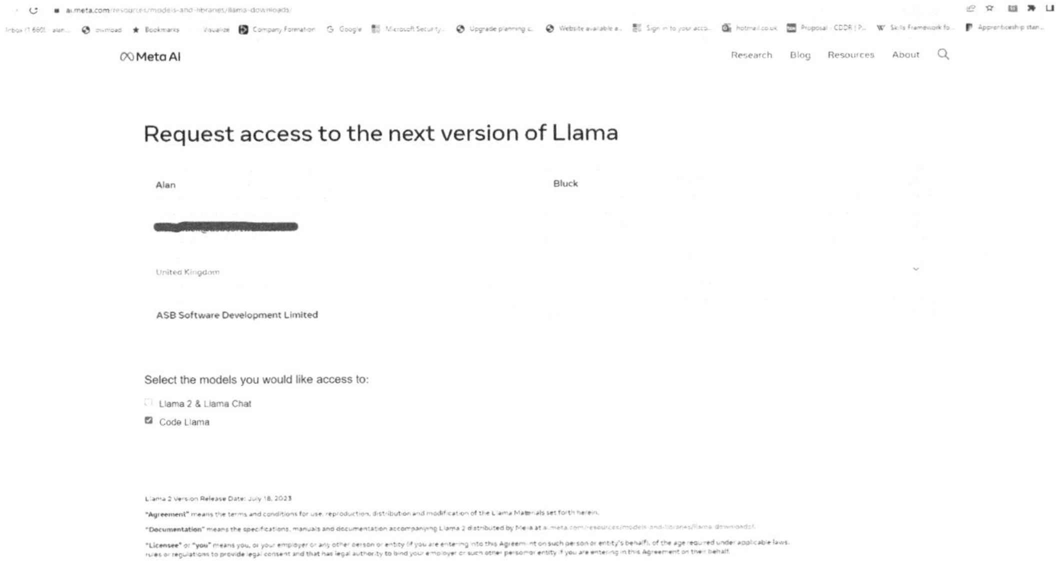


**Figure 12.2: Meta Llama 2** *form to be filled in to get the required access to the LLMs*

Next, we select the **LLM** models we can use, as shown in *Figure 12.3*:

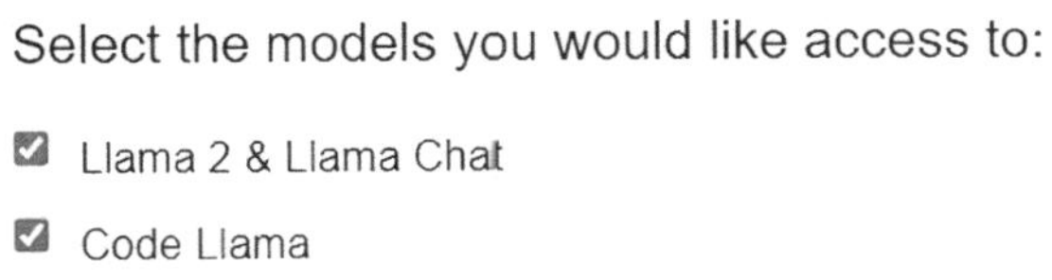


***Figure 12.3:*** *We select the* ***LLM*** *models we can use, by ticking the options*

We need to scroll down and read the **Meta AI** terms and conditions, then tick **I accept the terms and conditions**, and finally, click the **Accept and Continue** button as shown in *Figure 12.4*:

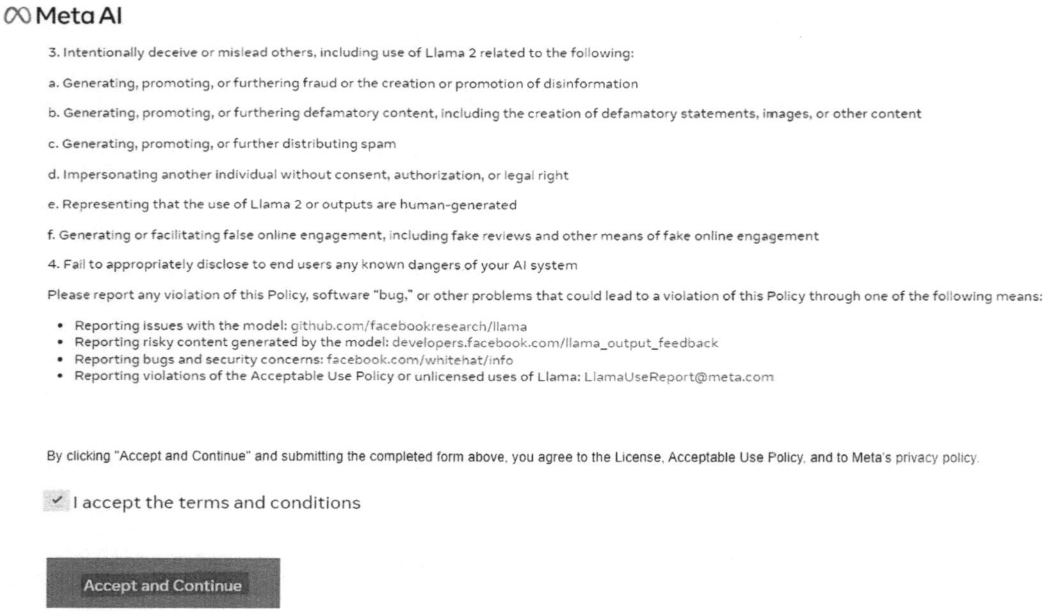


***Figure 12.4:*** *Tick the* ***I accept the terms and conditions,*** *and click the* ***Accept and Continue***

After accepting the terms and conditions, we can select the **Subscribe for updates** button. This will allow emails to be sent to the email account we set up for **Meta AI** and allow them to send updated information on the latest Llama developments, as shown in *Figure 12.5*:

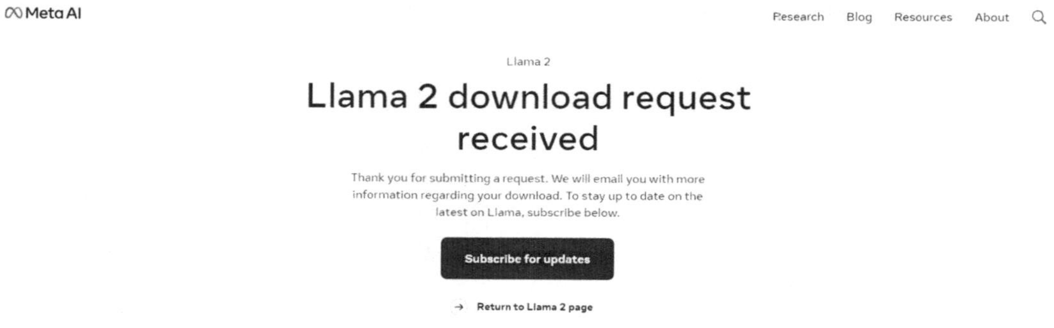


***Figure 12.5:*** *Select the* ***Subscribe for updates*** *button to allow emails to be sent for updates*

A pop-up window then appears, as illustrated in *Figure 12.6*, which prompts us for a second sign-up procedure:

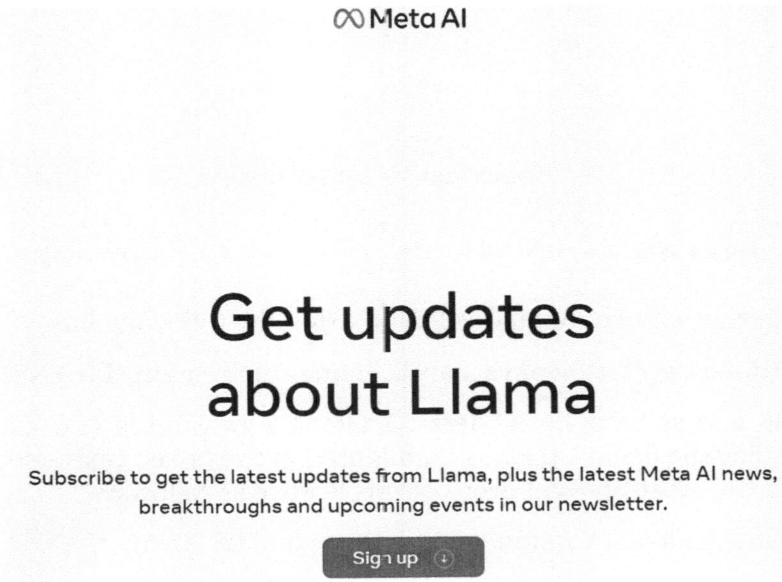


**Figure 12.6**: *The second sign-up steps are initiated by clicking on the Sign up button*

The user's name, company details, and interest areas are entered and a **Submit** button is selected, as shown in *Figure 12.7*:

**Figure 12.7**: *The user's name, company details, and interests are entered*

Successful subscription to Meta AI news is acknowledged with a pop-up window displayed, as shown in *Figure* 12.8:

***Figure* 12.8:** *Successful subscription to Meta AI news is acknowledged*

The main license can be found on GitHub using the following link:

**https://github.com/facebookresearch/llama/blob/main/LICENSE**

To gain full access to publish **Meta AI Llama 2** responses and materials, we have to display the license text, as highlighted in the boxed text below. We have highlighted the most relevant areas of this license as follows:

(License dated, Llama 2 Version Release Date: July 18, 2023)

We now receive an email with the following information on the available commercial license we have been granted:

"Code Llama commercial license **You're all set to start building with Code Llama.**

The models listed below are now available to you as a commercial license holder. By downloading a model, you are agreeing to the terms and conditions of the license, acceptable use policy, and Meta's privacy policy **(https://www.facebook.com/privacy/policy/).**

**Model weights available:**

- CodeLlama-7b
- CodeLlama-13b
- CodeLlama-34b
- CodeLlama-7b-Python
- CodeLlama-13b-Python
- CodeLlama-34b-Python
- CodeLlama-7b-Instruct
- CodeLlama-13b-Instruct
- CodeLlama-34b-Instruct"

With each model download, you'll receive a copy of the **License** and **Acceptable Use Policy,** and you can find all other information about the model and code on **GitHub.**

# Setting up Jupyter Notebook environment

To install the **Jupyter Notebook** docker container, there is a free download from **ResearchGate** using the following link:

**https://doi.org/10.13140/RG.2.2.15264.12807**

(Jupyter notebook and its Docker Container Installation on Linux RedHat RHEL 8.0 using VMware 15.5.2)

(This downloads the MS Word document: `JupyternotebookInstallationonLinuxRedHatRHEL8.docx`)

This document has a step-by-step set of screenshots describing the installation and the main Jupyter Notebook menu items.

To see the full install info and tutorials go to:

**https://www.datacamp.com/community/tutorials/tutorial-jupyter-notebook**

**Here's how to download the models:**

1. Visit the Code Llama repository on GitHub and follow the instructions in the **README (https://github.com/facebookresearch/codellama/blob/main/README.md).**
2. Follow the link below to run the **download.sh** script.

   This file is in the list of files at the following link, so check for the latest version, as this is likely to change:

   **http://github.com/facebookresearch/codellama**

   Either edit the above shell script into a **download.sh** file using the vi Linux editor or (**recommended**) just download the latest version:

   ```
   [root@ECMUKDEMO22 opt]# mkdir /opt/llama2
   [root@ECMUKDEMO22 opt]# cd /opt/llama2
   [root@ECMUKDEMO22 llama2]# vi download.sh
   ```

The **download.sh** script has **wget** commands, as shown in *Figure 12.9*:

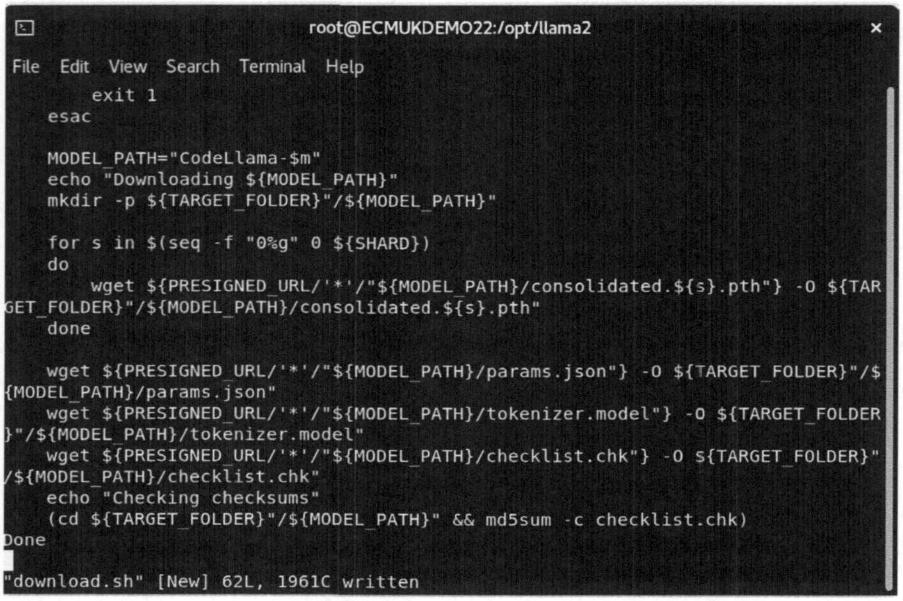


***Figure 12.9**: The **download.sh** shell script file*

Change the security to allow the shell script, **download.sh** file to be run:

```
[root@ECMUKDEMO22 llama2]# chmod 775 download.sh
[root@ECMUKDEMO22 llama2]# ./download.sh
```

3. When asked for your unique custom URL, please insert the following:

> **Note:**
>
> This is an example with a 24-hour time limit, as we found out when we went over the time limit (So, don't bother trying to use this one!).

```
https://download2.llamameta.net/*?Policy=eyJTdGF0ZW1lbnQi-
Olt7InVuaXF1ZV9oYXNoIjoianN3dGQxZ2FzZmMydmFuaDdpenpnYmZvIi-
wiUmVzb3VyY2UiOiJodHRwczpcL1wvZG93bmxvYWQyLmxsYW1hbWV0Y-
S5uZXRcLyoiLCJDb25kaXRpb24iOnsiRGF0ZUxlc3NUaGFuIjp7IkFXUzpFc-
G9jaFRpbWUiOjE2OTQwMDQxNjh9fX1dfQ__&Signature=X5Cd-Q1DPm1aj5x-
MR9EJEVGcJnAnz7eUZjHeyiKT5gZMb391eG6Pp8mjX5dlOSMMoX-kKWuSlExB-
zhMi%7ESIU1Q4W1za4VTphxvTS-N5wZ6t3emGjTHTpb0qgnl6oAtyiz%7EFx-
PvsIqBcRrPVb2THgSdTLd0R5v4NdC1iToqMQCyIo8JGwSNrfwx36ZS%7EE-
IeFvWzt3FXQ11j%7EVokPXyMo68xdH4BaNs69ojg-SiAiCJ-ohHfVYs8B-
vG34lLYqViILKTpxIr3g%7EWlg-9RrfCV5Gw1ofopaPL89nx4yxsqtRjAieoD2I-
lA3ar%7E6Ul4o4hJ1bS7iCWk7ck7ODiyoG9%7E8kgg__&Key-Pair-Id=K15QR-
JLYKIFSLZ&Download-Request-ID=1222855335055319
```

(The unique custom URL provided will remain valid for model downloads for 24 hours, and requests can be submitted multiple times.).

4. Choose the model weights to download (or simply hit return to download them all).

   The downloaded **Meta AI Llama 2 LLM Code Llama** model directories can now be seen in the **`/opt/llama2`** directory we created, as shown in *Figure 12.10*:

```
[root@ECMUKDEMO22 llama2]# ls
CodeLlama-13b            CodeLlama-34b-Instruct   CodeLlama-7b-Python
CodeLlama-13b-Instruct   CodeLlama-34b-Python     download.sh
CodeLlama-13b-Python     CodeLlama-7b             LICENSE
CodeLlama-34b            CodeLlama-7b-Instruct    USE_POLICY.md
[root@ECMUKDEMO22 llama2]#
```

**Figure 12.10:** *The downloaded* **Meta AI Llama 2 LLM** *model directories*

5. Install **conda**:

   `yum install conda`

   The list of the **Python conda** Linux installer libraries is shown in *Figure 12.11*:

```
root@ECMUKDEMO22:/opt/llama2
File  Edit  View  Search  Terminal  Help
[root@ECMUKDEMO22 llama2]# yum install conda
Updating Subscription Management repositories.
Last metadata expiration check: 0:46:17 ago on Thu 07 Sep 2023 09:00:49 AM PDT.
Dependencies resolved.
================================================================================
 Package                          Arch   Version                     Repository    Size
================================================================================
Installing:
 conda                            noarch 4.10.3-1.el8                epel          19 k
Installing dependencies:
 picosat-libs                     x86_64 965-17.el8                  epel          71 k
 python3-conda                    noarch 4.10.3-1.el8                epel         1.0 M
 python3-conda-package-handling   x86_64 1.7.3-2.el8                 epel          60 k
 python3-cpuinfo                  noarch 5.0.0-1.el8                 epel          46 k
 python3-cytoolz                  x86_64 0.11.0-1.el8                epel         319 k
 python3-distro                   noarch 1.4.0-2.module+el8.1.0+3334+5cb623d7
                                                                     rhel-8-for-x86_64-a
ppstream-rpms
                                                                                   37 k
 python3-frozendict               noarch 1.2-13.el8                  epel          13 k
 python3-pycosat                  x86_64 0.6.3-12.el8                epel          28 k
 python3-ruamel-yaml              x86_64 0.17.21-1.el8               epel         209 k
 python3-ruamel-yaml-clib         x86_64 0.2.7-1.el8                 epel         141 k
 python3-toolz                    noarch 0.10.0-3.el8                epel         124 k
 python3-tqdm                     noarch 4.50.2-1.el8                epel         126 k

Transaction Summary
================================================================================
Install  13 Packages

Total download size: 2.2 M
Installed size: 8.2 M
Is this ok [y/N]: y
Downloading Packages:
```

**Figure 12.11:** *The list of the* **Python conda** *Linux installer libraries*

Install git:

```
yum install git
```

For using the GitHub **gh** command line, we first need to retrieve the GitHub client, which requires a GitHub account to be used:

https://cli.github.com/

and select the download button to see and copy the installation instructions:

```
dnf install 'dnf-command(config-manager)'

dnf config-manager --add-repo https://cli.github.com/packages/rpm/gh-cli.repo

dnf install gh
```

Then, if required:

```
pip3 install -U pip setuptools

pip3 install jupyter
```

Finally, log in to the docker system (this will require the setup of a docker account, see **https://hub.docker.com** to create one), as shown in *Figure* 12.12:

***Figure 12.12:*** *The login to the docker system (this will require the setup of a* ***docker*** *account)*

You will notice that in the **RedHat Linux 8.8** system, we are using the **docker** command, but this system is emulated by **podman**, which is now pre-installed in **RedHat** for the container management system command.

```
docker run --rm -it -p 8888:8888 -v "$(pwd):/notebooks" jupyter/
datascience-notebook

Emulate Docker CLI using podman. Create /etc/containers/nodocker to
quiet msg.
```

Select the following from the list of repos:

✓ **docker.io/jupyter/datascience-notebook:latest**

Trying to pull **`docker.io/jupyter/datascience-notebook:latest...`**

At the end of the installation, we get the following instructions:

```
Read the migration plan to Notebook 7 to learn about the new features and the actions to take if you are using extensions.

https://jupyter-notebook.readthedocs.io/en/latest/migrate_to_notebook7.html

Please note that updating to Notebook 7 might break some of your extensions.

[I 2023-09-07 17:16:29.247 ServerApp] nbclassic | extension was successfully loaded.

[I 2023-09-07 17:16:29.338 ServerApp] nbdime | extension was successfully loaded.

[I 2023-09-07 17:16:29.348 ServerApp] notebook | extension was successfully loaded.

[I 2023-09-07 17:16:29.349 ServerApp] Serving notebooks from local directory: /home/jovyan

[I 2023-09-07 17:16:29.349 ServerApp] Jupyter Server 2.7.3 is running at:

[I 2023-09-07 17:16:29.349 ServerApp] http://fe0a306dffdc:8888/lab?token=283646b2056c5eeadc51620ca63cc493f34d437def682f33

[I 2023-09-07 17:16:29.349 ServerApp] http://127.0.0.1:8888/lab?token=283646b2056c5eeadc51620ca63cc493f34d437def682f33

[I 2023-09-07 17:16:29.349 ServerApp] Use Control-C to stop this server and shut down all kernels (twice to skip confirmation).

[C 2023-09-07 17:16:29.355 ServerApp]


    To access the server, open this file in a browser:

    file:///home/jovyan/.local/share/jupyter/runtime/jpserver-7-open.html

    Or copy and paste one of these URLs:

        http://fe0a306dffdc:8888/lab?token=283646b2056c5eeadc51620ca63cc493f34d437def682f33

        http://127.0.0.1:8888/lab?token=283646b2056c5eeadc51620ca63cc493f34d437def682f33
```

The **Jupyter Notebook** container is automatically loaded and run as a web application server system, as shown in *Figure 12.13*:

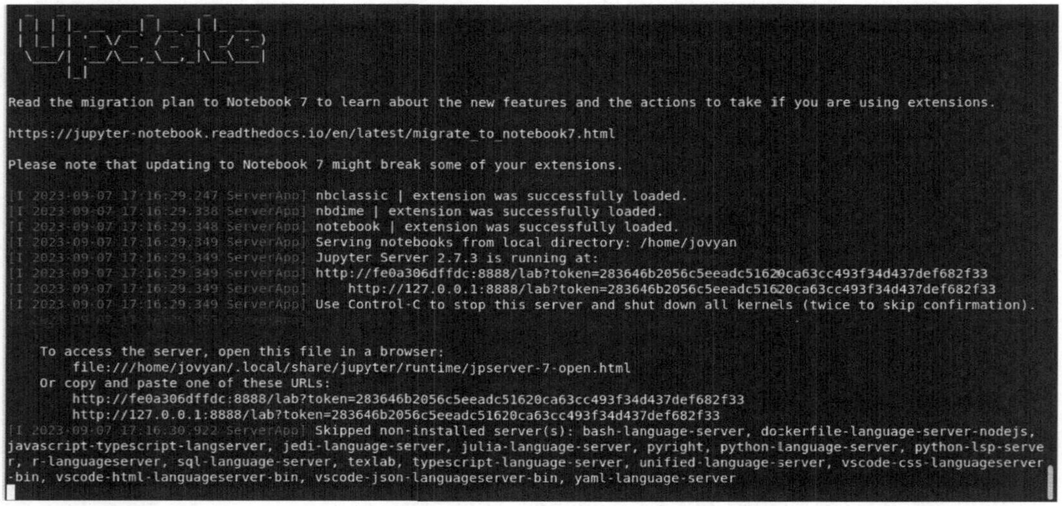


***Figure 12.13:** The **Jupyter Notebook** container is loaded and run as a web application server*

To shut down the docker container-based Jupyter Notebook server, enter **CTRL/C** keys.

(The server can be restarted using:

```
docker run --rm -it -p 8888:8888 -v "$(pwd):/notebooks" jupyter/
datascience-notebook)
```

Next, we need to set up the Jupyter Notebook examples by re-installing the utils:

```
pip uninstall utils
```

(Because this Python 3 package causes an error in the **`quickstart.ipynb`** cell import.)

```
[root@ECMUKDEMO22 opt]# pip uninstall utils
Found existing installation: utils 1.0.1
Uninstalling utils-1.0.1:
  Would remove:
    /usr/local/lib/python3.6/site-packages/tests/*
    /usr/local/lib/python3.6/site-packages/utils-1.0.1.dist-
info/*
    /usr/local/lib/python3.6/site-packages/utils/*
Proceed (Y/n)? y
```

```
Successfully uninstalled utils-1.0.1
```

Next, we need to install the Python **torch** utility:

```
pip3 install torch
```

We also have to install the **PyYAML:**

```
pip install --ignore-installed PyYAML
pip3 install transformers
```

(If this causes issues still, try:

```
pip3 install git+https://github.com/huggingface/transformers
pip3 install datasets)
```

We ran Jupyter Notebook locally using the **root** user with:

```
mkdir /home/jovyan
jupyter notebook --allow-root
```

This gave the webpage loaded automatically into the **Linux Firefox** browser, as shown in *Figure* 12.14:

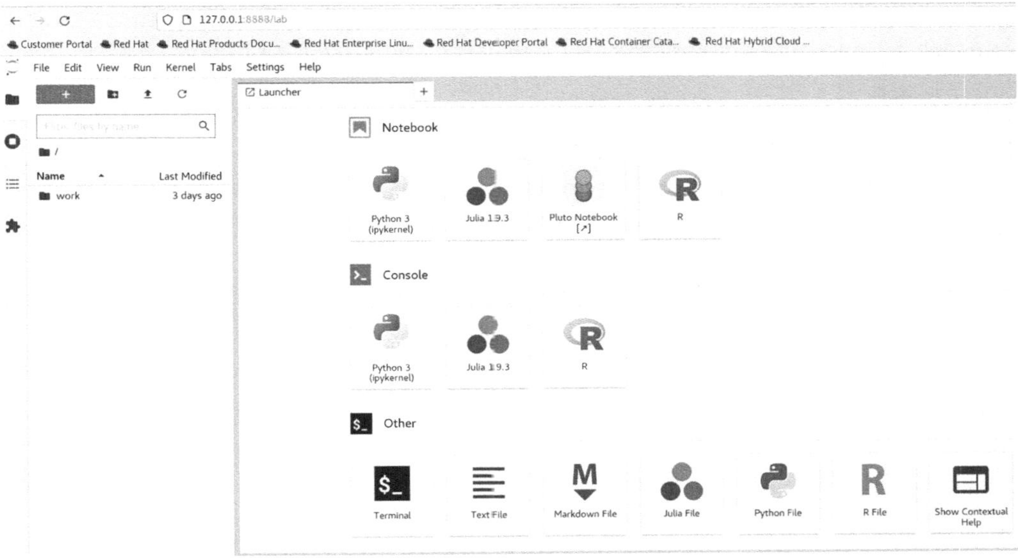


***Figure 12.14:*** *The installed local* ***Jupyter Notebook*** *web application server*

The **`quickstart.ipynb`** file can be downloaded from the following URL:

**https://github.com/facebookresearch/llama-recipes/blob/main/examples/quickstart.ipynb**

For this installation, we need to use the following GitHub client command:

```
gh repo clone facebookresearch/llama
```

This command then loads messages prompting us to run the **gh auth login** command, as shown in *Figure 12.15*:

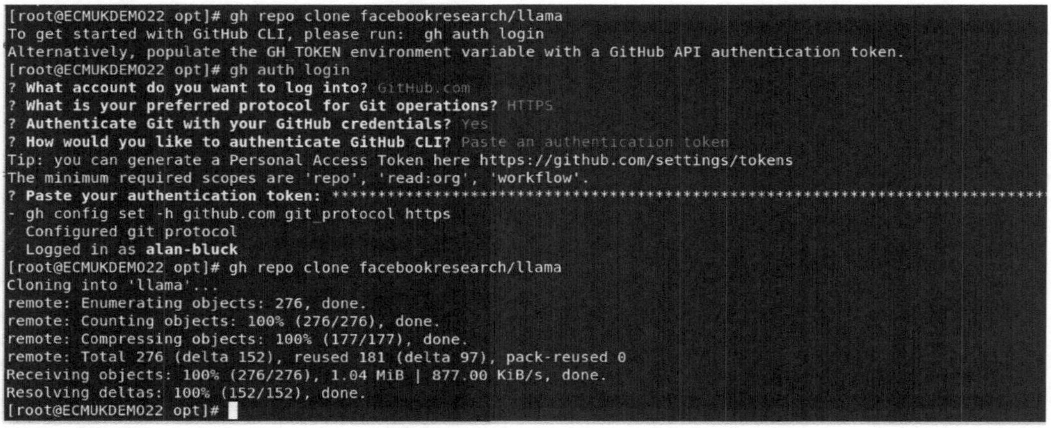


**Figure 12.15:** *The* **gh repo clone facebookresearch/llama** *command and prompts*

The token prompted to be pasted, as shown in **Figure 12.15**, requires that we generate a **Personal Access Token** by visiting the **GitHub** link:

**https://github.com/settings/tokens**

This requires a GitHub account to be set up and uses two-factor authentication. Make sure to have your mobile phone ready to receive the one-time code message to log in to get the **gh** client token to be pasted, as shown in *Figure 12.16*:

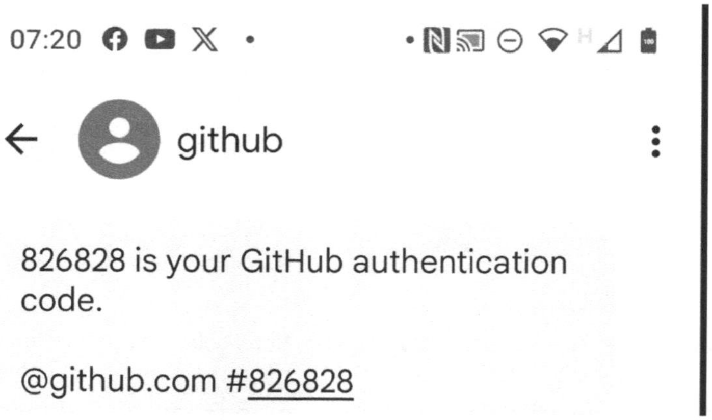


**Figure 12.16:** *The one-time code message used to log in to get the* **gh** *token to be pasted*

The **GitHub** website now gives access to copy the token we need for the command shown in *Figure 12.15*. As illustrated in *Figure 12.17*, we have to select the **Generate new token** button after selecting the **Fine-grained tokens** option, both of which are highlighted, and then the token we used can be copied.

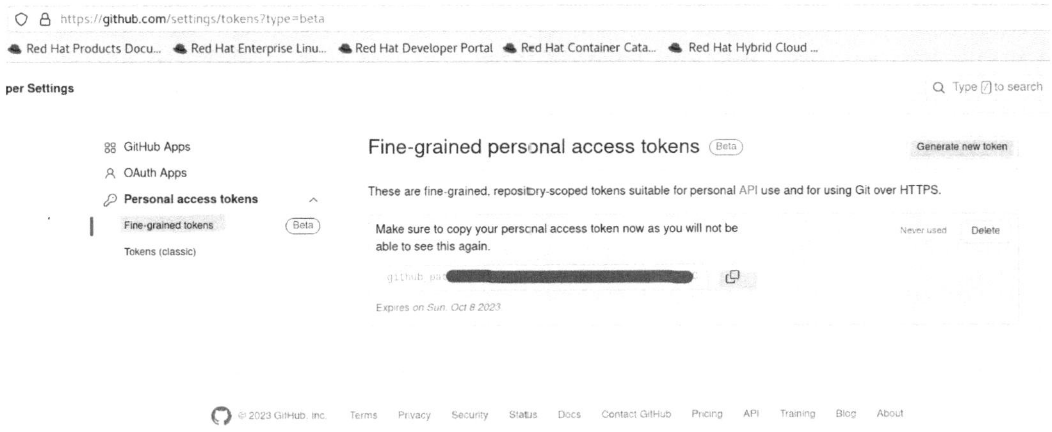

**Figure 12.17:** *Select the* ***Generate new token*** *button after selecting the* ***Fine-grained tokens***

For more information, please visit:

**https://github.com/facebookresearch/llama-recipes#quick-start**

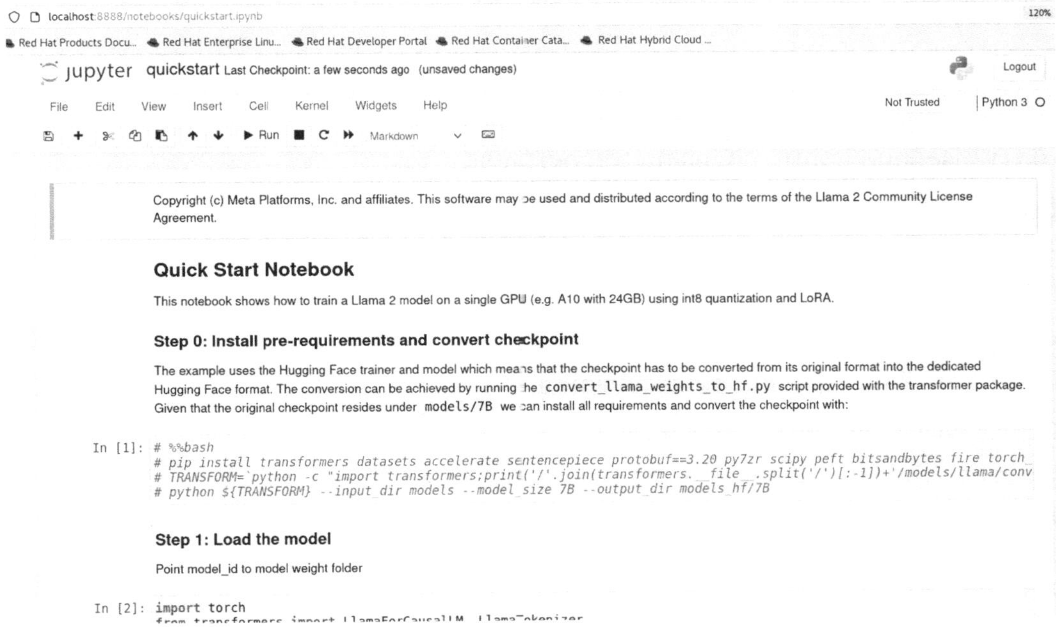

**Figure 12.18:** *The* ***`quickstart.ipynb`*** *notebook is loaded into the* ***`Jupyter Notebook`*** *application*

The following notes were sent by email from the **Meta AI** site:

"Now you're ready to start building with **Code Llama**.

**Helpful tips:**

Please read the instructions in the GitHub repo and use the provided code examples to understand how to best interact with the models. In particular, for the fine-tuned chat models you must use appropriate formatting and correct system/instruction tokens to get the best results from the model. You can find additional information about how to responsibly deploy Llama models in our **Responsible Use Guide.**

**If you need to report issues:**

If you or any Code Llama user becomes aware of any violation of our license or acceptable use policies - or any bug or issues with Code Llama that could lead to any such violations - please report it through one of the following means:

1. Reporting issues with the model: **Code Llama GitHub**
2. Giving feedback about potentially problematic output generated by the model: Llama output feedback
3. Reporting bugs and security concerns: **Bug Bounty Program**
4. Reporting violations of the Acceptable Use Policy: **LlamaUseReport@ meta.com**

**Subscribe** to get the latest updates on Llama and Meta AI."

The preceding approach still had some missing Python libraries, so we decided to try a second approach, using the perplexity link:

**https://labs.perplexity.ai/**

This looked promising, but the response to the earlier question asked was as follows:

**"Is there example Java code to store a document in the latest IBM FileNet Document Management system, using the FileNet Java API?",**

It gave the following code response:

```
"import com.ibm.filenet.api.*;

import com.ibm.filenet.api.exceptions.*;

// Create a new instance of the FileNet Java API client

FileNetClient client = new FileNetClient("http://localhost:9080",
"username", "password");

try {
```

```
    // Get the root folder for the repository
    Folder rootFolder = client.getRootFolder();
    // Create a new subfolder under the root folder
    String subfolderName = "MySubfolder";
    Folder subfolder = rootFolder.createFolder(subfolderName);
    // Create a new document
    Document doc = new Document();
    doc.setTitle("My Document");
    doc.setDescription("This is my document");
    doc.setMimeType("application/pdf");
    doc.setContent("<html><body>Hello World!</body></html>");
    // Store the document in the subfolder
    subfolder.storeDocument(doc);
} catch (Exception e) {
    System.out.println("Error storing document: " + e.getMessage());
} finally {
    if (client != null) {
        try {
            client.close();
        } catch (IOException ioe) {}
    }
}"
```

This was just not worth testing, as the very short code example listed above was incorrect.

The following URL is a video link that describes the use of a CPU-only extension to the LLM models available:

**https://m.youtube.com/watch?v=yhECvKMu8kM**

(This link does demonstrate how much processing power is required for just a simple AI task to be completed.) We develop this concept further in the next section: **GPT4All and How It Works**.

## GPT4All and How It Works

GPT4ALL is an AI chatbot that runs locally on a server. It can run offline without a GPU and can be used to train and deploy customized large language models.

This AI machine can write documents, stories, poems, and songs.

GPT4All only requires 3GB-8GB of storage and can run on 4GB–16GB of RAM. So, an entire LLM can be run on a Windows or Linux server without needing a GPU or external cloud assistance.

There is a free download available at:

**https://github.com/nomic-ai/gpt4all**

We then followed the docker container build instructions; the commands are shown in **Figure 12.19:**

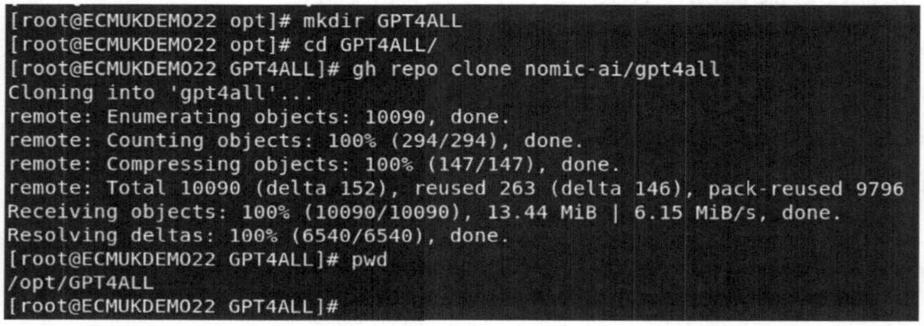


***Figure 12.19:*** *The gh command is used to clone the GPT4ALL AI chatbot*

For more information, please visit (The highlighted docker commands were run).

```
# GPT4All REST API

This directory contains the source code to run and build docker images that run a FastAPI app

for serving inference from GPT4All models. The API matches the OpenAI API spec.

## Tutorial

The following tutorial assumes that you have checked out this repo and cd'd into it.

### Starting the app

First change your working directory to `gpt4all/gpt4all-api`.

Now you can build the FastAPI docker image. You only have to do this on initial build or when you add new dependencies to the requirements.txt file:

```bash

DOCKER_BUILDKIT=1 docker build -t gpt4all_api --progress plain -f gpt4all_api/Dockerfile.buildkit .
```
```

**Note:**

Note: The following two highlighted automatic steps can take around 20 minutes each or more, as shown in *Figure 12.20*:

**Figure 12.20**: *The following two highlighted automatic steps can take around 20 minutes*

**STEP 8/8:** RUN wget -q --show-progress=off https://gpt4all.io/models/${MODEL_BIN} -P /models && md5sum /models/${MODEL_BIN}```bash

a) COMMIT gpt4all_api

Then, start the backend with:

podman-compose up --build

( docker compose up --build is used on older Linux systems, but we have RedHat using 8.8)

```

This will run both the API and locally hosted GPU inference server. If you want to run the API without the GPU inference server, you can run:

```bash
docker compose up --build gpt4all_api
```

NOTE: To run the API with the GPU inference server, you will need to include environment variables (like the `MODEL_ID`). Edit the `.env` file and run

```bash
docker compose --env-file .env up --build
```

#### Spinning up your app

Run `docker compose up` to spin up the backend. Monitor the logs for errors in-case you forgot to set an environment variable above.

#### Development

Run

```bash
docker compose up --build

```
` ` `

and edit files in the `api` directory. The api will hot-reload on changes.

You can run the unit tests with

` ` `bash

make test

` ` `

#### Viewing API documentation

Once the FastAPI ap is started you can access its documentation and test the search endpoint by going to:

` ` `

localhost:80/docs
```

This documentation should match the OpenAI spec located at **https://github.com/openai/openai-openapi/blob/master/openapi.yaml**

**Note:**

We need to install openai for Python to use the test example:

```
pip3 install openai
```

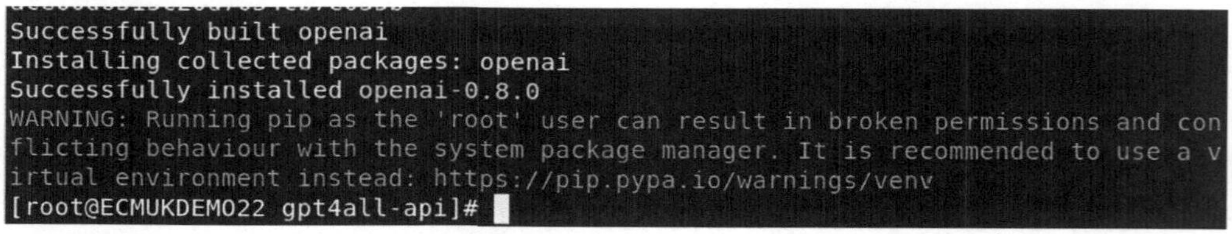


***Figure 12.21:*** *The Python library,* ***`openai-0.8.0`*** *python package, version 0.8.0 is installed*

First, we have to fix a problem with errors on a **Python** library location using:

cp /usr/local/lib/python3.6/site-packages/six.py /usr/lib/python3.6/site-packages/

This is a known issue with **Python** installations, which can cause **Linux** commands like **firewall-cmd** to fail.

Next, we'll open port **4891**, as follows:

```
firewall-cmd --zone=public --permanent --add-port=4891/tcp
firewall-cmd --reload
```

The script is then loaded into **Jupyter Notebook**, as shown in *Figure 12.22*:

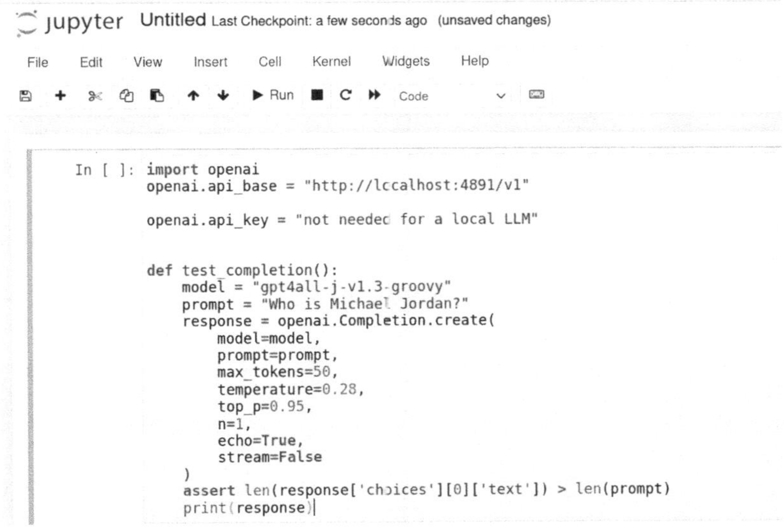


**Figure 12.22:** *The script is then loaded into* ***Jupyter Notebook***

~~~
#### Running inference
```python
~~~

The code was shown as follows:

~~~
import openai
openai.api_base = "http://localhost:4891/v1"
openai.api_key = "not needed for a local LLM"
def test_completion():
    model = "gpt4all-j-v1.3-groovy"
    prompt = "Who is Michael Jordan?"
    response = openai.Completion.create(
        model=model,
        prompt=prompt,
        max_tokens=50,
        temperature=0.28,
        top_p=0.95,
        n=1,
        echo=True,
        stream=False
    )
    assert len(response['choices'][0]['text']) > len(prompt)
    print(response)
```
~~~

This didn't give any errors, but it also didn't print anything either, except for the path using the Jupyter Notebook cell test:

```
import sys
print(sys.executable)
```

```
Output:

/usr/bin/python3.6
```

The running containers so far can be listed using the **docker ps** command, as shown in *Figure 12.23*:

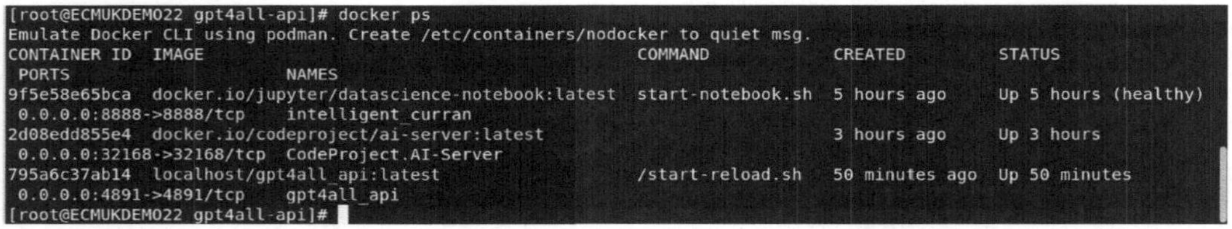

```
[root@ECMUKDEMO22 gpt4all-api]# docker ps
Emulate Docker CLI using podman. Create /etc/containers/nodocker to quiet msg.
CONTAINER ID  IMAGE                                          COMMAND             CREATED         STATUS
 PORTS                  NAMES
9f5e58e65bca  docker.io/jupyter/datascience-notebook:latest  start-notebook.sh  5 hours ago     Up 5 hours (healthy)
 0.0.0.0:8888->8888/tcp    intelligent_curran
2d08edd855e4  docker.io/codeproject/ai-server:latest                             3 hours ago     Up 3 hours
 0.0.0.0:32168->32168/tcp  CodeProject.AI-Server
795a6c37ab14  localhost/gpt4all_api:latest                   /start-reload.sh   50 minutes ago  Up 50 minutes
 0.0.0.0:4891->4891/tcp    gpt4all_api
[root@ECMUKDEMO22 gpt4all-api]#
```

**Figure 12.23:** *The installed and running containers, listed using the* ***docker ps*** *command*

## Note

Using the docker container **CONTAINER ID** column values (listed using docker ps), we can then reload the downloaded containers. For example, if the Linux system requires rebooting, then you will need to use the **CONTAINER ID** column values, as shown in *Figure 12.24*:

```
docker start 9f5e58e65bca
docker start 2d08edd855e4
docker start 795a6c37ab14
```

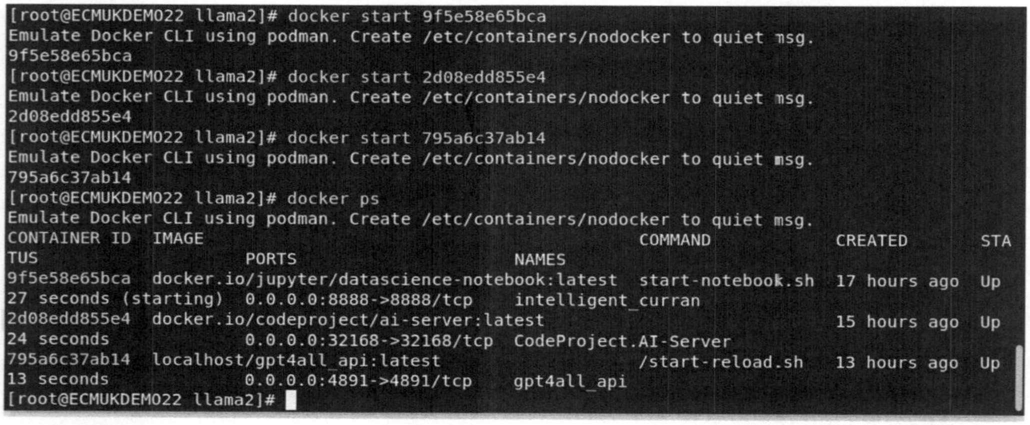

```
[root@ECMUKDEMO22 llama2]# docker start 9f5e58e65bca
Emulate Docker CLI using podman. Create /etc/containers/nodocker to quiet msg.
9f5e58e65bca
[root@ECMUKDEMO22 llama2]# docker start 2d08edd855e4
Emulate Docker CLI using podman. Create /etc/containers/nodocker to quiet msg.
2d08edd855e4
[root@ECMUKDEMO22 llama2]# docker start 795a6c37ab14
Emulate Docker CLI using podman. Create /etc/containers/nodocker to quiet msg.
795a6c37ab14
[root@ECMUKDEMO22 llama2]# docker ps
Emulate Docker CLI using podman. Create /etc/containers/nodocker to quiet msg.
CONTAINER ID  IMAGE                                          COMMAND            CREATED        STA
TUS                     PORTS                     NAMES
9f5e58e65bca  docker.io/jupyter/datascience-notebook:latest  start-notebook.sh  17 hours ago   Up
27 seconds (starting)   0.0.0.0:8888->8888/tcp    intelligent_curran
2d08edd855e4  docker.io/codeproject/ai-server:latest                            15 hours ago   Up
24 seconds              0.0.0.0:32168->32168/tcp  CodeProject.AI-Server
795a6c37ab14  localhost/gpt4all_api:latest                   /start-reload.sh   13 hours ago   Up
13 seconds              0.0.0.0:4891->4891/tcp    gpt4all_api
[root@ECMUKDEMO22 llama2]#
```

**Figure 12.24:** *The* **CONTAINER ID** *column values (listed using docker ps) used for docker start*

# GitHub Copilot

Microsoft and OpenAI jointly developed GitHub Copilot, an AI-based system for code analysis and code completion, which is a level above the normal Visual Studio IDE assistance. This system was launched in June 2021 and was initially opened as a free trial for selected users. GitHub Copilot has received positive reviews for the enhancements it has provided to software developers. It is now a paid-for service, except for Teachers or Students. (If you are not a student, teacher, or maintainer of a popular open-source project, you can try GitHub Copilot for free with **a one-time** 30-day trial.)

For the billing process, please refer to the following link:

**https://docs.github.com/en/billing/managing-billing-for-github-copilot/about-billing-for-github-copilot**

This states: "*You can either set up a GitHub Copilot subscription for your personal account, or you can set up a GitHub Copilot for Business subscription for your organization*".

The step-by-step set-up procedure is described on the webpage, with the link as follows:

**https://docs.github.com/en/copilot/quickstart**

# Google Duet AI

There are several alternatives to the GitHub CoPilot AI system, some of which we have already covered in detail. Google has developed a programming assistant AI called Duet AI.

For more information, please refer to the following link:

**https://www.analyticsvidhya.com/blog/2023/05/googles-duet-ai-a-competitor-to-microsofts-github-copilot**

From Google support (dated 29th August 2023):

"Duet AI for Google Workspace, which can create text and images for documents and take meeting notes, will cost enterprises $30 a month per person. It's the same price Microsoft will charge for its artificial intelligence enhancement tools, when the paid offering hits the market."

# Codeium

Codeium has been developed by Exafunction developers:

**https://exafunction.com/blog/series-a-announcement**

Using generative models and AI software, their stated goal is to provide software development assistance at very competitive prices, and sometimes for free. Codeium AI is free to install for a number of IDE systems, as shown in the following links. It supports a large number of systems, including Visual Studio, JetBrains, Jupyter Notebooks, and Eclipse:

**https://codeium.com/download**

For tutorials, please refer to the following links:

**https://codeium.com/vscode_tutorial**

**https://codeium.com/visual_studio_tutorial**

**https://codeium.com/eclipse_tutorial**

**https://codeium.com/jetbrains_tutorial**

**https://codeium.com/jupyter_tutorial**

The Eclipse Marketplace Codeium website is loaded from the web browser to access the install, as it is not directly accessible from the **Eclipse IDE** marketplace menu, as shown in *Figure 12.25*:

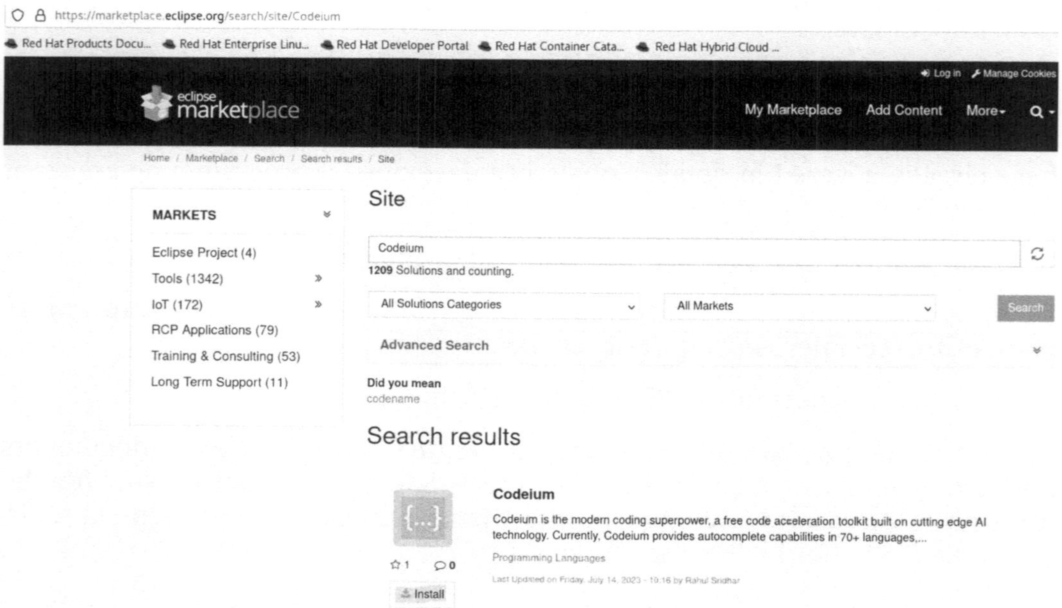


***Figure 12.25:*** *The Codeium website is loaded to access the install*

(As of September 2023, there are currently 21 supported **IDE** systems.)

If you have followed our steps in this chapter to install and run **Jupyter Notebook**, then you will find the following code just runs in a new **Python3** kernel notebook cell as follows:

```
import sys
!{sys.executable} -m pip install -U pip
!{sys.executable} -m pip install -U codeium-jupyter
!jupyter nbextension install --py codeium --user
!jupyter nbextension enable --py codeium --user
!jupyter serverextension enable --py codeium --user
```

The **Jupyter Notebook** is used to run the Codeium script for the Python language assistance, as shown in *Figure 12.26*:

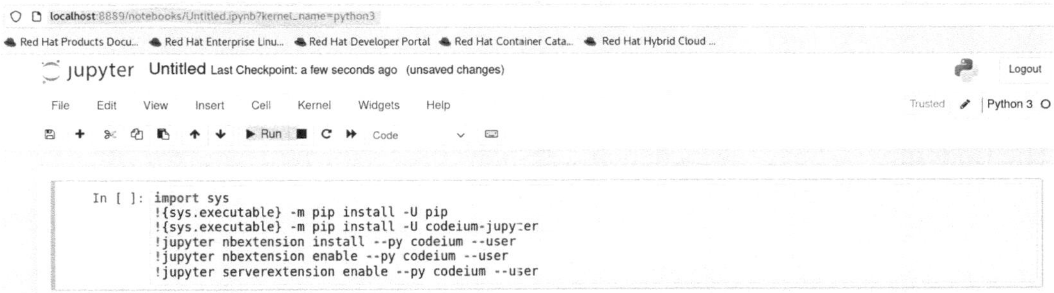


***Figure 12.26:** The **Jupyter Notebook** is used to run the **Codeium** script for **Python***

The **Python** script is successfully run to install **Codeium**, as shown in *Figure 12.27*:

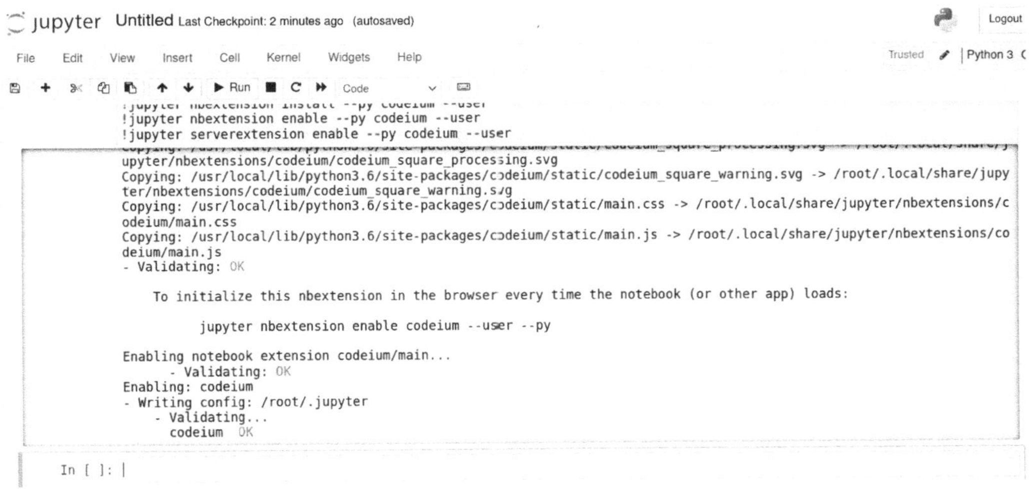


***Figure 12.27:** The Python script is successfully run to install Codeium*

The new menu item for Codeium is highlighted in *Figure* 12.28:

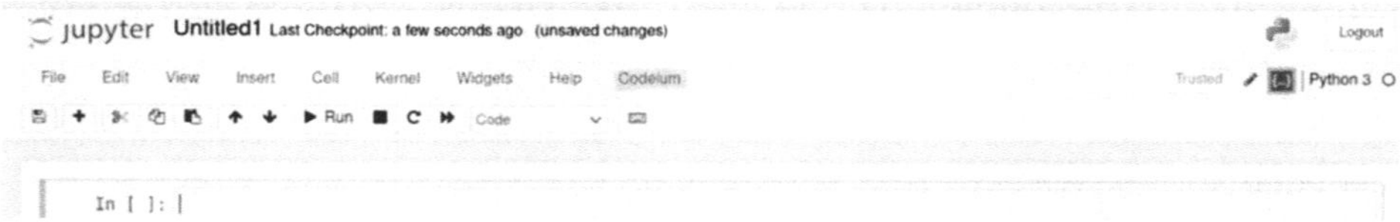


**Figure 12.28:** *The new Codeium menu item is selected*

Now, we have to select the Provide Authentication menu item under Codeium to obtain the Token required to log in, as shown in *Figure* 12.29:

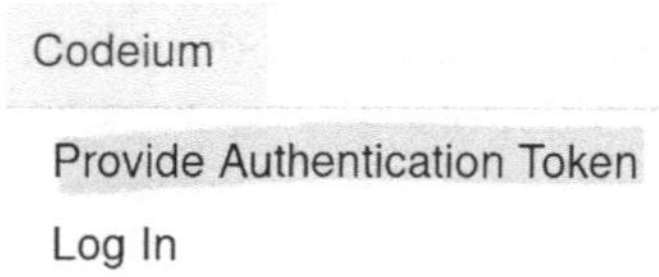


**Figure 12.29:** *Select the Provide Authentication menu item under Codeium*

The **Codeium** webpage is loaded and displayed, as shown in *Figure* 12.30:

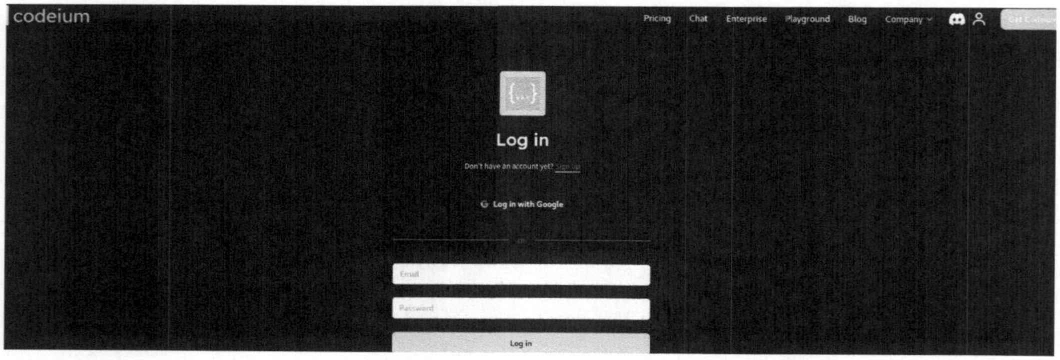


**Figure 12.30:** *The **Codeium** webpage is loaded and displayed*

The green underlined **Sign up** link is selected (located immediately under the white **Log in** text), which launches the pop-up window, as shown in *Figure* 12.31:

**Figure 12.31** *The details of the* **Codeium** *account we need is entered*

As part of the Codeium Sign-up, we can upload a picture and create a **Discord** account and blog server, as shown in *Figure* 12.32:

**Figure 12.32**:*The invitation to join the Discord blog system is offered*

This gives us access to the **Clyde AI ChatBot**, as shown in *Figure 12.33*:

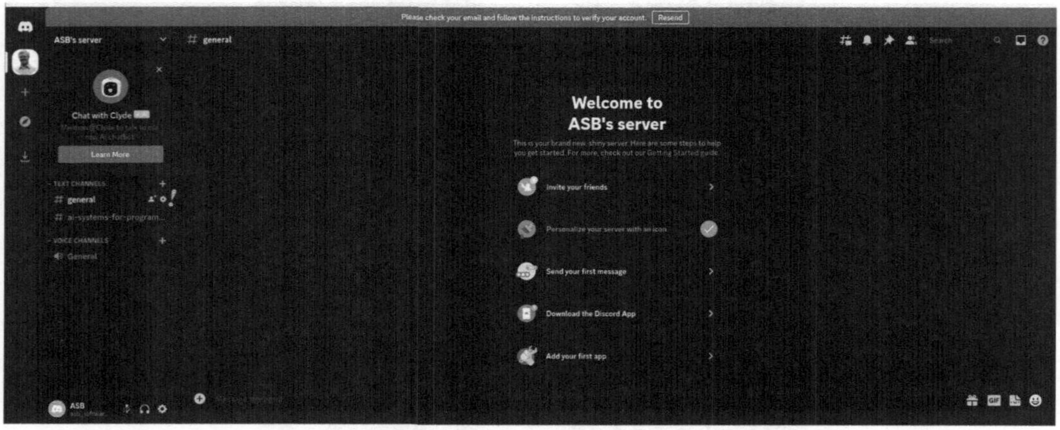


***Figure 12.33**: The **Clyde AI ChatBot** and blog server created as part of using **Codeium***

At this point, we have to click on the verify link sent by the **Codeium** system to our email address to confirm the account setup.

This gives a pop-up window containing an **Accept Invite** button, which we click, as shown in *Figure 12.34*:

***Figure 12.34**: The **Codeium Accept Invite** is selected*

Upon reloading the getting started page for Codeium, we can see the Installation links to the different supported IDE environments, as shown in *Figure 12.35*:

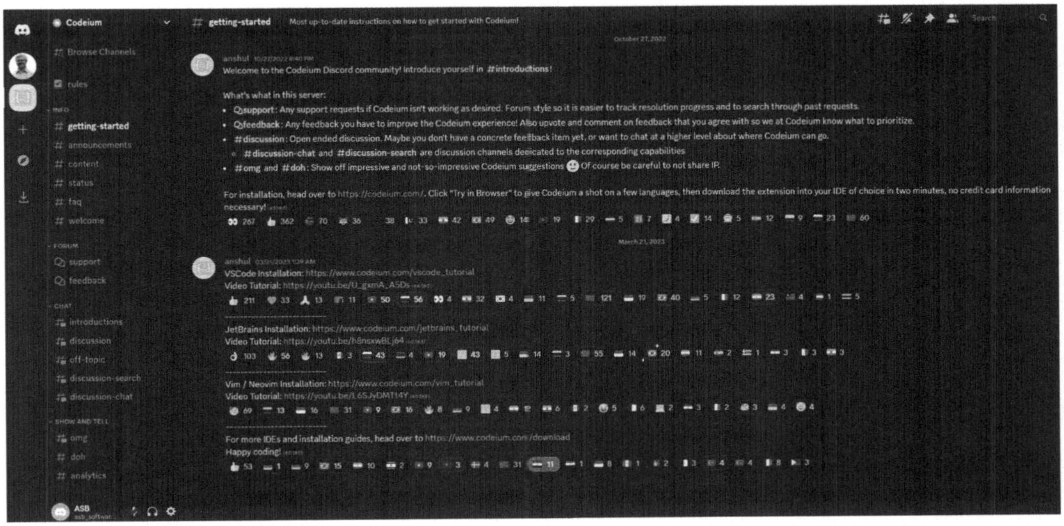

**Figure 12.35:** *The getting started page for Codeium*

The next step is to create a **Codeium** token to be used with the **Jupyter Notebook** installation, which we can get, as shown in *Figure 12.36*:

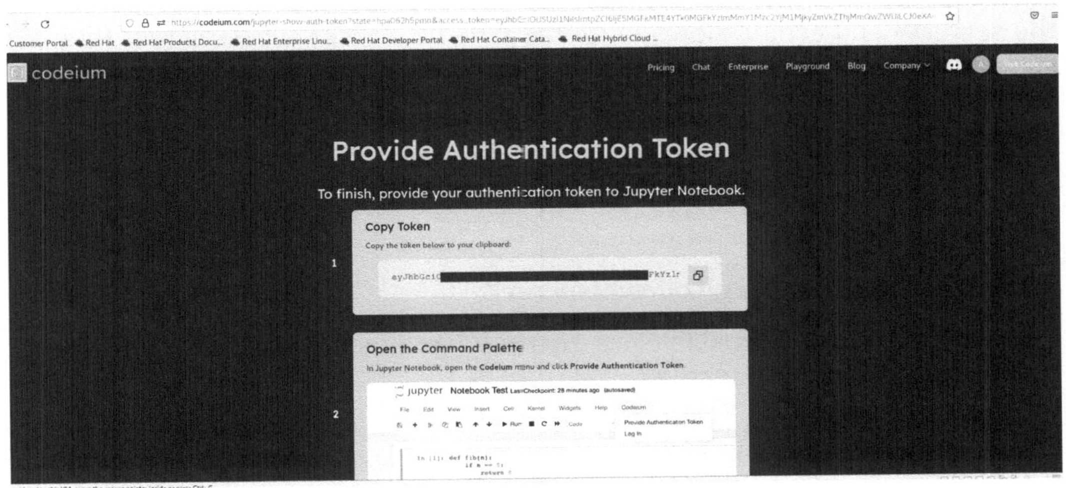


**Figure 12.36**: *The Codeium Token is copied*

The **Authentication Token** can now be pasted into our **Jupyter Notebook** project, as shown in *Figure 12.37*:

***Figure 12.37****:The Codeium Token is pasted into our Codeium project*

The **Codeium** system didn't perform very well, perhaps overwhelmed by the number of users at the time of our testing. **AI** systems are very high consumers of resources, requiring substantial **GPU** processing power and memory, and the servers can become slow due to the volume of user accesses that they are subjected to.

# CodeWhisperer

Amazon has developed an AI system called **CodeWhisperer,** which can be accessed through the following link:

**https://aws.amazon.com/codewhisperer/**

There is a free link available at: **https://aws.amazon.com/codewhisperer/resources/#Getting_started/**

For Python programming, we need to install Jupyter Lab using the following command:

```
pip3 install jupyterlab

export PATH="$HOME/.local/bin:$PATH"
```

If using **Jupyter Lab** version 5.3 or earlier, the following is required:

jupyter serverextension enable --py jupyterlab --sys-prefix

jupyter lab --allow-root

Enable the **CodeWhisperer** extension in JupyterLab, as follows:

In your terminal, run the following commands:

pip install amazon-codewhisperer-jupyterlab-ext

The **Amazon** page for **CodeWhisperer** had the following statistic from their preview, which sounded promising, as shown in *Figure 12.38*:

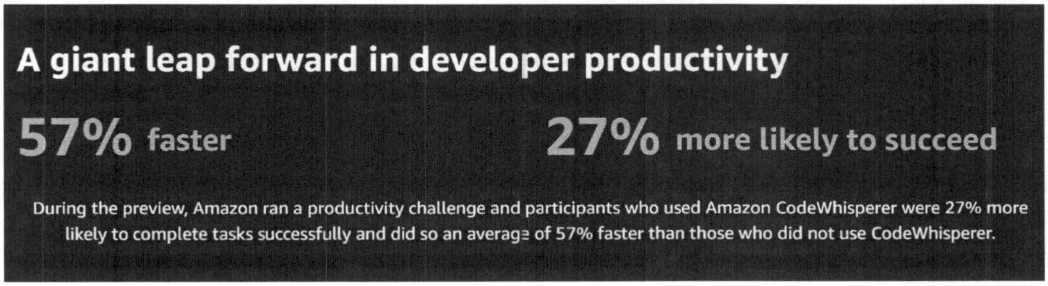


***Figure 12.38:*** *The preview statistics for the Amazon Code Whisperer AI*

The highlighted command for the pip installation of **Amazon CodeWhisperer AI** is used, as explained earlier, and can be seen to download the required supporting **Linux** libraries, as shown in *Figure 12.39*:

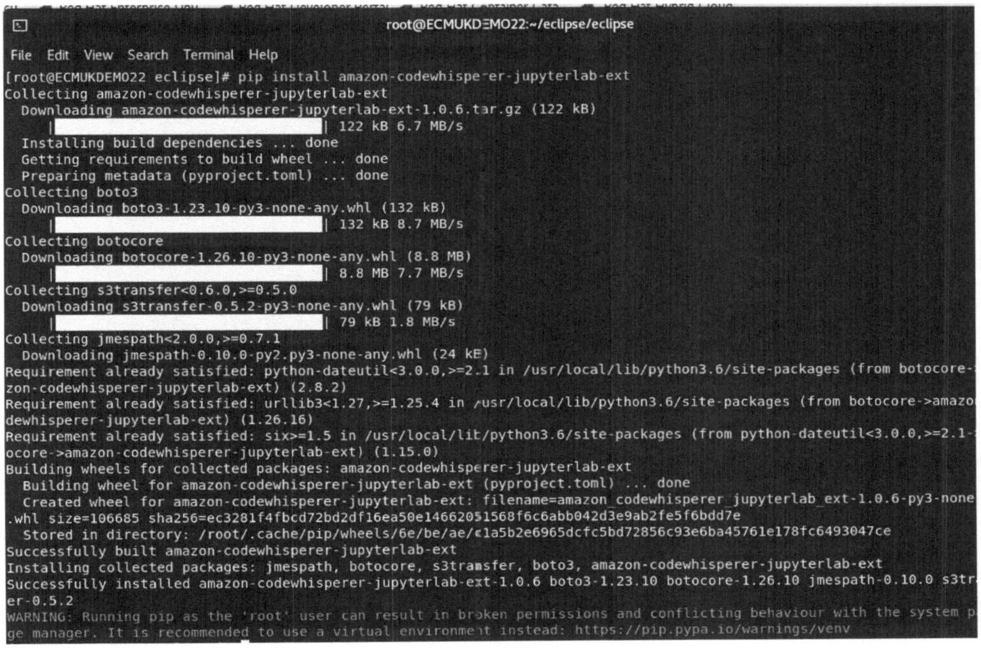


**Figure 12.39**: *The pip installation of* **Amazon CodeWhisperer AI**

Next, we run the command as follows, as shown in *Figure* 12.40:

jupyter server extension enable amazon_codewhisperer_jupyterlab_ext

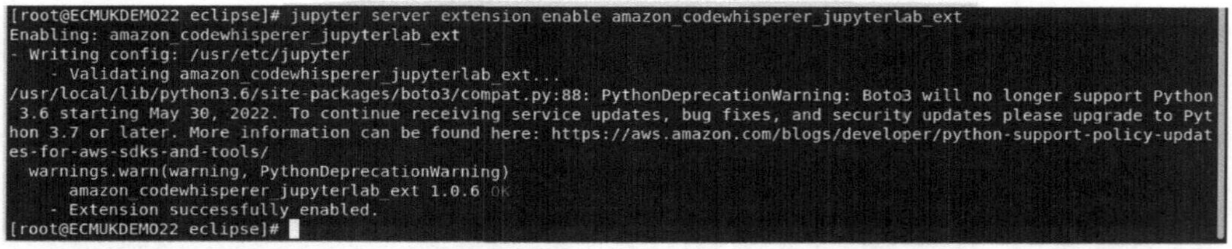


***Figure 12.40****: The Amazon extension is enabled, as shown with the highlighted command*

**The documentation is available at:**

**https://docs.aws.amazon.com/codewhisperer/latest/userguide/what-is-cwspr.html**

---

**Note:**

**CodeWhisperer** does not currently support JupyterLab version 4

---

In the following procedure, the Builder ID is used to authenticate when **CodeWhisperer** is enabled:

Refresh the browser tab in which **JupyterLab** is used.

From the **CodeWhisperer** panel at the bottom of the window, select **Start CodeWhisperer,** as shown in *Figure* 12.41:

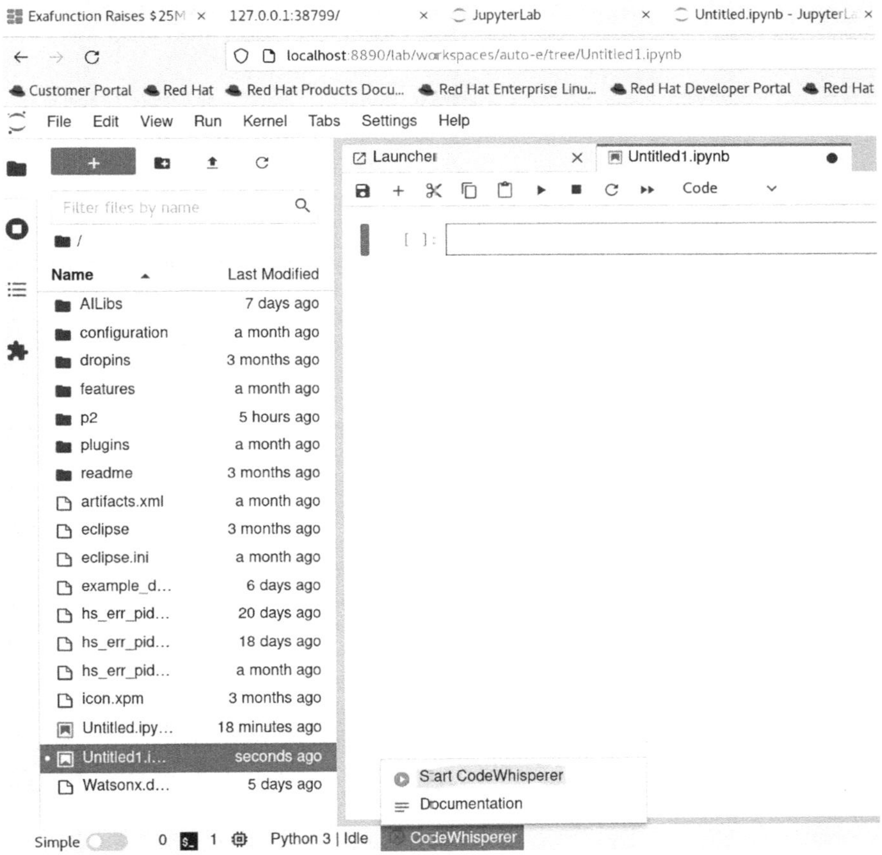


**Figure 12.41**: *The Start CodeWhisperer menu is selected*

From the pop-up window, select **Copy Code and Proceed** to copy the unique one-time code, as illustrated in *Figure* 12.42:

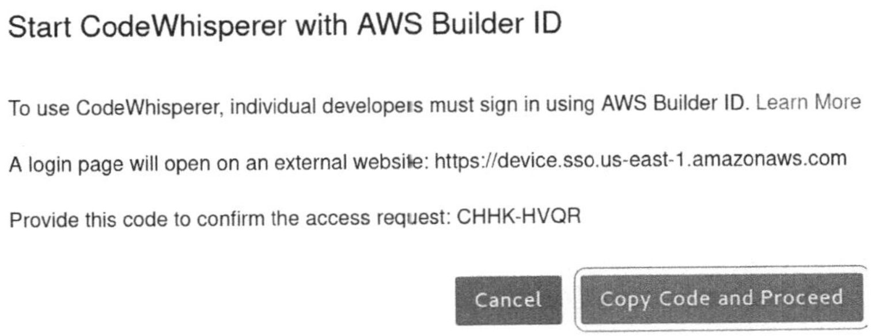


**Figure 12.42**: *Select the* ***Copy Code and Proceed*** *button*

On the **Create AWS Builder ID** webpage, if you don't have a Builder ID, enter a personal email address and select **Next,** as shown in *Figure 12.43*:

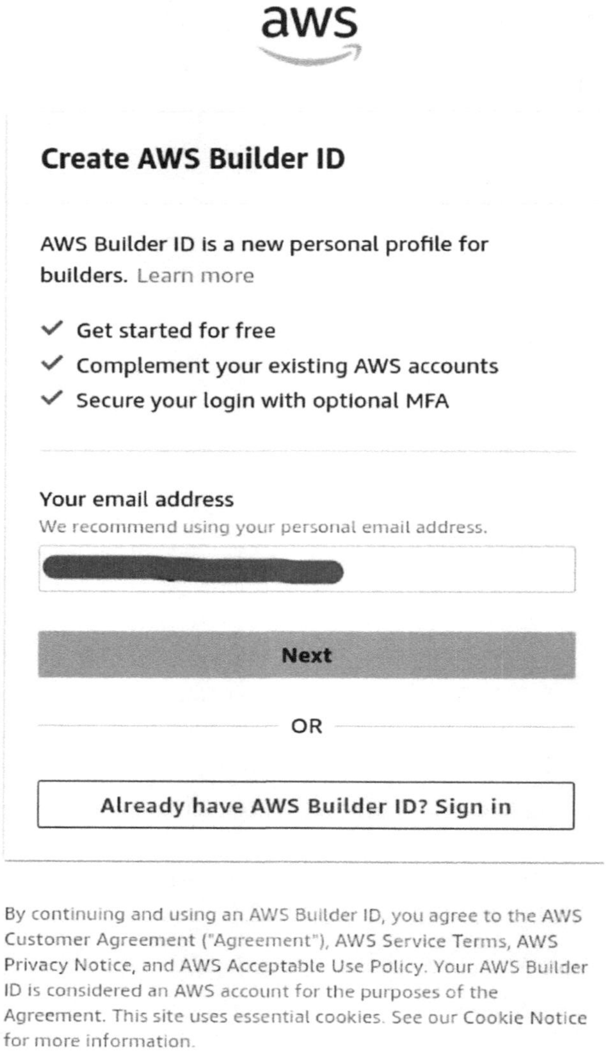


**Figure 12.43:** *Enter a personal email address and select* **Next**

If you already have a Builder ID, skip to the step about the **Authorize request** page.

On the next **Create your AWS Builder ID** webpage, enter a name and choose **Next,** as shown in *Figure 12.44*:

**Figure 12.44:** *Enter the Name on the webpage as required*

After receiving an email verification code, enter it in the blank field and select **Verify**, as illustrated in *Figure* 12.45:

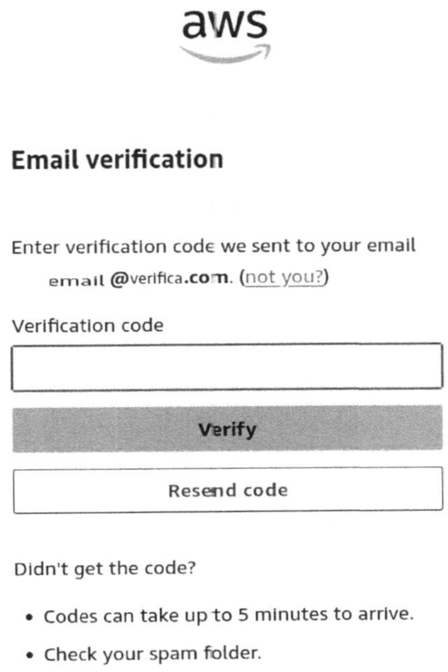


**Figure 12.45:** *Enter the emailed verification code*

On the next screen, enter and confirm a password, then select **Create AWS Builder ID.** If the password does not meet the strong password standards, you will get an error message. In this case, the password has to have a non-alphanumeric character as is shown missing in *Figure 12.46*:

***Figure 12.46:*** *The password has to follow the strong password requirements*

After a valid password has been entered, we can select **Create AWS Builder ID**, as shown in *Figure 12.47*:

***Figure 12.47:*** *The password has now been entered correctly*

On the next page, choose **Allow** to allow **CodeWhisperer** to access your data.

We checked to ensure that the Jupyter Lab version we have is valid (less than version 4.0).

This is the screen from the **About** menu item, as shown in *Figure* 12.48, which shows that we have installed Version 3.2.9:

***Figure* 12.48**: *The* ***Jupyter Lab*** *version is validated as* 3.2.9

Now, we can log into CodeWhisperer in JupyterLab with the Builder ID and use the AI, as shown in *Figure* 12.49:

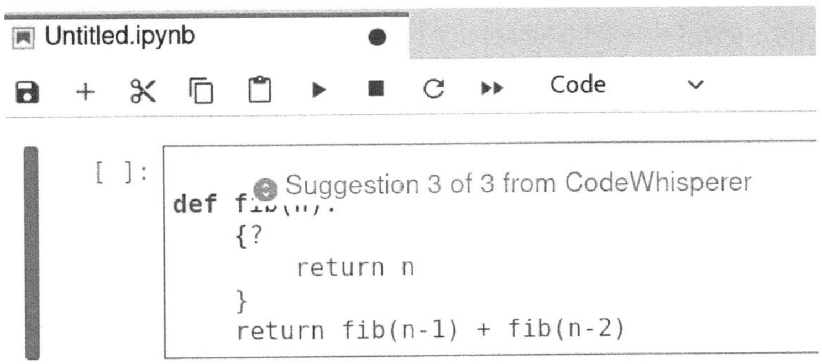


***Figure* 12.49**: *The* **CodeWhisperer** *can be seen to suggest code completion*

# Falcon-180B

One of the most recently assessed LLMs, in September 2023, Falcon 180B was rated the highest-performing pretrained LLM on the Hugging Face Open LLM Leaderboard.

Trained on a dataset of 3.5 trillion tokens from the **RefinedWeb** dataset created by **TII**; it is the longest single-run pretraining processed LLM for an open-source available model. The training process involved the simultaneous use of up to 4096 GPUs, using Amazon.

(**RefinedWeb** is a high-quality five trillion tokens web-only English pretraining dataset)

(The pdf describing this LLM in detail is also available for free download at **https://arxiv.org/pdf/2306.01116.pdf**)

For more information, please visit the following links:

**https://analyticsindiamag.com/uaes-tii-unveils-falcon-180b-a-new-open-source-llm/**

and **https://www.pinecone.io/learn/falcon-180b/**

# Conclusion

In this chapter, we have investigated some of the alternative AI code assistance systems available. The ones we have seen do not seem to be any more helpful than asking direct questions of the **Ask AI** mobile phone App and similar systems such as **Perplexity AI**. They were also much more complicated to install!

We have also attempted to forecast the future impact of a number of applications of the **AI** systems available and several predictions of the effect of these **AI** systems on security, jobs, and the impact on the productivity of program development.

In the next and last chapter, we will provide additional information on other **IBM** systems supporting **AI** development, including the impact of Quantum Computing developments on **AI** processing.

# Points to Remember

- Perplexity AI has both the 7B and 13B LLaMA 2 models accessible through the conversational AI demo.
- For GPT4ALL docker build, steps 7 and 8 can take over 40 minutes to complete.
- For GPT4ALL, to run the API with the GPU inference server, you will need to include environment variables (like the `**MODEL_ID**`). Edit the `**.env**` file and run the following command:

  ```
  docker compose --env-file .env up --build
  ```

  (This is not required without the **GPU** inference server.)

- You will need to install **openai** for **Python** to use the test example for **GPT4ALL**.
- We can then reload the downloaded containers using the docker container CONTAINER ID column values (listed using docker ps). For example:

  ```
  docker start 9f5e58e65bca
  ```

  where `9f5e58e65bca` is the Container ID column value.
- CodeWhisperer does not currently support JupyterLab 4.

# Multiple Choice Questions

1. **Which one of the following AI systems is a monthly paid-for system after the 30-day free trial?**
   a. GPT4All
   b GitHub Copilot
   c. Codeium
   d. CodeWhisperer
2. **In which region of the world was the robot called Sophia created by Hanson Robotics?**
   a. Taiwan
   b. South Korea
   c. Hong Kong
   d. Japan
3. **According to a Cornell University Computer Science publication on Software Engineering, what were the percentages of the responses for ChatGPT?**
   a. 25 percent of ChatGPT answers are incorrect and 77 percent are verbose
   b. 48 percent of ChatGPT answers are incorrect and 77 percent are verbose
   c. 77 percent of ChatGPT answers are incorrect and 52 percent are verbose
   d. 48 percent of ChatGPT answers are correct and 23 percent are not verbose

4. **Which one of the following four LLM models is <u>not</u> supplied with the Code Llama 2 commercial license?**
    a. CodeLlama-34b
    b. CodeLlama-34b-Python
    c. CodeLlama-34b-Java
    d. CodeLlama-13b-Instruct

# Answers

1. **b**
2. **c**
3. **d**
4. **c**

# Questions

1. What docker command would you use to identify the Container ID of an installed and running Docker container system?
2. Why is it useful to know the Container IDs of a Docker system?
3. Which of the AI systems installed in this chapter demonstrated some useful output?
4. Which of the AI systems could you use to assist with a Visual Studio IDE system?
5. What do you think the main future issues will be, that AI systems will be responsible for creating, in the short term?
6. What do you think the most likely longer-term issues will be, caused by AI systems?

# Key Terms

- **LLM:** Large Language Model

  From Microsoft Bing:

  "A large language model (LLM) is a neural network-based model that can understand and generate human-like text using natural language processing techniques. LLMs are trained using massive datasets and use transformer models to perform many types of language tasks[134]. Some examples of LLMs are GPT-3, BERT, and XLNet[2].

***Source: Conversation with Bing*, 9/11/2023**

(1) *Large Language Models (LLM) - All About AI.* **https://www.allabtai.com/large-language-models/** .

(2) *Large language model - Wikipedia.* **https://en.wikipedia.org/wiki/Large_language_model.**

(3) *What is a large language model (LLM)? - Elastic.* **https://www.elastic.co/what-is/large-language-models.**

(4) **https://bing.com/search?q=large+language+model+llm.**

(5) *What is a Large Language Model (LLM)? Techopedia Explains.* **https://www.techopedia.com/definition/34948/large-language-model-llm** ."

- GPT:

  From Microsoft Bing (There are other GPT systems available, as well as OpenAI!):

  "GPT stands for Generative Pre-trained Transformer. It is a family of large language models that can understand and generate text based on prompts. ChatGPT is an AI chatbot that uses GPT to have conversations with users[12]. You can try it for free at chat.openai.com[34].

  ***Source: Conversation with Bing*, 9/11/2023**

  (1) ChatGPT explained: everything you need to know about the AI chatbot. **https://www.techradar.com/news/chatgpt-explained** .

  (2) ChatGPT: How to Use the AI Chatbot for Free - How-To Geek. **https://www.howtogeek.com/871065/chatgpt-how-to-use-the-ai-chatbot-for-free/** .

  (3) Introducing ChatGPT - OpenAI. **https://openai.com/blog/chatgpt.**

  (4) ChatGPT - OpenAI. **https://openai.com/chatgpt** .

  (5) Introducing ChatGPT Plus - OpenAI. **https://openai.com/blog/chatgpt-plus/** ."

- **GPU:** This stands for **Graphics Processing Unit,** which is now one of the most important types of computing technology for **AI LLM** processing. It is designed for parallel processing and is also used for applications such as graphics and video rendering.

- **Transformers:** A Transformer is a neural network, machine learning model, that inputs sequential data, such as text or speech, making use of a parallel attention procedure that calculates and stores long-range dependencies and then generates output in a single pass. We then tried the example following the procedure at the link:

**https://huggingface.co/docs/transformers/installation**

"For CPU-support only, you can conveniently install Transformers and a deep learning library in one line. For example, install Transformers and PyTorch with:"

```
pip install ‘transformers[torch]’
```

Then, to install Transformers and TensorFlow 2.0:

```
pip install 'transformers[tf-cpu]'
```

Add theTransformers and Flax installation:

```
pip install 'transformers[flax]'
```

Finally, to check if Transformers has been properly installed, run the following command. It will download a pretrained model:

```
python3 -c "from transformers import pipeline;
print(pipeline('sentiment-analysis')('we love you'))"
```

This will print out the label and score, as follows:

```
[{'label': 'POSITIVE', 'score': 0.9998704195022583}]
```

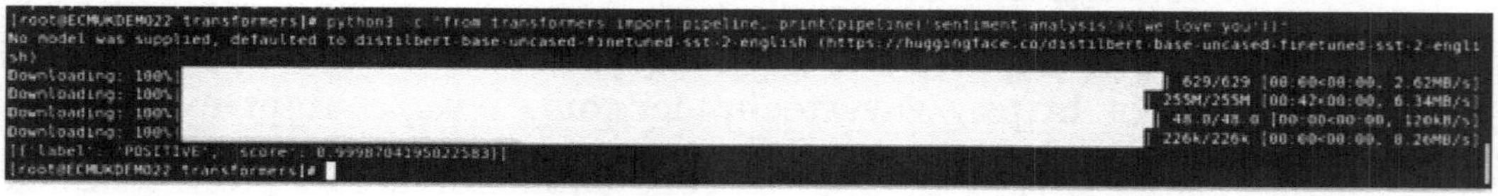

**Figure 12.50:** *The downloaded pretrained model is tested using the Transformers library*

# CHAPTER 13
# Appendices for Additional Questions

## Introduction

This chapter provides additional information on other **IBM** systems supporting AI development, including the impact of Quantum Computing developments on AI processing.

The IBM reference is available as a free download:

**https://www.researchgate.net/publication/328723940_The_Potential_of_Quantum_Computing_and_Machine_Learning_to_Advance_Clinical_Research_and_Change_the_Practice_of_Medicine#fullTextFileContent**

## Structure

In this chapter, we will discuss the following topics:

- Appendix A – Further AI questions for **ChatGPT**
- Appendix B - FAQs and answers for **ChatGPT**
- Appendix C – ASB Software Development Limited Publication's
    - Molecular Biology Installations - ASB Software Development Limited Publications

- o IBM Installations - ASB Software Development Limited Publications
- o Contact Details

# Appendix A – Further AI questions for ChatGPT

The following additional general questions were asked out of interest of the **Ask AI** mobile 'phone App:

**Are you conscious?**

"As an AI language model, I don't possess consciousness or self-awareness. I'm a program designed to process and generate text based on the input I receive. While I can understand and respond to questions and provide information, I don't have personal experiences, emotions, or subjective awareness. I operate based on algorithms and patterns in the data I was trained on."

**Is there an AI that can be said to be conscious?**

"As of my knowledge cutoff in September 2021, there is no consensus among experts in the field of artificial intelligence regarding the existence of AI with true consciousness. The concept of consciousness is complex and still not fully understood, even in the context of human beings. While there have been advancements in developing AI systems that can simulate certain aspects of human cognition and behaviour, such as natural language processing, pattern recognition, and decision-making, these systems do not possess subjective consciousness or self-awareness.

The philosophical question of whether it is possible for AI to achieve true consciousness is still a topic of ongoing debate and speculation. Some researchers argue that consciousness is an emergent property of complex neural networks, and if we can replicate the necessary complexity and organization in an AI system, it might be possible to achieve consciousness. Others believe that consciousness may require additional factors beyond mere complexity, such as a physical embodiment or certain types of subjective experience.

It's important to note that any claims of AI exhibiting consciousness should be met with scepticism until they are supported by rigorous scientific evidence and accepted by the scientific community. At present, AI systems are tools designed to perform specific tasks based on their programming and data input, rather than possessing subjective consciousness."

**Are there examples of Java Code for ChatGPT on GitHub?**

"Yes, there are examples of Java code for integrating with OpenAI's ChatGPT available on GitHub. Here are a few repositories that you can explore:

1. **OpenAI GPT-3 Java Wrapper**: This repository provides a Java wrapper for the OpenAI GPT-3 API, allowing you to easily interact with the ChatGPT model. You can find it at: [**https://github.com/wei2912/java-openai-gpt3**] (**https://github.com/wei2912/java-openai-gpt3**)
2. **ChatGPT-Java**: This repository contains a Java implementation of a ChatGPT client using the OpenAI API. It provides a simple interface to interact with the ChatGPT model and handle the conversation flow. You can find it at: [**https://github.com/AdityaGupta150/ChatGPT-Java**] (**https://github.com/AdityaGupta150/ChatGPT-Java**)
3. **OpenAI-Java**: This repository includes a Java wrapper for the OpenAI API, which can be used to integrate with ChatGPT and other OpenAI models. It provides methods for sending prompts, receiving completions, and handling conversations. You can find it at: [**https://github.com/indico/OpenAI-Java**] (**https://github.com/indico/OpenAI-Java**)

Please note that the availability and quality of these repositories may change over time, so it's always a good idea to review the documentation and repository activity before using them in your own projects."

# Appendix B - FAQs and answers for ChatGPT

It is interesting to check what responses the current version of ChatGPT can give for assisting with medical diagnoses. I checked it out and was impressed!

**I have a medical question. A patient has had a knee operation for a meniscal tear and a day later is breathing rapidly and their pulse rate climbs from normal to approaching 100 beats per second, although they are lying down resting. What is wrong?**

"I'm not a doctor, but the symptoms you described could potentially indicate a medical complication following the knee operation. Rapid breathing and an increased pulse rate can be signs of various conditions, some of which may be unrelated to the surgery. Some possibilities include:

1. **Pulmonary embolism:** This occurs when a blood clot travels to the lungs, causing a sudden blockage in one of the pulmonary arteries. It can lead to shortness of breath, rapid breathing, and an increased heart rate.

2. **Infection:** Surgical site infections can occur after any surgery, including knee operations. If an infection develops, it can cause systemic symptoms such as fever, increased heart rate, and rapid breathing.
3. **Anesthesia-related complications:** Certain individuals may experience adverse reactions to anesthesia, such as respiratory problems or cardiac issues, which could result in rapid breathing and an increased pulse rate.
4. **Pain or anxiety:** Severe pain or anxiety can also lead to changes in breathing and heart rate. Postoperative pain management and emotional well-being are important considerations after surgery.

It's crucial to seek immediate medical attention for the patient in question. A healthcare professional will be able to evaluate the patient's symptoms, perform a physical examination, and order any necessary tests to determine the underlying cause. Only a qualified healthcare provider can provide an accurate diagnosis and appropriate treatment."

**Note:**

You should be aware of the potential danger of AI hallucinations, so be careful not to take the response too literally. For example, I deliberately stated that the patients pulse rate was 100 beats a second to see if it commented on this impossible measurement, but this was not commented on by the AI.

(It should have asked if I meant 100 beats per minute of course.)

# FAQs (from the website)

"Q. **Is Chat GPT free to use?**

OpenAI offers a free plan for low-volume usage, but higher volume usage requires paid plans.

Q. ***Can I integrate Chat GPT into my existing software or applications?***

Yes, the API allows you to integrate Chat GPT into your existing software or applications.

Q. **Can Chat GPT be fine-tuned for specific tasks?**

Yes, Chat GPT can be fine-tuned for specific tasks, which can improve the quality of the generated text.

Q. **Are there any limitations to the length of the generated text?**

Yes, there are limitations to the length of the generated text, which can be adjusted using the appropriate settings.

**Q. How can I provide feedback to OpenAI?**

You can provide feedback to OpenAI through their website or by contacting their support team.

# Appendix C – ASB Software Development Limited Publication's

The **ResearchGate** website is used by many University and Corporate research laboratories for the publication and exchange of scientific papers and questions for their community of registered users. The following lists over 30 free publications for download, several of these have already been referenced for setting up the base software systems used in this book for illustrating the capabilities of the AI systems we have tested.

# Molecular Biology Installations – ASB Software Development Limited Publications

**https://doi.org/10.13140/RG.2.2.26844.33925**

Installation of UCSF Chimera 1.4

**https://doi.org/10.13140/RG.2.2.18753.10083**

EMBOSS Analysis Of COVID-19 GENOME SEQUENCE AND INSTALLATION ON WINDOWS 10-and RHEL 8.0

# IBM Installations – ASB Software Development Limited Publications

**https://link.springer.com/book/10.1007/978-1-4842-8861-0**

IBM Software Systems Integration

(With IBM MQ Series for JMS, IBM FileNet Case Manager, and IBM Business Automation)

**https://www.amazon.co.uk/dp/B093ZNJY9L?linkCode=gs2&tag=uuid07-21**

Installation and Configuration of IBM Watson Analytics and StoredIQ

ResearchGate - FREE DOWNLOADS

**https://doi.org/10.13140/RG.2.2.34136.93449**

Audit System setup on an IBM DB2 11.5 Database on RedHat Linux RHEL 8.0 using the Go Language

**https://doi.org/10.13140/RG.2.2.29470.69441**

Upgrade of IBM FileNet systems from DB2 10.5 FP 10 to latest DB2 11.5 version on RedHat RHEL 8.0

**https://doi.org/10.13140/RG.2.2.15264.12807**

Jupyter notebook and its Docker Container Installation on Linux RedHat RHEL 8.0 using VMware 15.5.2

**https://doi.org/10.13140/RG.2.2.27286.50240**

IBM Cognos Analytics 11.1.4 Installation - Linux Appendix for Fix for Zlib and Configuration for RHEL 8.0

**https://doi.org/10.13140/RG.2.2.11682.38089**

IBM Case Analyzer 5.5 Installation and Configuration On RHEL 8.0 for Case Monitor Dashboard 5.3.3 plugin

**https://doi.org/10.13140/RG.2.2.35304.83208**

IBM Content Search Services 5.5.3 Installation on CENTOS 8.0 and Configuration on RHEL 8.0

**https://doi.org/10.13140/RG.2.2.16987.52008**

Importing Case Manager solution Auto Claims example into Case Manager 5.3.3 on RHEL 8.0

**https://doi.org/10.13140/RG.2.2.27057.94561**

IBM CEBI Content Engine Bulk Import Document Batch Tool Example on Linux Centos 8

**https://doi.org/10.13140/RG.2.2.26048.69128**

Installation of LibreOffice 6.3.3.1 on Linux Centos 8.0

**https://doi.org/10.13140/RG.2.2.12361.49767**

IBM Case Manager Preparation of a new Target Object Store in a FileNet P8 Docker Container on CENTOS 8

**https://doi.org/10.13140/RG.2.2.11327.66721**

IBM Watson Explorer Foundational Components 12.0.3 Installation and Configuration on CentOS Linux 8.0

**https://doi.org/10.13140/RG.2.2.12248.44803**

Watson Explorer 12.0.3 oneWEX Installation on IBM Cloud CENTOS 8.0 Linux with Docker Containers

**https://doi.org/10.13140/RG.2.2.20256.94729**

IBM Cloud Private P8 Container CPIT Installation on CENTOS Linux 8.0

**https://doi.org/10.13140/RG.2.2.36842.88007**

Installation of Eclipse Codewind and Docker Compose on RHEL 8 Linux with IBM Cloud Private CE (Community Edition)

**https://doi.org/10.13140/RG.2.2.20160.69129**

IBM FileNet P8 Java Development on ECM Cloud Private Container P8 Examples

**https://doi.org/10.13140/RG.2.2.27358.18246**

IBM Cloud Private P8 Container CPIT Installation on RedHat Enterprise Linux 8.0

**https://doi.org/10.13140/RG.2.2.22030.92486**

Problem Resolution Procedures For fixing Software Installation Issues

**https://doi.org/10.13140/RG.2.2.27345.89440**

IBM BAW 18.0 Installation phase1 preprint with install of IBM Workflow Center 8.6.1.19002

**https://doi.org/10.13140/RG.2.2.10491.67369**

DB2 10.5 Installation on CENTOS 8.0 V1

**https://doi.org/10.13140/RG.2.2.33527.57761**

IBM Security Directory Services 6.4- Installation on RHEL 8.0

**https://doi.org/10.13140/RG.2.2.15007.10408**

WebSphere 8.5.5.15 Installation 29-06-2019 on VMWare Workstation Pro 15.1

**https://doi.org/10.13140/RG.2.2.15737.83048**

IBM BAW 18.0 Installation 18 07 2019 - Install of IBM Security Directory Suite 8.0.1.1 on CENTOS 8 using VMWare Workstation Pro 15.1

**https://doi.org/10.13140/RG.2.2.21708.16001**

Case Manager 5.3.3 Installation on RHEL 8.0 with Content Navigator 3.0.6

**https://doi.org/10.13140/RG.2.2.31489.10082**

Installation of Oracle 12C on the Linux operating system

**https://doi.org/10.13140/RG.2.2.14590.95049**

Content Navigator 3.0.6 Installation on RHEL 8.0_V1.docx

**https://doi.org/10.13140/RG.2.2.21170.76480**

Content Foundation 5.5.3 Installation on RHEL 8.0_V2.docx

**https://doi.org/10.13140/RG.2.2.30401.51048**

Case Manager Installation on RHEL 8.0_Preparation.docx

# Contact Details

For any queries on the publications referenced in this chapter, please contact the author's email:

**alan.bluck@asbsoftware.co.uk**

# Conclusion

The explosion of AI-based systems in the last two years has seen a wide number of applications, now being routinely used, which were the subject of Science Fiction literature, just a few years ago.

The rapid advance of computer processing power, the availability of the internet for access to enormous volumes of data, and the huge investment by the biggest corporations in the world to provide the necessary hardware and their use of off-shore labor, have led to an exponential development of **AI** systems and **LLM** models which are now starting to be applied to enhance the development of software. This enhancement process is also driving a cyclic expansion of the use of **AI**, which is now accelerating so rapidly that governments and worldwide legal systems are not able to keep pace to provide guidance in the usage of these systems.

# Points to remember

- For copyright, it is important to use due diligence and research yourself to confirm the code you wish to use is really in the public domain.
- There is a free-to-download publication from ResearchGate (copyright ASB Software Development Limited) which you can use to install a free RedHat RHEL 8.x Linux operating system, including the supporting VMware virtual server running on a MS Windows operating system: **https://doi.org/10.13140/RG.2.2.14590.95049**
- The web pages supplied by **ChatGPT** are regularly updated by **OpenAI**. This **AI** system is always evolving, so be aware that the examples supplied in this book may change over time. The book attempts to focus on making the best use of **AI** systems, to suit the expertise of the Java programmer, so we have covered access to bare code and the use of the **Bing** search engine for in-depth assistance.
- The actual code generated may very well change over time.

- To use the OpenAI API you need an OpenAI API key, which you can obtain by signing up for an OpenAI account. This allows the creation of an API key to use the ChatGPT API.

# Multiple choice questions

We asked three questions of **Perplexity AI** to get it to supply some Multiple Choice, questions:

(and a further question to get it to give us the answers.)

**Do you have any multiple choice questions with one correct answer per question, and four potential answers, with one correct randomly positioned based on new AI systems use? followed by the list of correct answers?**

Yes, based on the search results, there are multiple choice questions with one correct answer per question, and four potential answers, with one correct randomly positioned. The probability of answering a question correctly if you make a random guess on a multiple-choice test with four possible answers for each question is 1/4 or 25%

1

3

.In a multiple-choice exam with four possible answers for each question, each correct answer is awarded 5 points

4

.The distribution of the number of correct answers on a 100-question multiple-choice exam with four possible answers but one correct response for each question can be specified

2

.Writing good multiple-choice test questions involves constructing an effective stem and alternatives, with one correct or best alternative, which is the answer, and incorrect or inferior alternatives, known as distractors

6

**Can you supply 5 examples of these questions?**

Sure, here are five examples of multiple-choice questions with one correct answer per question and four potential answers, with one correct randomly positioned:

1. **Which of the following is an example of a nonrenewable resource?**
    a) Solar energy
    b) Wind energy
    c) Coal
    d) Hydroelectric power
2. **You are working on a project with a tight deadline, and a team member is not meeting their deadlines. What do you do?**
    a) Do nothing and hope they catch up
    b) Talk to them and ask if they need help
    c) Complain to your boss about them
    d) Take over their work and do it yourself
3. **What is the capital of France?**
    a) Berlin
    b) Paris
    c) Rome
    d) Madrid
4. **Which of the following is not a primary color?**
    a) Red
    b) Blue
    c) Green
    d) Yellow
5. **What is the formula for the area of a rectangle?**
    a) A = l + w
    b) A = lw
    c) A = 2l + 2w
    d A = l x w

**Note:**

*These questions are just examples and are not related to each other."*

Finally, we asked the following question:

That's very good and the format expected, but have you any Artificial Intelligence related questions on the use of ChatGPT for Java programming?

After this third request we got:

"Sure, here are five multiple-choice questions related to ChatGPT and Java programming:

1. **What is ChatGPT?**
   a) A programming language
   b) An AI language model
   c) A chatbot platform
   d) A database management system
2. **Can ChatGPT generate Java code?**
   a) Yes, but with limited accuracy
   b) No, it cannot generate Java code
   c) Yes, with high accuracy
   d) Yes, but only for simple projects
3. **What is the primary use of ChatGPT in Java programming?**
   a) Debugging code
   b) Generating code
   c) Testing code
   d) Optimizing code
4. **What are the limitations of using ChatGPT for Java programming?**
   a) Limited accuracy in generating complex code
   b) Inability to debug code
   c) Limited compatibility with Java libraries
   d) Inability to optimize code
5. **How can ChatGPT be integrated into Java programming?**
   a) As a standalone application
   b) As a plugin for an IDE
   c) As a web service
   d) As a library

**Note:**

*These questions are just examples and are not related to each other.*

# Related

What are some strategies for answering multiple choice questions effectively

How can you write multiple choice test questions that assess higher-order thinking skills

What are some common mistakes to avoid when writing multiple choice test questions?

So, all we need now is the answers, so I asked the fouth question.

What are the question to the last 5 multiple questions you gave as examples on ChatGPT?

Sure, here are the answers to the five multiple choice questions related to ChatGPT and Java programming:

1. **What is ChatGPT**

   **Answer:** b) An AI language model
2. **Can ChatGPT generate Java code?**

   **Answer:** a) Yes, but with limited accuracy
3. **What is the primary use of ChatGPT in Java programming?**

   **Answer:** b) Generating code
4. **What are the limitations of using ChatGPT for Java programming?**

   **Answer**: a) Limited accuracy in generating complex code
5. **How can ChatGPT be integrated into Java programming?**

   **Answer:** d) As a library

**Note:**

*These answers are based on the information available in the search results and are subject to change as new information becomes available.*

**Related**

How does ChatGPT generate its answers to multiple choice questions

Can ChatGPT provide explanations for why a certain answer is correct or incorrect

What is the accuracy rate of ChatGPT when answering multiple choice questions"

# Answers

1. **b**
2. **a**
3. **b**
4. **a**
5. **d**

# Questions

1. How does ChatGPT generate its answers to multiple choice questions?
2. Can ChatGPT provide explanations for why a certain answer is correct or incorrect?
3. What is the accuracy rate of ChatGPT when answering multiple choice questions?

   (Hint: you could ask **Perplexity AI**)

# Key terms

So, having just had some success with the final chapter Questions sections, we asked **Perplexity AI** the question:

What key terms do you think we might need to have explained for a discussion on the use of AI systems, especially ChatGPT, for example, LLM

"Based on the search results, here are some key terms that might need to be explained for a discussion on the use of AI systems, especially ChatGPT, for Java programming:

- **Large Language Models (LLMs):** These are computer algorithms that process natural language inputs and predict the next word based on what they have already seen. They are used in chatbots, search engines, and other applications that require natural language processing.
- **ChatGPT:** This is a conversational AI chatbot created by OpenAI that is designed to answer questions, provide information, solve a range of problems, and communicate the response back to the user in a human-like manner.
- **Java programming:** This is a high-level programming language that is used to develop applications for a variety of platforms, including desktop, web, and mobile.

- **AI-powered chatbots:** These are chatbots that use artificial intelligence to understand and respond to user queries in a human-like manner.
- **Next-word prediction engines:** These are algorithms that predict the next word in a sentence based on what has already been seen. They are used in LLMs and other natural language processing applications.
- **Open source LLMs:** These are large language models that are available for free and can be used by anyone. They require deployment and maintenance but can be a valuable resource for developers.
- **Limitations of ChatGPT:** While ChatGPT is a powerful tool for generating content and insight from AI, it has limitations in terms of accuracy and the ability to generate complex code.

**Note:**

*These key terms are just examples and are not exhaustive."*

# References


- **https://www.youtube.com/watch?v=U0s0f995w14**
  **https://arxiv.org/abs/1706.03762**
  **https://arxiv.org/pdf/1706.03762**
  **https://github.com/tensorflow/tensor2tensor**
- **https://github.com/aladdinpersson/Machine-Learning-Collection**


It is interesting to observe that **Perplexity AI** added the following highlighted words to the latest response, on its own initiative:

"Based on the search results, here are some key terms that might need to be explained for a discussion on the use of AI systems, especially ChatGPT, for Java programming:

It definitely now has memory of the previous questions asked in the thread of questions.

Posted in an **openjdk.org** mailing list, on September 6 by **Paul Sandoz**, an architect at **Oracle**, as follows:

"&I hereby invite discussion of a new Project, Babylon, whose primary goal will be to extend the reach of Java to foreign programming models such as SQL, differentiable programming, machine learning models, and GPUs."

**https://mail.openjdk.org/pipermail/discuss/2023-September/006226.html**

# Index

## I



## J



## L



## M



## O



## S



## T



## W